Handbook of
Programming Languages

Handbook of Programming Languages

Edited by
Samuel Green

STATES
ACADEMIC PRESS
www.statesacademicpress.com

Published by States Academic Press,
109 South 5th Street,
Brooklyn, NY 11249, USA

ISBN: 978-1-63989-266-2

Cataloging-in-Publication Data

Handbook of programming languages / edited by Samuel Green.
p. cm.
Includes bibliographical references and index.
ISBN 978-1-63989-266-2
1. Programming languages (Electronic computers). 2. Languages, Artificial. 3. Electronic data processing.
4. Computer science. I. Green, Samuel.
QA76.7 .H36 2022
005.13--dc23

For information on all States Academic Press publications
visit our website at www.statesacademicpress.com

Contents

Preface

Over the recent decade, advancements and applications have progressed exponentially. This has led to the increased interest in this field and projects are being conducted to enhance knowledge. The main objective of this book is to present some of the critical challenges and provide insights into possible solutions. This book will answer the varied questions that arise in the field and also provide an increased scope for furthering studies.

A programming language is a scientific language that comprises a set of instructions producing various kinds of output. Programming languages are essential in computer science and are used in computer programming to implement algorithms. Programming language theory is a branch of computer science that is concerned with the design, implementation, analysis, characterization, and classification of programming languages and of their individual characteristics. Java, Python, C, Ruby, Javascript, C#, and PHP are some of the prominent programming languages. They are used for front-end web development, back-end web development, desktop application, mobile development, and game development. The topics included in this book on programming languages are of utmost significance and bound to provide incredible insights to readers. There has been rapid progress in this field and its applications are finding their way across multiple industries. This book is a resource guide for experts as well as students.

I hope that this book, with its visionary approach, will be a valuable addition and will promote interest among readers. Each of the authors has provided their extraordinary competence in their specific fields by providing different perspectives as they come from diverse nations and regions. I thank them for their contributions.

Editor

Emulating Multiple Inheritance in Fortran 2003/2008

Karla Morris

Sandia National Laboratories, 7011 East Avenue, Livermore, CA 94550-9610, USA

Correspondence should be addressed to Karla Morris; knmorri@sandia.gov

Academic Editor: Can Özturan

Although the high-performance computing (HPC) community increasingly embraces object-oriented programming (OOP), most HPC OOP projects employ the C++ programming language. Until recently, Fortran programmers interested in mining the benefits of OOP had to emulate OOP in Fortran 90/95. The advent of widespread compiler support for Fortran 2003 now facilitates explicitly constructing object-oriented class hierarchies via inheritance and leveraging related class behaviors such as dynamic polymorphism. Although C++ allows a class to inherit from multiple parent classes, Fortran and several other OOP languages restrict or prohibit explicit multiple inheritance relationships in order to circumvent several pitfalls associated with them. Nonetheless, what appears as an intrinsic feature in one language can be modeled as a user-constructed design pattern in another language. The present paper demonstrates how to apply the facade structural design pattern to support a multiple inheritance class relationship in Fortran 2003. The design unleashes the power of the associated class relationships for modeling complicated data structures yet avoids the ambiguities that plague some multiple inheritance scenarios.

1. Introduction

Object-oriented programming originated in the late 1960s with the invention of the Simula 67 computer programming language. Since the early 1980s several modern programming languages, including C++, Java, Python, and Ruby, have been developed with explicit support for OOP from their inception. Several older languages, including Ada, BASIC, Lisp, Pascal, and Fortran, have evolved to support OOP in their modern versions [1]. Of these two groups, Fortran and C++ find the most frequent use in high-performance computing [2]. Due to the longer history of C++ support for OOP, a much more extensive body of literature exists for describing best practices in C++. The recent advent of widespread compiler support for the OOP features of the Fortran 2003 and 2008 standards offers an exciting opportunity to develop and promulgate idioms for expressing OOP concepts in Fortran [3]. The current article focuses on one such idiom: multiple inheritance.

The primary unit of decomposition in OOP is the object. The early stages of any object-oriented software design process involve defining classes of objects encapsulating the problem data and methods that manipulate the encapsulated data. The methods, referred to as *type-bound procedures* (TBP) in Fortran, provide functionality to the objects and the objects' users [4]. The objects can be organized into class hierarchies to define complex data relationships. One important feature most OOP language provide is dynamic polymorphism: the ability of an object at one level in the hierarchy to respond to invocations of methods inherited from one of the object's ancestors in the hierarchy.

Numerous designs can accomplish a desired task, but certain recurring design problems arise. In object-oriented design, the set of common solutions for recurring problems are termed *design patterns*. Designs that express these patterns typically exhibit higher quality in various respects [5]. Experienced software developers leverage design patterns to implement class hierarchies that have proven effective in solving a specific design problem across a variety of application domains. HPC projects that employ patterns include the open-source parallel solver libraries Trilinos (http://trilinos.sandia.gov/) and Parallel Sparse Basic Linear Algebra Subroutines (PSBLAS) (http://www.ce.uniroma2.it/psblas/).

Design patterns imbue several desirable properties in software: flexibility, maintainability, reusability, and scalability. As an example, consider the Mediator pattern. Common design problems involving a fully connected graph connecting interacting objects can be reduced to simple star graph by the Mediator pattern [6]. A Mediator is a single object that directs communication between N other objects, thereby reducing the communication links from $O(N^2)$ to $O(N)$. The resultant reduction in complexity increases the maintainability of the code and the scalability of the design up to more classes than would otherwise prove feasible. PSBLAS, for example, defines different compressed storage schemes for its sparse matrix objects. Because the scalability of certain operations is improved by using specific storage representations, there is functionality within the library to transform the storage scheme of its objects. The library uses the Mediator pattern to manage the number of procedures that must be implemented to convert the compressed storage representation of sparse matrix objects [7].

Interface reusability is another desirable software property. The Factory Method pattern defines a unifying interface for constructing objects across different classes that support the unified construction interface. Xpetra, a package in Trilinos, uses the Factory Method pattern to defer the instantiation of actual objects to an appropriate subclass implemented in other packages.

Inheritance addresses another important concern in software design: implementation reuse. Inheritance involves constructing child classes that automatically acquire attributes and methods of a parent class. One form of inheritance, multiple inheritance, incorporates functionality from more than one ancestor class.

Multiple inheritance also proves useful in applications where a programmer prefers class relationships structured into a lattice rather than a strict tree hierarchy class relationship structure [8]. Lattices and multiple inheritance find specific use in separating an application's interface from its implementation [9].

OOP language designers have chosen different levels of support for multiple inheritance. Each language that explicitly supports multiple inheritance must resolve ambiguities that might arise. The diamond problem, a common ancestor delegation dilemma problem, is an example of an ambiguity that arises when two classes B and C inherit from a class A. If a class D in turn inherits from B and C, then any method in A overridden with implementations in B and C but not in D has two alternative and ambiguous implementations when invoked on D: the implementation from parent B or that from parent C (if the method is not overwritten by D) [10].

Several OOP languages fully support multiple inheritance. These languages include C++, Python, Perl, and Curl. C++ partially resolves ambiguities such as those previously cited by enforcing explicit qualification, as each path in the inheritance structure is followed separately [8]. Java, Ruby, and C# limit support to inheritance from only one class implementation; however, a class can implement multiple interfaces (Java terminology), which would correspond to extending multiple abstract classes in Fortran terminology, but Fortran prohibits even this limited form of multiple inheritance.

What appears as an intrinsic feature of one language, however, might appear as a user-defined design pattern in another language. In this sense, design patterns are programming-language-independent. Only the degree of language support for the pattern varies. The Prototype pattern [6], for example, is a common user-defined pattern in C++ that is an intrinsic language feature in Fortran 2008 [7].

Publishing techniques for emulating unsupported aspects of OOP in Fortran has a long history. Starting in the mid-1990s, several groups published strategies for emulating OOP in Fortran 90/95 [11–15]. Scientific programming developers have also implemented design patterns in Fortran 90/95 before object-oriented compiler support [16]. No publication of which the current author is aware addresses emulating multiple inheritance in Fortran. Section 2 of this paper describes a multiple inheritance pattern using Unified Modeling Language (UML) diagrams [17]. Section 3 presents a sample implementation of the pattern leveraging the OOP features of the Fortran 2003 standard. The latest released versions of at least six Fortran compilers support all of the OOP features employed in Section 3: the IBM, Intel, Cray, Numerical Algorithms Group (NAG), Portland Group, and GNU Compiler Collection (GCC) compilers [3]. Section 4 discusses the results. Section 5 concludes the paper.

2. Methodology: Multiple Inheritance Pattern

The model presented in this section applies a Facade software design pattern to support the implementation of a multiple inheritance pattern in Fortran 2003. In general, the Facade structural design pattern can be used to reduce the complexity of a system and decouple multiple dependencies between subsystems. The client interacts directly with the facade, which provides a simple and unified interface to a set of subsystems [6]. In following a format similar to that prescribed by Gamma et al., this section describes the proposed multiple inheritance design pattern by using a set of key features: intent, motivation, applicability, participants, collaborators, and implementation.

(i) *Intent*: create a superclass that inherits functionality from a set of subclasses. Support class modularity by allowing a program structure where the capabilities of a superclass result from inheriting the features that are implemented by different subclasses.

(ii) *Motivation*: the collection of capabilities of a system is better implemented by using a structure set of subsystems. Each subsystem is responsible for implementing a specific capability. This module structure contributes to data and functionality encapsulation and enables the reusability of the different subsystems. The complexity of the system is managed by minimizing the communication and dependencies between the different components in the system.

Consider for example the basic constructs involved in a linear algebra application such as vectors, scalars, and matrices. In a parallel programming environment these constructs could take the form of superclasses that encapsulate distributed data, and basic functionality for data redistribution and communication, as well as functionality for basic computations, floating-point operations, and memory management, among others. If each of the different functionalities previously mentioned is implemented separately both the vector and matrix classes can reuse each of the classes responsible for the implementation of their common capabilities.

(iii) *Applicability*: the multiple inheritance pattern is used when a newly created class, which we refer to as a superclass, inherits the properties and behavior of multiple classes. The superclass delegates to its appropriate subclass any request for functionality implemented within the subclass, whether the request is generated inside the superclass or by an outside client using the superclass.

(iv) *Participants and Collaborators*: Figure 1 shows a UML class diagram of the multiple inheritance pattern. A similar data structure is commonly used within the Epetra (http://trilinos.sandia.gov/packages/epetra/) foundational package of the Trilinos library. In this case, the classes object_distribution and object_computation are part of the subsystems responsible for implementing the specific features related to data distribution and computation of floating-point operations, respectively.

The object_distribution class is one of the classes in a subsystem that implements all the functionality required to address data redistribution and enable import and export capabilities. The class object_computation is included in a subsystem that computes and reports computation of floating-point operations. The system, embodied by the vector class, makes use of the collection of capabilities.

The vector class could modify the implementation of any TBP of the two inherited classes or implement new functionality using both inherited classes. In an OOP language that explicitly supports multiple inheritance, the vector class inherits from both object_distribution and object_computation. All procedures attached to these classes thereby would be directly available to vector objects.

(v) *Implementation*: the proposed multiple inheritance pattern emulates the language-provided multiple inheritance of C++ and can be viewed as an application of the Facade pattern. Figure 2 provides a UML class diagram describing the proposed multiple inheritance pattern.

The model embeds a Facade pattern to collect all the classes that are to be inherited by the vector class. The created lattice structure comprises three classes: object_distribution, object_computation, and facade. The facade class combines the functionality provided by two demonstrative classes: object_distribution and object_computation.

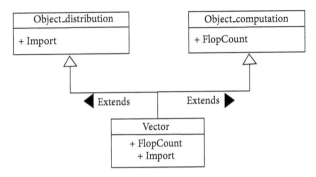

FIGURE 1: UML class diagram for multiple inheritance pattern, which is provided by the compiler in languages like C++. The vector class inherits from two other classes: object_distribution and object_computation.

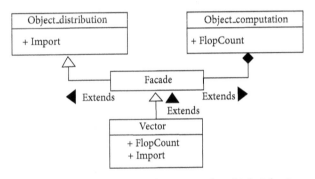

FIGURE 2: UML class diagram for proposed multiple inheritance pattern Fortran implementation. The facade class aggregates the functionality encapsulated in object_distribution and object_computation and provides a unified interface for the classes the vector class inherits.

The vector class shown could be any class that must extend the collection of classes handled by facade.

3. Results: Fortran Implementation

The Fortran implementation for emulating multiple inheritance with the previously described model is shown in Listings 1–4. Multiple inheritance is applied to enhance the number of capabilities available to a superclass. The design uses a Facade to collect all inherited functionality from a set of subclasses that form the lattice data structure. In this example, the data structure encapsulates functionality related to data distribution and computation capabilities.

As part of a subsystem that enables data distribution the object_distribution class, in Listing 1, includes the import method. This type-bound procedure allows vector to change the layout of its data in memory. The object_computation class, shown in Listing 2, encapsulates floating point operation functionality and allows vector objects access to the floating-points operations performed by the superclass.

```
(1) module object_distribution_concrete
(2)    implicit none
(3)    private
(4)    public:: object_distribution
(5)    type:: object_distribution
(6)      contains
(7)        procedure:: import
(8)    end type
(9)      contains
(10)       subroutine import(this)
(11)         class(object_distribution), intent(in):: this
(12)         print *, 'Import_Data_Functionality'
(13)       end subroutine
(14) end module
```

LISTING 1: Implementation for object_distribution class.

```
(1) module object_computation_concrete
(2)    implicit none
(3)    private
(4)    public:: object_computation
(5)    type:: object_computation
(6)      contains
(7)        procedure:: FlopCount
(8)    end type
(9)      contains
(10)       subroutine FlopCount(this)
(11)         class (object_computation), intent(in):: this
(12)         print *, 'Count_floating_point_operations'
(13)       end subroutine
(14) end module
```

LISTING 2: Implementation for object_computation class.

The source code in Listing 1 illustrates several OOP features, including data encapsulation support. In Fortran, the private and public keywords (lines 3-4) control access to members of the type. Members defined with public are accessible to any part of the program. Conversely, members defined with private are not accessible to code outside the scope of the module in which the type is defined. The implicit none statement on line 2 prevents implicit variable instantiation and forces programmers to declare all variables before they are used.

The facade class collects the functionality of the subclasses through inheritance and composition (see Listing 3). The constructor function (lines 16–19) returns a facade object after invoking intrinsic structure constructors for each data member, my_flop, and the extended object_distribution class. Fortran automatically provides an intrinsic structure constructor that returns an object wherein any private data components inside the object take on programmer-defined default initializations. Public state variables can be initialized by passing arguments to

the structure constructor or by overloading the derived type name and providing a programmer-defined constructor function. The later is a more desired approach when following an object-oriented programming paradigm, which requires private state variables for the derived type data components. In this code example, (lines 17-18) construction relies upon default initializations and therefore requires no arguments. Through inheritance, object_distribution gives facade objects, and any of its extended classes, full access to object_distributions's TBP. The composition relationship use for object_computation forces facade to create a TBP, FlopCount. This procedure invokes the implementation of FlopCount associated with the facade my_flop component.

The Vector superclass, shown in Listing 4, represents any derived type that accesses, through the inheritance of facade, all the collective functionality from the subclasses in the lattice structure.

The design described aggregates within facade all the classes that must be inherited by the vector derived data

```
(1) module facade_concrete
(2)    use object_distribution_concrete, only: object_distribution
(3)    use object_computation_concrete, only: object_computation
(4)    implicit none
(5)    private
(6)    public :: facade
(7)    type, extends(object_distribution):: facade
(8)      type(object_computation):: my_flop
(9)      contains
(10)       procedure:: FlopCount
(11)   end type
(12)   interface facade
(13)     module procedure constructor
(14)   end interface
(15)   contains
(16)     type(facade) function constructor()
(17)       constructor%object_distribution=object_distribution()
(18)       constructor%my_flop=object_computation()
(19)     end function
(20)     subroutine FlopCount(this)
(21)       class(facade), intent(in):: this
(22)       call this%my_flop%FlopCount()
(23)     end subroutine
(24) end module
```

LISTING 3: Additional level of abstraction used to incorporate all classes to be inherited.

```
(1) module foo_concrete
(2)    use facade_concrete, only: facade
(3)    implicit none
(4)    private
(5)    public:: foo
(6)    type, extends(facade):: foo
(7)    end type
(8)    interface foo
(9)      module procedure constructor
(10)   end interface
(11)    contains
(12)     type(foo) function constructor()
(13)       constructor%facade=facade()
(14)     end function
(15) end module
```

LISTING 4: Vector class taking advantage of multiple inheritance.

type. The facade class adds a level of indirection to encapsulate the multiple classes that are to be inherited. The type-bound procedures in the facade class provide Vector with direct access to the implementations in the parent classes in Listings 1 and 2.

The aforementioned diamond problem could occur when implementing the UML diagram shown in Figure 3. The object class holds some common, high-level, required functionality such as memory management. As such, any derived data type that implements a new capability must extend the object class. This behavior is enforced through an Object pattern and has been used in a reference-counting package [18, 19]. The Object pattern named after a like-named feature in Java propagates common functionality throughout a class hierarchy by establishing a base class that serves as a universal ancestor of all classes in a given package [20, 21]. If an abstract class defines the universal parent object, a designer could employ deferred bindings, which comprise type-bound procedures with only their function signatures specified. Writing deferred bindings provides a hook for accessing a particular capability in all concrete classes further down the hierarchy. Another approach provides a default implementation within the parent class; in this case, subclasses have the option to overwrite the procedure unless the deferred binding has the non_overridable attribute.

In an application where the object class publishes an interface for a TBP free_memory, the diamond problem will arise if concrete implementations are furnished by the concrete classes object_distribution and object_computation. Given that the vector class extends both concrete classes, invoking the free_memory method poses a dilemma: it is unclear which concrete implementation should be used. The pattern implementation shown in Figure 2 avoids this common ancestor dilemma; in this case, if we were to invoke the free_memory method, the implementation used would be given by object_distribution class with no ambiguity.

The pattern implemented in Listings 1–4 can also address the needs of a software application where the desired behavior requires the use of both concrete implementations of

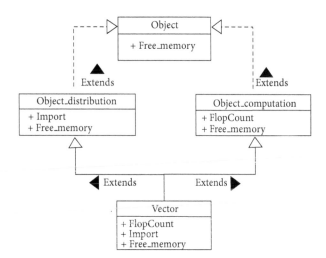

FIGURE 3: Unified modeling language (UML) class diagram for multiple inheritance diamond problem, given an interface for type-bound procedure free_memory.

the free_memory type-bound procedure. In such cases, the procedure should be overwritten within the object class, to invoke the implementations of the different parent classes. If the user code requires knowledge of the parent TBP invoked by facade, that could be discovered at runtime with Fortran's extends_type_of intrinsic procedure.

4. Discussion

The multiple inheritance pattern implementation discussed in Section 3 requires little work to incorporate additional functionality into the lattice structure. The facade used to emulate multiple inheritance with this pattern can be better exploited when the application requires that this collective functionality be used by several different superclasses. New functionality can be added to all the objects in the application, or all superclasses of interest, by specifying a new component in the facade class, corresponding to the derived type of the new features.

In the model described, the inheritance of multiple classes is achieved by inheriting one of the classes and aggregating the rest of the classes in the set providing the collective functionality. In the example, the set is given by classes at the hierarchy level of object_distribution and object_computation. The class that should be inherited by the facade derived data type, which encapsulates the multiple inheritance, is given by the class with the procedure implementation that would generally satisfy the inheritance path appropriate for the specific application.

In applications where all inheritance paths must be followed, the free_memory type-bound procedure should be overwritten within the facade class. Its new implementation will invoke the concrete implementation of the method for each one of the classes providing the collective functionality. Overwriting methods within this pattern's facade class affords the programmer the flexibility of implementing the desired behavior and at the same time circumvents the occurrence of possible ambiguities in the subclasses. A multiple

inheritance design pattern implementation solely based on aggregation could prove valuable if the collective functionality requires a complex interaction between the different methods provided by the subclasses.

5. Conclusion

The discussed model presents a safe solution for emulating multiple inheritance in Fortran 2003/2008. The pattern avoids the ambiguities that commonly arise when dealing with lattice data structures and at the same time provides the means for supporting different implementations. Different behaviors within a given software application can be supported depending on the inheritance path that needs to be followed. The pattern can successfully address the needs of applications where either a single concrete implementation of a method is required or applications where the implementation of the methods for each of the subclasses in the structure must be invoked.

Conflict of Interests

The author declares that there is no conflict of interests regarding the publication of this paper.

Acknowledgments

Sandia National Laboratories is a multiprogram laboratory managed and operated by Sandia Corporation, a wholly owned subsidiary of Lockheed Martin Corporation, for the U.S. Department of Energy under Contract DE-AC04-94AL85000. The author thanks Damian Rouson for the helpful discussions and guidance.

References

[1] G. O'Regan, *A Brief History of Computing*, Springer, London, UK, 2nd edition, 2011.

[2] M. Bull, X. Guo, and I. Liabotis, "Applications and user requirements for tier-0 systems," Tech. Rep. INFRA-2010-2.3.1, Partnership for Advanced Computing in Europe (PRACE) Consortium Partners, 2011.

[3] I. D. Chivers and J. Sleightholme, "Compiler support for the Fortran 2003 and 2008 standard," *ACM SIGPLAN Fortran Forum*, vol. 31, no. 1, pp. 23–33, 2012.

[4] M. Metcalf, J. K. Reid, and M. Cohen, *Fortran 95/2003 Explained*, Oxford University Press, Oxford, UK, 2004.

[5] A. Shalloway and J. R. Trott, *Design Patterns Explained*, Addison-Wesley, Reading, Mass, USA, 2002.

[6] E. Gamma, R. Helm, R. Johnson, and J. Vlissides, *Design Patterns: Elements of Reusable Object-Oriented Software*, Addison-Wesley, New York, NY, USA, 1995.

[7] D. Barbieri, V. Cardellini, S. Filippone, and D. Rouson, "Design patterns for scientific computations on sparse matrices," in *Euro-Par 2011: Parallel Processing Workshops*, vol. 7155 of *Lecture Notes in Computer Science*, pp. 367–376, Springer, 2012.

[8] B. Stroustrup, "Multiple inheritance for C++," in *European UNIX Users' Group Conference*, Helsinki, Finland, May 1987.

[9] B. Martin, "The separation of interface and implementation in C++," in *Proceedings of the 3rd USENIX C++ Conference*, pp. 51–63, Washington, DC, USA, April 1991.

[10] E. Tuyen, W. Joosen, B. N. Jorgensen, and P. Verbaeten, "A generalization and solution to the common ancestor dilemma problem in delegation-based object systems," in *Dynamic Aspects Workshop (DAW '04)*, pp. 103–119, March 2004.

[11] V. K. Decyk, C. D. Norton, and B. K. Szymanski, "How to express C++ concepts in Fortran 90," *ACM Fortran Forum*, vol. 15, pp. 13–18, 1997.

[12] V. K. Decyk, C. D. Norton, and B. K. Szymanski, "How to support inheritance and run-time polymorphism in Fortran 90," *Computer Physics Communications*, vol. 115, no. 1, pp. 9–17, 1998.

[13] E. Akin, *Object-Oriented Programming via Fortran 90/95*, Cambridge University Press, Cambridge, UK, 2003.

[14] D. W. I. Rouson, K. Morris, and X. Xu, "Dynamic memory deallocation in Fortran95/2003 derived type calculus," *Scientific Programming*, vol. 13, no. 3, pp. 189–203, 2005.

[15] M. Ljungberg, K. Otto, and M. Thuné, "Design and usability of a PDE solver framework for curvilinear coordinates," *Advances in Engineering Software*, vol. 37, no. 12, pp. 814–825, 2006.

[16] V. K. Decyk and H. J. Gardner, "Object-oriented design patterns in Fortran 90/95: mazev1, mazev2 and mazev3," *Computer Physics Communications*, vol. 178, no. 8, pp. 611–620, 2008.

[17] D. W. I. Rouson, J. Xia, and X. Xu, *Scientific Software Design: The Tao of SOOP*, Cambridge University Press, New York, NY, USA, 2010.

[18] K. Morris, D. W. I. Rouson, and J. Xia, "On the object-oriented design of reference-counted shadow objects," in *Proceedings of the 4th International Workshop on Software Engineering for Computational Science and Engineering (SE-CSE '11)*, pp. 19–27, May 2011.

[19] D. W. I. Rouson, K. Morris, and J. Xia, "Managing C++ objects with Fortran in the driver's seat: this is not your parents' Fortran," *Computing in Science and Engineering*, vol. 14, no. 2, pp. 46–54, 2012.

[20] D. W. I. Rouson, J. Xia, and X. Xu, "Object construction and destruction design patterns in Fortran 2003," in *Proceedings of the 10th International Conference on Computational Science (ICCS '10)*, pp. 1495–1504, June 2010.

[21] D. W. I. Rouson, J. Xia, and X. Xu, *Scientific Software Design: The Object-Oriented Way*, Cambridge University Press, New York, NY, USA, 2011.

2

A Survey on Visual Programming Languages in Internet of Things

Partha Pratim Ray

Department of Computer Applications, Sikkim University, Gangtok, Sikkim 737102, India

Correspondence should be addressed to Partha Pratim Ray; ppray@cus.ac.in

Academic Editor: Alok Mishra

Visual programming has transformed the art of programming in recent years. Several organizations are in race to develop novel ideas to run visual programming in multiple domains with Internet of Things. IoT, being the most emerging area of computing, needs substantial contribution from the visual programming paradigm for its technological propagation. This paper surveys visual programming languages being served for application development, especially in Internet of Things field. 13 such languages are visited from several popular research-electronic databases and compared under four key attributes such as programming environment, license, project repository, and platform supports. Grouped into two segments, open source and proprietary platform, these visual languages pertain few crucial challenges that have been elaborated in this literature. The main goal of this paper is to present existing VPLs per their parametric proforma to enable naïve developers and researchers in the field of IoT to choose appropriate variant of VPL for particular type of application. It is also worth validating the usability and adaptability of VPLs that is essential for selection of beneficiary in terms of IoT.

1. Introduction

User interaction is the main concern in today's software industry. Among many existing techniques, the implication behind Visual Programming Language (VPL) is the most promising and prevalent. A VPL is like any available programming language that lets user create programs by manipulating program elements graphically (while allowing programming with visual expressions, spatial arrangement of graphic symbol, etc.) rather than by specifying them textually [1]. For instance, many VPLs which are also known as Dataflow Languages are designed based on the idea of utilizing arrows and boxes, where arrows are used to connect the boxes by establishing a seamless relationship between boxes (i.e., entity). VPLs are normally used for educational, multimedia, video games, system development/simulation, automation, and data warehousing/business analytics purposes. For example, (a) Scratch [2], a platform of Massachusetts Institute of Technology, is designed for the kids in class 12 and after school programs; (b) Pure Data (Pd) [3] is designed for creating interactive multimedia and computer music; (c) Unreal Engine 4 [4] uses "Blueprints" to program video games; (d) VisSim [5] allows user to make complex mathematical models in smarter and faster way while executing them in real-time; (e) CiMPLE [6] is used for teaching automation through robotics; and (f) IBM Cognos Business Intelligence [7] is used for front-end programming in Business Intelligence (BI) applications whereby generating SQL queries to run against Relational Data Base Management Systems (RDBMS). Figure 1 presents the percentagewise distribution of VPLs in the illustrated domains. Out of 89 differently surveyed VP/Ls, system simulation and multimedia hold 60% of the market, marking 35% and 25%, respectively.

Although, several domains of applications are under the practice of VPLs, an emerging field of computing-Internet of Things (IoT) is still lingering far behind other sectors. In IoT, researchers direct main attention towards interconnection between several heterogenous objects or "things" with each

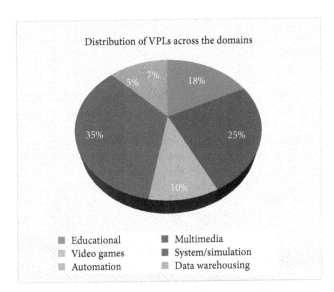

Distribution of VPLs across the domains

7%
5%
18%
35%
25%
10%

■ Educational   ■ Multimedia
■ Video games   ■ System/simulation
■ Automation   ■ Data warehousing

FIGURE 1: Percentagewise distribution of VPLs.

other by means of interoperable and unified platform creation to provide smarter and more efficient way of communication between digital and physical world. Applications of IoT include key areas like domotics, healthcare, smart city, automation, transport, education, environment monitoring, and industry [8–15]. In this context, we may refer to Gartner which has envisioned that about 50 billion of things will be connected to the Internet by 2020. This has already created a huge buzz in the IT industry especially in manufacturing sector where 12.4 billion USD's business was recorded at the end of 2015 [16].

Despite IoT's prospect, very few attentions have been given over the development and designing process of programming languages, mainly at Device-to-Device (D2D) relationship [17]. VPL would in this regard act as a key tool for further enhancement, progress, and motivation towards developers in this field (i.e., IoT) while reducing time-to-market in product (software/hardware) development life cycle. This, in turn, necessitates the need of study and analysis of VPL and its impact on IoT that has not been yet proved by existing literatures. This paper surveys current VPLs being used for application developments in IoT specific framework. The key contributions of this paper are given as follows:

(i) To use state-of-the-art survey of 13 existing VPLs for development of applications using IoT

(ii) To obtain parametric results on various aspects of VPLs

(iii) To discuss and analyze current trends towards selection of VPLs into an IoT specific application

(iv) To identify key issues in augmentation of VPLs in IoT application scenario

This paper is organized as follows. Section 2 presents the state-of-the-art survey of VPLs in IoT. Section 3 illustrates the discussion and analysis in this regard as well as presenting key challenges that need urgent consideration by the educators, industries, and developers. Section 4 concludes this paper.

2. State of the Art

IoT relates to numerous kinds of heterogeneous microcontroller enabled hardware platforms for multiple number of applications' development. Each of these platforms paves dedicated Integrated Development Environment (IDE) and separates programming languages that creates difficulty in seamless transformation from one domain to another, hence delaying product development while incurring excessive expenditure in terms of cost and man power. This section surveys the VPLs being used and developed by several organizations for smooth and ease of programming hardware platforms for IoT based applications with just few clicks/drag-drop procedures, without knowing much about the language (i.e., expression, statement, loop clause, and functional orientation). Popular electronic research databases (such as IEEE Xplore, Google Scholar, Web of Science, Science Direct, and Springer Link) and IoT specific web blogs (Postscapes, Internet of Things-Wired UK, IoT analysis and commentary-O'Reilly Radar, Internet of Things-The Guardian, and Internet of Things Council) are searched in detail while finding these VPLs.

The existing VPLs, involved in this study, are sometimes not just language by itself but a full-fledged IDE. They have been divided into two segments based on their usage licensing, that is, (a) open source and (b) proprietary platform. Further the survey is performed on four classes of characteristics such as programming environment, license, project repository, and platform support.

2.1. Open Source Platforms

(1) Node-Red. It is a visual tool developed for wiring IoT centric applications being hosted on the Github repository (https://github.com/node-red/node-red). It can be run on variety of hardware and software platforms such as Raspberry Pi, BeagleBone Black, Docker, Arduino, Android, IBM Bluemix, Amazon Web Services, and Microsoft Azure under Open Source-Apache 2.0 license. During development of IoT applications, the following APIs are taken into consideration: Admin HTTP API, Runtime API, Storage API, and Editor UI API for administration, embedding other application, runtime data storage and running jQuery template, respectively. It further supports JavaScript, HTML, and JSON language for node creation activities normally found at following port http://localhost:1880.

(2) NETLab Toolkit. It is helpful for drag and drop based IoT based applications development process hosted at http://www.netlabtoolkit.org. Further it provides a simple web interface to connect sensors, actuators, media, and networks associated with smart widgets for development of quick prototype iteration, experiment, and testing just by sketching in heterogenous genre of hardware and building the connected systems. Arduino and latest Linux embedded

systems like the Raspberry Pi, Intel Galileo, and Arduino Tre are currently supported. HTML5, Node.JS, and JavaScript are used for application sketching and server programming purposes under the GNU General Public License.

(3) Ardublock. It is a dedicated GPL, hosted at http://blog .ardublock.com, for programming Arduino and its variant platforms. It runs on Eclipse IDE (as well as Arduino IDE) while allowing developer to code in Java under the GNU General Public License. It is a popular web based VPL platform that helps user to connect and visually program Arduino to create an IoT based application.

(4) Scratch for Android (s4a). It is Scratch modification, made for integration and experimentation with Arduino base IoT products, currently hosted at http://s4a.cat. The s4a has designated protocol stack for communication with Arduino boards. It also supports Android users to get associated with Arduino through HTTP by means of Scratch based remote sensor protocol under the GNU General Public License v2 (GPL2).

(5) Modkit. It is another drag and drop VPL, designed for popular microcontrollers including Arduino, littleBits, Particle Photon, MSP340, Tiva C launch pad, and Wiring S, being hosted at http://modkit.io. It also supports Scratch like event driven and multithreaded model for building IoT related products at ease. This VPL belongs to get build in desktop environment under the GNU General Public License.

(6) miniBloq. This VPL platform is for programming Multiplo™, Arduino, RedBot, and RedBoard in desktop environment. It is available at http://blog.minibloq.org under the Robot Group Multiplo Pacifist License (RMPL) that is an MIT license with a restriction over the development on defence and military projects. C++ language is key of this VPL that runs with help of wxWidgets (http://www.wxwidgets.org).

(7) NooDL. It provides an efficient and effortless web based visual programming environment for IoT related product developments, currently hosted at http://www.getnoodl.com. It supports Arduino and any other physical devices while considering underlying "virtual things" aspect with it. Besides, Bluetooth based local communication with the devices is also possible that allows MQTT broker agent (API) for seamless connection. Dynamic data visualization and analytics are also integrated with this VPL that may be used to access the data stored at local or remote cloud servers with support of Android. NooDL is restricted with the NooDL End User License (NEUL) [18]. It does not provide any external programming language support for coding the applications however.

2.2. Proprietary Platforms

(1) DGLux5. It is a drag and drop based VPL platform for development of IoT applications, currently hosted at http://www.dglogik.com/products/dglux5-ioe-application-platform. This desktop centric approach has link, command, and control data dash board. It provides a personalized interaction by leveraging flexible deployment options (hardware platforms), customized chart, and real-time visualization tool under DGLux Engineering License.

(2) AT&T Flow Designer. It is built upon cloud based time-series data storage platform while involving an intuitive visual tool that enables developer to create IoT supported prototype, being hosted at https://flow.att.com. It offers a special inclusion named "nodes" that is already preconfigured to allow seamless and smooth access to multiple data sources, communication methods, cloud services, and device profiles. Thus, it reduces time-to-market phase in business development process. It supports several third party commercial platforms/APIs (e.g., Twilio and SMTP push mail/notification) for real-time data aggregation and communication between user and applications under the GNU General Public License v3 (GPL3).

(3) Reactive Blocks. It is a visual cum model-driven desktop development environment designed for supporting following tasks, such as, formal model analysis, hierarchical modeling, and automated code generation, available at http://www.bitreactive.com/reactive-blocks. It also provides built-in Java library so that a developer can create reusable and complex IoT applications graphically. Further, OSGi, Kura, and ESF IoT platforms can get merged with Reactive Blocks. MQTT, HTTP, and other IoT related APIs are also used for application development. Java is the key behind the production of Reactive Blocks VPL platform that helps to connect with Modbus, Raspberry Pi, and USB Camera. It is distributed in the market under the Eclipse Public License (EPL).

(4) GraspIO. It provides a drag and drop based, cloud assisted desktop application development platform for interaction with Arduino, Raspberry Pi, GIO Arm, GIO TetraPod, and GraspIO boards, currently hosted at http://www.graspio .com. It is able to support the USR-WiFi 232-G module to provide standard wireless communication by linking 3 Analog/Digital input, 11 touch points, ultrasonic, and GP2D port as sensors and 2 DC motor ports and 8 servo ports as actuators under BSD license.

(5) Wyliodrin. It is a browser enabled VPL that offers communication and development opportunities with Arduino, BeagleBone Black, Raspberry Pi, Intel Galileo, Intel Edison, UDOO, ZedBoard, and Red Pitaya platforms. It also offers multiple programming languages like C, C++, Objective-C, Shell Script, Perl, Python, JavaScript, PHP, C#, Java, Pascal, and so on to develop IoT applications. It is particularly efficient when developer wants to connect IoT devices from smart phones running on either Android or iOS under GNU General Public License v3 (GPL3).

(6) Zenodys. It a browser based specially designed VPL for leveraging IoT based industry 4.0 revolution that is evitable in coming years, hosted at https://www.zenodys.com. Its run-time environment can be deployed to the Raspberry Pi or similar other prospective Linux based industrial IoT

TABLE 1: Comparison between open source and proprietary VPLs.

Type of VPLs	Name of VPLs	Programming environment	License	Project repository	Platforms supported
Open source	Node-Red	Web	Open Source-Apache 2.0	Github	Raspberry Pi, BeagleBone Black, Docker, Arduino, Android, IBM Bluemix, Amazon Web Services, Microsoft Azure under
	NETLab Toolkit	Web	GPL	Self	Arduino and latest Linux embedded systems like the Raspberry Pi, Intel Galileo, and Arduino
	Ardublock	Web	GPL	Self	Arduino
	Scratch for Android (s4a)	Web	GPL2	Self	Arduino
	Modkit	Desktop	GPL2	Self	Arduino, littleBits, Particle Photon, MSP340, Tiva C
	miniBloq	Desktop	RMPL	Self	Multiplo, Arduino, RedBot, and RedBoard
	NooDL	Web	NEUL	Self	Arduino, Android
Proprietary	DGLux5	Desktop	DGLux Engineering License	Self	Raspberry Pi, BeagleBone, DGBox
	AT&T Flow Designer	Desktop	GPL3	Github	AT&T IoT SIM
	Reactive Blocks	Desktop	EPL	Self	Modbus, Raspberry Pi and USB Camera
	GraspIO	Desktop	BSD	Self	Arduino, Raspberry Pi, GIO Arm, GIO TetraPod, and GraspIO boards, Android
	Wyliodrin	Web	GPL3	Self	Arduino, BeagleBone Black, Raspberry Pi, Intel Galileo, Intel Edison, UDOO, ZedBoard and Red Pitay
	Zenodys	Desktop	—	Self	Raspberry Pi, Zenobox

gateways (e.g., Zenobox). This cloud supported platform (e.g., ZenoCloud and Microsoft Azure) encourages developers to associate 3rd party hardware, protocols (e.g., Modbus TCP/RTU, I2C, HTTP, TCP/IP, UDP, RS232, RF, BLE, One Wire, En-Ocean, and Z-Wave), devices, data, APIs, and applications to interact with it easily.

3. Discussions

Table 1 compares the VPLs per open source and proprietary segments while incorporating programming environment, license, project repository, and supported platforms. The reason behind choosing these four parameters is quite linear, that is, comparativeness metrics. Comparative metrics is usually designed in such a way that research can be progressed by means of equal opportunity in inclusiveness scenario. Here, 13 VPLs are being studied not only for the sake of informing the readers about what solutions are available in market, but also for the sake of disseminating applicability and selectivity while developing an IoT based application. An IoT designer must be helpful by gaining the preface made herein this article before going for an application development environment (i.e., desktop or web) as well as the convergence with a particular genre of hardware boards. Licensing is a factor in IoT based product development not only for its incurred cost of royalty service the vender, but also for its code stratification and technological adaptation purposes.

The results have been obtained by surveying the VPLs per various metrics. Few surprising items emerged which are described as follows, showing that open source and

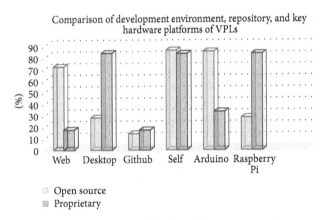

Comparison of development environment, repository, and key hardware platforms of VPLs

FIGURE 2: Percentagewise positioning of development environment, project repository, and key hardware platforms.

proprietary VPLs do infer in many ways from each other. Figure 2 illustrates the comparative analysis between these two portions of VPLs. For ease of understanding and analysis, only three crucial parameters are considered such as development environment, project repository, and hardware boards. It is observed that 72% of open source and 17% of proprietary VPLs are run from the web browser without any need of installation of packages in the host machine. In context of the desktop usage (i.e., nonweb browser based), this situation is just opposite (i.e., 28% of open source and 83% of proprietary). Going to the next parameter, that is, project repository, it is seen that Github is almost equalled by both the segments (i.e., 15.5% on average) which is followed by the self-server storage facility (i.e., 85.5% on average). Among variety of hardware platforms, Arduino and Raspberry Pi are the top two mostly compatible devices boards. Arduino leads the race, marking 85% and 33% in open source and proprietary segment, respectively. Again, the case is different in the usage of Raspberry Pi, where 28% of open source VPLs do practice on to it and 83% of proprietary. However, BeagleBone Board is also approaching to hold the first two boards. Other devices are less frequently getting accustomed with the deployments by VPLs. The GNU GPL is marking the top of the list, whereas Apache 2.0, EPL, BSD, and DGLux Engineering License are similarly gradually getting attention in the VPLs' market. The applicability of JavaScript has emerged as one of the key programming languages in terms of coding the VPLs. Out of 13 surveyed VPLs, 7 belong to open source and the rest belong to proprietary. This also shows the trend of current scenario in VPLs market for IoT development. Although there is slight difference of division among the two segments, it seems that open source VPLs are in the verge of domination of existing VPL supported IoT domain in coming times. As of Section 1, where 89 VPLs were studied over distribution among multiple domains of applications, none of these 13 VPLs was included in that list, which, surely points towards some technical and organizational challenges that are hampering the growth and adaptation of VPLs in IoT. The following section describes the challenges associated with integration of VPLs with IoT.

Challenges

(i) Extensibility. This is probably the vital problem in the surveyed VPLs. VPLs allow developer/user to perform a limited set of operations (things) easily, but precise edge cases are too far difficult (even impossible) to achieve in practice. These VPLs should give user more power, instead of constricting. This might give an opportunity for the IoT enabled application development process where extensibility is a fundamental need.

(ii) Slow Code Generation. Performance diagnosis is a key part of any developer's testing phase, especially in IoT where lots of devices are engaged into the system. It is always important to detect and solve the underlying problems. But, in case of these VPLs, it seems that they work on leaky abstractions, resulting in slow code generation which is nearly impossible to optimize by a developer.

(iii) Integration. Developers live in Integrated Development Environments (IDEs) and simulators world. If the IDEs and simulators are poor in effort and performance, they can make lives miserable! Hence, VPLs and IDEs (design editor) should be designed together for leverage ease of programming environment which is necessary for IoT.

(iv) Standard Model. This is another serious challenge in VPLs of IoT; there is no existing way to have a global standard model such as "mental model," used to give explanation of every human's thought process on working of "anything." Different service professionals like scientists, electrical engineers, mathematicians, IT industry programmers, and so on

are taught and trained how to model the problem statement in different manner, for example, an electrical engineer who would be well qualified and able enough to predict and feel what an electrical system does by just looking at that very circuit diagram. Existing VPLs for IoT do pave the environment to the developer in many ways. Hence, there is a strong need of a standard modular structure or method so that a well-trained developer would be able to build any sort of applications on different genre of platforms.

(v) Abstraction. VPLs are designed for better presenting and working with the existing "abstractions," a metaphor that is used to let the developer manipulate something complex in terms of logic, for example, a function lets programmer present logical operations in form of mapping from an input section to an output section.

(vi) User Interface. VPLs in IoT may be broken into three broad categories of programming tools for different situations such as (a) nonprogrammers (naïve users) to perform basic automation tasks; (b) program learning environments, where it is not feasible to have typing or structuring of the program; and (c) advanced data-flow aggregator; it is well modeled by appropriate data-flows between self-contained logical boxes that essentially mimic the physical world.

4. Conclusion

At this end, we may finally seek for pros and cons of VPLs implied into IoT summarized as follows:

Pros: easy to "visualize" the programming logic (e.g., flow chart), good for naïve users to get associated with the concept of interactions among the logical structures, meant for rapid development of IoT products, less burden over handling "syntax error," and portable on a tablet (or hand held smart phone/device) or in situations where no physical keyboard is present.

Cons: sometimes large amount of time is spent over designing small IoT applications. For example, programming for blinking an LED with Arduino requires lot of graphical interconnections.

Despite VPLs' huge facilities and limited disadvantages, IoT seems to be suitably getting empowered by smooth entanglement and promotion with promising reduction in physical-digital interface.

This paper presents state-of-the-art survey in 13 existing VPLs being used for IoT application development. Popular electronic research databases such as IEEE Xplore, Google Scholar, Web of Science, Science Direct, and Springer Link and IoT specific web blogs (Postscapes, Internet of Things-Wired UK, IoT analysis and commentary-O'Reilly Radar, Internet of Things-The Guardian, and Internet of Things Council) are searched in detail while finding these VPLs. A comparative study has been performed between theses VPLs based on open source and proprietary mode of procurement. Analysis is done on four sections on each VPL that includes (1) programming environment, (2) licensing, (3) project repository, and (4) supported platforms. Presented results show a trendy inference towards implications for Arduino and Raspberry Pi based hardware prototyping boards. Most of the VPLs are presently being hosted in their self-repository. Choice of the programming environment is more or less equally distributed among desktop and web versions. Licensing of such VPLs is somewhat aggregated in and around GPL but other specific types are also under the coverage. Out of the selected issues, poor user interface, slow code generation, lack of standardized model, and absence of abstraction layer seem to resist the growth of VPLs in present time.

However, naïve as well as expert researchers in collaboration with the company incorporations may join to work for the improvement of present issues to facilitate upcoming start-ups (i.e., industry-academia) while paving a prosperous future in this field.

Conflicts of Interest

The author declares that there are no conflicts of interest regarding the publication of this paper.

References

[1] B. Jost, M. Ketterl, R. Budde, and T. Leimbach, "Graphical programming environments for educational Robots: open Roberta—yet another one?" in *Proceedings of the 16th IEEE International Symposium on Multimedia (ISM '14)*, pp. 381–386, IEEE, Taichung, Taiwan, December 2014.

[2] Scratch—Imagine, Program, Share, https://scratch.mit.edu.

[3] Pur Data, "Get Pure Data for Windows/Mac/Linux," January 2017, https://puredata.info/.

[4] Unreal Engine 4, https://www.unrealengine.com/.

[5] VisSim, http://vision-traffic.ptvgroup.com/en-us/products/ptv-vissim/.

[6] CiMPLE, January 15, http://cimple.software.informer.com/.

[7] IBM Cognos Analytics, https://www.ibm.com/software/in/analytics/cognos/platform/.

[8] E. Fleisch, "What is the internet of things—an economic perspective," Auto-ID labs white paper, https://www.alexandria.unisg.ch/60578/1/AutoID%20-%20What%20is%20the%20Internet%20of%20Things%20-%20An%20Economic%20Perspective%20-%20E.%20Fleisch.pdf.

[9] H.-L. Truong and S. Dustdar, "Principles for engineering IoT cloud systems," *IEEE Cloud Computing*, vol. 2, no. 2, pp. 68–76, 2015.

[10] S. W. Kum, J. Moon, T. Lim, and J. I. Park, "A novel design of IoT cloud delegate framework to harmonize cloud-scale IoT services," in *Proceedings of the IEEE International Conference on Consumer Electronics (ICCE '15)*, pp. 247–248, Las Vegas, Nev, USA, January 2015.

[11] A. Celesti, M. Fazio, M. Giacobbe, A. Puliafito, and M. Villari, "Characterizing cloud federation in IoT," in *Proceedings of the 30th IEEE International Conference on Advanced Information Networking and Applications Workshops (WAINA '16)*, pp. 93–98, Crans-Montana, Switzerland, March 2016.

[12] A. Taherkordi and F. Eliassen, "Scalable modeling of cloud-based IoT services for smart cities," in *Proceedings of the 13th IEEE International Conference on Pervasive Computing and Communication Workshops (PerCom Workshops '16)*, Sydney, Australia, March 2016.

[13] G. Fortino, A. Guerrieri, W. Russo, and C. Savaglio, "Integration of agent-based and Cloud Computing for the smart objects-oriented IoT," in *Proceedings of the 18th IEEE International Conference on Computer Supported Cooperative Work in Design (CSCWD '14)*, pp. 493–498, May 2014.

[14] F. Wortmann and K. Flüchter, "Internet of things: technology and value added," *Business and Information Systems Engineering*, vol. 57, no. 3, pp. 221–224, 2015.

[15] H. Lasi, P. Fettke, H.-G. Kemper, T. Feld, and M. Hoffmann, "Industry 4.0," *Business and Information Systems Engineering*, vol. 6, no. 4, pp. 239–242, 2014.

[16] L. Columbus, "Roundup Of Internet of Things Forecasts And Market Estimates," 2015, http://www.forbes.com/sites/buiscolumbus/2015/12/27/roundup-of-internet-of-things-forecasts-and-market-estimates-2015/#60f94aab48a0.

[17] Y. Chen and G. D. Luca, "VIPLE: visual IoT/robotics programming language environment for computer science education," in *Proceedings of the IEEE International Parallel and Distributed Processing Symposium Workshops (IPDPSW '16)*, pp. 963–971, Chicago, Ill, USA, May 2016.

[18] NEUL, http://www.getnoodl.com/eula.

3

Prefiltering Strategy to Improve Performance of Semantic Web Service Discovery

Samira Ghayekhloo and Zeki Bayram

Department of Computer Engineering, Eastern Mediterranean University, Famagusta, Northern Cyprus, Mersin 10, Turkey

Correspondence should be addressed to Samira Ghayekhloo; sghayekhloo@gmail.com

Academic Editor: Wan Fokkink

Discovery of semantic Web services is a heavyweight task when the number of Web services or the complexity of ontologies increases. In this paper, we present a new logical discovery framework based on semantic description of the capability of Web services and user goals using F-logic. Our framework tackles the scalability problem and improves discovery performance by adding two prefiltering stages to the discovery engine. The first stage is based on ontology comparison of user request and Web service categories. In the second stage, yet more Web services are eliminated based upon a decomposition and analysis of concept and instance attributes used in Web service capabilities and the requested capabilities of the client, resulting in a much smaller pool of Web services that need to be matched against the client request. Our prefiltering approach is evaluated using a new Web service repository, called WSMO-FL test collection. The recall rate of the filtering process is 100% by design, since no relevant Web services are ever eliminated by the two prefiltering stages, and experimental results show that the precision rate is more than 53%.

1. Introduction

Semantic Web has been a popular topic of research since its introduction by Berners-Lee et al. in 2001 [1]. Based on this idea, automation of many tasks on the Internet is facilitated through the addition of machine understandable semantic information to Web resources. For instance, automatic discovery of Web services based on their functionality or composition of Web services which cannot fulfil the user requests individually becomes possible [2].

In recent years, complexity of conceptual models (e.g., WSMO [3] and OWL-S [4]) for semantic description of Web services as well as the increasing number of advertised services in repositories made the discovery processes of semantic Web services a heavyweight task [5]. In order to deal with the problem of scalability, researchers proposed various methods, such as indexing and caching mechanism [6], preprocessing strategies before actual matching [7, 8], and hybrid matchmakers that combine logic-based and non-logic-based reasoning [9, 10].

This paper presents a new logical framework and two prefiltering strategies to improve the speed and accuracy of automated Web service discovery. Our discovery framework is based on the WSMO conceptual model for semantically describing user requests (goals), Web services, and domain ontologies. During the discovery process, goal capability descriptions such as inputs, outputs, preconditions, and postconditions (effects) are compared with advertised Web service capability descriptions in order to determine whether they match or not. Logical inference is utilized for matching, which guarantees that the capability requested by the goal is indeed satisfied by the capability of the Web service and also that the Web service has all it needs before it starts execution. Capability reasoning of goal and advertised services relies on ontologies which are used both to describe the services and goals and also to describe the common vocabulary needed by the services and goals.

Our two prefiltering stages are used to eliminate Web services that cannot possibly be successfully matched and reduce the number of Web services which go through the logic-based matching stage. Our first prefiltering stage uses a categorization scheme of Web services. Our second prefiltering stage uses a new technique of extracting attributes and concepts of objects utilized in the goal and the Web service pre- and postconditions. Our technique can deal with objects and predicates that occur in a logical formula with usage of the conjunction (and) logical operator. We also make use of ontology-based mediation between concepts and attributes, so that two syntactically different symbols may be declared to denote the same thing semantically.

The remainder of this paper is organized as follows. Section 2 presents background information on the WSMO model, F-Logic, FLORA-2, and our logical discovery framework. In Section 3, F-Logic formalization of goal and Web services is described. Section 4 describes our preprocessing algorithms and shows how they work to reduce the run-time processing requirements in the matching phase. Section 5 shows experimental results of utilizing our proposed algorithms, as well as the evaluation of these results. In Section 6 we briefly describe related works on this field, and finally in Section 7 we have the conclusions and future works.

2. Background

Our semantic Web service discovery framework focuses on Web services, goals, ontologies, and mediators that are semantically described based on the WSMO [11] model and using the F-Logic [12] language as implemented in the FLORA-2 [13] logic system. The following subsections briefly introduce WSMO and its core elements, F-Logic, along with its reasoner FLORA-2 and our logical semantic Web service discovery framework.

2.1. WSMO Definition. Web services are semantically described by providing a high level declarative specification of Web service functionality and nonfunctional properties in order to facilitate automatic discovery, composition, and invocation of Web Services. Two prominent models in semantic Web service descriptions are Web Service Modelling Ontology (WSMO) [3] and Web Ontology Language for Services (OWL-S) [4]. There also exist other special purpose languages for the semantic description of Web services, such as DIANE Service Description (DSD) language [14] and Semantic Annotation for WSDL and XML schema (SAWSDL) [15].

WSMO comprises four core elements, namely, ontology, goal, Web service, and mediator. *Ontology* is defined as a formal, explicit specification of a shared conceptualization [16]. In the context of semantic Web services, ontology provides a common vocabulary to denote the types in the form of classes or concepts, properties, and interrelationships of concepts in a domain. *Goal* describes what the requester can provide and what it expects from a Web service. *Web service* description represents different functional and nonfunctional features of a deployed Web service. Finally, *Mediator* handles heterogeneity problems that possibly arise between goals, Web services, and ontologies.

2.2. F-Logic and FLORA-2. F-Logic (frame logic) is a powerful logic language with object modelling capabilities. It is used as a foundation for object-oriented logic programming and knowledge representation. Two popular reasoners of

F-Logic are FLORA-2 and OntoBroker [17]. Our proposed intelligent agent for semantic Web service discovery uses the FLORA-2 reasoning engine. FLORA-2 is considered as a comprehensive object-based knowledge representation and reasoning platform. The implementation of FLORA-2 is based on a set of run-time libraries and a compiler to translate a unified language of F-Logic [12], HiLog [18], and Transaction Logic [19, 20] into tabled Prolog code [13]. Basically, FLORA-2 supports a programing language that is a dialect of F-Logic including numerous extensions that involves a natural way to do meta-programming in the style of HiLog, logical updates in the style of Transaction Logic, and a form of defeasible reasoning described in [21].

2.3. Our Logical Semantic Web Service Discovery Framework. In general, Web service discovery is the process of finding appropriate Web services with respect to the user request and ranking of discovered services based on user preference. Our discovery framework receives WSMO goal descriptions and WSMO Web service descriptions, all coded in F-Logic, along with related mediators and ontologies as input entities and for each goal returns an ordered list of Web services that can satisfy the needs of the goal.

Figure 1 depicts the architecture of our discovery framework. The framework consists of four stages: (i) the creation and maintenance of goals and Web services along with related domain ontologies and mediators, (ii) prefiltering stages, (iii) matchmaker, and (iv) ranking stage. In the *creation and maintenance* stage, Web service and goal descriptions which are specified based on our modified WSMO model, along with domain ontologies and mediators, are stored in different repositories. In the *prefiltering* stages, for a given goal, advertised Web services are filtered in two steps in order to narrow down the list of Web services that can be possible matches for the goal, the rest of the Web services being eliminated from consideration. In the *matchmaker* stage, the logical matchmaker checks whether each filtered Web service can really execute in a way such that the user goal is achieved. Finally, the *ranking* stage returns lists of matched Web services based on user preference regarding the minimization of some numeric result (e.g., the cost of a flight between two cities).

Focus of this paper is on our novel filtering strategies that we explain in detail in Section 4. Here we briefly describe our logical matchmaker mechanism.

Our logical matchmaker algorithm makes use of preconditions and postconditions of goals and Web services, as well as related domain ontologies and mediators which are imported in service descriptions. The proof commitments (i.e., what must be proven before a match can succeed) required for our logical inference based matching are given as follows:

(1) *Onts* $\wedge$ *Mediator* $\wedge$ *Goal.Pre* $\vDash$ *Ws.pre*: the precondition of the Web service (*Ws.Pre*) should be logically entailed by imported ontologies, mediators, and what is provided/guaranteed by the goal precondition (*Goal.Pre*).

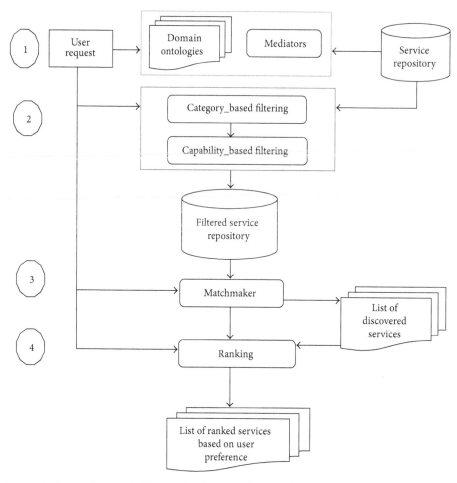

FIGURE 1: Proposed semantic Web service discovery framework including two prefiltering stages.

(2) *Onts* ∧ *Mediator* ∧ *Goal.Pre* ∧ *(Ws.pre ⇒ Ws.post)* ⊨ *Goal.post*: if the postconditions for the Web service were satisfied, then the requirements of the goal should be satisfied. Note how we assume that the execution of the Web service guarantees the validity of the implication in *Ws.pre ⇒ Ws.post*.

3. Web Service and Goal Specification in F-Logic

In Listings 1, 2, and 3 we have the meta-level concept definitions of WSMO [11], with several enhancements. Listing 1 contains the Goal concept, instances of which are used to specify a user's request. It has attributes for nonfunctional properties (such as quality of service, response time, and security), category information (such as transportation, education, and food), ontologies that need to be consulted that contain specific information about a domain (e.g., flight information ontology and geographical information ontology), mediator information (ontologies that deal with discrepancies in terms of defining equivalence classes of terms and synonymous relationship between them), capability needed from the Web service, and the interface demanded from the Web service (i.e., orchestration and choreography).

The *hasCategory* attribute has been newly introduced in our framework in order to allow for filtering based on categories.

The *Service* concept given in Listing 2 is almost identical to the *Goal* concept. Its two differences are as follows: (i) it specifies the *provided* capability instead of the *requested* capability, and (ii) it has an extra attribute called *otherSource* (not in the original WSMO specification) which lists the concepts that should be excluded from consideration in the filtering phase, since objects that are instances of the listed concepts should come from other sources, such as imported ontologies, and are not in the goal.

Listing 3 is the definition of the *Capability* concept. It has attributes for nonfunctional properties, imported ontologies, mediators used, precondition, assumption, postcondition, effect, and optimization. The *optimization* attribute allows the user to specify that the Web service returned by the discovery engine should be optimized with respect to some measure (e.g., price of a flight) and is an enhancement of the original WSMO specification.

When a capability object is part of a goal, precondition is a conjunction of embedded objects in the form of F-logic molecules which specify the information provided by the request to the Web service, and postcondition is a logical expression possibly containing embedded objects, predicates,

```
Goal [|
        hasNonFunctionalProperty ⇒ NonFunctionalProperty,
        hasCategory ⇒ Category,
        importsOntology ⇒ Ontology,
        usesMediator ⇒ Mediator,
        requestsCapability ⇒ Capability,
        requestsInterface ⇒ Interface
    |].
```

LISTING 1: Goal concept in our extended version of WSMO.

```
Service [|
        hasNonFunctionalProperty ⇒ NonFunctionalProperty,
        hasCategory ⇒ Category,
        importsOntology ⇒ Ontology,
        usesMediator ⇒ Mediator,
        hasCapability ⇒ Capability,
        hasInterface ⇒ Interface,
        otherSource ⇒ OntologyConcept
    |].
```

LISTING 2: Web service concept in our extended version of WSMO.

```
Capability [|
        hasNonFunctionalProperty ⇒ NonFunctionalProperty,
        importsOntology ⇒ Ontology,
        usesMediator ⇒ Mediator,
        hasPrecondition ⇒ Axiom,
        hasAssumption ⇒ Axiom,
        hasPostcondition ⇒ Axiom,
        hasEffect ⇒ Axiom,
        optimization ⇒ OptSpecification
        |].
```

LISTING 3: Capability concept in our extended version of WSMO.

conjunction, disjunction, and negation operators. All logic variables in a goal postcondition are implicitly existentially quantified.

However, inside a Web service specification, precondition is a logical expression possibly containing embedded objects in the form of F-Logic molecules, predicates, conjunction, disjunction, and negation operators, where all logic variables are existentially quantified, and postcondition is a conjunction of embedded objects which specify the information provided by the Web service to the requester that is the result of the Web service execution. Note the similarities between the goal postcondition and Web service precondition, as well as the goal precondition and Web service postcondition.

Listings 4 and 5 show the main parts of a goal and a Web service specifications, respectively, among various available types of goals and Web services in our repository.

Listing 4 depicts capability descriptions of a goal instance, which belongs to *AirTransportation* category and describes a request for a flight ticket from Berlin to Istanbul and specifies that the user wants *Sabiha_Gokcen* as a destination airport. The requester also demands flights that have a total cost less than 500$ for 2 people, and each returned flight must have the minimum cost among all other relevant flights. Note that logic variables start with the "?" symbol.

Listing 5 depicts part of the capability and category descriptions of a Web service instance in our Web service repository. The Web service instance belongs to the *Plane-Transportation* category and provides flight reservation for users who request a flight from one place to another. This Web service asks for source and destination cities, desired departure and arrival date, and number of people who would like to reserve this flight, consults two ontologies containing

```
Goal Instance
"Book a flight from Berlin to Istanbul"
hasCategory → AirTransportation,
requestsCapability → ${goal_1[
        hasPrecondition →
              ${reqFlight[
                      originateCity → berlin,
                      terminalCity → istanbul,
                      departureDate → ?DDate,
                      returnDate → ?RDate,
                      numberPeople → 2
                              ]:RequestTicket
              },
        hasPostcondition →
              (${?BookTicket[
                      departureDate → ?DDate,
                      returnDate → ?RDate,
                      fromAirport → ?FromAirport,
                      toAirport → ?ToAirport,
                      cost → ?TotalCost
                              ]:Response
              },
              is_equal(?ToAirport, Sabiha_Gokcen),
              less(?TotalCost, 500)
              ),
        optimization →
              ${optObj[optCost → ?TotalCost]}
                      ]
              }
```

LISTING 4: Part of goal instance specification dealing with the capability desired and the category of the desired service.

```
Web service
"Reserve a flight"
hasCategory → PlaneTransportation,
importsOntology →
              {'.../FlightInfo_ont.flr',
               '.../Geographical_ont.flr'},
hasCapability → ${ ws_x[
        hasPrecondition →
              (${?ReqFlight[
                      startCity → ?FromCity,
                      endCity → ?ToCity,
                      departureDate → ?DDate,
                      returnDate → ?RDate,
                      numberPeople → ?HNumber
                              ]: RequestAirplainTicket }
                      ,
              ${?SomeFlight[
                      departureDate → ?DDate,
                      returnDate → ?RDate,
                      fromAirport → ?FromAirport,
                      toAirport → ?ToAirport,
                      cost → ?Cost
                              ]:Flight  }
                      ,
              mult(?Cost, ?HNumber, ?TotalCost)),
        hasPostcondition →
              ${response[
                      departureDate → ?DDate,
                      returnDate → ?RDate,
                      fromAirport → ?FromAirport,
                      toAirport → ?ToAirport,
                      cost → ?TotalCost
                              ]:Response}
                      ]
              }
```

LISTING 5: Part of Web service instance specification dealing with the capability and the category of the provided service.

flight information (*FlightInfo_ont*) and geographical information (*Geographical_ont*), and returns the list of matching flights ordered according to minimum cost. The precondition needs two objects, one coming from the goal (instance of *RequestFlightTicket*) and one coming from an imported ontology (instance of *Flight*). The predicate *mult* multiplies its first and second parameters and binds its third parameter to the result. It is user-defined.

4. Proposed Two-Phase Prefiltering Mechanism

We propose a solution to tackle the scalability problem by adding two prefiltering stages before the logical matchmaker stage of our discovery framework. We call these two pre-processing algorithms, which offer different filtering levels, *Category_based Filtering* (Cat_Filt) and *Capability_based Filtering* (Cap_Filt).

Our algorithms that perform preprocessing reduce the input data of service matchmaking, so that the matching process is more streamlined; only logical reasoning about Web services that really matter with respect to the goal is carried out.

These preprocessing steps are performed through the main predicate which is called *%filterMain* in Listing 6.

Output of this predicate is list of goals and their related Web services which are inserted into the knowledge base called *RelatedGoalWsModule* for the subsequent logical match-maker phase. Listing 6 shows two filtering stages of this predicate.

To facilitate understanding of the code, let us give a brief introduction to object-oriented notation used in FLORA-2. Suppose that O and C are two objects. O : C means that O is an instance of C (in FLORA-2, an object can simultaneously be a class). C :: D means that C is a subclass of D. Also for user-defined equality, suppose that O1 and O2 are different names (called id-terms in FLORA-2 terminology) that are supposed to denote the same object. This fact is stated in FLORA-2 with the notation O1 :=: O2. This facility enables the user to state that two syntactically different (and typically nonunifiable) terms represent the same object and can be used to define synonymy between such terms.

For each goal-Web service pair, the first stage, *Cat_Filt*, uses the *Global_Cat_Ont* to check semantic similarity of the goal category (Cat_g) against the Web service category (Cat_w).

```
(1) %FilterMain:- ?_Inserted = setof{ ?Ins |
                    //---------First stage of filtering- Cat_Filt--------------
(2)              ?GoalName[hasCategory → ?GoalCat]@?_GoalModule,
(3)              ?WsName[hasCategory → ?WsCat]@?_WsModule,
(4)              ((?WsCat :=: ?GoalCat); (?WsCat :: ?GoalCat); (?GoalCat ::?WsCat)),
                    //---------Second stage of filtering- Cap_Filt---------
(5)              %Filter_Cap (?GoalName, ?WsName),
(6)              alreadySelected(?WsName, GOAL)@FilteredWsModule,
(7)              alreadySelected(?WsName, WEBSERVICE)@FilteredWsModule,
(8)
(9)              insert{related(?GoalName, ?WsName)}@RelatedGoalWsModule,
(10)             ?Ins=related(?GoalName, ?WsName)
(11)                          }.
```

LISTING 6: Prefiltering process containing two filtering stages (lines 2 to 4: *Cat_Filt*; lines 5 to 10: *Cap_Filt*).

$$
\begin{aligned}
&(1) \; Cat\_Filt(g) = \{w \mid g \text{ has a category specified,} \\
&(2) \qquad\qquad w \in W, \\
&(3) \qquad\qquad Cat_w \in Global\_Cat\_Ont, \\
&(4) \qquad\qquad Cat_g \in Global\_Cat\_Ont, \\
&(5) \qquad\qquad (Cat_w :: Cat_g \text{ or } Cat_g :: Cat_w \text{ or } Cat_w :=: Cat_g)\} \cup \\
&(6) \qquad\qquad \{w \mid w \in W, w \text{ does not have a category specified}\} \cup \\
&(7) \qquad\qquad \{w \mid g \text{ does not have a category specified, } w \in W\}.
\end{aligned}
$$

FORMULA 1: Definition of *Cat_Filt* as a function.

According to Listing 6 line (4), if Cat_g and Cat_w are equal, synonymous, or in an inheritance relationship with one another, the Web service is kept for the next stage; otherwise it is discarded. In the second stage, *Cap_Filt*, first attributes and concepts of objects utilized in the goal and the Web service pre- and postconditions are extracted by our new algorithm (described in Section 4.2). Then, extracted concepts and attributes as well as our ontology-based mediation are used to select Web services which satisfy the following conditions.

(i) Their precondition concepts and attributes are a subset of, equal to or synonymous with the goal precondition concepts and attributes, and (ii) their postconditions' concepts and attributes are a superset of, equal to or synonymous with the goal postcondition concepts and attributes. Each goal is then logically tested for an exact match with only the Web services that survive the two-phase filtering process.

Our current scheme of *Cap_Filt* deals with logical expressions involving only the conjunction operator, positive molecules, and predicates. We shall consider extension of the scheme to deal with any logical expression involving the negation and disjunction operators as well as the conjunction operator in future works.

In the following sections, we describe the two filtering stages in more detail.

4.1. Filtering according to Categories (Cat_Filt).

The *Cat_Filt* stage filters the original Web services repository according to both specified categories and synonyms defined in the *Global_Cat_Ont* ontology. Figure 2 illustrates part of hierarchical structure of our specified domains in *Global_Cat_Ont*, which currently contains the three major categories for *transportation*, *food*, and *education*.

Global_Cat_Ont contains both structural knowledge (i.e., it defines subclass and superclass relationships between concepts of three specified domains) and a dictionary of synonymous concepts.

Formula 1 hows the abstract definition of *Cat_Filt* in the form of a function that takes a goal as a parameter. Here, g and w stand for goal instance and Web service instance, respectively, and W is the Web service repository. The result of the function is the union of three sets: (i) if the goal specifies a category (Cat_g), advertised Web services in the registry which have categories matching the goal's category, (ii) Web services that have no category specified, and (iii) all Web services in case no category is specified for the goal. This definition guarantees that if there is any possibility of a Web service matching the goal, it is never eliminated from consideration in the next phase.

In order to better illustrate previous definitions, consider a scenario where a user is searching for a flight lookup service among the existing Web services described in the repository. Suppose that goal category is *PlaneTransportation* and categories of advertised Web services are *AeroplaneTransportation*, *RailwayTransportation*, and *AirTransportation* consecutively. Result of *Cat_Filt* based on *Global_Cat_Ont* ontology on the described scenario is illustrated in Table 1.

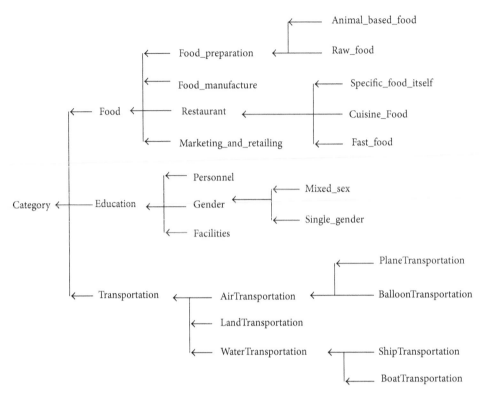

FIGURE 2: Part of the hierarchical structure of our specified domains in the category ontology *Global_Cat_Ont*.

TABLE 1: Results of *Cat_Filt* algorithm on described scenario.

Cat_G	Cat_{WA} AeroplaneTransportation	Cat_{WB} RailwayTransportation	Cat_{WC} AirTransportation
PlaneTransportation	√	×	√

According to the concept relationships definition in *Global_Cat_Ont* ontology, Cat_{WA}, *AeroplaneTransportation*, is a synonym of *PlaneTransportation* and Cat_{WC}, *AirTransportation*, is a subclass of *PlaneTransportation*. Thus, Web services A and C remain as inputs of *Cap_Filt*, and Web service (B) is discarded as irrelevant.

The result of the *Cat_Filt* stage is fed into the second stage *Cap_Filt* in order to eliminate even more Web services that cannot possibly be a match for the given goal.

4.2. Filtering according to Capability Decomposition (Cap_Filt). Unlike other proposals mentioned in related works, our *Cap_Filt* algorithm eliminates irrelevant Web services based on checking the attributes and concepts of objects employed in the goal and the Web service pre- and postconditions. This algorithm first extracts attributes and concepts of objects in goal and Web service specifications (it can deal with predicates and objects that occur in a logical formula possibly including the conjunction logical connective) and then analyzes semantic equivalency between extracted attributes and concepts in order to filter out unrelated Web services.

The level of similarity between such parameters is obtained based on their hierarchical relationships inside this ontology. In this work levels of semantic similarity between parameters are defined as *exact*, *plug-in*, *subsume*, and *fail*. *Exact* means two concepts or two attributes are exactly identical in the same domain ontology. Similarity degree of two concepts or two attributes is *plug-in* only if concept or attribute of goal request is superclass of concept or attribute of the Web service. Degree of two concepts or two attributes is *subsume* only if concept or attribute of goal request is subclass of concept or attribute of the Web service. Finally *fail* degree expresses that there is no semantic-based relationship between two concepts or two attributes.

Also, our work, in order to gain more precise results and tackle the problem that two concepts or two attributes which are going to be investigated may not be equal syntactically, uses WordNet [28], a dictionary of synonymous words. Thus, synonym similarity between the goal and Web service parameters in the *Cap-Filt* algorithm is calculated by making use of the WordNet [29] online synonym dictionary.

As an illustration of the above definition, consider the instances of a matched goal and Web service defined in Section 3. List of concepts and attributes of our goal and Web service preconditions are shown in Table 2.

```
(1) %Filter_Cap (?GoalName, ?WsName):-
                    //----------Pre-Condition--------
(2)     ?GoalName[requestsCapability → ?GCap]@?GoalModule,
(3)     ?GCap ~ ${?_GCapability[
(4)     hasPrecondition → ?GoalPre, hasPostcondition → ?GoalPost]}@?GoalModule,
(5)     ?WsName[hasCapability → ?Wcap]@?WsModule,
(6)     ?Wcap ~ ${?_WSCapability[
(7)     hasPrecondition → ?WsPre, hasPostcondition → ?WsPost]}@?WsModule,
(8)     %FindGoalOrWsAtt (?GoalPre, GoalWsAttModule),
(9)     %DC (?WsPre, ?Ws_Pre_Att_Cnp),
(10)    %Check_Att_Cnp (?WsName, ?Ws_Pre_Att_Cnp, WEBSERVICE),
                    //----------Post-Condition--------
(11)    deleteall{?_A[?_B → ?_V]:?_C @GoalWsAttModule},
(12)    %FindGoalOrWsAtt (?WsPost,GoalWsAttModule),
(13)    %DC (?GoalPost, ?Goal_Post_Att_Cnp),
(14)    %Check_Att_Cnp (?WsName, ?Goal_Post_Att_Cnp, GOAL).
```

LISTING 7: Critical parts of the %*filter_Cap* predicate.

TABLE 2: List of concepts and attributes obtained as a result of %DC/2 predicate.

Name	[(ConceptName, [List of attributes])]
Goal.Pre	[[(RequestTicket, [originateCity, terminalCity, departureDate, returnDate, numberPeople])]].
Ws.Pre	[[(RequestAirplainTicket, [startCity, endCity, departureDate, returnDate, numberPeople]), (Flight, [departureDate, returnDate, fromAirport, toAirport, cost])]].

As it is shown in Table 2, *originateCity* and *startCity* are the first attribute of goal precondition and Web service precondition, respectively. Although the spelling of these two attributes is different and they may not have any relation in domain ontology, they have the identical meaning. Our approach tackles this problem and considers the attributes similar to each other through the dictionary of synonymous words. We employ both semantic and synonymous equivalency of pre- and postconditions.

Listing 7 depicts the critical parts of the %*Filter_Cap* predicate. The filtering, which is based on concepts and attributes of objects in the capability specification of the Web service and goal, is carried out in the following manner:

(1) Lines (2) to (7) read goal and Web service pre- and postconditions from their individual's modules.

(2) As the process of checking semantic and synonymous similarity of goal and Web service specifications are done in knowledge base module (*GoalWsAttModule*), in Listing 7 line (8), attributes and concepts of goal preconditions are inserted into *GoalWsAttModule* through %*FindGoalOrWsAtt/2* predicate.

(3) Attributes and concepts of Web service preconditions are extracted via the %*DC/2* predicate.

This transactional predicate decomposes a Web service precondition, and then extracted concepts and attributes are stored in different lists. Listing 7 line (9) depicts the calling of this predicate with parameters ?*WsPre* (bound to a precondition) and ?*Ws_Pre_Att_Cnp* (a free variable). As a result of the call, ?*Ws_Pre_Att_Cnp* gets bound to the list of concepts and their corresponding attributes in the Web service precondition.

(4) Finally, line (10) depicts %*Check_Att_Cnp* predicate that implements Algorithm 1. It compares concepts and attributes related to goal preconditions with concepts and attributes associated with Web service preconditions based on semantic equivalency between them. Output is the name of related Web services whose concepts and attributes exist in requested goal, as explained below. Web service names that pass through this level of filtering are stored in the knowledge base called *FilteredWsModule*.

Comparison of goal and Web service postconditions is similar to that of the preconditions, except for some changes in predicates' parameters.

(5) As it is shown in line (11) of Listing 7, contents of knowledge base *GoalWsAttModule* which already consisted of goal precondition's attributes and concepts are erased in order to be replaced with the new data.

(6) Attributes and concepts of Web service postconditions are moved into *GoalWsAttModule* by %*FindGoalOrWsAtt* predicate in line (12) of Listing 7.

(7) Attributes and concepts of goal postconditions are extracted via %*DC/2* predicate, and the results are stored in ?*Goal_Post_Att_Cnp* variable as it is shown in line (13).

```
Input: List1 of the form [(Concept, [ListOfAttributes]), ...]
          (extracted from either Goal.Pre or Ws.Post)
       List2 of the form [(Concept, [ListOfAttributes]), ...]
          (extracted from either Ws.Pre or Goal.Post)
       Tag (either GOAL or WEBSERVICE)
Output: (WsName, Tag) (as insertion into module FilteredWsModule)
(1)        Let equiv(A, B) = (A :: B) or (B :: A) or (A :=: B)
(2)        PossibleMatch ← True
(3)        for all (Concept2, [ListOfAttributes2]) ∈ List2 do
(4)          if not ∃ (Concept1, [ListOfAttributes1]) ∈ List1 (
(5)                    equiv(Concept1, Concept2) and
(6)                    ∀ (attribute2 ∈ [ListOfAttributes2]) (
(7)                        ∃ (attribute1 ∈ [ListOfAttributes1]) (
(8)                            equiv(attribute1, attribute2)
(9)                        )
(10)                    )
(11)                )
(12)          then
(13)              PossibleMatch ← False
(14)          end if
(15)        end for
(16)        if
(17)            PossibleMatch = True
(18)        then
(19)            Insert (WsName, Tag) into FilteredWsModule
(20)        end if
```

ALGORITHM 1: Filtering by comparing concepts and attributes.

(8) In line (14), similar to line (10), %Check_Att_Cnp predicate implements Algorithm 1. But this time it checks concepts and attributes related to Web service postconditions with concepts and attributes associated with goal postconditions based on semantic equivalency between them.

If all these checks succeed, then the pair of goal and its related Web services is inserted into the knowledge base so that full checking of the proof commitments can be carried out in the next stage.

5. Experimental Results and Discussions

Proper test collection is needed in order to evaluate the suitability and performance of service discovery frameworks. Currently, two de facto test collections are OWLS-TC [30] and SAWSDL-TC [31]. OWLS-TC, which mainly considers input and output parameters, is applicable for approaches that deal with OWL-S Web services descriptions, and approaches which employ SAWSDL Web service descriptions use the SAWSDL-TC test collection.

The latest version of OWLS-TC at this time is version 4 [32]; it consists of 1083 Web services and 42 queries which are written in the OWL-S language. Unfortunately, the majority of Web services in OWLS-TC are only partially described, being based on input and output types. Only in the last version (version 4), 160 Web services contain preconditions and postconditions (effects) which are described in different

languages such as SWRL (SWRL: A Semantic Web Rule Language, [33]) and PDDL (International Planning Competition, [34]).

The SAWSDL-TC test collection is established to support the performance appraisal of SAWSDL matchmakers. The latest version of SAWSDL-TC, at this time, is version 3; it consists of 1080 semantic Web services and 42 queries which are described in the SAWSDL language. However, descriptions of Web services and queries are only based on input and output parameters [35].

The majority of approaches (such as [7, 9, 23–26]) that work in our field and are mentioned in related works evaluated efficiency and accuracy of their works based on OWLS-TC version 3 test collection. Among all related works, authors of [36] evaluated their proposal based on last version of OWLS-TC test collection, but only input and output parameters are considered for evaluation of their work.

Therefore, due to unavailability of an appropriate test collection that covers main functional descriptions of Web services such as preconditions and postconditions, as well as a categorization scheme of Web services, we generated our own test collection of Web service/goal specifications and used this test collection to measure the gains in efficiency obtained by employing our proposed prefiltering strategy. We called our test collection WSMO-FL [37].

WSMO-FL contains three different domains, namely, transportation, food, and education, with 250 different F-Logic Web services descriptions, 6 different F-Logic goals descriptions, 22 concepts, and 1225 instances.

In this section, in order to validate our proposal, we performed experimental evaluations described and the results of that experimental study. For analysis, each test has been run 20 times performed on a machine with Windows 7, a 2.93 GHz Intel processor, and 4.00 GB of RAM.

In order to determine the actual improvements of our proposed prefiltering stages, we measured several indicators: (i) the average response time of our semantic Web service matchmaker with filtering (*Filt_Disc*) and without filtering (*Naive_Disc*), (ii) the number of Web services that have been effectively eliminated from the initial pool of available Web services at each prefiltering stage, (iii) precision, and (iv) recall. Due to the fact that our filtering stages never eliminate any Web service from consideration unless they are guaranteed to fail at the logical matching stage, it is no surprise that recall rate is always 100%.

The results of the performed tests for the goal are given in Table 3, showing the mean and median of the time it took to match the goal against varying number of Web services. The statistical measures (mean, median) were computed over 20 runs which yielded the raw data. Timing data was recorded for the two cases of matchmaker using the prefiltering phases *Filt_Disc* and matchmaker using no filtering at all *Naive_Disc*.

Figure 3 graphically depicts the same information as a line chart. It can be seen that when using *Filt_Disc*, the average response time is in range of 0.08 to 0.062 seconds, while for the same goal and Web services in *Naive_Disc* it dramatically increases and is in range of 0.08 to 17.5 seconds.

Figure 4 depicts the dramatic number of reductions in the number of Web services that remain after each prefiltering phase. The data has been collected by matching six different goals and varying number of Web services for each goal. The chart indicates that *Cap_Filt* through the semantic equivalency of goal and Web service concepts and attributes does a very good job of eliminating irrelevant Web services, given that most of the remaining Web services after its application pass the *Cat_Filt* stage.

To analyse the accuracy of our prefiltering stages, Table 4 gives the precision and recall values of the combined prefiltering stages for the same set of data obtained by running 6 requested goals against 250 Web services in the repository.

Precision is percentage of the retrieved Web services that are actually relevant. In our context, "retrieved Web services" means the Web services that survived the two-stage elimination process, and a Web service is "relevant" to a goal if the logical matchmaker says so. With these definitions, precision is formalized as follows [38]:

Precision

$$= \frac{\text{Number of Relevant Web services in the retrieved set}}{\text{Number of Retrieved Web services}}. \quad (1)$$

Recall is the portion of the relevant Web services that are successfully retrieved. It is formalized as follows [38]:

Recall

$$= \frac{\text{Number of relevant Web services in the retrieved set}}{\text{Number of all relevant Web services in the repository}}. \quad (2)$$

TABLE 3: Statistical comparison of *Filt_Disc* and *Naive_Disc*.

Number of WSs	Engine	Mean time (sec)	Median time (sec)
5	Filt_Disc	0.08	0.09
	Naive_Disc	0.08	0.08
50	Filt_Disc	0.27	0.27
	Naive_Disc	3.93	4.02
150	Filt_Disc	0.45	0.51
	Naive_Disc	12.39	12.39
250	Filt_Disc	0.62	0.60
	Naive_Disc	17.43	17.33

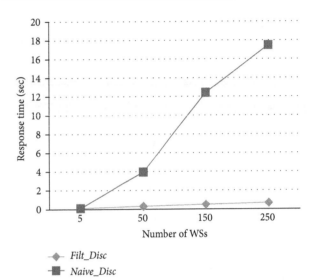

FIGURE 3: Comparison of *Filt_Disc* and *Naive_Disc*.

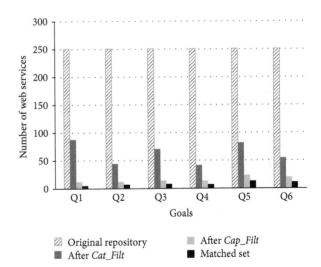

FIGURE 4: Effectiveness of the two prefiltering stages in eliminating irrelevant Web services.

As shown in Table 4, average precision for all request queries is 53.72% which to some extent can be considered a good precision rate. It means that around 55% of retrieved Web services are exactly matched with the requested goal and the others, around 45%, are irrelevant. However, the average recall of queries has the highest possible rate, 100%. With this

TABLE 4: Precision and recall of combined prefiltering stages in each requested goal.

Goal	Q1	Q2	Q3	Q4	Q5	Q6	Average
Precision	41.6%	58.3%	57.1%	53.8%	56.5%	55%	53.72%
Recall	100%	100%	100%	100%	100%	100%	100%

100% recall rate, all the relevant Web services in Web service repository are retrieved through the proposed prefiltering stages, an important feature that sets out filtering strategy apart from all the other proposals.

Figure 5 graphically shows the precision and recall rate of each requested goal together with the average precision line. The chart illustrates that precision rate of all requests except the first one (Q1) is higher than the average. Low precision rate of Q1 indicates that there exist many Web services in the repository whose attributes and concepts are semantically similar to the concepts' name and attributes' name of requested goal; however, the value of Web service attributes defined in ontologies does not match the requested value of goal attributes. Such Web services fail in the actual logical matching procedure.

As we explained before, the reason of top average recall rate is that all relevant Web services are retrieved by *Cat_Filt* and *Cap_Filt* algorithms, which is another way of saying that in the prefiltering stages, we only eliminate Web services that the matcher would definitely reject. The reason for the not-so-high average precision rate in prefiltering stages is that although the retrieved Web services are similar to requested goal due to semantic and synonymous equivalency of their concepts and attributes in domain ontology, maybe some Web services that will eventually be rejected pass through the filters. However, in a real world situation where thousands of categories exist and Web services, as well as goals, are annotated by categories, precision would be expected to rise significantly, since the majority of Web services under consideration would be eliminated by the first stage of filtering (Cat_Filt).

Since our framework evaluation is based on our newly generated test collection, WSMO-FL, a comparison between the accuracy and performance of our work and the other available works in the literature would not be very informative. However, an average of 100% for recall and 53.72% for precision indicates a satisfactory accuracy of this work. It should be pointed out that this accuracy was observed in a more complex condition of goals and Web services due to pre- and postcondition parameters. The other studies mentioned in related works did not consider these many complexities in their goals and Web services.

6. Overview of Related Works

Recently, although a wealth of insightful efforts have proposed different solutions to improve the semantic Web discovery process and their related scalability issues, we could not find any work that addresses the performance challenge of discovery process in a similar way to our work. In this section, we discuss proposals related to this field and analyse

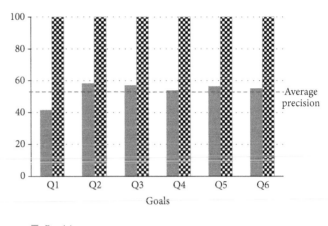

FIGURE 5: Precision and recall of each requested goal along with the average precision line.

their relationship with our solution, and their advantages are compared to our approach.

Table 5 compares our work with the related works based on several dimensions with respect to semantic Web service discovery improvement. These dimensions are preprocessing, discovery method, parameters, and frameworks. First three dimensions are further subdivided into subdimensions.

Preprocessing is subdivided into nonfunctional properties (NFPs) and functional properties (FPs). *NFP* here stands for methods of adding some NFP elements to the Web service and goal descriptions (e.g., categorization of each advertised/requested Web service at design time). *FP* stands for methods to compare functional parameters of goal and Web services. One more level of subdivision used in preprocessing factor is taxonomy (TX) (i.e., relationship between two concepts/attributes is described by using a hierarchical diagram), synonymity (SY) (i.e., syntactically two concepts/attributes are different but they have the same or identical meaning), and syntax (ST) (i.e., no synonymous or hierarchical relationships exist between two concepts/attributes and they are compared based on similarity of their string) similarity method measurements for each mentioned NFP and FP.

Discovery method represents which kinds of service matchmakers are used in the approaches: logic (LOG), nonlogic (NLOG), or hybrid method (HY) which is combination of both logic and nonlogic methods.

Parameters demonstrates degree of completeness of a research (whether it uses the major functional parameters of goal and Web services or not). Major functional parameters of goal and Web services in OWL-S and WSMO models are input (I), output (O), precondition (PRE), and Postcondition or effect (POS/EFF).

We summarise the result of the comparative study of Web service discovery approaches in Table 5, where each row represents an approach and the columns stand for main dimensions in Web service discovery improvement. The symbol "$\sqrt{}$" is used to denote that the specified approach supports the corresponding dimension, and "—" means that it does not.

TABLE 5: Comparison of this work with related works.

App.	Preprocessing					Discovery method			Parameters				Framework
	NFP		FP										
	TX	SY	TX	SY	ST	LOG	NLOG	HY	I	O	PRE	POS/EFF	
[9]	—	—	—	—	—	—	—	√	√	√	—	—	OWL-S
[10]	—	—	—	—	—	—	—	√	√	√	—	—	WSMO
[6, 22]	—	—	—	—	—	√	—	—	√	√	√	√	WSMO
[23]	—	—	—	—	—	√	—	—	√	√	√	√	OWL-S
[24]	—	—	—	—	—	—	—	√	√	√	—	—	OWL-S
[25]	√	—	—	—	—	√	—	—	√	√	—	—	OWL-S
[26]	—	√	—	—	—	—	—	—	√	√	—	—	OWL-S
[7]	—	—	√	—	—	—	—	—	√	√	—	—	OWL-S
[8]	—	—	√	—	—	—	—	—	√	√	—	—	WSMO
[27]	—	—	—	—	√	√	—	—	√	√	√	√	WSMO
Our work	√	√	√	√	—	√	—	—	√	√	√	√	WSMO

Approach name (APP). Hybrid method (HY). Taxonomy (TX). Synonymity (SY). Syntax (ST). Logic (LOG). Functional properties (FPs). Output (O). Input (I). Nonlogic (NLOG). Nonfunctional properties (NFPs). Precondition (PRE). Postcondition or effect (POS/EFF).

In order to highlight the advantages of our work with respect to the prior researches, we classified the related works into two groups: approaches that optimize semantic Web service discovery through (a) improvement of matchmakers and (b) application of prefiltering mechanism before actual matchmakers. The former discusses the related works where the only focus is to improve the performance of their matchmaker engines by employing various methods. The latter tries to reduce the size of original repository and the filtered repository is used as input of actual matchmaker.

(a) Approaches That Improve the Matchmaker Engine. Regarding the need to improve the discovery process and make it more scalable, some approaches attempt to improve the performance of the matchmaker engine without introducing any extra preprocessing stages.

Klusch et al. [9] implemented a hybrid matchmaker consisting of both approximated Information Retrieval (IR) matching, such as syntactic similarity technique, and OWL-DL logical reasoner to discover semantic Web services. Authors used four variants to calculate the text similarity of parameters, called *cosine, loss-of-information, extended Jacquard,* and *Jensen-Shannon.* In *OWLS-MX*, the logical reasoner only considers degree of semantic similarity between input and output parameters of OWL-S advertised/requested services and available concepts in the specified domain ontology. Later they developed their system to support WSMO services, called *WSMO-MX* [10]. Their comprehensive evaluations demonstrate that both approaches presented high precision in the S3 contest [39]. However, shortcomings of their solution are as follows. (i) They are time consuming because of high calculation costs related with both logic-based matching and text-based similarity matching; (ii) they retrieve Web services which are not related to the request.

The Klusch et al. approach can be improved if they utilize our preprocessing strategies on top of their actual matchmakers. For instance, by applying our prefiltering stages before the hybrid matchmakers, especially on the logic-based matchmaker, they can potentially decrease the size of the initial Web service repository and consequently improve the overall performance of matchmaker.

Stollberg et al. in [6, 22] improved the matching process by implementing a caching mechanism that decreases the size of search space and reduces the matchmaker operations. The presented cache uses a *Semantic Discovery Caching* (SDC) graph that stores connections between client requests described as WSMO goal templates and their relevant Web services. Thus, when a goal instance is received, first, the system compares the goal instance with cached templates with respect to semantic similarity and if there is a match, merely the relevant Web services that are stored in the SDC graph are used for subsequent discovery.

Authors of [6, 22] claim that they presented a standard approach where both advertised and requested functionalities are formally expressed in terms of preconditions and effects (postcondition). Also they used first-order logic as the specification language for formal description of these terms. Since our proposal also has been established in the spirit of WSMO framework and developed to work on goals and Web services capability which consist of inputs, outputs, and pre- and postcondition, proposed caching approach can be completed when our prefiltering mechanisms are implemented before creating the caching graph. Thus, the number of relevant Web services which are stored in graph can be possibly decreased.

Authors of [23] introduced SPARQL as a language to describe the preconditions and postconditions of OWL-S Web services as well as user requests. They implemented a matchmaker that works through agents called *SPARQLent* (SPARQL agent). In this approach, a complete discovery solution of their algorithm is discussed and shows how SPARQL queries are used to modify and query the agent's knowledge base. Finally, they evaluated their proposal against OWLS-MX via SME_2 test tool [40].

Although the method offered in [23] is based on pre- and postconditions of Web services and goals, their evaluation is performed based on OWLS-TC V3, while presented Web services descriptions in this test collection are without pre- and postconditions. In addition, our prefiltering stages could be also useful in avoiding SPARQL agent to load all available Web services on the repository and as a result cause further improvement to their agent performance.

Amorim et al. discuss a hybrid matchmaker called *OWL-S Discovery*. It is a combination of semantic filters based on input and output parameters of requested/advertised services and analysing each neighbour relationship in domain ontology [24]. Authors employed five levels of semantic similarity between input and output parameters, namely, exact, plug-in, subsume, fail, and sibling. Also, in order to analyse each neighbour relationship in the concepts, they use a dictionary to classify the concepts. Based on this dictionary, concepts are either identical or synonymous or neither synonymous nor identical, as in our work. At the end they compare their work with Paolucci's approach [41] and the hybrid algorithm OWLS-MX through OWLS-TC v3 test collection. Our proposal also can be applied to the top of *OWL-S Discovery* to further improve discovery processes. But our work uses a more expressive model to describe user requests and Web services descriptions as they contain pre- and postconditions.

(b) Approaches Using Preprocessing Mechanisms. These approaches make use of preprocessing mechanisms that help optimization of automated Web service discovery by narrowing down the set of existing Web services in the repository that will be considered by the service matchmaker. Preprocessing mechanisms are further subdivided into two categories: (1) preprocessing mechanisms based on categorization schemes of NFPs and (2) preprocessing mechanisms based on semantic similarity of FPs.

(1) Prefiltering Based on Categorization Schemes of NFPs. Most of the efforts related to prefiltering techniques follow the classification methods: either exploit hierarchical categorization schemes of Web services on the basis of domain ontologies [25] or use dictionary of synonymous words [26]. The filtering process is separate from matchmaker, so the results of this prefiltering stage are then inspected through any actual process of service matchmaking. The majority of the mentioned proposals adapted OWLS-TC v3 test collection by adding one element to the request and Web service NFPs that refer to service application domain.

Authors of [25, 26] implemented their categorization proposals on OWL-S Web services and verified them with respect to the OWLS-TC v3 data set. However, OWL-S service description in this test collection does not contain any information about service's application domain. Thus, in order to overcome the limitation of current OWL-S service profile elements both approaches added one NFP to the OWL-S service profile. Although both used the same idea, their solution is different. In [25] the defined category concept of the service request is compared with the defined category concept of advertised Web services via hierarchical categorization scheme in global category ontology. A Web service is eliminated if it has no category relationship with the request category. However, in [26] equivalency of requested and advertised Web services category concepts are computed via their relationship in the WordNet [28] dictionary of synonyms words. This approach is lacking in its own matchmaker (i.e., evaluation is done via OWLS-MX matchmaker).

Although the idea of our first filtering stage is similar to the mentioned proposals, it has the following novelties. (i) Our proposed *Cat_filt* stage enriches the WSMO framework by adding an attribute called hasCategory to both goal and Web service descriptions. (ii) In order to increase the accuracy and performance of our categorization schemes, this work takes into account semantic similarity relationship between goal category and Web service category (i.e., if two categories mean the same thing or inherit the same class).

(2) Prefiltering Based on Semantic Similarity of FPs. Authors of [7, 8] also used preprocessing strategies before the actual matching process. Their prefiltering is based on only FPs of Web services. They present two different SPARQL queries to facilitate the search process on a semantic Web service registry. They automatically create SPARQL queries (called Q_{all}, Q_{some}) by analysing the user request, and by using these two filtering queries they are able to perform two levels of filtering on the initial Web service repository. Based on these two queries, only Web services containing all (in the case of Q_{all}) or some (in the case of Q_{some}) concepts referred by a user request are returned.

Our second filtering stage (*Cap_Filt*) is similar to the method proposed in [8]. Four major differences between our work and theirs are that

(i) since in our prefiltering stage service descriptions consist of all information about inputs, outputs, and pre- and postconditions, we can obtain more accurate results than their strategies;

(ii) our algorithm not only considers the hierarchical relationship of concepts and attributes but also takes into account the similarity of requested/advertised Web service concepts and attributes based on their synonyms;

(iii) we employ an initial filtering phase based upon a categorization scheme, which could actually improve their performance as well if they used it before Q_{all} or Q_{some} algorithm;

(iv) their approach consists only of a preprocessing stage to filter the preliminary Web service repository and they did not implement any service matchmaking, so they cannot be evaluated on their own.

Among all the mentioned approaches, [27] is the closest to our work. The INFRAWEBS project implements a discovery framework which consists of two components, prefiltering and discovery. In the prefiltering stage it uses traditional Information Retrieval techniques, and a logic-based matching implemented in Prolog is utilized as a service matchmaker.

Although the INFRAWEBS project has similarities with our work, some differences do stand out. Our prefiltering stage considers semantic equivalency of both NFP and FP of the requested/advertised services, analyzing objects, attributes, and concepts. Our discovery engine works with much richer descriptions of Web services and requests, encoded in frame logic. Our implementation uses the FLORA-2 language and execution environment, a much more powerful alternative to plain Prolog. It is conceivable that a combination of our approach and theirs can yield a discovery framework that is more effective at eliminating useless Web services than either approach alone.

7. Conclusions and Future Works

We have shown that the overall performance and accuracy of semantic Web service discovery frameworks can be improved significantly through the introduction of prefiltering stages that eliminate most of the irrelevant Web services from consideration at the computationally expensive matching stage. Specifically, in this paper, we proposed *Category_based* and *Capability_based* prefiltering mechanisms for narrowing down the number of Web service descriptions that need to be considered in the matching phase to determine their relevance to the current goal.

We evaluated the effectiveness of our proposal in a novel test collection, *WSMO-FL*, which consists of 250 Web service specifications of varying complexities and 6 goals. Our filtering stages stand out due to their 100% recall rate that is a consequence of their design, their ability to deal with complex specifications of goals and Web services written in an enhanced version of WSMO, and a reasonably high precision rate, as demonstrated experimentally, which is bound to increase considerably in the presence of a large number of categories and goals/Web services that make use of those categories. Our results also indicate that when the prefiltering stages are employed in the system, as expected, the search space is considerably reduced, and consequently response time of the system is improved dramatically.

Our work has several further advantages, summed up in the following:

(i) Unlike the majority of semantic Web service discovery approaches which are only performed on input and output concepts, our semantic Web service discovery framework deals with concepts and attributes of Web service and goal pre- and postconditions.

(ii) Our prefiltering stages are generic, so that they can be applied (after necessary adaptations) to improve the performance of other available service matchmakers.

(iii) 100% recall rate of our framework implies that our method does not result in false negatives (FN) (i.e., Web services which are relevant but are classified as irrelevant): all relevant Web services are retrieved through the prefiltering algorithms.

(iv) Due to incomplete service descriptions in OWLS-TC test collections (i.e., Web services are partially described only based on input/output concepts), for the first time we created a new test collection called WSMO-FL, which contains fully defined Web services and goals capabilities (i.e., Web services and goals are described based on pre- and postconditions).

(v) To the best of our knowledge WSMO-FL is the first larger test collection which is established based on the WSMO conceptual model. It uses frame logic (F-Logic) as a fully adequate expression language for specifying pre- and postconditions which is missing in currently available test collections.

For future work, we are planning to improve our scheme in the following ways:

(i) extending the second stage so that it can work on *any* logical expression containing the logical connectives *conjunction (and), disjunction (or),* and *negation (not)* to any nesting depth;

(ii) extending our new *WSMO-FL* test collection to (a) have a much larger number of Web services and goals, as well as categories, (b) increase complexity of Web service and goal pre- and postconditions, and (c) expand the dictionary of synonymous words in the existing domain ontologies.

Conflict of Interests

The authors declare that there is no conflict of interests regarding the publication of this paper.

References

[1] T. Berners-Lee, J. Hendler, and O. Lassila, "The semantic web," *Scientific American*, vol. 284, no. 5, pp. 34–43, 2001.

[2] S. A. McIlraith, T. C. Son, and H. Zeng, "Semantic web services," *IEEE Intelligent Systems*, vol. 16, no. 2, pp. 46–53, 2001.

[3] D. Roman, U. Keller, H. Lausen et al., "The Web service modelling ontology," *Applied Ontology*, vol. 1, no. 1, pp. 77–106, 2005.

[4] D. Martin, M. Burstein, J. Hobbs et al., "OWL-S: Semantic Markup for Web Services," W3C member submission 22, 2004.

[5] L. D. Ngan and R. Kanagasabai, "Semantic Web service discovery: State-of-the-art and research challenges," *Personal and Ubiquitous Computing*, vol. 17, no. 8, pp. 1741–1752, 2013.

[6] M. Stollberg, M. Hepp, and J. Hoffman, "A caching mechanism for semantic web service discovery," in *The Semantic Web: 6th International Semantic Web Conference, 2nd Asian Semantic Web Conference, ISWC 2007 + ASWC 2007, Busan, Korea, November 11–15, 2007. Proceedings*, vol. 4825 of *Lecture Notes in Computer Science*, pp. 480–493, Springer, Berlin, Germany, 2007.

[7] J. M. García, D. Ruiz, and A. Ruiz-Cortés, "Improving semantic web services discovery using SPARQL-based repository filtering," *Web Semantics: Science, Services and Agents on the World Wide Web*, vol. 17, pp. 12–24, 2012.

[8] J. Mara García, D. Ruiz, and A. Ruiz-Corts, "A lightweight prototype implementation of SPARQL filters for WSMO-based discovery," Tech. Rep., Applied Software Engineering Research Group-University of Seville., ISA-11-TR-01, 2011.

[9] M. Klusch, B. Fries, and K. Sycara, "OWLS-MX: a hybrid Semantic Web service matchmaker for OWL-S services," *Web Semantics*, vol. 7, no. 2, pp. 121–133, 2009.

[10] M. Klusch and F. Kaufer, "WSMO-MX: a hybrid Semantic Web service matchmaker," *Web Intelligence and Agent Systems*, vol. 7, no. 1, pp. 23–42, 2009.

[11] D. Fensel, H. Lausen, A. Polleres et al., "The concepts of WSMO," in *Enabling Semantic Web Services: The Web Service Modeling Ontology*, pp. 63–81, Springer Science+Business Media, 2007.

[12] M. Kifer, G. Lausen, and J. Wu, "Logical foundations of object-oriented and frame-based languages," *Journal of the ACM*, vol. 42, no. 4, pp. 741–843, 1995.

[13] M. Kifer, G. Yang, H. Wan, and C. Zhao, *FLORA-2: User's Manual, Version 1.0*, Stony Brook University, Stony Brook, NY, USA, 2014.

[14] U. Küster, B. König-Ries, M. Klein, and M. Stern, "DIANE: a matchmaking-centered framework for automated service discovery, composition, binding, and invocation on the web," *International Journal of Electronic Commerce*, vol. 12, no. 2, pp. 41–68, 2007.

[15] H. Lausen and J. Farrell, "Semantic annotations for WSDL and XML schema," W3C recommendation, 2007.

[16] T. R. Gruber, "A translation approach to portable ontology specifications," *Knowledge Acquisition*, vol. 5, no. 2, pp. 199–220, 1993.

[17] J. Angele, "OntoBroker: mature and approved semantic middleware," *Semantic Web*, vol. 5, no. 3, pp. 221–235, 2014.

[18] W. Chen, M. Kifer, and D. S. Warren, "HiLog: a foundation for higher-order logic programming," *Journal of Logic Programming*, vol. 15, no. 3, pp. 187–230, 1993.

[19] A. Bonner and M. Kifer, "A logic for programming database transactions," in *Logics for Databases and Information Systems*, pp. 117–166, 1998.

[20] A. J. Bonner and M. Kifer, "Overview of transaction logic," *Theoretical Computer Science*, vol. 133, no. 2, pp. 205–265, 1994.

[21] H. Wan, B. Grosof, M. Kifer, P. Fodor, and S. Liang, "Logic programming with defaults and argumentation theories," in *Logic Programming*, vol. 5649 of *Lecture Notes in Computer Science*, pp. 432–448, Springer, Berlin, Germany, 2009.

[22] M. Stollberg, J. Hoffmann, and D. Fensel, "A caching technique for optimizing automated service discovery," *International Journal of Semantic Computing (World Scientific)*, vol. 5, no. 1, pp. 1–31, 2011.

[23] M. L. Sbodio, D. Martin, and C. Moulin, "Discovering Semantic Web services using SPARQL and intelligent agents," *Journal of Web Semantics*, vol. 8, no. 4, pp. 310–328, 2010.

[24] R. Amorim, D. B. Claro, D. Lopes, P. Albers, and A. Andrade, "Improving web service discovery by a functional and structural approach," in *Proceedings of the IEEE 9th International Conference on Web Services (ICWS '11)*, pp. 411–418, IEEE, Washington, DC, USA, July 2011.

[25] T. Khdour, "Towards semantically filtering web services repository," in *Digital Information and Communication Technology and Its Applications*, vol. 167 of *Communications in Computer and Information Science*, pp. 322–336, Springer, Berlin, Germany, 2011.

[26] K. Mohebbi, S. Ibrahim, and M. Zamani, "A pre-matching filter to improve the query response time of semantic web service discovery," *Journal of Next Generation Information Technology*, vol. 4, no. 6, 2013.

[27] L. Kovács, A. Micsik, and P. Pallinge, "Two-phase semantic web service discovery method for finding intersection matches using logic programming," in *Proceedings of the Workshop on Semantics for Web Services*, Zurich, Switzerland, December 2006.

[28] C. Fellbaum, *WordNet: An Electronic Lexical Database*, Blackwell Publishing, Oxford, UK, 1998.

[29] https://wordnet.princeton.edu/.

[30] http://projects.semwebcentral.org/projects/owls-tc/.

[31] http://projects.semwebcentral.org/projects/sawsdl-tc.

[32] M. Klusch, M. A. Khalid, P. Kapahnke, B. Fries, and M. V. Saarbrücken, *OWLS-TC -OWL-S Service Retrieval Test Collection, User Manual*, 2010.

[33] http://www.w3.org/Submission/SWRL/.

[34] C. Aeronautiques, A. Howe, C. Knoblock et al., *The Planning Domain Definition Language (PDDL)*, 1998.

[35] M. A. Khalid, B. Fries, M. Vasileski, P. Kapahnke, and M. Klusch, *SAWSDL-TC Service Retrieval Test Collection, User Manual*, Version 3.0, SAWSDL, Saarbrücken, Germany, 2010.

[36] Z. Cong, A. Fernandez, H. Billhardt, and M. Lujak, "Service discovery acceleration with hierarchical clustering," *Information Systems Frontiers*, vol. 17, no. 4, pp. 799–808, 2014.

[37] http://cmpe.emu.edu.tr/samira/WSMO-FL.htm.

[38] R. Baeza-Yates and B. Ribeiro-Neto, *Modern Information Retrieval*, vol. 463, ACM Press, New York, NY, USA, 1999.

[39] M. Klusch, "Overview of the S3 contest: performance evaluation of semantic service matchmakers," in *Semantic Web Services: Advancement through Evaluation*, pp. 17–34, Springer, Berlin, Germany, 2012.

[40] http://projects.semwebcentral.org/projects/sme2/.

[41] M. Paolucci, T. Kawamura, T. R. Payne, and K. Sycara, "Semantic matching of web services capabilities," in *The Semantic Web—ISWC 2002: First International Semantic Web Conference Sardinia, Italy, June 9–12, 2002 Proceedings*, vol. 2342 of *Lecture Notes in Computer Science*, pp. 333–347, Springer, Berlin, Germany, 2002.

4

OpenCL Performance Evaluation on Modern Multicore CPUs

Joo Hwan Lee, Nimit Nigania, Hyesoon Kim, Kaushik Patel, and Hyojong Kim

School of Computer Science, College of Computing, Georgia Institute of Technology, Atlanta, GA 30332, USA

Correspondence should be addressed to Joo Hwan Lee; joohwan.lee@gatech.edu

Academic Editor: Xinmin Tian

Utilizing heterogeneous platforms for computation has become a general trend, making the portability issue important. OpenCL (Open Computing Language) serves this purpose by enabling portable execution on heterogeneous architectures. However, unpredictable performance variation on different platforms has become a burden for programmers who write OpenCL applications. This is especially true for conventional multicore CPUs, since the performance of general OpenCL applications on CPUs lags behind the performance of their counterparts written in the conventional parallel programming model for CPUs. In this paper, we evaluate the performance of OpenCL applications on out-of-order multicore CPUs from the architectural perspective. We evaluate OpenCL applications on various aspects, including API overhead, scheduling overhead, instruction-level parallelism, address space, data location, data locality, and vectorization, comparing OpenCL to conventional parallel programming models for CPUs. Our evaluation indicates unique performance characteristics of OpenCL applications and also provides insight into the optimization metrics for better performance on CPUs.

1. Introduction

The heterogeneous architecture has gained popularity, as can be seen from AMD's Fusion and Intel's Sandy Bridge [1, 2]. Much research shows the promise of the heterogeneous architecture for high performance and energy efficiency. However, how to utilize the heterogeneous architecture considering performance and energy efficiency is still a challenging problem. OpenCL is an open standard for parallel programming on heterogeneous architectures, which makes it possible to express parallelism in a portable way so that applications written in OpenCL can run on different architectures without code modification [3]. Currently, many vendors have released their own OpenCL framework [4, 5].

Even though OpenCL provides portability on multiple architectures, portability issues still remain in terms of performance. Unpredictable performance variations on different platforms have become a burden for programmers who write OpenCL applications. The effective optimization technique is different depending on the architecture where the kernel is executed. In particular, since OpenCL shares many similarities with CUDA, which was developed for NVIDIA GPUs, many OpenCL applications are not well optimized for modern multicore CPUs. The performance of general OpenCL applications on CPUs lags behind the performance expected by programmers considering conventional parallel programming models. The expectation comes from programmers' experience with conventional programming models. OpenCL applications show very poor performance on CPUs when compared to applications written in conventional programming models.

The reasons we consider CPUs for OpenCL compute devices are as follows.

(1) CPUs can also be utilized to increase the performance of OpenCL applications by using both CPUs and GPUs (especially when a CPU is idle).

(2) Because modern CPUs have more vector units, the performance gap between CPUs and GPUs has been decreased. For example, even for the massively parallel kernels, sometimes CPUs can be better than GPUs, depending on input sizes. On some workloads with high branch divergence or with high instruction-level parallelism (ILP), the CPU can also be better than the GPU.

A major benefit of using OpenCL is that the same kernel can be easily executed on different platforms. With OpenCL,

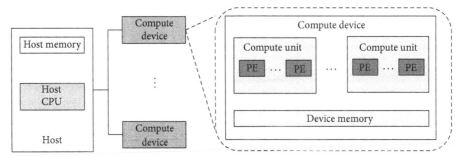

FIGURE 1: OpenCL platform model.

it is easy to dynamically decide which device to use at run-time. OpenCL applications that select a compute device between CPUs and GPUs at run-time can be easily implemented. However, if the application is written in OpenMP, for example, it is not trivial to split an application to use both CPUs and GPUs.

Here, we evaluate the performance of OpenCL applications on modern out-of-order multicore CPUs from the architectural perspective, regarding how the application utilizes hardware resources on CPUs. We thoroughly evaluate OpenCL applications on various aspects that could change their performance. We revisit generic performance metrics that have been lightly evaluated in previous works, especially for running OpenCL kernels on CPUs. Using these metrics, we also verify the current limitation of OpenCL and the possible improvement in terms of performance. In summary, the contributions of this paper are as follows.

(i) We provide programmers with a guideline to understand the performance of OpenCL applications on CPUs. Programmers can verify whether the OpenCL kernel fully utilizes the computing resources of the CPU.

(ii) We discuss the effectiveness of OpenCL applications on multicore CPUs and possible improvement.

The main objective of this paper is to provide a way to understand OpenCL performance on CPUs. Even though OpenCL can be executed on CPUs and GPUs, most previous work has focused on only GPU performance issues. We believe that our work increases the understandability of OpenCL on CPUs and helps programmers by reducing the programming overhead to implement a separate CPU-optimized version from scratch. Some previous studies about OpenCL on CPUs discuss some aspects presented in this paper, but they lack both quantitative and qualitative evaluations, making them hard to use when programmers want to estimate the performance impact of each aspect.

Section 2 describes the background and architectural aspects to understand the OpenCL performance on CPUs. Then, we evaluate OpenCL applications regarding those aspects in Section 3. We review related work in Section 4 and conclude the paper.

2. Background and Criteria

In this section, we describe the background of several aspects that affect OpenCL application performance on CPUs: API overhead, thread scheduling overhead, instruction-level parallelism, data transfer, data locality, and compiler autovectorization. These aspects have been emphasized in academia and industry to improve application performance on CPUs on multiple programming models. Even though most of the architectural aspects described in this section are well-understood fundamental concepts, most OpenCL applications are not written considering these aspects.

2.1. API Overhead. OpenCL has high overhead for launching kernels, which is negligible on other conventional parallel programming models for CPUs. In addition to the kernel execution on the compute device, OpenCL needs OpenCL API function calls in the host code to coordinate the executions of kernels that are overheads. The general steps of an OpenCL application are as follows [3]:

(1) Open an OpenCL context.

(2) Create a command queue to accept the execution and memory requests.

(3) Allocate OpenCL memory objects to hold the inputs and outputs for the kernel.

(4) Compile and build the kernel code online.

(5) Set the arguments of the kernel.

(6) Set workitem dimensions.

(7) Kick off kernel execution (enqueue the kernel execution command).

(8) Collect the results.

The complex steps of OpenCL applications are due to the OpenCL design philosophy emphasizing portability over multiple architectures. Since the goal of OpenCL is to make a single application run on multiple architectures, they make the OpenCL programming model as flexible as possible. Figure 1 shows the OpenCL platform model and how OpenCL provides portability. The OpenCL platform consists of a host and a list of compute devices. A host is connected to one or more compute devices and is responsible for managing resources on compute devices. The compute device is an abstraction of the processor, which can be any type of processor, such as a conventional CPU, GPU, and DSP. A compute device has a separate device memory and a list of compute units. A compute unit can have multiple processing elements (PEs). By this abstraction, OpenCL enables portable execution.

On the contrary, flexibility for various platform supports does not exist on conventional parallel programming models for multicore CPUs. Many of the APIs in OpenCL, which take a significant execution time on OpenCL application do not exist on conventional parallel programming models. The compute device and the context in OpenCL are implicit on conventional programming models. Users do not have to query the platform or compute devices and explicitly create the context.

Another example of the unique characteristics of OpenCL compared to conventional programming models is the "just-in-time compilation" [6] during run-time. In many OpenCL applications, kernel compilation time by the JIT compiler incurs the execution time overhead. On the contrary, compilation is statically done and is not performed during application execution for the application written in other programming models.

Therefore, to determine the actual performance of applications, the time cost to execute the OpenCL API functions also should be considered. From evaluation, we find that the API overhead is larger than the actual computation in many cases.

2.2. Thread Scheduling. Unlike other parallel programming languages such as TBB [7] and OpenMP [8], the OpenCL programming model is a single-instruction and multiple-thread (SIMT) model just like CUDA [9]. An OpenCL kernel describes the behavior of a single thread, and the host application explicitly declares the number of threads to express the parallelism of the application. In OpenCL terminology, a single thread is called a `workitem` (a `thread` in CUDA). The OpenCL programmer can form a set of workitems as a `workgroup` (a `threadblock` in CUDA), where the programmer can synchronize among workitems by `barrier` and `mem_fence`. A single workgroup is composed of a multi-dimensional array of workitems. Figure 2 shows the OpenCL execution model and how an OpenCL kernel is mapped on the OpenCL compute device. In OpenCL, a kernel is allocated on a compute device, and a workgroup is executed on a compute unit. A single workitem is processed by a processing element (PE). For better performance, programmers can tune the number of workitems and change the workgroup size.

It is common for OpenCL applications to launch a massive number of threads for kernels expecting speedup by parallel execution. However, portability of OpenCL applications in terms of performance is not maintained on different architectures. In other words, an optimal decision of how to parallelize (partition) a kernel on GPUs does not usually guarantee good performance on CPUs. The partitioning decision of a kernel is done by changing *the number of workitems* and *workgroup size*.

2.2.1. Number of Workitems. First, the number of workitems and the amount of work done by a workitem affect

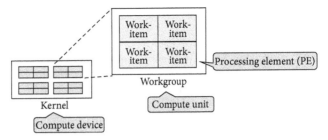

FIGURE 2: OpenCL execution model.

performance differently on CPUs and GPUs. A massive number of short workitems hurts performance on CPUs but helps performance on GPUs. The performance difference comes from the different architectural characteristics between CPUs and GPUs. On GPUs, a single workitem is processed by a scalar processor (SP) or one single SIMD lane. As is widely known, GPUs are specialized for supporting a large number of concurrently running threads, and high thread-level parallelism (TLP) is critical to achieve high performance [10–13]. On the contrary, on CPUs, the TLP is limited by the number of cores, so using more threads to do the same amount of work does not help performance on CPUs but hurts it due to the overhead of emulating a large number of concurrently executing workitems on a small number of cores.

2.2.2. Number of Workitems and Instruction-Level Parallelism (ILP). The number of workitems affects the instruction-level parallelism (ILP) of the OpenCL kernel on CPUs. Increasing ILP in GPU applications has not been a popular performance optimization technique. The reasons are as follows. First, the hardware can explore much TLP so ILP will not affect the performance significantly. Second, the hardware does not explore too much ILP. The GPU processor is an in-order scheduler processor and does not also support branch prediction to increase ILP. However, on CPUs, the hardware has been designed to increase ILP with multiple features such as superscalar execution and branch predictors.

A modern superscalar processor executes more than one instruction concurrently by dispatching multiple independent instructions during a clock cycle to utilize the multiple functional units in CPUs. Superscalar CPUs use hardware that checks data dependencies between instructions at run-time and schedule instructions to run in parallel [14].

One of the performance problems of OpenCL applications on CPUs is that usually the kernel is written mostly to utilize the TLP, not for ILP. The OpenCL programming model is an SIMT model, and it is common for an OpenCL application to have a massive number of threads. Since independent instructions computing different elements are separated into different threads, most instructions in a single workitem in the kernel are usually dependent on previous instructions, so that typically most OpenCL kernels have ILP one; only one instruction can be dispatched to execute in a workitem. On the contrary, on conventional programming models such as OpenMP, independent instructions exist between different loop iterations. For better performance on CPUs, the

OpenCL kernel should be written to have more independent instructions.

2.2.3. Workgroup Size.

The second important component is the workgroup size. Workgroup size determines the amount of work in a workgroup and the number of workgroups of a kernel. On GPUs, a workgroup or multiple groups are executed on a streaming multiprocessor (SM), which is equivalent to a physical core on the multicore CPU. Similarly, a workgroup is processed by a logical core of the CPU [15, 16]. (Even though it depends on the implementation, many implementations have this characteristic in common.). A workload size that is too small per workgroup makes the scheduling overhead more significant in total execution time on CPUs since the thread context switching overhead becomes bigger.

An OpenCL programmer can explicitly set workgroup size or let the OpenCL implementation decide. If NULL value is passed for workgroup size when the host application calls clEnqueueNDRangeKernel, the OpenCL implementation automatically partitions global workitems into the appropriate number of workgroups.

2.2.4. Proposed Solutions and Limitations.

Many proposals to reduce the scheduling overhead by serialization have been presented [15–17]. Scheduling overhead is not a fundamental problem with the OpenCL programming model. Better OpenCL implementation can have less overhead than other suboptimal implementations. Serialization is a technique that serializes multiple workitems into a single workitem. For example, SnuCL [15] overcomes the overhead of a large number of workitems by serializing them to have fewer workitems in the run-time. However, even with serialization, multiple OpenCL implementations for CPUs still have high scheduling overhead due to the complexity of compiler analysis. Therefore, instead of using many workitems, as is usually the case for OpenCL applications on GPUs, we are better off assigning more work to each workitem with fewer workitems on CPUs. The results from our experiments agree with the above inferences.

2.3. Memory Allocation and Data Transfer.

In general, a parallel programming model can have two types of address space options: unified memory space and disjoint memory space [18]. Conventional programming models for CPUs provide the unified memory address space both for the sequential code and for parallel code. The benefit of unified memory space is easy programming, with no explicit data transfer for kernel execution.

On the contrary, even though it is hard for programmers to program, OpenCL provides disjoint memory space to programmers. This is because most heterogeneous computing platforms have disjoint memory systems due to the different memory requirements of different architectures. OpenCL assumes for its target a system where communication between the host and compute devices are performed explicitly by a system network, such as PCI-Express. But, the assumption of discrete memory systems is not true when we use CPUs as compute devices for kernel execution. The

host and compute devices share the same memory system resources such as last-level cache, on-chip interconnection, memory controllers, and DRAMs.

The drawback of disjoint memory address space is that it requires the programmer to explicitly manage data transfer between the host and compute devices for kernel execution. In common OpenCL applications, the data should be transferred back and forth in order to be processed by the host or the compute device [3], which becomes unnecessary when we use only the host for computation. To minimize the data transfer overhead on a specific architecture, OpenCL programmers usually have to rewrite the host code [3]. Often, they need to change the memory allocation flags or use different data transfer APIs for performance. For example, the programmer should allocate memory objects on host memory or device memory depending on target platform. These rewriting efforts have been a burden for programmers and have even been a waste of time due to the lack of architectural or run-time knowledge of a specific system in most cases.

2.3.1. Memory Allocation Flags.

One of rewriting efforts is changing the memory allocation flag. OpenCL provides the programmer multiple options for memory object allocation flags when the programmer calls clCreateBuffer that could affect the performance of data transfer and kernel execution. The memory allocation flag is used to specify how the object is accessed by a kernel and where it is allocated.

Access Type. First, programmers can specify if the memory object is a read-only memory object (CL_MEM_READ_ONLY) or write-only one (CL_MEM_WRITE_ONLY) when referenced inside a kernel. The programmer can set memory objects used as input to the kernel as read-only and memory objects used as output from the kernel as write-only. If the programmer does not specify access type, the default option is to create a memory object that can be read and written by the kernel (CL_MEM_READ_WRITE). CL_MEM_READ_WRITE can also be explicitly specified by programmers.

Where to Allocate. The other option that programmers can specify is where to allocate a memory object. When the programmer does not specify allocated location, the memory object is allocated on the device memory in the OpenCL compute device. OpenCL also supports the pinned memory. When the host code creates memory objects using the CL_MEM_ALLOC_HOST_PTR flag, the memory object is allocated on the host-accessible memory that resides on the host. Different from allocating the memory object in the device memory, there is no need to transfer the result of kernel execution back to the host memory when the result is required by the host.

2.3.2. Different Data Transfer APIs.

OpenCL also provides different APIs for data transfer between the host and compute devices. The host can enqueue commands to read data from an OpenCL memory object that is created by clCreateBuffer call to the memory object that is mostly created by malloc call in the host memory (by clEnqueueReadBuffer API). The host can also enqueue commands to write data to the OpenCL memory object from the memory object in the host memory (by clEnqueueWriteBuffer API). The programmer can also map an OpenCL memory object to have the host-accessible pointer of the mapped object (by clEnqueueMapBuffer API).

2.4. Vectorization and Thread Affinity

2.4.1. Vectorization. Utilizing SIMD units has been one of the key performance optimization techniques for CPUs [19]. Since SIMD instructions can perform computation on more than one data item at the same time, SIMD utilization could make the application more efficient. Many vendors have released various SIMD instruction extensions on their instruction set architectures, such as MMX [20].

Various methods have been proposed to utilize the SIMD instruction: using optimized function libraries such as Intel IPP [21] and Intel MKL [22], using C++ vector classes with Intel ICC [23], or using DSL compilers such as the Intel SPMD Program Compiler [24]. Programmers can also program in assembly or use intrinsic functions. However, all of these methods assume rewriting the code. Due to this limitation, and to help programmers easily write applications utilizing SIMD instruction, autovectorization has been implemented in many modern compilers [19, 23].

It is quite natural for programmers to expect that a programming model difference has no effect on compiler autovectorization on the same architecture. For example, if a kernel is written in both OpenCL and OpenMP and both implementations are written in a similar manner, programmers would expect that both codes are vectorized in a similar fashion, thereby giving similar performance numbers. Even though it depends on the implementation, this is not usually true. Unfortunately, today's compilers are very fragile about vectorizable patterns, which depend on the programming model. Applications should satisfy certain conditions in order to fully take advantage of compiler autovectorization [19]. Our evaluation in Section 3.5.1 shows an example of this fragility and verifies the possible effect of programming models on vectorization.

2.4.2. Thread Affinity. Where to place threads can affect the performance on modern multicore CPUs. Threads can be placed on each core in different ways, which can create a performance difference. The performance impact of the placement would increase with more processors on the system.

The performance difference can occur for multiple reasons. For example, because of the different latency on the interconnection network, threads that are far away will take longer to communicate with each other, whereas threads close to the adjacent core can communicate more quickly. Also, an application that requires data sharing among adjacent threads can benefit if we assign these adjacent threads to nearby cores. Proper placement can also eliminate the communication overhead by utilizing shared cache. For the

TABLE 1: Experimental environment.

CPUs	Intel Xeon E5645
# Cores	4
Vector width	SSE 4.2, 4 single precision FP
Caches	L1D/L2/L3: 64 KB/256 KB/12 MB
FP peak performance	230.4 GFlops
Core frequency	2.40 GHz
DRAM	4 GB
GPUs	NVidia GeForce GTX 580
# SMs	16
Caches	L1/Global L2: 16 KB/768 KB
FP peak performance	1.56 TFlops
Shader Clock frequency	1544 MHz
O/S	Ubuntu 12.04.1 LTS
Platform	Intel OpenCL Platform 1.5 for CPU NVidia OpenCL Platform 4.2 for GPU
Compiler	Intel C/C++ compiler 12.1.3

performance reason, most conventional parallel programming models support affinity, such as CPU_AFFINITY in OpenMP [8].

Unfortunately, thread affinity is not supported in OpenCL. An OpenCL workitem is a logical thread, which is not tightly coupled with a physical thread even though most parallel programming languages provide this feature. The reason for the lack of this functionality is that the OpenCL design philosophy emphasizes portability over efficiency.

We present the lack of affinity support as one of the performance limitations of OpenCL on CPUs compared to other programming languages for CPUs. We would like to present a potential solution to enhance OpenCL performance on CPUs. We found the benefit of better utilizing cache on OpenCL applications by thread affinity. An example is presented in Section 3.5.2.

3. Evaluation

Given the preceding background on the anticipated effects of architectural aspects to understand the OpenCL performance on CPUs, the goal of our study is to quantitatively explore these effects.

3.1. Methodology. The experimental environment for our evaluation is described in Table 1. Our evaluation was performed on a heterogeneous computing platform consisting of a multicore CPU and a GPU; the OpenCL kernel was executed either on the Intel OpenCL platform [4] or the NVidia OpenCL platform [5]. We implemented an execution framework so that we can vary and control many aspects on the applications without code changes. The execution framework is built as an OpenCL delegator library that invokes OpenCL libraries from vendors: the one from Intel for kernel execution on CPUs and the other from NVidia for kernel execution on GPUs.

TABLE 2: List of NVidia OpenCL benchmarks for API overhead evaluation.

Benchmark
oclBandwidthTest, oclBlackScholes, oclConvolutionSeparable, oclCopyComputeOverlap,
oclDCT8x8, oclDXTCompression, oclDeviceQuery, oclDotProduct, oclHiddenMarkovModel,
oclHistogram, oclMatrixMul, oclMersenneTwister, oclMultiThreads, oclQuasirandomGenerator,
oclRadixSort, oclReduction, oclSimpleMultiGPU, oclSortingNetworks, oclTranspose,
oclTridiagonal, oclVectorAdd

We use different applications for each evaluation. To verify the API overhead, We use NVIDIA OpenCL Benchmarks [5]. For other aspects, including scheduling overhead, memory allocation, and data transfer, we first use simple applications for evaluation. We also vary the data size of each application. The applications are ported to the execution framework we implemented. After evaluation with simple applications, we also use the Parboil benchmarks [25, 26]. Tables 2, 3, and 4 describe evaluated applications and their default parameters.

We use the wall-clock execution time. To measure stable execution time without fluctuation, we iterate the kernel execution until the total execution time of an application reaches a long enough running time, 90 seconds in our evaluation. This is sufficiently long to have a multiple number of kernel executions for all applications in our evaluation. Using the average kernel execution time per kernel invocation calculated, we use normalized throughput to clearly present the performance difference on multiple sections.

3.2. API Overhead. As we discussed in Section 2.1, the OpenCL application has API overhead. To verify the API overhead, we measured the time cost of each API function in executing the OpenCL application in NVIDIA OpenCL Benchmarks [5]. The workload size for each benchmark is the size the application provides as a default. Figure 3 shows the ratio of the execution time of kernel execution and auxiliary API functions to the total execution time of each OpenCL benchmark. (Auxiliary API functions are OpenCL API functions called in the host code to coordinate kernel execution.) The last column `total` means the arithmetic mean of the data from each benchmark. From the figure, we can see that a large portion of execution time is spent on auxiliary API functions instead of kernel execution.

For detailed analysis, we categorized OpenCL APIs into 16 categories. We group multiple categories for visibility in the following. Figure 4 provides a detailed example of API overheads by showing the execution time distribution of each API function category for `oclReduction`. `Enqueued Commands` category includes kernel execution time and data transfer time between the host and compute device and accounts for 12.1% of execution time. We find that the API overhead is larger than the actual computation.

3.2.1. Overhead due to Various Platform Supports. Figure 5 shows the ratio of the execution time of each category to the total execution time of each OpenCL benchmark. The figure shows the performance degradation due to the flexibility of various platforms. We see that the API functions in `Platform`, `Device`, and `Context` categories consume over 80 percent of the total execution time of each OpenCL benchmark on average. The need to call API functions in these categories comes from the fact that each OpenCL application needs to set up an execution environment for which the detailed mechanism would change, depending on the platform. From our evaluation, we also see that each call to the API functions in these categories requires a long execution time. In particular, context management APIs incur a large execution time overhead. Figure 6 shows the execution time distribution of `clCreateContext` and `clReleaseContext` to total execution time in each benchmark. These functions are called at most once on each OpenCL benchmark. But in conventional parallel programming models, context and device are implicit, so there is no need to call such management functions.

3.2.2. Overhead due to JIT Compilation. The list of OpenCL kernels in the application is represented by the `cl_program` object. `cl_program` object is created using either `clCreateProgramWithSource` or `clCreateProgramWithBinary`. JIT compilation is performed by either calling the `clBuildProgram` function or a sequence of `clCompileProgram` and `clLinkProgram` functions for the `cl_program` object to build the program executable for one or more devices associated with the program [3].

JIT compilation overhead is another source of the API overhead. Figure 7 shows the execution time distribution of `Program` category to the sum of execution time of all categories except `Platform`, `Device`, and `Context` categories. We exclude these 3 categories that we have evaluated in previous section. The figure clearly shows the performance degradation due to the JIT compilation. We see that the API functions in `Program` category consume around 33% of the total execution time for 13 categories of the API functions including kernel execution. Execution time overhead of `clBuildProgram` is not negligible in most benchmarks.

Caching. Caching JIT compiled code can help reduce the overhead. Some of the caching ideas are available in OpenCL. Programmers can extract compiled binary by using the `clGetProgramInfo` API function and store it using FILE I/O functions. When the kernel code is not modified since caching, programmers can load the cached binary on disk and use the binary instead of performing JIT compilation on every execution of the application.

3.2.3. Summary. In this section, we can see the high overhead of explicit context management (Section 3.2.1) and JIT compilation (Section 3.2.2) in OpenCL applications. These are unique characteristics of OpenCL compared to conventional programming models for portable execution over multiple architectures.

TABLE 3: Configurations of simple applications.

Benchmark	Kernel	Global work size	Local work size
Square	Square	10000, 100000, 1000000, 10000000	NULL
Vectoraddition	vectoadd	110000, 1100000, 5500000, 11445000	NULL
Matrixmul	matrixMul	800×1600, 1600×3200, 4000×8000	16×16
Reduction	reduce	640000, 2560000, 10240000	256
Histogram	histogram256	409600	128
Prefixsum	prefixSum	1024	1024
Blackscholes	blackScholes	1280×1280, 2560×2560	16×16
Binomialoption	binomialoption	255000, 2550000	255
Matrixmul(naive)	matrixMul	800×1600, 1600×3200, 4000×8000	16×16

TABLE 4: Configurations of the Parboil benchmarks.

Benchmark	Kernel	Global work size	Local work size
CP	Cenergy	64×512	16×8
MRI-Q	computePhiMag	3072	512
	computeQ	32768	256
MRI-FHD	RhoPhi	3072	512
	computeFHD	32768	256

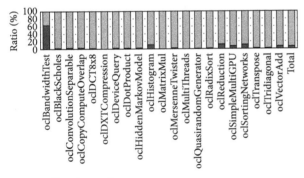

■ Kernel execution
▨ Auxiliary

FIGURE 3: Execution time distribution of kernel execution and auxiliary API functions.

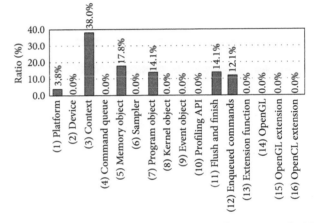

FIGURE 4: Execution time distribution of each category of API function for `oclReduction`.

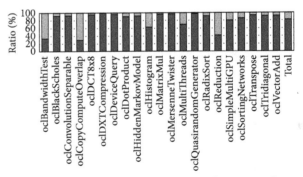

▨ Command queue, memory object, sampler, program object, kernel object, event object, profiling API, flush and finish, enqueued commands, extension function, openGL, openGL extension, openCL extension
■ Platform, device, context

FIGURE 5: Execution time distribution of each category of API functions.

It should be noted that the workload size for the evaluation in Section 3.2 is the size that the application provides as the default workload size, which is relatively small. Therefore, these overheads can be reduced with a large workload size and thus a long kernel execution time. But it is also true that these overheads are not negligible with small workload size, so the programmer should consider the workload size when they decide whether to use OpenCL or not.

3.3. Thread Scheduling

3.3.1. Number of Workitems. Associated with the discussion in Section 2.2.1, to evaluate the effect of the number of workitems and the workload size per workitem, we perform an experiment on OpenCL applications by allocating more computation per workitem. We coalesce multiple workitems into a single workitem by forming a loop inside the kernel.

To keep the total amount of computation the same, we reduce the number of workitems to execute the kernel. The number of workitems coalesced increases from 1 to 1000 workitems by multiplying by 10 for each step. Figure 8 shows the performance of `Square` and `Vectoraddition` applications with a different amount of computation per

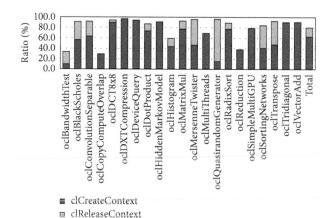

FIGURE 6: Execution time distribution of clCreateContext and clReleaseContext.

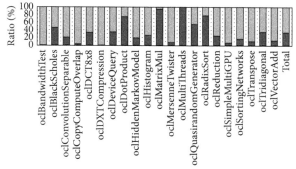

FIGURE 7: Execution time distribution of Program category API functions except Platform, Device, and Context categories.

workitem. Table 5 shows the number of workitems used in this evaluation.

From Figure 8, we find a performance gain for allocating more work per workitem on CPUs. A noticeable example is a case of Vectoraddition, where we add an array of numbers. If we create as many workitems as the size of arrays, we end up creating significant overhead on CPUs. When we reduce the number of workitems, we see a major performance improvement for CPUs. We could also find that the performance is saturated sometimes when the workload assigned per each workitem goes over a certain threshold. This shows that when each workitem has a sufficient workload, scheduling overhead is reduced.

Compared to CPUs with high overhead of handling many workitems, GPUs have low overhead for maintaining a large number of workitems, as our evaluation shows. Furthermore, reducing the number of workitems degraded performance on GPUs significantly. The large performance degradation on GPUs is because we could no longer take advantage of many processing units on GPUs.

One of the reasons for performance improvement by allocating more workload per workitem is the reduced number of instructions. Figure 9 shows the number of dynamic instructions of Square and Vectoraddition applications with a different amount of computation per workitem. The left figure of Figure 9 shows the dynamic instruction count including instructions from OpenCL APIs on top of instructions from the OpenCL kernel. And the right figure of Figure 9 represents the instructions only from the kernel.

For this evaluation, we implement a tool based on Pin [27] that counts the number of instructions. The tool also identifies the function to which the instruction belongs. From Figure 9, we can see that the number of instructions is reduced with more workload per workitem even though the amount of computation is the same regardless of the number of workitems. The number of instructions from OpenCL APIs as well as that from the kernels increases, so that the scheduling overhead exists on both OpenCL APIs and the JIT compiled OpenCL kernel binary. Figure 10 shows reduced overhead on OpenCL APIs with increased workload per workitem. The instructions from OpenCL APIs are for scheduling, not for computation intended by programmers represented as an OpenCL kernel. So a reduced number of instructions from OpenCL APIs means reduced overhead.

Figure 11 shows the performance of Parboil benchmarks with a similar experiment [25, 26]. The number of workitems coalesced is different depending on the benchmark since we could not increase the workload per workitem in the same manner for all kernels. We find a similar performance gain of allocating more work per workitem. Figure 12 represents the reduced number of dynamic instructions with increased workload per workitem.

3.3.2. Number of Workitems and Instruction-Level Parallelism (ILP). As we discussed in Section 2.2.2, the number of workitems, and therefore how to parallelize the computation, also affects the instruction-level parallelism (ILP) of the OpenCL kernel on CPUs. Coalescing multiple workitems can not only reduce the scheduling overhead but also improve the performance by utilizing ILP.

To evaluate the ILP effect on both the CPU and the GPU, we implemented a set of compute-intensive microbenchmarks that share common characteristics. Every benchmark has an identical number of dynamic instructions and memory accesses. Each benchmark also has the same instruction mixture, such as a ratio of the number of branch instructions over the total number of instructions. The only difference between each benchmark is ILP by varying the number of independent instructions. From the baseline implementation, we increase the number of operand variables, so that the number of independent instructions can increase. For example, in the case of ILP 1, the next instruction depends on the output of the previous instruction so that the number of independent instructions is one; but in the case of ILP 2, an independent instruction exists between two dependent instructions.

Figure 13 shows the performance with increasing ILP. We provide enough workitems to fully utilize TLP. The number of workitems remains the same for all microbenchmarks. The

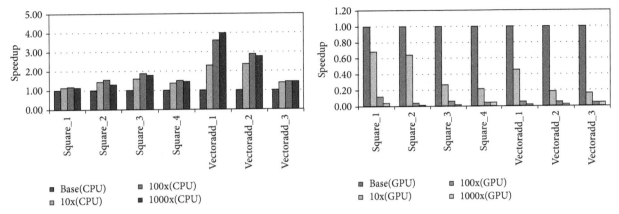

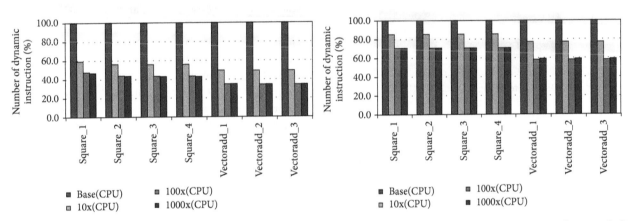

FIGURE 8: Performance of Square and Vectoraddition applications with different workload per workitem.

FIGURE 9: The number of dynamic instructions of Square and Vectoraddition applications with different workload per workitem including (L) instructions from OpenCL APIs and (R) kernel only.

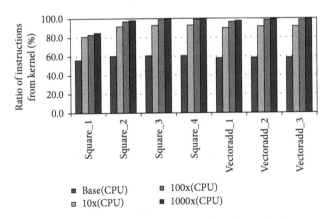

FIGURE 10: The ratio of instructions from kernel over the instructions around clEnqueueNDRangeKernel for Square and Vectoraddition applications with different workload per workitem.

left y-axis represents the throughput of the CPUs, and the right one represents the throughput of the GPUs. From the figure, we find that performance improves depending on the ILP value of the OpenCL kernel on CPUs. On the contrary, there is no performance variation on GPUs with different degrees of instruction-level parallelism.

3.3.3. Workgroup Size. Associated with the discussion in Section 2.2.3, the number of workitems in workgroups can affect the performance of the OpenCL application. We evaluate the effect of workgroup size, both on CPUs and GPUs. We vary the number of workitems in a workgroup by passing a different argument for workgroup size (`local_work_size`) on kernel invocation. We maintain the total number of workitems of the kernel as the same. Table 6 shows the different workgroup size for each benchmark, and Figures 14, 16, and 18 show the performance of applications with different workgroup sizes. When the NULL argument is passed on kernel invocation, the workgroup size is implicitly defined by the OpenCL implementation.

The benchmarks can be categorized into three categories, depending on the behavior. The first group consists of Square, Vectoraddition, and naive implementation of Matrixmul; Matrixmul belongs to the second group; and Blackscholes belongs to the last.

Square, Vectoraddition, and naive implementation of Matrixmul show a performance increase with increased workgroup sizes on the CPU, as can be seen in Figure 14. On the Square and Vectoraddition applications, performance achieved with the NULL workgroup size is less than the peak performance we achieve. This implies that

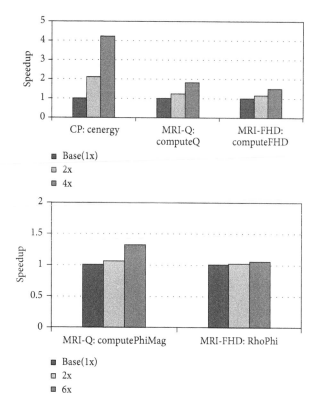

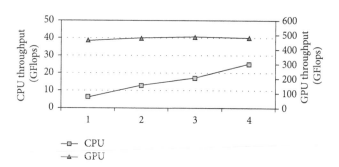

FIGURE 13: Performance of ILP microbenchmark on the CPU and the GPU.

TABLE 5: Number of workitems for each application.

Benchmark	Base	10x	100x	1000x
Square_1	10000	1000	100	10
Square_2	100000	10000	1000	100
Square_3	1000000	100000	10000	1000
Square_4	10000000	1000000	100000	10000
Vectoradd_1	110000	11000	1100	110
Vectoradd_2	1100000	110000	11000	1100
Vectoradd_3	5500000	550000	55000	5500

FIGURE 11: Performance of Parboil benchmarks with different workloads per workitem.

TABLE 6: Workgroup size for each application.

Benchmark	Base	Case_1	Case_2	Case_3	Case_4
Square	NULL	1	10	100	1000
Vectoraddition	NULL	1	10	100	1000
Matrixmul	16×16	1×1	2×2	4×4	8×8
Blackscholes	16×16	1×1	1×2	2×2	2×4
Matrixmul(naive)	16×16	1×1	2×2	4×4	8×8

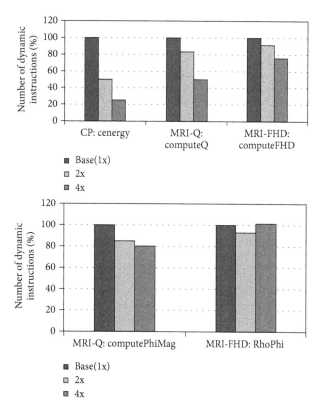

programmers should explicitly set the workgroup size for the maximum performance. The performance with a small workgroup size is also bad on GPUs since the workgroup is allocated per SM, so that the small workgroup size makes GPUs unable to utilize many warps in an SM. Even though no hardware TLP is available inside a logical core on CPUs (the evaluated CPU is an SMT processor, so multiple logical cores share one physical core), performance increases with a large workgroup size. This is because the overhead of managing a large number of workgroups, many threads in many implementations, is reduced. We also find that performance is saturated at a certain workgroup size.

The left figure of Figure 15 shows the number of dynamic instructions of Square, Vectoraddition, and naive implementation of Matrixmul with different workgroup size on CPUs. The right figure of Figure 15 shows the ratio of instructions from kernel over the instructions around clEnqueueNDRangeKernel for those applications with a different workgroup size. From the left figure of Figure 15, we can see that the number of instructions is reduced with larger workgroup size. This is because the number of instructions from OpenCL APIs is reduced, as can be seen from the right figure of Figure 15. The number

FIGURE 12: The number of dynamic instructions of Parboil benchmarks with different workload per workitem.

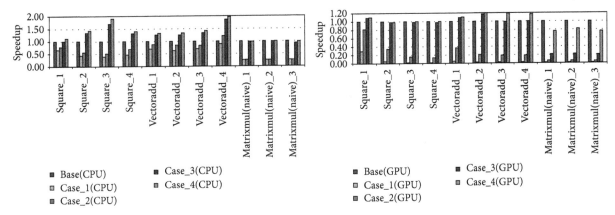

FIGURE 14: Performance of applications with different workgroup size on CPUs and GPUs.

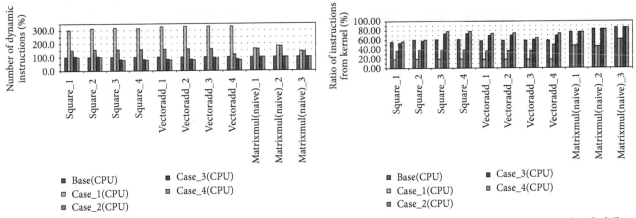

FIGURE 15: (U) The number of dynamic instructions of Square, Vectoraddition, and naive implementation of Matrixmul with different workgroup size on CPUs. (L) The ratio of instructions from kernel over the instructions around clEnqueuNDRangeKernel for Square, Vectoraddition, and naive implementation of Matrixmul with different workgroup size.

of instructions from the OpenCL kernel remains the same regardless of workgroup size.

As we can see from Figure 16, we also see a significant performance increase on the Matrixmul application with an increased workgroup size. The optimal workgroup size of this application is different, depending on platforms. For inputs 1 and 2, the optimal workgroup size on CPUs is 8 × 8, but the optimal size on GPUs is 16 × 16. Here, the performance depends not only on the scheduling overhead, but also on the cache usage. Matrixmul utilizes the local memory in OpenCL by blocking. Workgroup size can change the local memory usage of the kernel. Since the size of the cache in CPUs and the scratchpad memory in GPUs are different, the optimal workgroup size can be different. Figure 17 shows the reduced number of dynamic instructions of Matrixmul with increasing workgroup size.

Unlike other applications, Blackscholes shows different performance behavior on CPUs and on GPUs. As we can see in Figure 18, the workgroup size does not change the performance on CPUs, but it affects the performance significantly on GPUs. Since the workload allocated on a single workitem is relatively long compared to other applications, the overhead of managing a large number of workgroups becomes negligible. On the contrary, the number of warps

in the SM is defined by the workgroup size on GPUs, which makes the performance on GPUs low on small workgroup sizes. Figure 19 shows that the number of instructions does not change much for Blackscholes, regardless of workgroup size.

Figure 20 shows the performance of Parboil benchmarks with different workgroup sizes. We increase the workgroup size from one to 16 times by multiplying by 2 for each step. Since the workgroup size for CP:cenergy kernel is two-dimensional, we increase the workgroup size of the kernel in two directions. CP:cenergy(x) represents the performance with workgroup sizes 1 × 8, 2 × 8, 4 × 8, 8 × 8, and 16 × 8. CP:cenergy(y) represents the performance with workgroup sizes 16 × 1, 16 × 2, 16 × 4, 16 × 8, and 16 × 16. In general, we find the performance gain with a large workgroup size. The performance saturates when there is enough computation inside the workgroup. Figure 21 shows that the performance gain is due to reduced scheduling overhead, which is represented by a reduced number of dynamic instructions.

3.3.4. Summary. Here, we summarize the findings on thread scheduling for OpenCL applications.

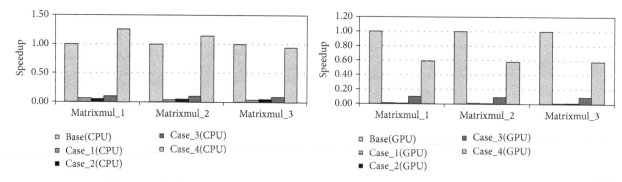

FIGURE 16: Performance of Matrixmul with different workgroup size on CPUs and GPUs.

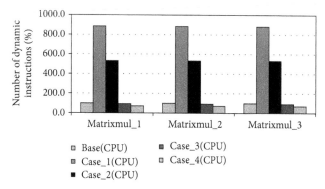

FIGURE 17: The number of dynamic instructions of Matrixmul with different workgroup size on CPUs.

(1) Allocating more work per workitem by manually coalescing multiple workitems reduces scheduling overhead on CPUs (Section 3.3.1).

(2) High ILP increase performance on CPUs but not on GPUs (Section 3.3.2).

(3) Workgroup size affect performance both on CPUs and GPUs. In general, large workgroup size increases performance by reducing scheduling overhead on CPUs and enables utilizing high TLP on GPUs. Workgroup size can also affect the cache usage (Section 3.3.3).

3.4. Memory Allocation and Data Transfer.
Associated with the discussion in Section 2.3, to evaluate the performance effect of different memory object allocation flags and different APIs for data transfer, we perform an experiment on OpenCL applications with different combinations of the following options. To measure exact execution performance, we use a blocking call for all kernel execution commands and memory object commands so that no command overlaps with other commands. The combination we use is three-dimensional as follows.

3.4.1. Evaluated Options for Memory Allocation and Data Transfer

(1) Different APIs for data transfer:

(i) explicit transfer: `clEnqueueReadBuffer` and `clEnqueueWriteBuffer` for explicit read and write;

(ii) mapping: `clEnqueueMapBuffer` with `CL_MAP_READ`, `CL_MAP_WRITE` for implicit read and write.

(2) Kernel access type when referenced inside a kernel:

(i) the kernel accesses the memory object as read-only/write-only:

(a) `CL_MEM_READ_ONLY` for the input to the kernel;

(b) `CL_MEM_WRITE_ONLY` for computation results from the kernel;

(ii) the kernel accesses the memory object as read/write: `CL_MEM_READ_WRITE` for all memory objects.

(3) Where to allocate a memory object:

(i) allocation on the device memory;

(ii) allocation on the host-accessible memory on the host (pinned memory).

3.4.2. Metric: Application Throughput.
The throughput we present here is the performance, including data transfer time, between the host and compute devices, not just the kernel execution throughput on the compute device. For example, the throughput of an application becomes half of the throughput when we consider only the kernel execution time if the data transfer time between the host and the compute device equals the kernel execution time. The way we calculate the throughput of an application is illustrated in

$$\text{Throughput\_app} = \frac{\text{Throughput\_kernel}}{\text{kernel\_time} + \text{transfer\_time}}. \quad (1)$$

3.4.3. Different Data Transfer APIs.
We compare the performance of different data-transfer APIs on all possible allocation flags. (The combinations are as follows: (1) read-only/write-only memory object + allocation on the device; (2) read-only/write-only memory object + allocation on the

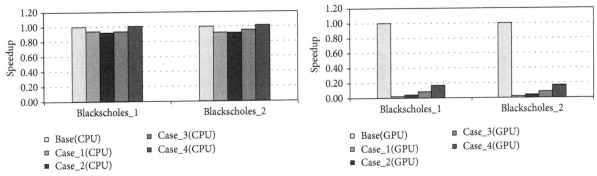

FIGURE 18: Performance of Blackscholes with different workgroup size on CPUs and GPUs.

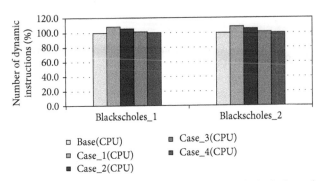

FIGURE 19: The number of dynamic instructions of Blackscholes with different workgroup size on CPUs.

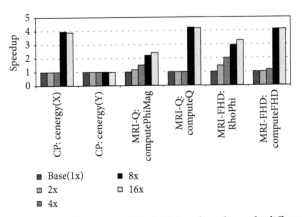

FIGURE 20: Performance of Parboil benchmarks with different workgroup size on CPUs.

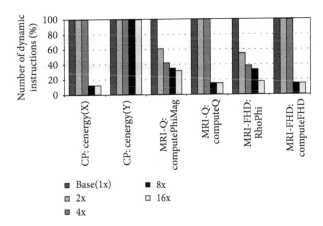

FIGURE 21: The number of dynamic instructions of Parboil benchmarks with different workgroup size on CPUs.

host; (3) read-write memory object + allocation on the device; (4) read-write memory object + allocation on the host.) Figure 22 shows the performance of the benchmarks with different APIs for data transfer. The y-axis represents the normalized application throughput (Throughput_app) when we use mapping for data transfer over the baseline when we use explicit data transfer APIs. We find that mapping APIs have superior performance compared to explicit data transfer APIs, regardless of the decision on other dimensions. First, the performance of mapping APIs is superior wherever the memory object is allocated: on device memory or on pinned memory on host. Second, mapping APIs also perform better

regardless of the decision for allocating the memory object as read-only/write-only or as read/write object.

Different APIs change data transfer time. Figure 23 shows the normalized data transfer throughput from the host to a compute device between different data transfer APIs. Figure 24 shows the one from compute device to host. The data transfer time is shorter with mapping APIs. The difference of data transfer throughput increases with increases in workload sizes and therefore increases in data transfer sizes.

We also report the performance of Parboil benchmarks with different APIs for data transfer [25, 26]. Since the data transfer time is much shorter than the kernel execution time on Parboil benchmarks, instead of using application throughput as shown in (1), we report the data transfer time from the host to device, and data transfer time from the device to host with different APIs. Figure 25 shows the different data transfer time of the Parboil benchmarks with different APIs for data transfer. The y-axis represents the data transfer time in milliseconds. The left figure in Figure 25 shows the data transfer time from the host to the compute device with different data transfer APIs. The right figure shows the one from the compute device to the host. As with simple applications, we find that the data transfer time is shorter with mapping APIs on these benchmarks.

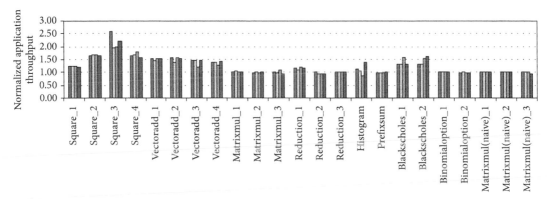

FIGURE 22: Normalized application throughput of mapping over explicit data transfer for all combinations on other dimensions. The performance of mapping APIs is superior to explicit data transfer on all possible combinations.

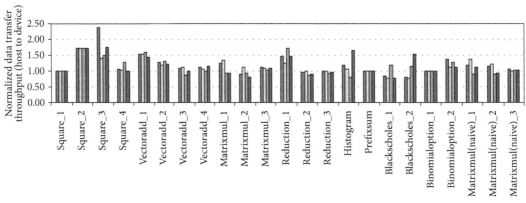

FIGURE 23: Normalized data transfer (host to device) throughput of mapping over explicit data transfer for all combinations on other dimensions.

The difference of data transfer time is due to the different behaviors of different APIs. When the host code explicitly transfers data between the host and the compute device, the OpenCL run-time library should allocate a separate memory object for the device and copy the data between the memory object allocated by the `malloc` call and the memory object allocated for the device that is allocated by the `clEnqueueReadBuffer` call. However, a separate memory object is not needed when the host code uses mapping; only returning a pointer of the memory object is needed. So, copying between memory objects becomes unnecessary.

3.4.4. Kernel Access Type When Referenced inside a Kernel. We also verify the performance effect of specifying a memory object as read-only/write-only or as read/write. Figure 26 shows the performance implication of this flag.

The *y*-axis represents the normalized throughput when we allocate the memory object as read-only/write-only from the baseline when we allocate the object as read/write. OpenCL implementations can utilize the detailed information of how the memory object is accessed in the OpenCL kernel for optimization instead of naively assuming all objects are read and modified in the OpenCL kernel. However, we do not see a noticeable performance difference with our evaluated workloads. Kernel execution time and data transfer time between the host and compute device do not differ regardless of this memory allocation flag.

3.4.5. Where to Allocate a Memory Object. Finally, we also verify the performance effect of the allocation location of memory objects. Programmers can allocate the memory object on the host memory or the device memory. Figure 27 shows the performance of benchmarks with

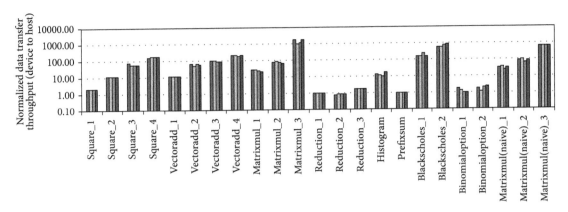

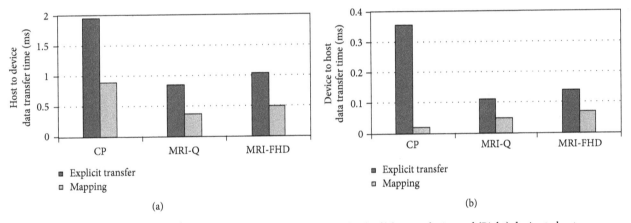

FIGURE 24: Normalized data transfer (device to host) throughput of mapping over explicit data transfer for all combinations on other dimensions.

(a)

(b)

FIGURE 25: Data transfer time with different APIs for data transfer. (Left) host to device and (Right) device to host.

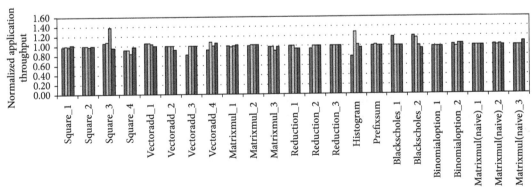

FIGURE 26: Normalized application throughput of read-only/write-only memory objects over read/write memory objects for all combinations on other dimensions. There is no noticeable performance difference.

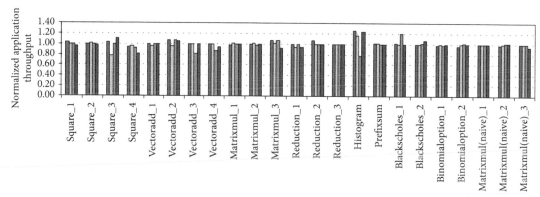

- ■ Read-only or write-only, explicit transfer
- ▨ Read write, explicit transfer
- ▢ Read-only or write-only, mapping
- ■ Read write, mapping

FIGURE 27: Normalized application throughput of the pinned memory over the device memory for all combinations on other dimensions. Where to allocate a memory object does not change the performance much on CPUs.

different allocation locations. The *y*-axis represents the normalized throughput when we allocate the memory object on the host memory from the baseline when we use the device memory. We find that an allocation location does not have a huge impact on performance both for kernel execution time and data transfer time. This is because the device memory and the host memory reference the same memory, the main memory of the system when the compute device is the CPU. Therefore, a different memory allocation location does not imply performance differences. On the contrary, when the compute device is not the CPU, memory allocation location can affect the performance significantly.

3.4.6. Summary. In this section we find that mapping APIs perform superior compared to explicit data transfer APIs with reduced data transfer time by eliminating the copying overhead on CPUs. Allocated location and kernel access type do not affect the performance on CPUs.

3.5. Vectorization and Thread Affinity

3.5.1. Vectorization. We evaluate the possible effect of programming models on vectorization, even though vectorization is more about compiler implementation. For evaluation, we port the OpenCL kernels to identical computations being performed by their OpenMP counterparts. We map multiple workitems on OpenCL to a loop to port OpenCL kernels to their OpenMP counterparts. We utilize the Intel C/C++ 12.1.3 compiler and the Intel OpenCL platform 1.5 for our evaluation. The programmer's expectation is that when we run the same computation in the OpenCL and OpenMP applications, both runs should give comparable performance numbers. However, the results show that this assumption does not hold. For the evaluated benchmarks, the OpenCL kernels outperform their OpenMP counterparts. Figure 28 shows the different performance of OpenMP and OpenCL implementations. The reason for this mismatch is the different way OpenMP and OpenCL compilers vectorize code.

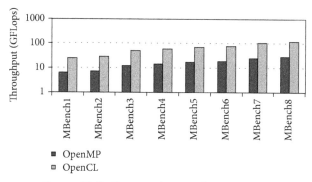

- ■ OpenMP
- ▢ OpenCL

FIGURE 28: Performance impact of vectorization.

OpenCL Vectorization. The vectorization by the OpenCL kernel compiler is coalescing workitems. OpenCL vectorization enables the execution of several workitems together by a single vector instruction. Vectorization enables multiple work items to be processed concurrently on a single thread. For example, if the target instruction set is SSE 4.2, and the computation is based on a single precision floating point, then four workitems could make progress concurrently, so they are coalesced into a single workitem. By doing this, vectorized OpenCL code would have fewer dynamic instruction counts compared to nonvectorized code.

OpenMP Vectorization. On the other hand, the OpenMP compiler vectorizes loops by unrolling a loop combined with the generation of packed SIMD instructions. To be vectorized, a loop should be countable, have single entry and single exit, and have a straight control flow graph inside the loop [28]. Many factors could prevent the vectorization of a loop in OpenMP. Two key factors are (1) `non-contiguous memory access` and (2) `data dependence`.

(1) Noncontiguous memory access:

(i) four consecutive floats may be loaded directly from the memory in a single SSE instruction;

```
/*OpenMP computation that doesn't vectorize due to dependencies.*/
int main(){
    ...
    for (int j = 0; j < 4; j++){
        FMUL(_a[j], _b[j])
        FMUL(_a[j], _b[j])
        FMUL(_a[j], _b[j])
        FMUL(_a[j], _b[j])
        FMUL(_a[j], _b[j])
        FMUL(_a[j], _b[j])
    }
    ...

}
/*Similar OpenCL kernel computation which vectorizes.*/
void VectorAdd (..., __global float *dm_src, __global float *dm_dst){
    ...
    for (int j = 0; j < 4; j++){
        FMUL(_a[j], _b[j])
        FMUL(_a[j], _b[j])
        FMUL(_a[j], _b[j])
        FMUL(_a[j], _b[j])
        FMUL(_a[j], _b[j])
        FMUL(_a[j], _b[j])
    }
    ...

}
```

ALGORITHM 1: Vectorization on OpenCL versus OpenMP. The equivalent code in OpenCL is vectorizable while OpenMP code is not vectorizable.

but if the four floats to be loaded are not consecutive, we will have a load using multiple instructions; loops with a nonunit stride are an example of the above scenario.

(2) Data dependence:

(i) vectorization requires changes in the order of operations within a loop since each SIMD instruction operates on several data elements at once; but such a change of order might not be possible due to data dependencies.

Example. Algorithm 1 shows an example of how different vectorization mechanisms from OpenMP and OpenCL compilers affect whether identical codes are to be vectorized or not. When there is a true data dependence inside an OpenCL kernel or inside a loop iteration in OpenMP parallel for section, the OpenCL kernel is vectorized, while the OpenMP code is not. Therefore, they show different performance even when vectorization of OpenMP loops seems possible. The vectorization of an OpenCL kernel is relatively straightforward because no dependency checks are required as in the case of traditional compilers. Even though we only show the example of when the OpenCL compiler shows the benefit, the opposite case is also possible: when the OpenMP compiler vectorizes code, but the OpenCL compiler fails.

New OpenMP Compiler. We have also evaluated OpenMP vectorization with OpenMP 4.0 SIMD extension and the newer compiler (Intel C/C++ compiler 15.0.1). The evaluation revealed comparable performance of OpenMP and OpenCL implementations. Compiler vectorization is dependent on the compiler implementation.

3.5.2. Thread Affinity. We evaluate the performance benefit using the CPU affinity in OpenMP. We use OMP_PROC_BIND and GOMP_CPU_AFFINITY to control the scheduling of threads on the processors [8]. When the OMP_PROC_BIND is set to be true, the threads will not be moved between processors. GOMP_CPU_AFFINITY enables us to control the allocation of a thread on a particular core.

We use a simple application for evaluation. The aim of the application is to verify the effects of binding threads to cores in terms of cache utilization. Performance can improve when the OpenCL run-time library maps logical threads of a kernel on physical cores so that it can utilize the cached data of the previous kernel execution. The application we use consists of two kernels: Vector Addition and Vector Multiplication. Computation of each kernel is distributed among eight cores: and the computation of second kernel is dependent on the first one, using the data produced by the first one.

Table 7 shows the method we use. The upper table in Table 7 represents the (a) Aligned case, and the lower table represents the (b) Misaligned case. The numbers in the table represent the logical thread IDs. Threads with identical IDs of both the kernels access the same data. On the (a) Aligned case, we bind threads of the second kernel to the cores on which the threads of the first kernel

TABLE 7: Performance impact of CPU affinity.

(a) Aligned

	Core 0	Core 1	Core 2	Core 3	Core 4	Core 5	Core 6	Core 7
Computation 1	0	1	2	3	4	5	6	7
Computation 2	0	1	2	3	4	5	6	7

(b) Misaligned

	Core 0	Core 1	Core 2	Core 3	Core 4	Core 5	Core 6	Core 7
Computation 1	0	1	2	3	4	5	6	7
Computation 2	6	3	4	0	2	1	7	5

```
/*First Kernel: Vector Addition.*/
#pragma omp parallel for shared(a, b, c) private (i)
for (int i = 0; i < MAX_INDEX; i++){
    c[i] = a[i] + b[i];
}
/*(a) Aligned Second Kernel: Vector Multiplication.*/
#pragma omp parallel for shared(b, c, d) private (i)
for (int i = 0; i < MAX_INDEX; i++){
    d[i] = b[i] + c[i];
}
/*(b) Misaligned Second Kernel: Vector Multiplication.*/
#pragma omp parallel for shared(b, c, d) private (i)
for (int i = 0; i < MAX_INDEX; i++){
    int j = MAX_INDEX - 1 - i;
    d[j] = b[j] + c[j];
}
```

ALGORITHM 2: Code snippet of simple application.

are bound. On the (b) Misaligned case, we shuffle this binding. Algorithm 2 shows the code snippet of this simple application.

As we expect, the (a) Aligned case shows higher performance than does the (b) Misaligned case. The (b) Misaligned one runs longer by 15%. This is because during the execution of the second kernel, the cores on the CPU encounter cache misses on their private caches. On the contrary, the (a) Aligned case would have more cache hits than the (b) Misaligned case because the data accessed by the second kernel would already be on the cache after the execution of the first kernel on the (a) Aligned case.

As the results show, even though OpenCL emphasizes portability, adding the affinity support to OpenCL may provide a significant performance improvement in some cases. Hence, we argue that coupling logical threads with physical threads (cores on the CPU) is needed on OpenCL, especially for CPUs. The granularity for the assignment could be a workgroup; in other words, the programmer can specify the core where a specific workgroup would be executed. This functionality would help to improve the performance of OpenCL applications. For example, data from different kernels can be shared without a memory request if the programmer allocates cores for specific workgroups in consideration of the data sharing of different kernels. The data can be shared through the private caches of cores.

4. Related Work

Multiple research studies have been done on how to optimize OpenCL performance on GPUs. The GPGPU community provides TLP [29] as a general guideline for optimizing GPGPU applications since GPGPUs are usually equipped with a massive number of processing elements. Since OpenCL has the same background as CUDA [9], most OpenCL applications are written to better utilize TLP. The widely used occupancy metric indicates the degree of TLP. However, this scheme cannot be applied on CPUs since even when the TLP of the application is large, the physical TLP available on CPUs is limited by the number of CPU cores, so that the context switching overhead is much higher on CPUs than on GPUs for which this overhead is negligible.

Several publications refer to the performance of OpenCL kernels on CPUs. Some focus on algorithms and some refer to the performance difference by comparing it with GPU implementation and OpenMP implementation on CPUs [16, 30, 31]. However, to the best of our knowledge, our work is the first to provide a broad summary, combining application with the architecture knowledge to provide a general guideline to understand OpenCL performance on multicore CPUs.

Ali et al. compare OpenCL with OpenMP and Intel's TBB on different platforms [30]. They mostly discuss the scaling effects and compiler optimizations. But it misses out on why the optimizations listed in the paper give the performance benefit mentioned and lacks quantitative evaluation. We, too, evaluate the performance of OpenCL and OpenMP for a given application. However, our work considers various aspects that can change application performance and provide quantitative evaluations to help programmers estimate the performance impact of each aspect.

Seo et al. discuss OpenCL performance implications for the NAS parallel benchmarks and give a nice overview of how they optimize the benchmarks by first getting an idea of the data transfer and scheduling overhead and then coming up with ways to avoid them [31]. They also show how to rewrite a good OpenCL code, given an OpenMP code. Stratton et al. describe a way to implement a compiler for fine-grained SPMD-thread programs on multicore execution platforms [16]. For the fine-grained programming model, they start with CUDA, saying that it will apply to OpenCL as well. They focus on the performance improvement over the baseline. Our work is more generalized and broad compared to these previous studies and also includes some of the important points that are not addressed in these papers.

One of the references that is very helpful to understand the performance behavior of OpenCL is a document from Intel [32]. It broadly lays out some general guidelines to follow to get better performance out of OpenCL applications on Intel processors. However, it does not discuss the performance improvement and also does not state how much benefit can be achieved.

5. Conclusion

We evaluate the performance of OpenCL applications on modern multicore CPU architectures. Understanding the performance in terms of architectural resource utilization is helpful for programmers. In this paper, we evaluate various aspects, including API overhead, thread scheduling, ILP, data transfer, data locality, and compiler-supported vectorization. We verify the unique characteristics of OpenCL applications by comparing them with conventional parallel programming models such as OpenMP. Key findings of our evaluation are as follows.

(1) OpenCL API overhead is not negligible on CPUs (Section 3.2).

(2) Allocating more work per workitem therefore reducing the number of workitems helps performance on CPUs (Section 3.3.1).

(3) Large ILP helps performance on CPUs (Section 3.3.2).

(4) Large workgroup size is helpful for better performance on CPUs (Section 3.3.3).

(5) On CPUs, Mapping APIs perform superior compared to explicit data transfer APIs. Memory allocation flags do not change performance (Section 3.4).

(6) Programming model can have possible effect on compiler-supported vectorization. Conditions for the code to be vectorized can be complex (Section 3.5.1).

(7) Adding affinity support to OpenCL may help performance in some cases (Section 3.5.2).

Our evaluation shows that considering the characteristics of CPU architectures, the OpenCL application can be optimized further for CPUs, and the programmer needs to consider these insights for portable performance.

Conflict of Interests

The authors declare that there is no conflict of interests regarding the publication of this paper.

Acknowledgments

The authors would like to thank Jin Wang and Sudhakar Yalamanchili, Inchoon Yeo, the Georgia Tech HPArch members, and the anonymous reviewers for their suggestions and feedback. We gratefully acknowledge the support of the NSF CAREER award 1139083 and Samsung.

References

[1] AMD, AMD Accelerated Processing Units (APUs), http://www.amd.com/en-us/innovations/software-technologies/apu.

[2] Intel, "Products (Formerly Sandy Bridge)," http://ark.intel.com/products/codename/29900/Sandy-Bridge.

[3] Khronos Group, "OpenCL: the open standard for parallel programming of heterogeneous systems," http://www.khronos.org/opencl.

[4] Intel, "Intel OpenCL SDK," http://software.intel.com/en-us/articles/intel-opencl-sdk/.

[5] NVIDIA, "NVIDIA OpenCL SDK," http://developer.nvidia.com/cuda/opencl/.

[6] J. Aycock, "A brief history of just-in-time," *ACM Computing Surveys*, vol. 35, no. 2, pp. 97–113, 2003.

[7] Intel, Intel Threading Building Blocks, http://threadingbuildingblocks.org/.

[8] The OpenMP Architecture Review Board, OpenMP, http://openmp.org/wp/.

[9] NVIDIA, CUDA Programming Guide, V4.0, 2011.

[10] S. Ryoo, C. I. Rodrigues, S. S. Baghsorkhi, S. S. Stone, D. B. Kirk, and W.-M. W. Hwu, "Optimization principles and application performance evaluation of a multithreaded GPU using CUDA," in *Proceedings of the 13th ACM SIGPLAN Symposium on Principles and Practice of Parallel Programming (PPoPP '08)*, pp. 73–82, February 2008.

[11] S. Ryoo, C. I. Rodrigues, S. S. Stone, S. S. Baghsorkhi, S.-Z. Ueng, and W.-M. W. Hwu, "Program optimization study on a 128-core GPU," in *Proceedings of the 1st Workshop on General Purpose Processing on Graphics Processing Units (GPGPU '07)*, October 2007.

[12] S. Ryoo, C. I. Rodrigues, S. S. Stone et al., "Program optimization space pruning for a multithreaded GPU," in *Proceedings of the 6th Annual IEEE/ACM International Symposium on Code Generation and Optimization (CGO '08)*, pp. 195–204, 2008.

[13] V. Volkov and J. W. Demmel, "Benchmarking GPUs to tune dense linear algebra," in *Proceedings of the International Conference for High Performance Computing, Networking, Storage and Analysis (SC '08)*, pp. 31:1–31:11, November 2008.

[14] R. Balasubramonian, S. Dwarkadas, and D. H. Albonesi, "Reducing the complexity of the register file in dynamic superscalar processors," in *Proceedings of the 34th Annual International Symposium on Microarchitecture*, pp. 237–248, December 2001.

[15] J. Kim, S. Seo, J. Lee, J. Nah, and G. Jo, "SnuCL: an OpenCL framework for heterogeneous CPU/GPU clusters," in *Proceedings of the 26th ACM International Conference on Supercomputing (ICS '12)*, pp. 341–351, June 2012.

[16] J. A. Stratton, V. Grover, J. Marathe et al., "Efficient compilation of fine-grained SPMD-threaded programs for multicore CPUs," in *Proceedings of the 8th International Symposium on Code Generation and Optimization (CGO '10)*, pp. 111–119, ACM, April 2010.

[17] G. Diamos, "The design and implementation Ocelot's dynamic binary translator from PTX to Multi-Core x86," Tech. Rep. GIT-CERCS-09-18, Georgia Institute of Technology, 2009.

[18] B. Saha, X. Zhou, H. Chen et al., "Programming model for a heterogeneous x86 platform," in *Proceedings of the ACM*

SIGPLAN Conference on Programming Language Design and Implementation (PLDI '09), pp. 431–440, June 2009.

[19] S. Maleki, Y. Gao, M. J. Garzarán, T. Wong, and D. A. Padua, "An evaluation of vectorizing compilers," in *Proceedings of the 20th International Conference on Parallel Architectures and Compilation Techniques (PACT '11)*, pp. 372–382, Galveston, Tex, USA, October 2011.

[20] L. Gwennap, "Intel's MMX speeds multimedia," Microprocessor Report, 1996.

[21] Intel, "Intel Integrated Performance Primitives," https://software.intel.com/en-us/intel-ipp.

[22] Intel, Intel Math Kernel Library, http://software.intel.com/en-us/intel-mkl.

[23] Intel, Intel C and C++ Compilers, https://software.intel.com/en-us/c-compilers.

[24] M. Pharr and W. R. Mark, "ispc: a SPMD compiler for high-performance CPU programming," in *Proceedings of the Innovative Parallel Computing (InPar '12)*, pp. 1–13, IEEE, San Jose, Calif, USA, May 2012.

[25] D. Grewe and M. F. P. O'Boyle, "A static task partitioning approach for heterogeneous systems using OpenCL," in *Proceedings of the 20th International Conference on Compiler Construction (CC '11)*, pp. 286–305, Saarbrücken, Germany, March 2011.

[26] The IMPACT Research Group and UIUC, "Parboil benchmark suite," http://impact.crhc.illinois.edu/Parboil/parboil.aspx.

[27] C.-K. Luk, R. Cohn, R. Muth et al., "Pin: building customized program analysis tools with dynamic instrumentation," in *Proceedings of the ACM SIGPLAN Conference on Programming Language Design and Implementation (PLDI '05)*, pp. 190–200, June 2005.

[28] Intel, A Guide to Auto-Vectorization with Intel C++ Compilers, http://software.intel.com/en-us/articles/a-guide-to-auto-vectorization-with-intel-c-compilers.

[29] S. Hong and H. Kim, "An analytical model for a gpu architecture with memory-level and thread-level parallelism awareness," in *Proceedings of the 36th Annual International Symposium on Computer Architecture (ISCA '09)*, pp. 152–163, June 2009.

[30] A. Ali, U. Dastgeer, and C. Kessler, "OpenCL for programming shared memory multicore CPUs," in *Proceedings of the MULTIPROG Workshop at HiPEAC*, 2012.

[31] S. Seo, G. Jo, and J. Lee, "Performance characterization of the NAS Parallel Benchmarks in OpenCL," in *Proceedings of the IEEE International Symposium on Workload Characterization (IISWC '11)*, pp. 137–148, Austin, Tex, USA, November 2011.

[32] Intel, "Writing Optimal OpenCL Code with Intel OpenCL SDK," http://software.intel.com/file/37171.

5

High-Performance Design Patterns for Modern Fortran

Magne Haveraaen,[1] **Karla Morris,**[2] **Damian Rouson,**[3]
Hari Radhakrishnan,[4] **and Clayton Carson**[3]

[1]*Department of Informatics, University of Bergen, 5020 Bergen, Norway*
[2]*Sandia National Laboratories, Livermore, CA 94550, USA*
[3]*Stanford University, Stanford, CA 94305, USA*
[4]*EXA High Performance Computing, 1087 Nicosia, Cyprus*

Correspondence should be addressed to Karla Morris; knmorri@sandia.gov

Academic Editor: Jeffrey C. Carver

This paper presents ideas for using coordinate-free numerics in modern Fortran to achieve code flexibility in the partial differential equation (PDE) domain. We also show how Fortran, over the last few decades, has changed to become a language well-suited for state-of-the-art software development. Fortran's new coarray distributed data structure, the language's class mechanism, and its side-effect-free, pure procedure capability provide the scaffolding on which we implement HPC software. These features empower compilers to organize parallel computations with efficient communication. We present some programming patterns that support asynchronous evaluation of expressions comprised of parallel operations on distributed data. We implemented these patterns using coarrays and the message passing interface (MPI). We compared the codes' complexity and performance. The MPI code is much more complex and depends on external libraries. The MPI code on Cray hardware using the Cray compiler is 1.5–2 times faster than the coarray code on the same hardware. The Intel compiler implements coarrays atop Intel's MPI library with the result apparently being 2–2.5 times slower than manually coded MPI despite exhibiting nearly linear scaling efficiency. As compilers mature and further improvements to coarrays comes in Fortran 2015, we expect this performance gap to narrow.

1. Introduction

1.1. Motivation and Background. The most useful software evolves over time. One force driving the evolution of high-performance computing (HPC) software applications derives from the ever evolving ecosystem of HPC hardware. A second force stems from the need to adapt to new user requirements, where, for HPC software, the users often are the software development teams themselves. New requirements may come from a better understanding of the scientific domain, yielding changes in the mathematical formulation of a problem, changes in the numerical methods, changes in the problem to be solved, and so forth.

One way to plan for software evolution involves designing variation points, areas where a program is expected to accommodate change. In a HPC domain like computational physics, partial differential equation (PDE) solvers are important.

Some likely variation points for PDE solvers include the formulation of the PDE itself, like different simplifications depending on what phenomena is studied, the coordinate system and dimensions, the numerical discretization, and the hardware parallelism. The approach of coordinate-free programming (CFP) handles these variation points naturally through domain-specific abstractions [1]. The explicit use of such abstractions is not common in HPC software, possibly due to the historical development of the field.

Fortran has held and still holds a dominant position in HPC software. Traditionally, the language supported loops for traversing large data arrays and had few abstraction mechanisms beyond the procedure. The focus was on efficiency and providing a simple data model that the compiler could map to efficient code. In the past few decades, Fortran has evolved significantly [2] and now supports class abstraction, object-oriented programming (OOP), pure functions, and a coarray model for parallel programming in shared or distributed memory and running on multicore processors and some many-core accelerators.

1.2. Related Work. CFP was first implemented in the context of seismic wave simulation [3] by Haveraaen et al. and Grant et al. [4] presented CFP for computational fluid dynamics applications. These abstractions were implemented in C++, relying on the language's template mechanism to achieve multiple levels of reuse. Rouson et al. [5] developed a "grid-free" representation of fluid dynamics, implementing continuous but coordinate-specific abstractions in Fortran 95, independently using similar abstractions to Diffpack [6]. While both C++ and Fortran 95 offered capabilities for overloading each language's intrinsic operators, neither allowed defining new, user-defined operators to represent the differential calculus operators, for example, those that appear in coordinate-free PDE representations. Likewise, neither language provided a scalable, parallel programming model.

Gamma et al. [7] first introduced the concept of patterns in the context of object-oriented software design. While they presented general design patterns, they suggested that it would be useful for subsequent authors to publish domain-specific patterns. Gardner et al. [8] published the first text summarizing object-oriented design patterns in the context of scientific programming. They employed Java to demonstrate the Gamma et al. general patterns in the context of a waveform analyzer for fusion energy experiments. Rouson et al. [9] published the first text on patterns for scientific programming in Fortran and C++, including several Gamma et al. patterns along with domain-specific and language-specific patterns. The Rouson et al. text included an early version of the PDE solver in the current paper, although no compilers at the time of their publication offered enough coverage of the newest Fortran features to compile their version of the solver.

The work of Cann [10] inspired much of our thinking on the utility of functional programming in parallelizing scientific applications. The current paper examines the complexity and performance of PDE solvers that support a functional programming style with either of two parallel programming models: coarray Fortran (CAF) and the message passing interface (MPI). CAF became part of Fortran in its 2008 standard. We refer the reader to the text by Metcalf et al. [2] for a summary of the CAF features of Fortran 2008 and to the text by Pacheco [11] for descriptions of the MPI features employed in the current paper.

1.3. Objectives and Outline. The current paper expands upon the first four author's workshop paper [12] on the CAF PDE solver by including comparisons to an analogous MPI solver first developed by the fifth author. We show how modern Fortran supports the CFP domain with the language's provision for user-defined operators and its efficient hardware-independent, parallel programming model. We use the PDE of Burgers [13] as our running theme.

Section 2 introduces the theme problem and explains CFP. Section 3 presents the features of modern Fortran used by the Burgers solver. Section 4 presents programming patterns useful in this setting, and Section 5 shows excerpts of code written according to our recommendations. Section 6 presents measurements of the approach's efficiency. Section 7 summarizes our conclusions.

2. Coordinate-Free Programming

Coordinate-free programming (CFP) is a structural design pattern for PDEs [3]. It is the result of domain engineering of the PDE domain. Domain engineering seeks finding the concepts central to a domain and then presenting these as reusable software components [14]. CFP defines a layered set of mathematical abstractions at the ring field level (spatial discretization), the tensor level (coordinate systems), and the PDE solver level (time integration and PDE formulation). It also provides abstractions at the mesh level, encompassing abstraction over parallel computations. These layers correspond to the variation points of PDE solvers [1], both at the user level and for the ever changing parallel architecture level.

To see how this works, consider the coordinate-free generalization of the Burgers equation [13]:

$$\frac{\partial \vec{u}}{\partial t} = \nu \nabla^2 \vec{u} - \vec{u} \cdot \nabla \vec{u}. \tag{1}$$

CFP maps each of the variables and operators in (1) to software objects and operators. In Fortran syntax, such a mapping of (1) might result in program lines of the form shown in Listing 1.

Fortran keywords are depicted in boldface. The first line declares that u and u_t are (distributed) objects in the tensor class. The second line defines the parameter value corresponding to ν. The third line evaluates the right-hand side of (1) using Fortran's facility for user-defined operators, in which the language requires to be bracketed by periods: laplacian (.laplacian.), dot product (.dot.), and gradient (.grad.). The mathematical formulation and the corresponding program code both are independent of dimensions, choice of coordinate system, discretisation method, and so forth. Yet the steps are mathematically and computationally precise.

Traditionally, the numerical scientist would expand (1) into its coordinate form. Deciding that we want to solve the 3D problem, the vector equation resolves into three component equations. The first component equation in Cartesian coordinates, for example, becomes

$$u_{1,t} = \nu \left(u_{1,xx} + u_{1,yy} + u_{1,zz} \right)$$
$$- \left(u_1 u_{1,x} + u_2 u_{1,x} + u_3 u_{1,x} \right). \tag{2}$$

Here, subscripted commas denote partial differentiation with respect to the subscripted variable preceded by the comma; for instance, $u_{1,t} \equiv \partial u_1 / \partial t$. Similar equations must be given for $u_{2,t}$ and $u_{3,t}$.

For one-dimensional (1D) data, (1) reduces to

$$u_{1,t} = \nu u_{1,xx} - u_1 u_{1,x}. \tag{3}$$

Burgers originally proposed the 1D form as a simplified proxy for the Navier-Stokes equations (NSE) in studies of

```
class(tensor):: u_t, u
real:: nu = 1.0
u_t = nu * (.laplacian.u) − (u.dot.(.grad.u))
```

LISTING 1

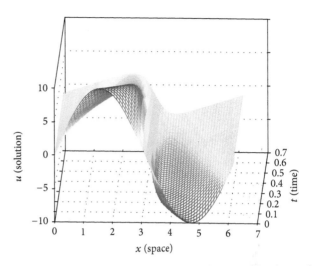

FIGURE 1: Unsteady, 1D Burgers equation solution values (vertical axis) over space (horizontal axis) and time (oblique axis). 1D Burgers equation solution surface: red (highest) and blue (lowest) relative to the $u = 0$ plane.

fluid turbulence. Equation (3) retains the diffusive nature of the NSE in the first right-hand-side (RHS) term and the nonlinear character of the NSE in the second RHS term. This equation has also found useful applications in several branches of physics. It has the nice property of yielding an exact solution despite its nonlinearity [15].

Figure 1 shows the solution values (vertical axis) as a function of space (horizontal axis) and time (oblique axis) starting from an initial condition of $u(x, t = 0) = 10 \sin(x)$ with periodic boundary conditions on the semiopen domain $[0, 2\pi)$. As time progresses, the nonlinear term steepens the initial wave while the diffusive term dampens it.

3. Modern Fortran

Fortran has always been a language with a focus on high efficiency for numerical computations on array data sets. Over the past 10–15 years, it has picked up features from mainstream programming, such as class abstractions, but also catered to its prime users by developing a rich set of high-level array operations. Controlling the flow of information allows for a purely functional style of expressions; that is, expressions that rely solely upon functions that have no side effects. Side effects influence the global state of the computer beyond the function's local variables. Examples of side effects include input/output, modifying arguments, halting execution, modifying nonlocal data, and synchronizing parallel processes.

There have been longstanding calls for employing functional programming as part of the solution to programming parallel computers [10]. The Fortran 2008 standard also includes a parallel programming model based primarily upon the coarray distributed data structure. The advent of support for Fortran 2008 coarrays in the Cray and Intel compilers makes the time ripe to explore synergies between Fortran's explicit support for functional expressions and coarray parallel programming. (Released versions of two free compilers also provide limited support for coarrays: g95 supports coarrays in what is otherwise essentially Fortran 95 and GNU Fortran (gfortran) supports the coarray syntax but runs coarray code as sequential code. Additionally, gfortran's prerelease development branch supports parallel execution of coarray code with communication handled by an external library (OpenCoarrays: http://www.opencoarrays.org) [16]. Ultimately, all compilers must support coarrays to conform to the Fortran standard.)

3.1. Array Language. Since the Fortran 90 standard, the language has introduced a rich set of array features. This set also applies to coarrays in the 2008 standard as we demonstrate in Section 3.4. Fortran 90 contained operations to apply the built-in intrinsic operators, such as + and *, to corresponding elements of similarly shaped arrays, that is, mapping them on the elements of the array. Modern Fortran also allows the mapping of user-defined procedures on arrays. Such procedures have to be declared "**elemental**," which ensures that, for every element of the array, the invocations are independent of each other and therefore can be executed concurrently. Operations for manipulating arrays also exist, for example, slicing out a smaller array from a larger one, requesting upper and lower range of an array, and summing or multiplying all elements of an array.

This implies that, in many cases, it is no longer necessary to express an algorithm by explicitly looping over its elements. Rather a few operations on entire arrays are sufficient to express a large computation. For instance, the following array expressions, given an allocatable real array X, will in the first line take 1-rank arrays A, B, and C, perform the elemental functions +, **sin**, and * on the corresponding elements from each of the arrays, and pad the result with 5 numbers:

$$X = [\mathbf{sin}(A + B) * C, 0., 1., 2., 3., 4., 5.];$$
$$X = X(1:5).$$

In the second line, only the 5 first elements are retained. Thus, for arrays A = [0., 0.5708], B = [0.5235988, 1.], and C = [3, 5], the result is an array X = [1.5, 5., 0., 1., 2.].

3.2. Class Abstraction. Class abstractions allow us to associate a set of procedures with a private data structure. This is the basic abstraction mechanism of a programming language, allowing users to extend it with libraries for domain-specific abstractions. The Fortran notation is somewhat verbose compared to other languages but gives great freedom in defining operator names for functions, both using standard symbols and introducing new named operators, for example, . dot . as used above.

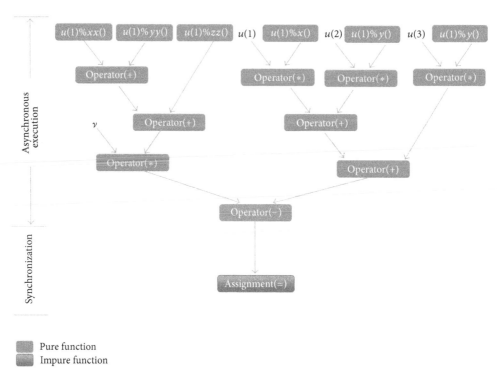

FIGURE 2: Calling sequence for evaluating the RHS of (2) and assigning the result.

The Fortran class abstractions allow us to implement the CFP domain abstractions, such as ring and tensor fields. Note that Fortran has very limited generic facilities. Fortran variables have three intrinsic properties: type, kind, and rank. Fortran procedures can be written to be generic in kind, which allows, for example, one implementation to work across a range of floating-point precisions. Fortran procedures can also be written to be generic in rank, which allows one implementation to work across a range of array ranks. Fortran procedures cannnot yet be generic in type, although there is less need for this compared to in languages where changing precision implies changing type. In Fortran, changing precision only implies changing kind, not type.

3.3. Functional Programming. A compiler can do better optimizations if it knows more about the intent of the code. A core philosophy of Fortran is to enable programmers to communicate properties of a program to a compiler without mandating specific compiler optimizations. In Fortran, each argument to a procedure can be given an attribute, **intent**, which describes how the procedure will use the argument data. The attribute "**in**" stands for just reading the argument, whereas "**out**" stands for just creating data for it, and "**inout**" allows both reading and modifying the argument. A stricter form is to declare a function as "**pure**," for example, indicating that the procedure harbors no side effects.

Purely functional programming composes programs from side-effect-free procedures and assignments. This facilitates numerous optimizations, including guaranteeing that invocations of such procedures can safely execute asynchronously on separate partitions of the program data. Figure 2 shows the calling sequence for evaluating the RHS

of (2) and assigning the result. Expressions in independent subtrees can be executed independently of each other, allowing concurrency.

When developing abstractions like CFP, the procedures needed can be implemented as subroutines that modify one or more arguments or as pure functions. Using pure functions makes the abstractions more mathematical and eases reasoning about the code.

3.4. Coarrays. Of particular interest in HPC are variation points at the parallelism level. Portable HPC software must allow for efficient execution on multicore processors, many-core accelerators, and heterogeneous combinations thereof. Fortran 2008 provides such portability by defining a partitioned global address space (PGAS), the coarray. This provides a single-program, multiple-data (SPMD) programming style that makes no reference to a particular parallel architecture. Fortran compilers may replicate a program across a set of images, which need to communicate when one image reaches out to a nonlocal part of the coarray. Images and communications are mapped to the parallel architecture of the compiler's choice. The Intel compiler, for example, maps an image to a message passing interface (MPI) process, whereas the Cray compiler uses a proprietary communication library that outperforms MPI on Cray computers. Mappings to accelerators have also been announced.

For example, a coarray definition of the form given in Listing 2 establishes that the program will index into the variable "a" along three dimensions (in parenthesis) and one codimension (in square brackets), so Listing 3 lets image 3, as given by the **this_image** () function, copy the first element of image 2 to the first element of image 1. If there are less

```
real, allocatable:: a(:,:,:)[:]
```

LISTING 2

```
if (this_image() == 3) then
   a(1, 1, 1)[1] = a(1, 1, 1)[2]
end if
```

LISTING 3

than 3 images, the assignment does not take place. The size of the normal dimensions is decided by the programmer. The run-time environment and compiler decide the codimension. A reference to the array without the codimension index, for example, a (1, 1, 1), denotes the local element on the image that executes the statement. Equivalently, the expression "a (1, 1, 1) [**this_image** ()]" makes the reference to the executing image explicit.

A dilemma arises when writing parallel operations on the aforementioned tensor object by encapsulating a coarray inside it; Fortran prohibits function results that contain coarrays. Performance concerns motivate this prohibition; in an expression, function results become input arguments to other functions. For coarray return values to be safe, each such result would have to be synchronized across images, causing severe scalability and efficiency problems. The growing gap between processor speeds and communication bandwidth necessitates avoiding interprocessor coordination.

To see the scalability concern, consider implementing the expression $(u * u)_x$ using finite differences with a stencil of width 1 for the partial derivative, with data u being spread across images on a coarray. The part of the partial derivative function u_x executing on image i requires access to data from neighboring images $i + 1$ and $i - 1$. The multiplication $u * u$ will be run independently on each image for the part of the coarray residing on that image. Now, for $(u * u)_x$ on image i to be correct, the system must ensure that $u * u$ on images $i - 1, i$, and $i + 1$ all have finished computing and stored the result in their local parts of the coarray. Likewise, for the computation of $(u * u)_x$ at images $i - 1$ and $i + 1$, the computation of $u * u$ at images $i - 2, i - 1$, and i and $i, i + 1$, and $i + 2$, respectively, must be ready. Since the order of execution for each image is beyond explicit control, synchronization is needed to ensure correct ordering of computation steps.

Because analyzing whether and when synchronization is needed is beyond the compiler, the options are either synchronizing at return (with a possibly huge performance hit) or not synchronizing at return, risking hard to track data inconsistencies. The aforementioned prohibition precludes these issues, by placing the responsibility for synchronization with the programmer yet allowing each image to continue processing local data for as long as possible. Consider the call graph in Figure 2. The only function calls requiring access to

nonlocal data are the 6 calls to the partial derivatives on the top row. The remaining 9 function calls only need local data, allowing each image to proceed independently of the others until the assignment statement calls for a synchronization to prepare the displacement function u for the next time-step by assigning to $u_{1,t}$.

4. Design Patterns

Programming patterns capture experience in how to express solutions to recurring programming issues effectively from a software development, a software evolution, or even a performance perspective. Standard patterns tend to evolve into language constructs, the modern "**while**" statement evolved from a pattern with "**if**" and "**goto**" in early Fortran.

Patterns can also be more domain-specific, for example, limited to scientific software [9]. Here we will look at patterns for high-performance, parallel PDE solvers.

4.1. Object Superclass and Error Tracing. Many object-oriented languages, from the origins in Simula [17] and onwards, have an object class that is the ultimate parent of all classes. Fortran, like C++, does not have a universal base class. For many projects, though it can be useful to define a Fortran object class that is the ultimate parent of all classes in a project, such an object can provide state and functionality that are universally useful throughout the project. The object class itself is declared **abstract** to preclude constructing any actual objects of type object.

The object class in Listing 4 represents a solution to the problem of tracing assurances and reporting problems in pure functions. Assertions provide one common mechanism for verifying requirements and assurances. However, assertions halt execution, a prohibited side effect. The solution is to have the possible error information as extra data items in the object class. If a problem occurs, the data can be set accordingly and passed on through the pure expressions until it ultimately is acted upon in a procedure where such side-effects are allowed, for example, in an input/output (I/O) statement or an assignment.

The object class in Listing 4 allows tracking of the definedness of a variable declared to belong to the object class or any of its subclasses. Such tracking can be especially useful when dynamically allocated structures are involved. The is_defined function returns the value of the user_defined component. The mark_as_defined subroutine sets the value of user_defined to .**true.**. Using this systematically in each procedure that defines or uses object data will allow a trace of the source of uninitialized data.

A caveat is that the object class cannot be a superclass of classes containing coarrays because the compiler needs to know if a variable has a coarray component or not. We therefore need to declare a corresponding co_object class to be the superclass for classes with coarray components.

4.2. Compute Globally, Return Locally. The behavioural design pattern *compute globally, return locally* (CGRL) [9] has been suggested as a way to deal with the prohibition on returning coarrays from functions.

```
type, abstract:: object
    logical:: user_defined = .false.
contains
    procedure:: is_defined
    procedure:: mark_as_defined
end type
```

LISTING 4

In CGRL, each nonlocal operator accepts operands that contain coarrays. The operator performs any global communication required to execute some parallel algorithm. On each image, the operator packages its local partition of the result in an object containing a regular array. Ultimately, when the operator of lowest precedence completes and each image has produced its local partition of the result, a user-defined assignment copies the local partitions into the global coarray and performs any necessary synchronizations to make the result available to subsequent program lines. The asymmetry between the argument and return types forces splitting large expressions into separate statements when synchronization is needed.

5. Implementation Example

In this section, we implement the functions needed to evaluate (2), as illustrated in Figure 2. We follow the CGRL pattern: the derivation functions take a coarray data structure and return an array data structure, the multiplication then takes a coarray and an array data structure and return an array data structure, and the remaining operators work on array data structures. The assignment then synchronizes after assigning the local arrays to the corresponding component of the coarray.

To avoid cluttering the code excerpts with error-forwarding boiler plate, we first show code without this and then show how the code will look with this feature in Section 5.4.

5.1. Array Data Structure. First, we declare a local_tensor class with only local array data. It is a subclass of object. The ampersand (&) is the Fortran line continuation character and the exclamation mark (!) precedes Fortran comments. The size of the data on each image is set by a global constant, the parameter local_grid_size (see Listing 5).

The procedure declarations list the procedures that the class exports. The generic declarations introduce the operator symbols as synonyms for the procedure names. The four functions that are of interest to us are implemented in Listing 6.

These are normal functions on array data. If executed in parallel, each image will have a local instance of the variables and locally execute each function. Notice how we use the Fortran operators "+" and "−" directly on the array data structures in these computations.

```
type, extends(object):: local_tensor
    real:: f(local_grid_size)
    contains
    !...
    procedure:: add
    procedure:: assign_local
    procedure:: state
    procedure:: subtract
    generic:: operator(+)    => add
    generic:: operator(−)    => subtract
    generic:: assignment(=) => assign_local
    !...
end type
```

LISTING 5

```
pure function add(lhs, rhs) result(total)
    class(local_tensor), intent(in):: lhs, rhs
    type(local_tensor):: total
    total%f = lhs%f + rhs%f
end function
pure subroutine assign_local(lhs, rhs)
    class(local_tensor), intent(inout):: lhs
    real, intent(in):: rhs(:)
    lhs%f = rhs
end subroutine
pure function state(this) result(my_data)
    class(local_tensor), intent(in):: this
    real:: my_data(local_grid_size)
    my_data = this%f
end function
pure function subtract(lhs, rhs) &
    result(difference)
    class(local_tensor), intent(in):: lhs, rhs
    type(local_tensor):: difference
    difference%f = lhs%f − rhs%f
end function
```

LISTING 6

5.2. Coarray Data Structure. Listing 7 is the declaration of a data structure distributed across the images.

The coarray declaration allows us to access data on other images.

The partial derivative function takes a coarray data structure as argument and returns an array data structure. The algorithm is a simple finite difference that wraps around the boundary. The processing differs depending on whether **this_image** () is the first image, an internal image, or the last image **num_images**(). An internal image needs access to data from the next image above or below. The extremal images do a wrap-around for their missing neighbors (see Listing 8).

In the tensor class, the local_tensor class is opaque, disallowing direct access to its data structure. Only procedures from the interface can be used. These include a user-defined assignment implicitly invoked in the penultimate

```
type, extends(co_object):: tensor
  private
  real, allocatable:: global_f(:)[:]
contains
  !...
  procedure:: assign_local_to_global
  procedure:: multiply_by_local
  procedure:: add_to_local
  procedure:: x              => df_dx
  generic:: operator(*)      => &
              multiply_by_local
  generic:: assignment(=)    => &
              assign_local_to_global
  !...
end type
```

LISTING 7

line of the df_dx function. Note again how most of the computation is done by using intrinsics on array data. We also make use of the Fortran 2008 capability for expressing the opportunity for concurrently executing loop traversals when no data dependencies exist from one iteration to the next. The "**do concurrent**" construct exposes this concurrency to the compiler.

The partial derivative functions, the single derivative shown here, and the second derivative (omitted) are the only procedures needing access to nonlocal data. Although a synchronization must take place before the nonlocal access, the requisite synchronization occurs in a prior assignment or object initialization procedure. Hence, the full expression evaluation generated by the RHS of (2) occurs asynchronously, both among the images for the distributed coarray and at the expression level for the pure functions.

The implementation of the add_to_local procedure has the object with the coarray as the first argument and a local object with field data as its second argument and return type (see Listing 9).

The rhs%state () function invocation returns the local data array from the rhs local tensor and this is then added to the local component of the coarray using Fortran's array operator notation.

Finally, the assignment operation synchronizes when converting the array class local_tensor back to the coarray class tensor (see Listing 10).

After each component of the coarray has been assigned, the global barrier "**sync all**" is called, forcing all images to wait until all of them have completed the assignment. This ensures that all components of the coarray have been updated before any further use of the data takes place. Some situations might also necessitate a synchronization at the beginning of the assignment procedure: to prevent modifying data that another image might be accessing. Our chosen 2ndorder Runge Kutta time advancement algorithm did not require this additional synchronization because no RHS expressions contained nonlocal operations on the data structure appearing on the LHS.

5.3. MPI Data Structure. Developing applications using MPI necessitates depending on a library defined outside any programming language standard. This often results in procedural programming patterns instead of functional or object-oriented programming patterns. To make a fair comparison, we will employ a MPI data structure that uses the array data structure shown in Section 5.1. In the MPI version, the 1D grid was partitioned across the cores using a periodic Cartesian communicator, as shown in the code listing in Listing 11.

Using this communicator allowed us to reorder the processor ranks to make the communication more efficient by placing the neighbouring ranks close to each other. The transfer of data between the cores was done using MPI_SENDRECV, as shown in Listing 12. As in the case of the coarray version, nonlocal data was only required during the computation of the partial derivatives. The MPI version of the first derivative function is shown in Listing 12.

MPI_SENDRECV is a blocking routine which means that the processor will wait for its neighbor to complete communication before proceeding. This works as a de facto synchronization of the data between the neighbours ensuring that the data is current on all the processors. The c_double kind parameter used to declare the real variables in Listing 12 is related to the kind parameter MPI DOUBLE PRECISION in the MPI communication calls. These must be in sync, ensuring that the Fortran data has the same format as that used in MPI calls, viz. double precision real numbers that are compatible with C.

5.4. Error Tracing. The error propagating pattern is illustrated in the code in Listing 13.

The ! Requires test in Listing 13 checks that the two arguments to the add function have the definedness attribute set. It then performs the actual computation and sets the definedness attribute for the return value. In case of an error in the input, the addition does not take place and the default object value of undefined data gets propagated through this function.

The actual validation of the assurance and reporting of the error takes place in the user-defined assignment or I/O that occurs at the end of evaluation of a purely functional expression. The listing in Listing 14 shows this for the assign_local_to_global procedure.

More detailed error reporting can be achieved by supplying more metadata in the object for such reporting purposes.

6. Results

6.1. Pattern Tradeoffs. This paper presents two new patterns: the aforementioned object and the CGRL patterns. The object pattern proved to be lightweight in the sense of requiring simple Boolean conditionals that improve the code robustness with negligible impact on execution time. The object pattern is, however, heavyweight in terms of source-code impact: the pattern encourages having every class extend the object superclass, and it encourages evaluating these conditionals at the beginning and end of every method. We found the robustness benefit to be worth the source-code cost.

```
function df_dx(this)
 class(tensor), intent(in):: this
 type(local_tensor):: df_dx
 integer:: i, nx, me, east, west
 real:: dx
 real:: local_tensor_data(local_grid_size)
  nx = local_grid_size
  dx = 2. * pi/(real(nx) * num_images())
  me = this_image()
 if (me == 1) then
  west = num_images()
  east = merge(1, 2, num_images() == 1)
 else if (me == num_images()) then
  west = me − 1
  east = 1
 else
  west = me − 1
  east = me + 1
 end if
  local_tensor_data(1) = 0.5 * (this%global_f(2) − this%global_f(nx)[west])/dx
  local_tensor_data(nx) = 0.5 * (this%global_f(1)[east] − this%global_f(nx − 1))/dx
  do concurrent(i = 2 : nx − 1)
   local_tensor_data(i) = 0.5 * (this%global_f(i + 1) − this%global_f(i − 1))/dx
  end do
  df_dx = local_tensor_data
end function
```

LISTING 8

```
function add_to_local(lhs, rhs) result(total)
 class(tensor), intent(in):: lhs
 type(local_tensor), intent(in):: rhs
 type(local_tensor):: total
 total = lhs%state() + rhs%global_f(:)
end function
```

LISTING 9

```
subroutine assign_local_to_global(lhs, rhs)
 class(tensor), intent(inout):: lhs
 class(local_tensor), intent(in):: rhs
 lhs%global_f(:) = rhs%state()
 sync all
end subroutine
```

LISTING 10

The CGRL pattern is the linchpin holding together the functional expression evaluation in the face of a performance-related language restriction on coarray function results. The benefit of CGRL is partly syntactical in that it enables the writing of coordinate-free expressions composed of parallel operations on coarray data structures. CGRL also offers potential performance benefits by enabling particular compiler optimizations. Fortran requires that user-defined operator to have the "**intent (in)**" attribute, which precludes a common side effect: modifying arguments. This goes a long way toward enabling the declaration of the operator as "**pure,**" which allows the compiler to execute multiple instances of the operator asynchronously. One cost of CGRL in the context of the CFP pattern lies in the frequent creation of temporary intermediate values. This is true for most compilers that deal naively with the functional programming style, as precluding the modification of arguments inherently implies allocating memory on the stack or the heap for each operator result. This implies a greater use of memory. It also implies latencies associated with each memory allocation. Balancing this cost is a reduced need for synchronization and the associated increased opportunities for parallel execution. A detailed evaluation of this tradeoff requires writing a numerically equivalent code that exploits mutable data (modifiable arguments) to avoid temporary intermediate values. Such a comparison is beyond the scope of this paper. More advanced approaches to compiling functional expressions exist, as demonstrated by the Sisal compiler [10]. It aggressively rearranges computations to avoid such memory overhead. Whether this is possible within the framework of current Fortran compilers needs to be investigated.

6.2. Performance. We have investigated the feasibility of our approach using the one-dimensional (1D) form of Burgers equation, (3). We modified the solver from [9] to ensure

```
subroutine mpi_begin
integer:: dims(1), periods(1), reorder
! prevent accidentally starting MPI
! if it has already been initiated
if (program_status .eq. 0) then
  call MPI_INIT(ierr)
  call MPI_COMM_SIZE(MPI_COMM_WORLD, num_procs, ierr)
  call MPI_COMM_RANK(MPI_COMM_WORLD, my_id, ierr)
  ! Create a 1D Cartesian partition
  ! with reordering and periodicity
  dims = num_procs
  reorder = .true.
  periods = .true.
  call MPI_CART_CREATE(MPI_COMM_WORLD, 1, dims, periods, reorder, MPI_COMM_CART, ierr)
  call MPI_COMM_RANK(MPI_COMM_CART, my_id, ierr)
  call MPI_CART_SHIFT(MPI_COMM_CART, 0, 1, left_id, right_id, ierr)
  program_status = 1
endif
end subroutine
```

LISTING 11

```
function df_dx(this)
  implicit none
  class(tensor), intent(in):: this
  type(tensor):: df_dx
  integer(ikind):: i, nx
  real(c_double):: dx, left_image, right_image
  real(c_double), dimension(:), allocatable, save:: local_tensor_data
    nx = local_grid_resolution
    if (.not.allocated(local_tensor_data)) allocate(local_tensor_data(nx))
    dx = 2. * pi/(real(nx, c_double) * num_procs)
    if (num_procs > 1) then
      call MPI_SENDRECV(this%global_f(1), 1,
          MPI_DOUBLE_PRECISION, left_id, 0, right_image, 1,
          MPI_DOUBLE_PRECISION, right_id, 0, MPI_COMM_CART,
          status, ierr)
      call MPI_SENDRECV(this%global_f(nx), 1,
          MPI_DOUBLE_PRECISION, right_id, 0, left_image, 1,
          MPI_DOUBLE_PRECISION, left_id, 0, MPI_COMM_CART,
          status, ierr)
    else
      left_image = this%global_f(nx)
      right_image = this%global_f(1)
    end if
    local_tensor_data(1) = 0.5 * (this%global_f(2) - left_image)/dx
    local_tensor_data(nx) = 0.5 * (right_image - this%global_f(nx - 1))/dx
    do concurrent(i = 2 : nx - 1)
      local_tensor_data(i) = 0.5 * (this%global_f(i + 1) - this%global_f(i - 1))/dx
    end do
    df_dx%global_f = local_tensor_data
  end function
```

LISTING 12

```
pure function add(lhs, rhs) result(total)
  class(local_tensor), intent(in):: lhs, rhs
  type(local_tensor):: total
  ! Requires
  if (lhs%user_defined() .and. &
      rhs%user_defined()) then
    total%f = lhs%f + rhs%f
    ! Ensures
    call total%mark_as_defined
  end if
end function
```

LISTING 13

```
subroutine assign_local_to_global(lhs, rhs)
  class(tensor), intent(inout):: lhs
  class(local_tensor), intent(in):: rhs
  ! Requires
  call assert(rhs%user_defined())
  ! update global field
  lhs%global_f(:) = rhs%state()
  ! Ensures
  call lhs%mark_as_defined
  sync all
end subroutine
```

LISTING 14

```
if (num_images() == 1 .or. &
    num_images() == 2) then
  sync all
else
  if (this_image() == 1) then
    sync images([2, num_images()])
  elseif (this_image() == num_images()) then
    sync images([1, this_image() − 1])
  else
    sync images([this_image() − 1, &
                 this_image() + 1])
  endif
endif
```

LISTING 15

explicitly pure expression evaluation. The global barrier synchronization in the code excerpt above was replaced by synchronizing nearest neighbors only (see Listing 15).

Figure 3 depicts the execution time profile of the dominant procedures as measured by the tuning and analysis utilities (TAU) package [18]. In constructing Figure 3, we emulated larger, multidimensional problems by running with 128^3 grid points on each of the 256 cores. The results demonstrate nearly uniform load balancing. Other than the main program (red), the local-to-global assignment occupies the largest inclusive share of the runtime. Most of that procedure's time lies in its synchronizations.

We also did a larger weak scaling experiment on the Cray. Here, we emulate the standard situation where the user exploits the available resources to solve as large a problem as possible. Each core is assigned a fixed data size of 2 097 152 values for 3 000 time steps, and the total size of the problem solved is then proportional to the number of cores available. The solver shows good weak scaling properties; see Figure 4, where it remains at 87% efficiency for 16 384 cores. We have normalized the plot against 64 cores. The Cray has an architecture of 24 cores per node, so our base measurement takes into account the cost due to off-node communication.

Currently, we are synchronizing for every time step, only reaching out for a couple of neighboring values (second derivative) for each synchronization. We may want to trade

some synchronization for duplication of computations. The technique is to introduce ghost values in the coarray, duplicating the values at the edge of the neighboring images. These values can then be computed and used locally without the need for communication or synchronization. The optimal number of ghost values depends on the relative speed between computation and synchronization. For example, using 9 ghost values on each side in an image, should reduce the need for synchronization to every 8th time step, while it increases computation at each core by 18/1283 = 1.4%. The modification should be local to the tensor class, only affecting the partial derivative (the procedures needing remote data) and assignment (the procedure doing the synchronization) procedures. We leave this as future work.

We also looked at the strong scaling performance of the MPI and coarray versions by looking at change in execution times for a fixed problem size. The strong scaling efficiency for two different problem sizes is shown in Figures 5(a) and 5(b). We expect linear scaling; that is, the execution time will halve when the number of processors are doubled. However, we see that we obtain superlinear speedup during the initial doubling of the number of processors. This superlinear speedup is caused by the difference in speeds of the cache memory. The large problems cannot fit entirely into the heap, and time is consumed in moving objects from the slower memory to the faster memory. As the problem is divided amongst more and more processors, the problem's memory requirements become smaller, and is able to fit in the faster memory that is closer to the processor. This causes the superlinear speedup. As more processors are added, communication between processors starts to become expensive, and the speedup drops. We observe superlinear speedup for both coarray and MPI versions. However, the much greater speedup seen for the coarray version suggest that its memory requirements are higher than those of the MPI version. (These numbers may be slightly misleading, as the MPI version used dynamically allocated data, while the CAF version used statically allocated data. This may cause the CAF version to use more memory than the MPI version. Fixing this will cause minor changes in the numbers and close

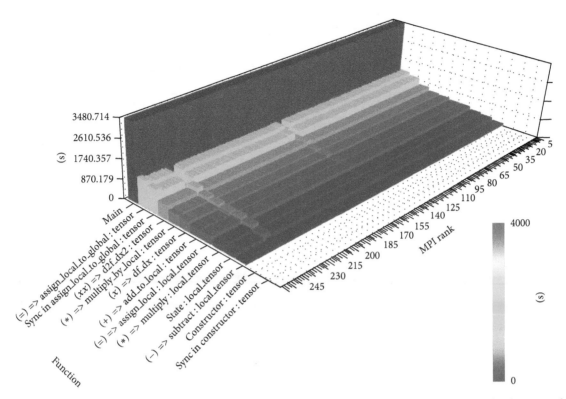

FIGURE 3: Runtime work distribution on all images. Each operator is shown in parenthesis, followed consecutively by the name of the type-bound procedure implementing the operator and the name of the corresponding module. The two points of synchronization are indicated by the word "sync" followed by the name of the type-bound procedure invoking the synchronization.

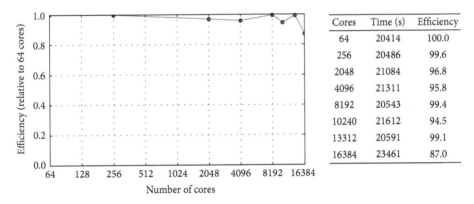

Cores	Time (s)	Efficiency
64	20414	100.0
256	20486	99.6
2048	21084	96.8
4096	21311	95.8
8192	20543	99.4
10240	21612	94.5
13312	20591	99.1
16384	23461	87.0

FIGURE 4: Weak scaling of solver for (3) using the coarray version on Cray.

the ratio between the MPI and CAF efficiency. We will have these numbers available for the revision of this document.)

The raw execution times using the different versions on Intel and Cray platforms are shown in Table 1. We chose a smaller problem for the strong scaling experiments than for the weak scaling experiments because of the limited resources available with the Intel platform. We see that the coarray version is slower than the MPI version on the same platform for the same problem size. Comparing the actual runtimes shown in Table 1 shows that using the Intel compiler, the MPI version is about 2 to 2.5 times faster than the coarray version. For the Cray compiler, the MPI version is about 1.5 to 2 times faster than the coarray version. To understand the difference

in runtimes, we analyzed the CAF and MPI versions using TAU and the Intel compiler. Using PAPI [19] with TAU and the Intel compiler to count the floating-point operations, we see that the MPI version is achieving approximately 52.2% of the peak theoretical FLOPS for a problem with 819200 grid points using 256 processors whereas the CAF version is achieving approximately 21% of the peak theoretical FLOPS. The execution times for some of the different functions are shown in Figure 6. We see that the communication routines are taking the longest fraction of the total execution time. However, the coarray syncing is taking significantly longer than the MPI_SENDRECV blocking operation. The Intel coarray implementation is based on its MPI library, and

TABLE 1: Execution times for the CAF and MPI versions of the Burgers solver for different problem sizes using Intel and Cray compilers.

Cores	409600 grid points				819200 grid points			
	MPI		CAF		MPI		CAF	
	Intel	Cray	Intel	Cray	Intel	Cray	Intel	Cray
32	52.675	59.244	154.649	187.204	128.638	131.048	333.682	512.312
64	29.376	28.598	71.051	46.923	58.980	58.887	152.829	192.396
128	19.864	14.169	38.321	21.137	31.396	26.318	69.612	42.939
256	12.060	9.109	23.183	13.553	21.852	12.953	51.957	27.226
512	7.308	6.204	19.080	12.581	12.818	8.413	31.437	18.577

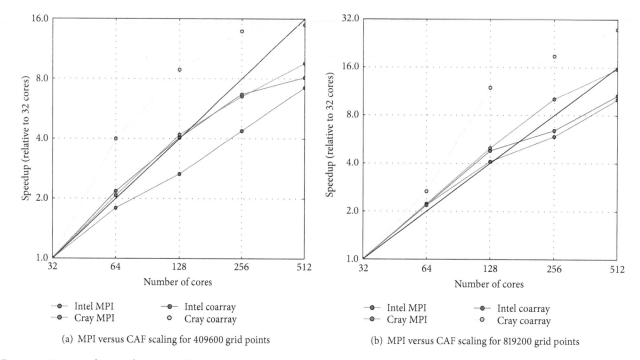

(a) MPI versus CAF scaling for 409600 grid points

(b) MPI versus CAF scaling for 819200 grid points

FIGURE 5: Strong scaling performance of the coarray and MPI versions of the solver for (3) using different platforms. The raw execution times are listed in Table 1.

the overheads of the coarray implementation are responsible for some of the slowdown. The greater maturity of the MPI library compared to CAF also probably plays a role in the superior performance of the MPI implementation. So, we are likely to see the performance gap lessen as compiler implementations of CAF improve over time.

6.3. Complexity. Other than performance considerations, we also wanted to compare the pros and cons of the coarray Fortran (CAF) implementation versus an MPI implementation of the 1D form of the Burgers equation (3) in terms of code complexity and ease of development.

The metrics used to compare the code complexity were lines of code (LOC), use statements, variable declarations, external calls, and function arguments. The results of this comparison may be found in Table 2. As seen in Table 2, the MPI implementation had significantly greater complexity compared to the CAF implementation for all of the metrics which were considered. This has potential consequences in terms of the defect rate of the code. For example, comparing

the MPI version with the coarray version listed in Section 5.2, we see that the basic structures of the functions are almost identical. However, the MPI_SENDRECV communication of the local grid data to and from the neighbours is achieved implicitly in the coarray version making the code easier to read. Counterbalancing its greater complexity, the MPI implementation had superior performance compared to the CAF code.

Software development time should also be taken into account when comparing CAF to MPI. Certain metrics of code complexity have been shown to correlate with higher defect rates. For instance, average defect rate has been shown to have a curvilinear relationship with LOC [20]. So, an MPI implementation might drive higher defect density and overall number of defects in a project, contributing to development time and code reliability. Likewise, external calls or fanout has shown positive correlation with defect density, also reducing the relative attractiveness of the MPI implementation [21]. In addition, the dramatically increased number of arguments for function calls, as well as the larger number of functions

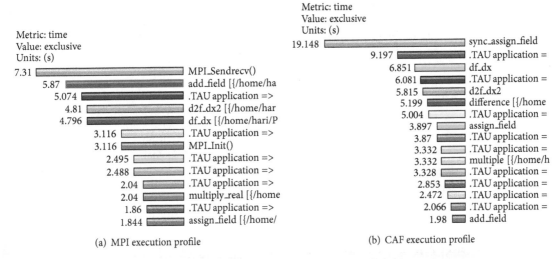

(a) MPI execution profile

(b) CAF execution profile

FIGURE 6: Execution profiles of MPI and CAF versions of Burgers solver.

TABLE 2: Code complexity of CAF versus MPI.

Metric	CAF	MPI
LOC	238	326
Use statements	3	13
Variables declared	58	97
External calls	0	24
Function arguments	11	79

which are used in the MPI implementation, suggests a higher learning curve for novice parallel programmers compared to CAF.

7. Conclusion

Motivated by the constant changing requirements on HPC software, we have presented coordinate-free programming [1] as an approach that naturally deals with the relevant variation points, resulting in flexibility and easy evolution of code. We then looked at the modern Fortran language features, such as pure functions and coarrays, and related programming patterns, specifically *compute globally, return locally* (CGRL), which make such programming possible. We also looked at implementing coordinate-free programming using MPI and the advantages and disadvantages of the MPI implementation vis-a-vis using only modern Fortran language features.

As a feasibility study for the approach, we used these techniques in a code that solves the one-dimensional Burgers equation:

$$u_t = \nu u_{xx} - u u_x. \tag{4}$$

(Subscripts indicate partial differentiation for t and x, time and space coordinates, resp.) The functional expression style enhances readability of the code by its close resemblance to the mathematical notation. The CGRL behavioural pattern enables efficient use of Fortran coarrays with functional expression evaluation.

A profiled analysis of our application shows good load balancing, using the coarray enabled Fortran compilers from Intel and Cray. Performance analysis with the Cray compiler exhibited good weak scalability from 64 to above 16 000 cores. Strong scaling studies using MPI and coarray versions of our application show that while the runtimes of the coarray version lag behind the MPI version, the coarray version's scaling efficiency is on par with the MPI version.

Future work includes going from this feasibility study to a full coordinate-free implementation in Fortran of the general Burgers equation. This will allow us to study the behaviour of Fortran on such abstractions. We also want to increase the parallel efficiency by introducing ghost cells in the code, seeing how well modern Fortran can deal with the complexities of contemporary hardware architecture.

Disclosure

This is an extended version of a workshop paper presented at SE-HPCSSE13 in Denver, CO, USA.

Conflict of Interests

The authors declare that there is no conflict of interests regarding the publication of this paper.

Acknowledgments

Thanks are due to Jim Xia (IBM Canada Lab) for developing the Burgers 1D solver and Sameer Shende (University of Oregon) for help with TAU. This research is financed in part by the Research Council of Norway. This research was also supported by Sandia National Laboratories, a multiprogram laboratory operated by Sandia Corporation, a Lockheed Martin Company, for the National Nuclear Security Administration under contract DE-AC04-94-AL85000. This work used resources of the National Energy Research Scientific Computing Center, which is supported by the Office of

Science of the US Department of Energy under Contract no. DE-AC02-05CH11231. This work also used resources from the ACISS cluster at the University of Oregon acquired by a Major Research Instrumentation grant from the National Science Foundation, Office of Cyber Infrastructure, "MRI-R2: Acquisition of an Applied Computational Instrument for Scientific Synthesis (ACISS)," Grant no. OCI-0960354.

References

[1] M. Haveraaen and H. A. Friis, "Coordinate-free numerics: all your variation points for free?" *International Journal of Computational Science and Engineering*, vol. 4, no. 4, pp. 223–230, 2009.

[2] M. Metcalf, J. Reid, and M. Cohen, *Modern Fortran Explained*, Oxford University Press, Oxford, UK, 2011.

[3] M. Haveraaen, H. A. Friis, and T. A. Johansen, "Formal software engineering for computational modelling," *Nordic Journal of Computing*, vol. 6, no. 3, pp. 241–270, 1999.

[4] P. W. Grant, M. Haveraaen, and M. F. Webster, "Coordinate free programming of computational fluid dynamics problems," *Scientific Programming*, vol. 8, no. 4, pp. 211–230, 2000.

[5] D. W. Rouson, R. Rosenberg, X. Xu, I. Moulitsas, and S. C. Kassinos, "A grid-free abstraction of the Navier-Stokes equations in Fortran 95/2003," *ACM Transactions on Mathematical Software*, vol. 34, no. 1, article 2, 2008.

[6] A. M. Bruaset and H. P. Langtangen, "A comprehensive set of tools for solvingpartial differential equations; Diffpack," in *Numerical Methods and Software Tools in Industrial Mathematics*, M. Dæhlen and A. Tveito, Eds., pp. 61–90, Birkhäuser, Boston, Mass, USA, 1997.

[7] E. Gamma, R. Helm, R. Johnson, and J. Vlissides, *Design Patterns: Elements of Reusable Object-Oriented Software*, Pearson Education, 1994.

[8] H. Gardner, G. Manduchi, T. J. Barth et al., *Design Patterns for E-Science*, vol. 4, Springer, New York, NY, USA, 2007.

[9] D. W. Rouson, J. Xia, and X. Xu, *Scientific Software Design: The Object-Oriented Way*, Cambridge University Press, Cambridge, Mass, USA, 2011.

[10] D. C. Cann, "Retire Fortran? A debate rekindled," *Communications of the ACM*, vol. 35, no. 8, pp. 81–89, 1992.

[11] P. S. Pacheco, *Parallel programming with MPI*, Morgan Kaufmann, 1997.

[12] M. Haveraaen, K. Morris, and D. Rouson, "High-performance design patternsfor modern fortran," in *Proceedings of the 1st International Workshop on Software Engineering for High Performance Computing in Computational Science and Engineering*, pp. 1–8, ACM, 2013.

[13] J. Burgers, "A mathematical model illustrating the theory of turbulence," in *Advances in Applied Mechanics*, R. V. Mises and T. V. Kármán, Eds., vol. 1, pp. 171–199, Elsevier, New York, NY, USA, 1948.

[14] D. Bjørner, *Domain Engineering: Technology Management, Research and Engineering*, vol. 4 of *COE Research Monograph Series*, JAIST, 2009.

[15] C. Canuto, M. Y. Hussaini, A. Quarteroni, and T. Zang, *Spectral Methods: Fundamentals in Single Domains*, Springer, Berlin, Germany, 2006.

[16] A. Fanfarillo, T. Burnus, S. Filippone, V. Cardellini, D. Nagle, and D. W. I. Rouson, "OpenCoarrays: open-source transport layers supporting coarray Fortran compilers," in *Proceedings of the 8th International Conference on Partitioned Global Address Space Programming Models (PGAS '14)*, Eugene, Ore, USA, October 2014.

[17] O.-J. Dahl, B. Myhrhaug, and K. Nygaard, *SIMULA 67 Common Base Language*, vol. S-2, Norwegian Computing Center, Oslo, Norway, 1968.

[18] S. S. Shende and A. D. Malony, "The TAU parallel performance system," *International Journal of High Performance Computing Applications*, vol. 20, no. 2, pp. 287–311, 2006.

[19] J. Dongarra, K. London, S. Moore, P. Mucci, and D. Terpstra, "Using PAPI for hardware performance monitoring on linux systems," in *Conference on Linux Clusters: The HPC Revolution*, Linux Clusters Institute, 2001.

[20] C. Withrow, "Error density and size in Ada software," *IEEE Software*, vol. 7, no. 1, pp. 26–30, 1990.

[21] S. H. Kan, *Metrics and Models in Software Quality Engineering*, Addison-Wesley, New York, NY, USA, 2nd edition, 2002.

6

Extracting UML Class Diagrams from Object-Oriented Fortran: ForUML

Aziz Nanthaamornphong,[1] **Jeffrey Carver,**[2] **Karla Morris,**[3] **and Salvatore Filippone**[4]

[1]*Department of Information and Communication Technology, Prince of Songkla University, Phuket Campus,*
Phuket 83120, Thailand

[2]*Department of Computer Science, University of Alabama, Tuscaloosa, AL 35487, USA*

[3]*Sandia National Laboratories, 7011 East Avenue, Livermore, CA 94550-9610, USA*

[4]*Department of Civil and Computer Engineering, University of Rome 'Tor Vergata', Roma 00173, Italy*

Correspondence should be addressed to Aziz Nanthaamornphong; aziz.nantha@gmail.com

Academic Editor: Selim Ciraci

Many scientists who implement computational science and engineering software have adopted the object-oriented (OO) Fortran paradigm. One of the challenges faced by OO Fortran developers is the inability to obtain high level software design descriptions of existing applications. Knowledge of the overall software design is not only valuable in the absence of documentation, it can also serve to assist developers with accomplishing different tasks during the software development process, especially maintenance and refactoring. The software engineering community commonly uses reverse engineering techniques to deal with this challenge. A number of reverse engineering-based tools have been proposed, but few of them can be applied to OO Fortran applications. In this paper, we propose a software tool to extract unified modeling language (UML) class diagrams from Fortran code. The UML class diagram facilitates the developers' ability to examine the entities and their relationships in the software system. The extracted diagrams enhance software maintenance and evolution. The experiments carried out to evaluate the proposed tool show its accuracy and a few of the limitations.

1. Introduction

Computational research has been referred to as the third pillar of scientific and engineering research, along with experimental and theoretical research [1]. Computational science and engineering (CSE) researchers develop software to simulate natural phenomena that cannot be studied experimentally or to process large amounts of data. CSE software has a large impact on society as it is used by researchers to study critical problems in a number of important application domains, including weather forecasting, astrophysics, construction of new physical materials, and cancer research [2]. For example, US capabilities in science and engineering are frequently called upon to address urgent challenges in national and homeland security, economic competitiveness, health care, and environmental protection [3]. Recently the

software engineering (SE) community has become more interested in the development of software for CSE research.

In this critical type of software, Fortran is still a very widely used programming language [4]. Due to the growing complexity of the problems being addressed through CSE, the procedural programming style available in a language like Fortran 77 is no longer sufficient. Many developers have applied the object-oriented programming (OOP) paradigm to effectively implement the complex data structures required by CSE software. In the case of Fortran developers, this OOP paradigm was first emulated following an object-based approach in Fortran 90/95 [5–7]. By including full support for OOP constructs, the Fortran 2003 language standard influenced the advent of several CSE packages [8–12].

One of the greatest challenges faced by CSE developers is the ability to effectively maintain their software over its generally long lifetime [13]. This challenge implies high development and maintenance costs during a software system's lifetime. The difficulty of the maintenance process is affected by at least three factors. First, most CSE developers are not formally trained in SE. Second, some existing SE tools are difficult to use in CSE development. In general, CSE developers request tools to accommodate documentation, correctness testing, and aid in design software for testability. Unfortunately, most SE tools were not designed to be used in the context of CSE development. Third, CSE software often lacks the formal documentation necessary to help developers understand its complex design. This lack of documentation presents an even larger software maintenance challenge. The objective of this work is to provide tool support for automatically extracting UML class diagrams from OO Fortran code.

To address this objective, we developed and evaluated the *ForUML* tool. *ForUML* uses a reverse engineering approach to transform Fortran source code into UML models. To ensure flexibility, our solution uses a Fortran parser that does not depend on any specific Fortran compiler and generates output in the XML Metadata Interchange (XMI) format. The tool then displays the results of the analysis (the UML class diagram) using the *ArgoUML* (http://argouml.tigris.org/) modeling tool. We evaluated the accuracy of *ForUML* using five CSE software packages that use object-oriented features from the Fortran 95, 2003, and 2008 compiler standards. This paper extends the workshop paper [14] by providing more background information and more details on the transformation process in ForUML. Additionally, this paper includes a discussion of the audience feedback during the *Workshop on Software Engineering for High Performance Computing in Computational Science and Engineering* (SE-HPCCSE'13).

The contributions of this paper are as follows:

(i) the ForUML tool that will help CSE developers extract UML design diagrams from OO Fortran code to enable them make good decisions about software development and maintenance tasks;

(ii) description of the transformation process used to develop ForUML, which may help other tool authors create tools for the CSE community;

(iii) the results of the evaluation and our experiences using ForUML on real CSE projects to highlight its benefits and limitations;

(iv) workshop feedback that should help SE develop practices and tools that are suitable for use in the CSE domain.

The rest of this paper is organized as follows. Section 2 provides the background concepts related to this work. Section 3 presents ForUML. Section 4 describes the evaluation and our experiences with ForUML. Section 5 discusses the evaluation results and limitations of ForUML. Finally, Section 6 draws conclusions and presents future work.

2. Related Work

This section first describes important CSE characteristics that impact the development of tool support. Next, it presents two important concepts used in the development of ForUML, reverse engineering and OO Fortran. Finally, because one of the benefits of using ForUML is the ability to recognize and maintain design patterns, the last subsection provides some background on design patterns.

2.1. Important CSE Characteristics. This section highlights three characteristics of CSE software development that differentiate it from traditional software development. First, CSE developers typically have a strong background in the theoretical science but often do not have formal training about SE techniques that have proved successful in other software areas. More specifically, because the complexity of the problems addressed by CSE generally requires a domain expert (e.g., a Ph.D. in physics or biology) to even understand the problem, and that domain expert generally must learn how to develop software [15]. Wilson [16] stated that one of the reasons why scientists tend to be less effective programmers is that they do not have the time to learn yet another programming language and software tool. Furthermore, the CSE culture, including most funding agencies, tends to view software as the means to a new scientific discovery rather than as a CSE instrument that must be carefully engineered, maintained, and extended to enable novel science.

Second, some SE tools are difficult to use in a CSE development environment [17]. CSE applications are generally developed with software tools that are crude compared to those used today in the commercial sector. Researchers and scientists seek easy-to-use software that enables analysis of complex data and visualization of complicated interactions. Consequently, CSE developers often have trouble identifying and using the most appropriate SE techniques for their work, in particular as it relates to reverse engineering tasks. Scientists interested in scientific research cannot spend most of their time understanding and using complex software tools. The limited interoperability of the tools and their complexity are major obstructions to their adaptation by the CSE community. For example, Storey noted that CSE developers who lack formal SE training need help with program comprehension when they are developing complex applications [18]. To address this problem, the SE community must develop tools that satisfy the needs of CSE developers. These tools must allow the developers to easily perform important reverse engineering tasks. More specifically, a visualization-based tool is appropriate for program comprehension in complex object-oriented applications [19].

Third, CSE software typically lacks adequate development-oriented documentation [20]. In fact, documentation for CSE software often exists only in the form of subroutine library documentation. This documentation is usually quite clear and sufficient for library users, who treat the library as a black box, but not sufficient for developers who need to understand the library in enough detail to maintain it. The lack of design documentation in particular leads to multiple problems. Newcomers to a project must invest a lot of effort to understand the code. There is an increased risk of failure when developers of related systems cannot correctly understand how to interact with the subject system.

In addition, the lack of documentation makes refactoring and maintenance difficult and error prone. CSE software typically evolves over many years and involves multiple developers [21], as functionality and capabilities are added or extended [22]. The developers need to be able to determine whether the evolved software deviates from the original design intent. To ease this process, developers need tools that help them identify changes that affect the design and determine whether those changes have undesired effects on design integrity. The availability of appropriate design documentation can reduce the likelihood of poor choices during the maintenance process.

2.2. Reverse Engineering.

2.2. Reverse Engineering. Reverse engineering is a method that transforms source code into a model [23]. ForUML builds upon and expands some existing reverse engineering work. The Dagstuhl middle metamodel(DMM) is a schema for describing the static structure of source code [24]. DMM supports reverse engineering by representing models extracted from source code written in most common OOP languages. We applied the idea of DMM to OO Fortran.

The transformation process in ForUML is based on the XMI format, which provides a standard method of mapping an object model into XML. XMI is an open standard that allows developers and software vendors to create, read, manage, and generate XMI tools. Transforming the model (Fortran code) to XMI requires use of the model driven architecture (MDA) technology [25], a modeling standard developed by the object management group (OMG) [26]. MDA aims to increase productivity and reuse by using separation of concerns and abstraction. A platform independent model (PIM) is an abstract model that contains the information to drive one or more platform specific models (PSMs), including source code, data definition language (DDL), XML, and other outputs specific to the target platform. MDA defines transformations that map from PIMs to PSMs.

The basic idea of using an XMI file to maintain the metadata for UML diagrams was drawn from four reverse engineering tools. Alalfi et al. developed two tools that use XMI to maintain the metadata for the UML diagrams: a tool that generates UML sequence diagrams for web application code [27] and a tool to create UML-entity relationship diagrams for the structured query language (SQL) [28]. Similarly, Korshunova et al. [29] developed *CPP2XMI* to extract various UML diagrams from C++ source code. CPP2XMI generates an XMI document that describes the UML diagram, which is then displayed graphically by DOT (part of the Graphviz framework) [30]. Duffy and Malloy [31] created *libthorin*, a tool to convert C++ source code into UML diagrams. Prior to converting an XMI document into a UML diagram, *libthorin* requires developers to use a third party compiler to compile code into the DWARF (http://www.dwarfstd.org/), which is a debugging file format used to support source level debugging. In terms of Fortran, DWARF only supports Fortran 90, which does not include all object-oriented features. This limitation may cause compatibility problems with different Fortran compilers. Conversely, ForUML is compiler independent and able to generate UML for all types of OO Fortran code.

Doxygen is a documentation tool that can use Fortran code to generate either a simple, textual representation with procedural interface information or a graphical representation. The only OOP class relationship Doxygen supports is inheritance. With respect to our goals, Doxygen has two primary limitations. First, it does not support all OOP features within Fortran (e.g., type-bound procedures and components). Second, the diagrams generated by Doxygen only include class names and class relationships but do not contain other important information typically included in UML class diagrams (e.g., methods, properties). Our work expands upon Doxygen by adding support for OO Fortran and by generating UML diagrams that include all relevant information about the included classes (e.g., properties, methods, and signatures).

There are a number of available tools (both open source and commercial) that claim to transform OO code into UML diagrams (e.g., Altova UModel, Enterprise Architect, StarUML, and ArgoUML). However, in terms of our work, these tools do not support OO Fortran. Although they cannot directly create UML diagrams from OO Fortran code, most of these tools are able to import the metadata describing UML diagrams (i.e., the XMI file) and generate the corresponding UML diagrams. ForUML takes advantages of this feature to display the UML diagrams described by the XMI files it generates from OO Fortran code.

This previous work has contributed significantly to the reverse engineering tools of traditional software. ForUML specifically offers a method to reverse engineering code implemented with modern Fortran, including features in the Fortran 2008 standard. Moreover, the tool was deliberately designed to support important features of Fortran, such as coarrays, procedure overloading, and operator overloading.

2.3. Object-Oriented Fortran. Fortran is an imperative programming language. Traditionally, Fortran code has been developed through a procedural programming approach that emphasizes the procedures and subroutines in a program rather than the data. A number of studies discuss approaches for expressing OOP principles in Fortran 90/95. For example, Decyk described how to express the concepts of data encapsulation, function overloading, classes, objects, and inheritance in Fortran 90 [6, 7, 32]. Moreover, several authors have described the use and syntax of OO features in Fortran 2003 [33–35]. Table 1 presents important Fortran-specific terms along with their OOP equivalent and some examples of Fortran keywords.

The Fortran 2003 compiler standard added support for OOP, including the following OOP principles: dynamic and static polymorphism, inheritance, data abstraction, and encapsulation. Currently, a number of Fortran compiler vendors support all (or almost all) of the OOP features included in the Fortran 2003 standard. These compilers include [36]

(i) NAG (http://www.nag.com/);

(ii) GNU Fortran (http://gcc.gnu.org/fortran/);

(iii) IBM XL Fortran (http://www-142.ibm.com/software/ products/us/en/fortcompfami/);

TABLE 1: Object-oriented Fortran terms (adapted from [12]).

Fortran	OOP equivalent	Fortran keywords
Module	Package	Module
Derived type	Abstract data type (ADT)	Type
Component	Attribute	—
Type-bound procedure	Method	Procedure
Parent type	Parent class	—
Extend type	Child class	Extends
Intrinsic type	Primitive type	For example, real, integer

(iv) Cray (http://www.nersc.gov/users/software/compilers/cray-compilers/);

(v) Intel Fortran (https://software.intel.com/en-us/fortran-compilers).

Fortran 2003 supports procedure overriding where developers can specify a type-bound procedure in a child type that has the same binding name as a type-bound procedure in the parent type. Fortran 2003 also supports user-defined constructors that can be implemented by overloading the intrinsic constructors provided by the compiler. The user-defined constructor is created by defining a generic interface with the same name as the derived type.

Algorithm 1 illustrates a snippet of Fortran 2003 code in which the parent type shape_ (Line 2) is extended by the type circle (Line 7). At runtime the compiler invokes the type-bound procedure add (Line 18) whenever an operator "+" (with the specified argument type) is used in the client code. This behavior conforms to polymorphism, which allows a type or procedure to take many object or procedural forms.

Data abstraction is the separation between the interface and implementation of the program. It allows developers to provide essential information about the program to the outside world. In Fortran, the private and public keywords control access to members of the type. Members defined with public are accessible to any part of the program. Conversely, members defined with private are not accessible to code outside the module in which the type is defined. In the example, the component radius (Line 11) cannot be accessed directly by other programs. Rather, the caller must invoke the type-bound procedure set_radius (Line 13).

With the increase in parallel computing, the CSE community needs to utilize the full processing power of all available resources. Fortran 2008 improves the performance for a parallel processing feature by introducing the Coarray model [37]. The Coarray extension allows developers to express data distribution by specifying the relationship between memory images/cores. The syntax of the Coarray is very much like normal Fortran array syntax, except with square brackets instead of parentheses. For example, the statement integer:: m[*] (Line 4) declares m to be an integer that is sharable across images. Fortran uses normal

```
(1)  module example
(2)     type shape_
(3)        real :: area
(4)        integer :: m[*]
(5)     end type
(6)     !  Inheritance
(7)     type, extends (shape_) :: circle
(8)        !  Data abstraction
(9)        private
(10)       !  Encapsulation
(11)       real :: radius
(12)    contains
(13)       procedure :: set_radius
(14)       procedure :: add
(15)       procedure :: area
(16)       !  Polymorphism
(17)       generic :: total => area
(18)       generic :: operator(+) => add
(19)    end type
(20)    !  Overloads intrinsic constructor
(21)    interface circle
(22)       module procedure new_circle
(23)    end interface
(24)    !  ...
(25)  end module
```

ALGORITHM 1: Samples code snippet of OOP constructs supported by Fortran 2003.

rounded brackets () to point to data in local memory. Although using Coarray requires the additional syntax, the coarray has been designed to be easy to implement and to provide the compiler scope both to apply its optimizations within each image and among images.

2.4. Design Patterns. A design pattern is a generic solution to a common software design problem that can be reused in similar situations. Design patterns are made of the best practices drawn from various sources, such as building software applications, developer experiences, and empirical studies. Generally, we can classify the design patterns of the software into classical and novel design patterns. The 23 classical design patterns were introduced by the "Gang of Four" (GoF) [38]. Subsequently, software developers and researchers have proposed a number of novel design patterns targeted at particular domains, for example, parallel programming [39, 40].

In general, a design pattern includes a section known as *intent*. Intent is "a short statement that answers the following questions: What does the design pattern do? What is its rationale and intent? What particular design issues or problem does it address?" [38]. For example, the intent of the template method pattern requires that developers define the skeleton of an algorithm in an operation, deferring some steps to subclasses. Template method lets subclasses redefine certain steps of an algorithm without changing the algorithm's structure. When using design patterns, developers have to understand the intent of each design pattern to determine whether the design pattern could provide a good solution to a given problem.

Several researchers have proposed design patterns for computational software implemented with Fortran. For example, Weidmann [41] implemented design patterns to enable sparse matrix computations on NVIDIA GPUs. They then evaluated the benefits of the implementation and reported that the design patterns provided a high level of maintainability and performance. Rouson et al. [12] proposed three new design patterns, called multiphysics design patterns, to implement the differential equations, which are integrated into multiphysics and numerical software. These new design patterns include the semidiscrete, surrogate and template class patterns. Markus demonstrated how some well-known design patterns could be implemented in Fortran 90, 95, and 2003 [42, 43]. Similarly, Decyk et al. [4] proposed the factory pattern in Fortran 95 based on CSE software. These researchers presented the proposed pattern implementation in their particle-in-cell (PIC) methods [44] in plasma simulation software. Decyk and Gardner [45] also described a way to implement the strategy, template, abstract factory, and facade patterns in Fortran 90/95.

3. ForUML

This section describes the rationale and benefits of developing ForUML and details the transformation process used by ForUML.

3.1. The Need for ForUML. The CSE characteristics described in Section 2.1 indicate that CSE developers could benefit from a tool that creates system documentation with little effort. The SE community typically uses reverse engineering to address this problem.

Although there are a number of reverse engineering tools [46] (see Section 2.2), those tools that can be applied to OO Fortran do not provide the full set of documentation required by developers. Therefore, we identified the need for a tool that automatically reverses engineers OO Fortran code into the necessary UML design documentation.

This work is primarily targeted at CSE developers who develop OO Fortran. The ForUML tool will provide the following benefits to the CSE community.

(1) The extracted UML class diagrams should support software maintenance and evolution and help maintainers ensure that the original design intentions are satisfied.

(2) The developers can use the UML diagrams to illustrate software design concepts to their team members. In addition, UML diagrams can help developers visually examine relationships among objects to identify code smells [47] in software being developed.

(3) Because SE tools generally improve productivity, ForUML can reduce the training time and learning curve required for applying SE practices in CSE software development. For instance, ForUML will help developers perform refactoring activities by allowing

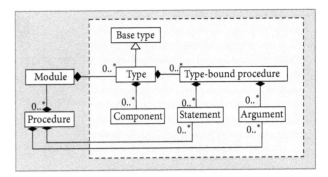

FIGURE 1: The Fortran model.

them to evaluate the results of refactoring using the UML diagrams rather than inspecting the code manually.

Since Fortran 2003 provides all of the concepts of OOP, tools like ForUML can help to place Fortran and other OOP program languages on equal levels.

3.2. Transformation Process. The primary goal of ForUML is to reverse engineering UML class diagrams from Fortran code. By extracting a set of source files, it builds a collection of objects associated with syntactic entities and relations. Object-based features were first introduced in the Fortran 90 language standard. Accordingly, ForUML supports all versions of Fortran 90 and later, which encompasses most platforms and compiler vendors. We implemented ForUML using Java Platform SE6 so that it could run on any client computing systems.

The UML object diagram in Figure 1 expresses the model of the Fortran language. The module object corresponds to Fortran modules, that is, containers holding type and procedure objects. The type-bound procedure and component objects are modeled with a composition association to instances of type. Both the procedure and type-bound procedure objects are composed of argument and statement objects. The generalization relation with base type object leads to the parents in the inheritance hierarchy. When generating the class diagram in ForUML, we consider only the objects inside the dashed-line box that separates object-oriented entities from the module-related entities.

Figure 2 provides an overview of the transformation process embodied in ForUML, comprising the following steps: parsing, extraction, generating, and importing. The following subsections discuss each step in more detail.

3.2.1. Parsing. The Fortran code is parsed by the Open Fortran Parser (OFP) (http://fortran-parser.sourceforge.net/). OFP provides ANTLR-based parsing tools [48], including Fortran grammars and libraries for performing translation actions. ANTLR is a parser generator that can parse language specifications in an EBNF-like syntax, a notation for formally describing programming language syntax, and generate the library to parse the specified language. ANTLR distinguishes three compilation phases: lexical analysis, parsing, and tree walking.

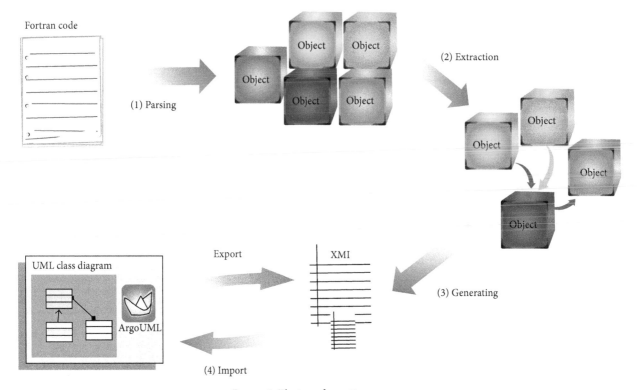

FIGURE 2: The transformation process.

We have customized the ANTLR libraries to translate particular AST nodes (i.e., type, component, and type-bound procedure) into objects. These AST nodes are only the basic elements of UML class diagrams. In fact, a UML class diagram includes classes, attributes, methods, and relations. The parsing actions include two steps. The first step verifies the syntax in the source file and eliminates source files that have syntax problems. It also eliminates source files that do not contain any instances of type and module. For example, ForUML will eliminate modules that contain only subroutines or functions. After this step, ForUML reports the results to the user via a GUI. In the second step, the parser manipulates all AST nodes, relying on the model described earlier. Note that ForUML only manipulates the selected input source files. Any associated type objects that exist in files not selected by the user are not included in the class diagram.

3.2.2. Extraction. During the extraction process, ForUML excerpts the objects and identifies their relationships. ForUML determines the type of each extracted relationship and maps each relationship to a specific relationship's type object. Based on the example code in Algorithm 1, the type circle inherits the type shape. As a consequence, the extraction process will create a generalization object. ForUML supports two relationship types: composition and generalization.

(i) Composition represents the whole-part relationship. The lifetime of the part classifier depends on the lifetime of the whole classifier. In other words, a

composition describes a relationship in which one class is composed of many other classes. In our case, the composition association will be produced when a type object refers to another type object in the component. The association refers to a type not provided by the user and as a result it does not appear in the class diagram. In the UML class diagram, a composition relationship appears as a solid line with a filled diamond at the association end that is connected to the whole class.

(ii) Generalization represents an *is-a* relationship between a general object and its derived specific objects, commonly known as an inheritance relation. Similar to the composition association, the generalization association is not shown in the class diagram if the source file of the base type is not provided by the user. This relationship is represented by a solid line with a hollow unfilled arrowhead that points from the child class to the parent class.

3.2.3. Generating. We developed the XMI generator module to convert the extracted objects into XMI notation based on our defined rules for mapping the extracted objects to the proper XMI notation. The rules for mapping the extracted objects and XMI document are specified in Table 2. In addition to these rules, we developed new stereotype notations for the constructor, coarray constructs, type-bound procedure overloading, and operator overloading, such as ≪Constructor≫, ≪Coarray≫, ≪Overloading≫, and ≪Overloading of +≫.

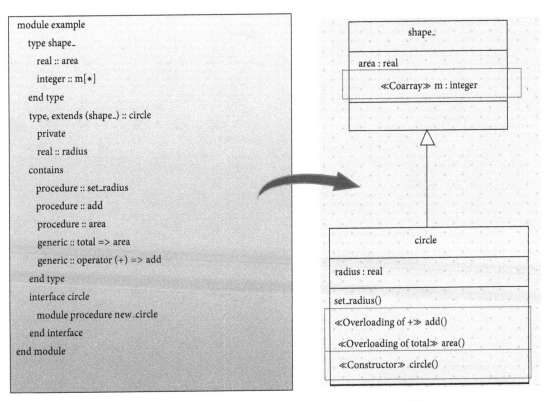

FIGURE 3: Sample code snippet of Fortran supported by ForUML.

TABLE 2: Fortran to XMI conversion rules.

Fortran	XMI elements
Derived type	UML: class
Type-bound Procedure	UML: operation
Dummy argument	UML: parameter
Component	UML: attribute
Intrinsic type	UML: DataType
Parent type	UML: Generalization.parent
Extended type	UML: Generalization.child
Composite	UML: association (the aggregation property as "composite")

Figure 3 provides the sample Fortran code without procedure implementation and its generated class diagram including stereotypes.

3.2.4. Importing. To visually represent the extracted information as a UML class diagram, we import the XMI document into a UML modeling tool. We decided to include a UML modeling tool directly in ForUML to prevent the user from having to install or use a second application for visualization. We chose to include ArgoUML as the UML visualization tool in the current version of ForUML. We had to modify the ArgoUML code to allow it to automatically import the XMI document. Of course, if a user would prefer to use a different modeling tool, he or she can manually import the generated XMI file into any tool that supports the XMI format.

After importing the XMI file, ArgoUML's default view of the class diagram does not show any entities in the editing pane. Like the WYSIWYG ("what you see is what you get") concept, the user needs to drag the target entity from a hierarchical view to the editing pane. To help with this problem, we added features so that ArgoUML will show all entities in the editing pane immediately after successfully importing the XMI document. Note that the XMI document does not specify how to present the elements graphically, so ArgoUML automatically adjusts the diagram when rendering the graphics. Each graphical tool may have its own method for generating the graphical layout of diagrams. The key reasons why we chose to integrate ArgoUML into ForUML are that (1) it has seamless integration properties as an open source and Java implementation; (2) it has sufficient documentation; and (3) it provides sufficient basic functions required by the users (e.g., export graphics, import/export XMI, zooming).

ForUML provides a Java-based user interface for executing the command. To create a UML class diagram, the user performs these steps.

(1) Select the Fortran source code

(2) Select the location to save the output.

(3) Open the UML diagram.

Figures 4–7 show screenshots from the ForUML tool. Figure 4 presents the graphical user interface (GUI) of

FIGURE 4: A graphical user interface of ForUML.

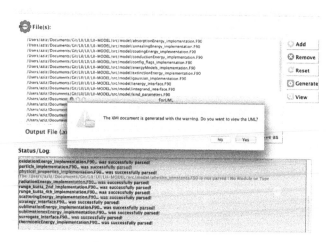

FIGURE 6: Generating the XMI.

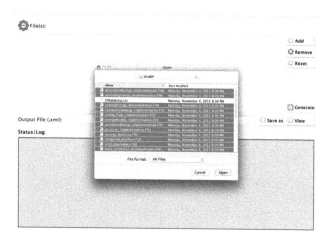

FIGURE 5: Selection of the Fortran code.

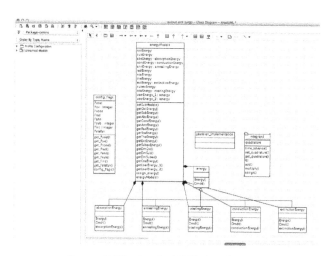

FIGURE 7: Viewing the UML class diagram.

ForUML. Figure 5 illustrates how a user can select multiple Fortran source files for input to ForUML. The *Add* button opens a new window to select target file(s). Users can remove the selected file(s) by selecting the *Remove* button. The *Reset* button clears all selected files. After selecting the source files, the user chooses the location to save the generated XMI document (.xmi file). The *Generate* button activates the transformation process. During the process, the user can see whether each given source file is successfully parsed or not (Figure 6). Once the XMI document is successfully generated, the user can view the class diagram by selecting the *View* button. Figure 7 illustrates the UML class diagram that is automatically represented in the editing pane with the ArgoUML. ArgoUML allows users to refine the diagram and then decide to either save the project or export the XMI document, which contains all the modified information.

4. Evaluation

To assess the effectiveness of ForUML, we conducted some small experiments to gather data about its accuracy in extracting UML constructs from code. This section also

provides some lessons learned from the studies and feedback from the SEC-HPC'13 workshop audience.

4.1. Controlled Experiment. The following subsections provide the details of a controlled experiment to evaluate ForUML. The accompanying website (http://aziz.students.cs.ua.edu/foruml-eval.htm) contains all of the class diagrams. The website also provides the ForUML executable (source code is not available yet) for download.

4.1.1. Experimental Design. We evaluated the *accuracy* of ForUML on five OO Fortran software packages by adopting the definitions of *recall* and *precision* defined by Tonella and Potrich [49].

(i) *Recall* measures the percentage of the various objects, that is, type, components, type-bound procedure, and associations, in the source code correctly identified by ForUML.

(ii) *Precision* measures the percentage of the objects identified by ForUML that are correct when compared with the source code.

We performed the evaluations as follows.

(1) We manually inspected the source code to document the number of relevant objects in each package. Note that we performed this step multiple times to ensure that the numbers were not biased by human error.

(2) We ran ForUML on each software package and documented the number of relevant objects included in the generated class diagram.

(3) To compute *recall*, we compared the number of objects manually identified in the source code (Step 1) with the number identified by ForUML (Step 2).

(4) To compute *precision*, we determined whether there were any objects produced by ForUML (Step 2) that we did manually observe in the code (Step 1).

(5) We investigated whether the generated class diagrams could present the design pattern classes existing in the subject systems.

4.1.2. Subject Systems. The five software packages we used in the experiments were (1) ForTrilinos (http://trilinos.sandia.gov/packages/fortrilinos/); (2) CLiiME; (3) PSBLAS (http://www.ce.uniroma2.it/psblas/); (4) MLD2P4 (http://www.mld2p4.it/); and (5) MPFlows. We selected these software packages because they were intentionally developed for use in the CSE environment. Two of the software packages (CLiiME and MPFlows) are not yet publicly available. A description of each software package follows.

(1) ForTrilinos: ForTrilinos consists of an OO Fortran interface to expand the use of Trilinos (http://trilinos.sandia.gov/) into communities that predominantly write Fortran. Trilinos is a collection of parallel numerical solver libraries for the solution of CSE applications in the HPC environment. To provide portability, ForTrilinos extensively exploits the Fortran 2003 standard's support for interoperability with C. ForTrilinos includes 4 subpackages (epetra, aztecoo, amesos, and fortrilinos), 36 files, and 36 modules.

(2) *CLiiME*: community laser induced incandescence modeling environment (CLiiME) is a dynamic simulation model that predicts the temporal response of laser-induced incandescence from carbonaceous particles. CLiiME is implemented with Fortran 2003. It contains 2 subpackages (model and utilities), 30 files, and 29 modules. Additionally, this application contains three design patterns, including factory method, strategy, and surrogate.

(3) *PSBLAS*: PSBLAS 3.0 is a library for parallel sparse matrix computations, mostly dealing with the iterative solution of sparse linear system via a distributed memory paradigm. The library assumes a data distribution consistent with a domain decomposition approach, where all variables and equations related to a given portion of the computation domain are assigned to a process; the data distribution can be specified in multiple ways allowing easy interfacing with many graph partitioning procedures. The library design also provides data management tools allowing easy interfacing with data assembly procedures typical of finite elements and finite volumes discretization. Researchers have used versions of the library in various application domains, mostly in fluid dynamics and structural analysis, where it has been successfully used to solve linear system with millions of unknowns arising in complex simulations. The PSBLAS library version 3.0 is implemented with Fortran 2003. PSBLAS contains 10 subpackages (prec, psblas, util, impl, krylov, tools, serial, internals, comm, and modules), 476 files, and 135 modules.

(4) *MLD2P4*: multi-level domain decomposition parallel preconditioners package based on PSBLAS (MLD2P4 version 1.2) is a package of parallel algebraic multilevel preconditioners. This package provides a variety of high-performance preconditioners for the Krylov methods of PSBLAS. A preconditioner is an operator capable of reducing the number of iterations needed to achieve convergence to the solution of a linear system; multilevel preconditioners are very powerful tools especially suited for problems derived from elliptic PDEs. This package is implemented with object-based Fortran 95. The MLD2P4 contains only one package (miprec), 117 files and 9 modules.

(5) *MPFlows*: multiphase flows (MPFlows) is a package developed for computational modeling of spray applications. MPFlows is implemented with Fortran 2003/2008. The use of coarrays within this application enables scalable CSE software package that works without requiring the use of external parallel libraries. MPFlows contains 2 subpackages (spray and utilities), 12 files, and 12 modules. Note that this package contains two design patterns, including strategy and surrogate.

4.1.3. Analysis. Table 3 shows the results of experiments. Each cell represents the recall as a ratio between extracted data and actual data. The results show that the recall reaches 100% for all subpackages. Overall, there was only one error in *precision* in the *ForTrilinos* subpackage of *ForTrilinos*. Our analysis of the code identified a conditional preprocessor statement (specified by the `#if` statement) as the source of the problem. ForUML currently does not handle preprocessor directives. During the experiments, only 6 files were not parsed (0.89% of all files). The notification messages informed the users which files were not processed and specifically why each file could not be processed. Based on code inspection, we found four files that do not conform to the Fortran model described earlier (Figure 1). Those files do not have the `module` keyword that is the starting point for the transformation process. Other files exceptions were due to ambiguous syntax; for example, Fortran keywords were used as part of a procedure name (e.g., `print`, `allocate`). Table 3 only shows the results for packages that have the

TABLE 3: Evaluation of ForUML: recall (extracted data/actual data).

Packages	Subpackages	Type	Procedure	Component	Inheritance	Composition
ForTrilinos	Epetra	16/16	304/304	17/17	12/12	2/2
	Aztecoo	1/1	12/12	1/1	0/0	0/0
	Amesos	1/1	7/7	1/1	0/0	0/0
	ForTrilinos	48/48	11/11	139/139	4/4	4/4
CLiiME	Model	23/23	167/167	61/61	32/32	32/32
PSBLAS	Modules	50/50	1309/1309	160/160	34/34	28/28
	prec	20/20	208/208	28/28	24/24	12/12
MLDP4	miprec	11/11	0/0	67/66	0/0	10/10
MPFlows	Spray	10/10	55/55	29/29	2/2	3/3
Overall		180/180 (100%)	2073/2073 (100%)	503/503 (100%)	108/108 (100%)	91/91 (100%)

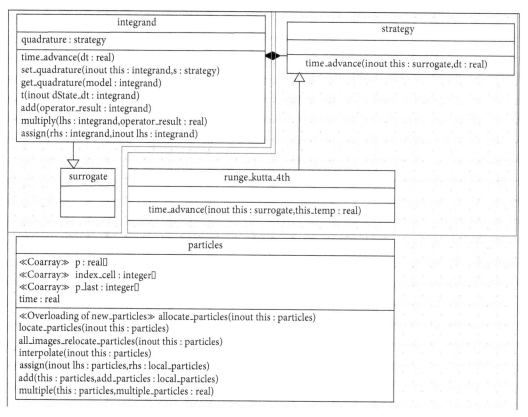

FIGURE 8: The class diagram (partial): MPFlows.

type construct. We only evaluated the correctness of ForUML current capabilities.

Figure 8 provides an example of an excerpt from a class diagram derived from MPFlows. This diagram consists of the implementation of two design patterns, including strategy (inside the red box) and surrogate (inside the blue box) patterns. In the strategy pattern, an interface class `strategy` defines only the time integration method, deferring to subclasses the implementation of the actual quadrature schemes. The concrete strategy class (derived class) `runge_kutta_4th` provides the algorithm that presents a part of the `time_advance` method declared by the `strategy` interface. Next, the surrogate pattern is very similar in concept to an ATM. An ATM holds a surrogate database for bank information that exists in another place. The bank's customer can perform transactions through the ATM and circumvent a visit to the bank. The implementation of the surrogate pattern introduces the `surrogate` abstract class (virtual class in C++). The class `integrand` has a component of class `strategy` meaning that

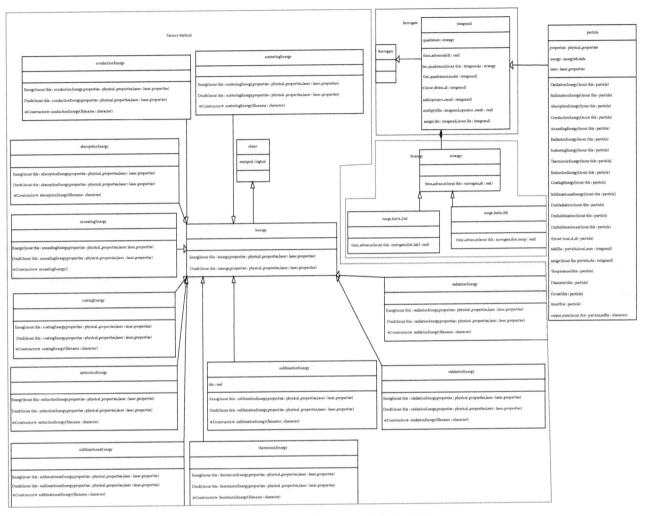

FIGURE 9: The class diagram (partial): CLiiME.

the surrogate allows us to pass an integrand child class dummy argument to the type-bound procedures implemented in runge_kutta_4th. The class particle contains components and type-bound procedures computing the energy of the particle. In Fortran, each dummy argument has three possible intent attributes including IN, OUT, and INOUT. Therefore, each parameter, which is passed to the operation in the diagram, needs to be specified with a specific intent. In the class diagram, the keyword IN is omitted because ArgoUML assumes that a parameter has the IN by default.

4.2. Experience.
The following subsections describe our experiences using ForUML on a real CSE project and discuss feedback on ForUML we received during the SE-HPCCSE'13 workshop.

4.2.1. CLiiME Project.
ForUML played a significant role in the development of the CLiiME package [50]. The developers used ForUML to validate the design after each code refactoring process. The developers compared the class diagram produced by ForUML with the originally agreed upon design. After comparison, they determined instances in which the code implementation deviated from the design. Instead of inspecting the source code manually, the developers were able to make the comparison/decision with less effort. Also, the developers were able to use the extracted UML diagrams to identify code smells, places where the code might induce some defects in the future. For instance, we inspected the UML class diagrams and identified places where classes had too many type-bound procedure or procedures with too many arguments, all of which we corrected during the refactoring process.

This project also deployed three design patterns. Figure 9 presents the UML class diagram of the CLiiME project, including the strategy (inside the red box), surrogate (inside the blue box), and factory method (inside the green box) patterns. The factory method pattern indicates encapsulating the subclass selection (*Energy class) and object construction processes into one class (ienergy). We used ForUML to confirm the correct implementation of those three design patterns rather than reviewing the source code. In addition to helping CLiiME developers, ForUML also influenced the

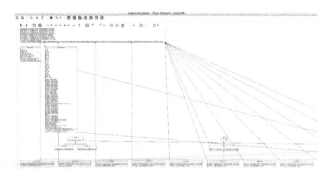

FIGURE 10: Example of larger classes.

development of PSBLAS version 3.1, by allowing a comprehensive and unitary view of the project.

The UML diagram must be properly arranged to foment design comprehension. A large class diagram that contains several classes and relationships requires additional effort from users' as they try to assimilate all the information. Unfortunately, the built-in function layout in ArgoUML does not refine the layout in diagrams that contain numerous elements. Although ArgoUML provides the ability to zoom in or zoom out, large diagrams can still be difficult to view. Figure 10 shows an example of a UML class diagram generated by ForUML that includes large classes. These problems can be addressed by dividing the collection of classes into smaller packages, which should improve the diagram's understandability. Another option is to provide different settings for the information included in the class diagrams, allowing a user to create diagrams with the level of detail required for a particular task. This option can ease the development and/or maintenance process by eliminating irrelevant information.

4.2.2. SEC-HPC'13 Workshop. In addition to our own experiences, we can make some observations based on the discussions during the SE-HPCCSE'13 workshop regarding the use of UML in CSE applications. UML helps partition the coding workloads in large projects. For larger projects, especially libraries, it is a matter of dwelling on the "use cases" and designing an interface perhaps with UML. Then feature coding tasks can be distributed to other developers. In contrast, CSE has been reluctant to adopt object-oriented design, whereas in other standard mathematics, linear algebra design bears some similarly to OOP considering larger mathematical structures as objects. Many audiences believed that better SE practices, including adoption ForUML could lead to a better adaptation of codes to multiple architectures. However, one reason for the lack of advance SE in CSE is that CSE developers try to use UML for everything. The audience suggested that other domain specific languages (DSLs) could be useful targets for generating information from legacy code. Further, during the workshop's discussion, there were some questions that inspired us to study the impact of ForUML on the CSE community. We believe that we can find answers to these questions by conducting human-based studies of ForUML. Below is a list of questions that arose during the workshop.

(i) Is UML really useful for CSE developers?

(ii) Can ForUML and UML support larger application sizes and multiple developers?

(iii) Many graphical design models serve multiple purposes. Some users can convey a high-level design for discussion, and others want to display the low-level of design. In the context of CSE software development, does UML serve all these needs well?

(iv) Which aspects of the CSE application should be documented in the UML?

5. Discussion

Based on the experimental results, ForUML provided quite precise outputs. ForUML was able to automatically transform the source code into correct UML diagrams. To illustrate the contributions of ForUML, Table 4 compares ForUML with other visualization-based tools [18] that have features to support program comprehension tasks. Based on this table, one of the unique contributions of ForUML is its ability to reverse engineered OO Fortran code. ForUML integrates the capabilities of ArgoUML to visually display the class diagram.

We believe that ForUML can be used by three types of people during the software development process, especially for CSE software.

(1) Stakeholders or customers: ForUML generates documentation that describes the high-level structure of the software. This documentation should make communication between developers and the stakeholders or customers more efficient.

(2) Developers: ForUML helps developers extract design diagrams from their code. Developers might need to validate whether the code under development conforms to the original design. Similarly, when developers refactor the code, they need to ensure that the refactoring does not break exiting functionality or decompose the architecture.

(3) Maintainers: they need a document that provides adequate design information to enable them to make good decisions. In particular, maintainers who are familiar with other OOP languages can understand a system implemented with OO Fortran.

However, ForUML has a few limitations that must be addressed in the future as follows.

(1) Provide more relationships: two other relationships that we frequently found in the Fortran applications are as follows.

(i) Dependency: in practice, dependency is most commonly used between elements (e.g., packages, folders) that contain other elements located in different packages. The relationship

TABLE 4: A brief comparison between UML tools.

Features	Rose enterprise [53]	Doxygen	Libthorin	ForUML + ArgoUML	Rigi [54]
Visualization	UML	Graph	UML	UML	Graph
Reverse eng. (Fortran)	No	No	Ver.90	Yes	No
Hide/show detail	Yes	No	Yes	No	No
Inheritance	Yes	No	Yes	Yes	No
Layout	A/M	A	A	A/M	A

Note: automatically adjusted (A) and manually adjusted (M).

is represented by a dashed line with an arrow pointing toward a class that is an argument in a procedure that is bound to another class.

(ii) Realization: it refers to the links between either the interface or abstract and its implementing classes. A dashed line is connected to an open triangle for a type that extends an abstract type.

Note that although the current version of ForUML does not support these relation types, the users can edit the relationships in the ArgroUML after importing the XMI document.

(2) Incorporation of other UML visualization tools: currently, ForUML integrates ArgoUML as the CASE tool. We plan to build different interfaces to integrate with other UML tools, so users can select their tool of preference. Although many UML CASE tools support the use of XMI documents, there are several XMI versions defined by object management group (OMG) and different tools support different versions. We also plan to develop a plugin for Photran (http://www.eclipse.org/photran/), to allow users to automatically generate UML diagrams within the IDE.

(3) Generate UML sequence diagram: a single diagram does not sufficiently describe the entire software system. Sequence diagrams are widely used to represent the interactive behavior of the subject system [51]. To create UML sequence diagrams, we would have to augment the ForUML extractor to build the necessary relationships among objects necessary for the generator to create the corresponding XMI code.

6. Conclusion and Future Work

This paper presents and evaluates the ForUML tool that can be used for extracting UML class diagram from Fortran code. Fortran is one of the predominant programming languages used in the CSE software domain. ForUML generates a visual representation of software implemented in OO Fortran in the same way as is done in other, more traditional OO languages. Software developers and practitioners can use ForUML to improve the program comprehension process. ForUML will help CSE developers adopt better SE approaches for the development of their software. Similarly, software engineers who are not familiar with scientific principles may be able to understand a CSE software system just based on information

in the generated UML class diagrams. Currently, ForUML can produce an XMI document that describes the UML class diagrams. The tool supports the inheritance and composition relationships that are the most common relationships found in software systems. The tool integrates ArgoUML, an open source UML modeling tool to allow users to view and modify the UML diagrams without installing a separate UML modeling tool.

We have run ForUML on five CSE software packages to generate class diagrams. The experimental results showed that ForUML generates highly accurate UML class diagrams from Fortran code. Based on the UML class diagrams generated by ForUML, we identified a few limitations of its capabilities. To augment the results of experiments, we have created a website that contains all of the diagrams generated by ForUML along with a video demonstrating the use of ForUML. We plan to add more diagrams to the website as we run ForUML on additional software packages. We believe that ForUML conforms to Chikofsky and Cross II [52] objectives of reverse engineering, which are identified as follows: (1) to identify the system's component and their relationships and (2) to represent the system in another form or at a higher level of abstraction.

In the future, we plan to address the limitations we have identified. We also plan to conduct human-based studies to evaluate the effectiveness and usability of ForUML by other members of the CSE software developer community. To encourage wider adoption and use of ForUML, we are investigating the possibility of releasing it as open source software. This direction can help us to get more feedback about the usability and correctness of the tool. Demonstrating that ForUML is a realistic tool for large-scale computational software will make it an even more valuable contribution to both the SE and CSE communities.

Conflict of Interests

The authors declare that there is no conflict of interests regarding the publication of this paper.

Acknowledgments

The authors gratefully thank Dr. Damian W. I. Rouson, at Stanford University, and Dr. Hope A. Michelsen, member of the Combustion Chemistry Department at Sandia National Laboratories, for their useful comments and helpful discussions which were extremely valuable.

References

[1] National Science Foundation, *Cyberinfrastructure for 21st Century Science and Engineering Advanced Computing Infrastructure (Vision and Strategies Plan)*, 2012, http://www.nsf.gov/pubs/2012/nsf12051/nsf12051.pdf.

[2] J. C. Carver, "Software engineering for computational science and engineering," *Computing in Science and Engineering*, vol. 14, no. 2, Article ID 6159198, pp. 8–11, 2011.

[3] J. H. Marburget, "Report of the high-end computing revitalization task force (hecrtf)," Tech. Rep., National Coordination Office for Information Technology Research and Development, 2004.

[4] V. K. Decyk, C. D. Norton, and H. J. Gardner, "Why fortran?" *Computing in Science and Engineering*, vol. 9, no. 4, Article ID 4263269, pp. 68–71, 2007.

[5] E. Akin, *Object-Oriented Programming via Fortran 90/95*, Cambridge University Press, Cambridge, UK, 2003.

[6] V. K. Decyk, C. D. Norton, and B. K. Szymanski, "Expressing object-oriented concepts in Fortran 90," *ACM SIGPLAN Fortran Forum*, vol. 16, no. 1, pp. 13–18, 1997.

[7] V. K. Decyk, C. D. Norton, and B. K. Szymanski, "How to support inheritance and run-time polymorphism in Fortran 90," *Computer Physics Communications*, vol. 115, no. 1, pp. 9–17, 1998.

[8] D. Barbieri, V. Cardellini, S. Filippone, and D. Rouson, "Design patterns for scientific computations on sparse matrices," in *Proceedings of the International Conference on Parallel Processing (Euro-Par '11)*, vol. 7155 of *Lecture Notes in Computer Science*, pp. 367–376, Springer, Berlin, Germany, 2012.

[9] S. Filippone and A. Buttari, "Object-oriented techniques for sparse matrix computations in Fortran 2003," *ACM Transactions on Mathematical Software*, vol. 38, no. 4, article 23, 2012.

[10] K. Morris, D. W. I. Rouson, M. N. Lemaster, and S. Filippone, "Exploring capabilities within ForTrilinos by solving the 3D Burgers equation," *Scientific Programming*, vol. 20, no. 3, pp. 275–292, 2012.

[11] D. W. Rouson, J. Xia, and X. Xu, "Object construction and destruction design patterns in fortran 2003," *Procedia Computer Science*, vol. 1, no. 1, pp. 1495–1504, 2003.

[12] D. W. I. Rouson, H. Adalsteinsson, and J. Xia, "Design patterns for multiphysics modeling in Fortran 2003 and C++," *ACM Transactions on Mathematical Software*, vol. 37, no. 1, article 3, 2010.

[13] Z. Merali, "Computational science: ...Error," *Nature*, vol. 467, no. 7317, pp. 775–777, 2010.

[14] A. Nanthaamornphong, K. Morris, and S. Filippone, "Extracting uml class diagrams from object-oriented fortran: Foruml," in *Proceedings of the 1st International Workshop on Software Engineering for High Performance Computing in Computational Science and Engineering (SE-HPCCSE '13)*, pp. 9–16, Denver, Colo, USA, November 2013.

[15] J. C. Carver, "Report: the second international workshop on software engineering for CSE," *Computing in Science and Engineering*, vol. 11, no. 6, Article ID 5337640, pp. 14–19, 2009.

[16] G. V. Wilson, "What should computer scientists teach to physical scientists and engineers?" *IEEE Computational Science & Engineering*, vol. 3, no. 2, pp. 46–55, 1996.

[17] J. C. Carver, R. P. Kendall, S. E. Squires, and D. E. Post, "Software development environments for scientific and engineering software: a series of case studies," in *Proceedings of the 29th International Conference on Software Engineering (ICSE '07)*, pp. 550–559, Minneapolis, Minn, USA, May 2007.

[18] M.-A. Storey, "Theories, tools and research methods in program comprehension: past, present and future," *Software Quality Journal*, vol. 14, no. 3, pp. 187–208, 2006.

[19] M. J. Pacione, "Software visualisation for object-oriented program comprehension," in *Proceedings of the 26th International Conference on Software Engineering (ICSE '04)*, pp. 63–65, May 2004.

[20] J. Segal, "Professional end user developers and software development knowledge," Tech. Rep., Open University, England, UK, 2004.

[21] M. T. Sletholt, J. E. Hannay, D. Pfahl, and H. P. Langtangen, "What do we know about scientific software development's agile practices?" *Computing in Science and Engineering*, vol. 14, no. 2, Article ID 6081842, pp. 24–36, 2012.

[22] R. N. Britcher, "Re-engineering software: a case study," *IBM Systems Journal*, vol. 29, no. 4, pp. 551–567, 1990.

[23] I. Jacobson, G. Booch, and J. Rumbaugh, *The Unified Software Development Process*, Addison Wesley Longman, Boston, Mass, USA, 1999.

[24] T. C. Lethbridge, S. Tichelaar, and E. Ploedereder, "The dagstuhl middle metamodel: a schema for reverse engineering," *Electronic Notes in Theoretical Computer Science*, vol. 94, pp. 7–18, 2004.

[25] OMG, OMG Model Driven Architecture (MDA), 1997, http://www.omg.org/mda/.

[26] Object Management Group (OMG), 1997, http://www.omg.org.

[27] M. H. Alalfi, J. R. Cordy, and T. R. Dean, "Automated reverse engineering of UML sequence diagrams for dynamic web applications," in *Proceedings of the IEEE International Conference on Software Testing, Verification, and Validation Workshops (ICSTW '09)*, pp. 287–294, Denver, Colo, USA, April 2009.

[28] M. H. Alalfi, J. R. Cordy, and T. R. Dean, "SQL2XMI: reverse engineering of UML-ER diagrams from relational database schemas," in *Proceedings of the 15th Working Conference on Reverse Engineering (WCRE '08)*, pp. 187–191, Antwerp, Belgium, October 2008.

[29] E. Korshunova, M. Petkovic, M. van den Brand, and M. Mousavi, "CPP2XMI: reverse engineering of UML class, sequence, and activity diagrams from C++ source code," in *Proceedings of the 13th Working Conference on Reverse Engineering (WCRE '06)*, pp. 297–298, Benevento, Italy, October 2006.

[30] E. Gansner, E. Koutsofios, S. North, and K.-P. Vo, "A technique for drawing directed graphs," *IEEE Transactions on Software Engineering*, vol. 19, no. 3, pp. 214–230, 1993.

[31] E. B. Duffy and B. A. Malloy, "A language and platform-independent approach for reverse engineering," in *Proceedings of the 3rd ACIS International Conference on Software Engineering Research, Management and Applications (SERA '05)*, pp. 415–422, Pleasant, Mich, USA, August 2005.

[32] V. K. Decyk, C. D. Norton, and B. K. Szymanski, "How to express C++ concepts in Fortran 90," *Scientific Programming*, vol. 6, no. 4, pp. 363–390, 1997.

[33] W. S. Brainerd, *Guide to Fortran 2003 Programming*, Springer, 1st edition, 2009.

[34] M. Metcalf, J. Reid, and M. Cohen, *Modern Fortran Explained*, Oxford University Press, New York, NY, USA, 4th edition, 2011.

[35] D. Rouson, J. Xia, and X. Xu, *Scientific Software Design: The Object-Oriented Way*, Cambridge University Press, New York, NY, USA, 1st edition, 2011.

[36] I. D. Chivers and J. Sleightholme, "Compiler support for the Fortran 2003 and 2008 Standards Revision 11," *ACM SIGPLAN Fortran Forum*, vol. 31, no. 3, pp. 17–28, 2012.

[37] J. Reid, "Coarrays in the next fortran standard," *SIGPLAN Fortran Forum*, vol. 29, no. 2, pp. 10–27, 2010.

[38] E. Gamma, R. Helm, R. Johnson, and J. Vlissides, *Design Patterns: Elements of Reusable Object-Oriented Software*, Addison-Wesley, Longman Publishing, Boston, Mass, USA, 1995.

[39] T. Mattson, B. Sanders, and B. Massingill, *Patterns for Parallel Programming*, Addison-Wesley Professional, 1st edition, 2004.

[40] J. L. Ortega-Arjona, *Patterns for Parallel Software Design*, John Wiley & Sons, 1st edition, 2010.

[41] M. Weidmann, "Design and performance improvement of a real-world, object-oriented C++ solver with STL," in *Scientific Computing in Object-Oriented Parallel Environments*, Y. Ishikawa, R. Oldehoeft, J. Reynders, and M. Tholburn, Eds., vol. 1343 of *Lecture Notes in Computer Science*, pp. 25–32, Springer, Berlin, Germany, 1997.

[42] A. Markus, "Design patterns and Fortran 90/95," *ACM SIGPLAN Fortran Forum*, vol. 25, no. 1, pp. 13–29, 2006.

[43] A. Markus, "Design patterns and Fortran 2003," *ACM SIGPLAN Fortran Forum*, vol. 27, no. 3, pp. 2–15, 2008.

[44] H. Neunzert, A. Klar, and J. Struckmeier, "Particle methods: theory and applications," Tech. Rep. 95-113, Fachbereich Mathematik, Universitat Kaiserslautern, Kaiserslautern, Germany, 1995.

[45] V. K. Decyk and H. J. Gardner, "Object-oriented design patterns in Fortran 90/95: mazev1, mazev2 and mazev3," *Computer Physics Communications*, vol. 178, no. 8, pp. 611–620, 2008.

[46] H. A. Muller, J. H. Jahnke, D. B. Smith, M.-A. Storey, S. R. Tilley, and K. Wong, "Reverse engineering: a roadmap," in *Proceedings of the Conference on The Future of Software Engineering*, pp. 47–60, Limerick, Ireland, June 2000.

[47] M. Fowler, *Refactoring: Improving the Design of Existing Code*, Addison-Wesley Longman, Boston, Mass, USA, 1999.

[48] T. J. Parr and R. W. Quong, "ANTLR: a predicated-LL(k) parser generator," *Software: Practice and Experience*, vol. 25, no. 7, pp. 789–810, 1995.

[49] P. Tonella and A. Potrich, "Reverse engineering of the UML class diagram from C++ code in presence of weakly typed containers," in *Proceedings of the IEEE International Conference on Software Maintenance (ICSM '01)*, pp. 376–385, Florence, Italy, November 2001.

[50] A. Nanthaamornphong, K. Morris, D. W. I. Rouson, and H. A. Michelsen, "A case study: agile development in the community laser-induced incandescence modeling environment (CLiiME)," in *Proceedings of the 5th International Workshop on Software Engineering for Computational Science and Engineering*, pp. 9–18, San Francisco, Calif, USA, May 2013.

[51] L. C. Briand, Y. Labiche, and Y. Miao, "Towards the reverse engineering of UML sequence diagrams," in *Proceedings of the 10th Working Conference on Reverse Engineering*, pp. 57–66, Victoria, Canada, November 2003.

[52] E. J. Chikofsky and J. H. Cross II, "Reverse engineering and design recovery: a taxonomy," *IEEE Software*, vol. 7, no. 1, pp. 13–17, 1990.

[53] IBM, *Rational Rose Enterprise*, 2013, http://www-03.ibm.com/software/products/en/enterprise/.

[54] Department of Computer Science University of Victoria, Rigi, 2001, http://www.rigi.cs.uvic.ca/rigi/blurb/rigi-blurb.html.

7

SDN Programming for Heterogeneous Switches with Flow Table Pipelining

Junchang Wang ⓘ, Shaojin Cheng ⓘ, and Xiong Fu ⓘ

Department of Computer Science, Nanjing University of Posts and Telecommunications, Nanjing, China

Correspondence should be addressed to Junchang Wang; junchangwang@gmail.com

Academic Editor: Emiliano Tramontana

High-level programming is one of the critical building blocks of the effective use of software-defined networking (SDN). Existing solutions, however, either (1) cannot utilize the state-of-the-art switches with flow table pipelining, a key technique to prevent flow rule set explosion or (2) force programmers to manually organize and manage hardware flow table pipelines, which is time-consuming and error-prone. This paper presents a high-level SDN programming framework to address these issues. The framework can automatically (1) generate rule sets for heterogeneous switches with different flow table pipelining designs and (2) update installed rules when the network state changes. As a result, the framework can not only generate efficient rule sets for switches but also provide programmers a centralized, intuitive, and hence easy-to-use programming API. Experiments show that the framework can generate compact rule sets that are 29–116 times smaller than those generated by other open-source SDN controllers. Besides, the framework is 5 times faster to recover from network link failures in comparison to other controllers.

1. Introduction

Software-defined networking (SDN) brings the appeal to manage complex networks more efficiently by shielding low-level details (e.g., setting up flow tables and handling network events such as link failures). In recent years, SDN is becoming more commonplace in scenarios such as high-performance computing and data centers [1–4].

To that end, a major research direction of SDN is to provide more sophisticated SDN programming interfaces, which we refer to as *high-level SDN programming* APIs. By using these APIs, SDN programmers can manage an SDN network in a centralized, intuitive, and hence easy-to-use manner [5–7]. The basic idea of existing programming APIs is to compile SDN programs statically and then to generate a specific flow table scheme for each network switch. We refer to this approach as *proactive high-level SDN programming model* [8] (henceforth simply *proactive programming*). Proactive programming, however, has limitations. Specifically, to manage network switches, programmers have to explicitly specify matching fields of each flow table, and hence it is programmers' responsibility to correctly handle hardware details.

In recent years, another promising approach, *reactive high-level SDN programming model (reactive programming* henceforth), has been proposed. *Reactive programming* depends on a runtime optimizer—rather than programmers—to (1) identify switch configurations when an SDN controller starts running, (2) generate flow table scheme for each switch, (3) and populate flow rules when necessary. With these unique features, reactive programming hides switch details and provides programmers a more general and easy-to-use abstraction. A few proactive programming systems [8, 9] have been proposed. In practice, however, we found that utilizing proactive programming can be complex and challenging, and many programming complexities remain. Following are two major challenges.

Firstly, flow table pipelining is a key technique to prevent flow rule set explosion and has been adopted by almost all of the major SDN switch vendors. For example, recent switches from P4 [6], Domino [10], OF-DPA [11], and POF [7] all support flow table pipelining. Unfortunately, existing implementations of *reactive programming* (e.g., Maple [8]) only generate rule set for switches with a single flow table. As far as we know, there is no implementation of *reactive programming* that can support switches with flow table pipelining yet. The major challenge is that to support flow table pipelining, each single flow rule must be split into multiple stages, and each of which is inserted into a flow table in the pipeline. And hence, smart strategies are required in splitting rules, inserting different stages into different flow tables, and invalidating all stages distributed among flow tables atomically (detailed in Section 3).

Secondly, when *reactive programming* is used, it is the controller's responsibility to automatically recalculate and update installed flow rules when network state (such as topology) changes. This job is nontrivial because multiple flow tables in the pipeline must be updated atomically; otherwise, performance issue or even security issue arises (detailed in Section 2). Unfortunately, no existing implementation of *reactive programming* can handle network state dependencies correctly and efficiently.

Overall, applying *reactive programming* to the state-of-the-art switches that support flow table pipelining is quite challenging. To the best of our knowledge, no existing work has successfully solved the aforementioned issues. In research, it remains an open question *if reactive programming can be applied to the state-of-the-art switches?* And if the answer is yes, *what is the expected benefit?*

This paper tries to answer the above questions by presenting Maple++, the first implementation of high-level SDN reactive programming for switches with flow table pipelining. Maple++ is an extension of Maple [8], a classic reactive programming model. Maple only supports switches with single flow table. In contrast, Maple++ can support switches with flow table pipeline designs, by addressing the aforementioned issues. Specifically, Maple++ introduces *forwarding tree*, a data structure maintained by the controller runtime system to manage forwarding rule sets of switches in a unified and centralized way. Each leaf in the forwarding tree consists of routing decision, dependencies, and handler to environment snapshots. Based on the forwarding tree, a novel tree compression algorithm is invented to remove redundancies. A compressed forwarding tree, which is basically a directed acyclic graph (DAG), can dramatically reduce the number of flow rules generated. To utilize flow table pipeline design in switches, Maple++ splits the compressed forwarding tree to multiple subtrees, according to the configuration of hardware switches. Then, a novel mapping algorithm maps subtrees to multiple flow tables and organizes them as a pipeline. Besides, to handle network events such as link failures, Maple++ includes a novel programmer-oblivious subscription/notification strategy to efficiently handle network events. The strategy not only provides an easy-to-use API to programmers but also helps Maple++ runtime to efficiently and atomically update retired flow rules. As far as we know, Maple++ is the first implementation of reactive programming for real SDN networks including heterogeneous switches with flow table pipeline designs (the authors emphasize that proactive programming

and reactive programming do not exclude each other. In practice, a system may adopt both approaches. This paper focuses on reactive programming).

Experiments show that rule sets generated by Maple++ are much more efficient than those generated by other SDN controllers, in the sense that the rule sets are more compact and consume less flow table space. For example, rule sets generated by Maple++ are 29–116x smaller than those generated by POX, Floodlight, and OpenDaylight, the three most widely used open-source SDN controllers. Besides, Maple++ is 5 times faster than other compilers to recover from link failures. We have implemented an open source version of Maple++ in Python. We hope this implementation could be useful for both the academia and industry.

The rest of the paper is organized as follows: Section 2 gives a motivating example of high-level SDN programming. Section 3 presents the design details of Maple++. We present evaluations in Section 4, discuss related work in Section 5, and conclude in Section 6.

2. A Motivating Example

To motivate challenges reactive programming is facing to manage heterogeneous switches with flow table pipeline designs, we use the following high-level SDN program.

Suppose a programmer is managing a local network by using a policy which consists of three parts: (1) the programmer wants to define a white list of hosts, named *recognizedHost*. Each time when a packet comes in, if either the source MAC address or destination MAC address does not exist in the white list, the packet should be dropped; (2) the programmer wants to derive the access switch of the host. If the access switch is in "programmer-defined" list *protectedAP*, a secure path should be used to forward the packet; (3) otherwise, the default shortest path should be used.

This policy is conceptually simple and straightforward. The reactive programming model allows the programmer to use familiar programming languages (such as Java and Python) and data structures (such as hash map and list) to implement the policy. Figure 1 presents the code that a programmer needs to program if he/she personally likes Python.

Specifically, the programmer defines a dictionary, *recognizedHost*, to save known MAC addresses and related access switches (Line 1 in Figure 1). And then, the programmer defines a list, *protectedAP*, to record the secure access switches. Each time when a switch receives a packet but does not know how to forward it, the switch sends a PACKET_IN message containing the header of the packet to the controller. The controller then invokes the *onPacket* function, which retrieves the source MAC and destination MAC addresses of the packet. If either the source MAC or the destination MAC address does not exist in *recognizedHost*, which is set up and maintained by another independent L2-learning program, the controller instructs the switch to drop the packet (Lines 6-7). Otherwise, the controller instructs the switch to route the packet either along a secure path or the shortest path, by checking if one of the

```
(1)   Map recognizedHost {key: macAddress, value: switchID}
(2)   List protectedAP [value: switchID]
(3)   def onPacket (p):
(4)      sw = recognizedHost [p . srcMac]
(5)      dw = recognizedHost [p . dstMac]
(6)      if sw == NULL || dw == NULL:
(7)         return DROP
(8)      elif sw in protectedAP or dw in protectedAP:
(9)         return securePath (sw, dw)
(10)     else:
(11)        return shortestPath (sw, dw)
```

FIGURE 1: Example of reactive high-level SDN programming (*secure-or-shortest-forwarding*).

access switches is in *protectedAP*. The controller finally inserts flow rules that match on the source MAC and destination MAC addresses. Despite its simplicity, reactive programming has the following shortcomings:

Flow Table Explosion. Existing implementations of reactive programming could not work efficiently. One problem is that *onPacket* is generating flow rules for single flow table, and as a result, the rule set generated may explode. For example, the number of rules generated by program *secure-or-shortest-forwarding* in Figure 1 is exponential to the number of MAC addresses (hosts) in network. In worst case, the network consists of 2^{48} source MAC addresses and 2^{48} destination MAC addresses, resulting in a rule set of about 2^{96} entries that is far beyond the capacity of forwarding tables in modern hardware switches (detailed in Section 3.4).

Network State Inconsistency. Another problem is that *onPacket* cannot handle network state dependencies correctly. Suppose the access switch of host A was not in *protectedAP*, and as a result, packets that were sent to or received from host A were forwarded to the shortest path. Then, one manager manually adds the switch to *protectedAP* for some security reasons. Merely forcing subsequent flows to route through secure paths is far from enough because rules that were inserted into network switches also need to be removed to avoid packets walking through unsecure links. We refer to this situation as *network state inconsistency* issues.

As far as we know, no existing work focuses on addressing these two fundamental issues in reactive programming. Maple++ tries to implement and deploy reactive programming in real networks, by solving the issues.

3. System Design

The objective of Maple++ is to implement reactive programming for heterogeneous switches with different flow table pipeline designs. Specifically, Maple++ addresses challenges including rule set explosion and network failure recovery.

To that end, Maple++ introduces a sophisticated SDN controller framework shown in Figure 2. Maple++ adopts the OpenFlow protocol to manage network switches and

provides an *algorithmic policy* programming API [8]. *Algorithmic policy* API allows programmers to use familiar programming languages (such as Java and Python) to design programs and manage network. The core of Maple++ consists of four modules, including *Runtime*, *Global Optimization*, *Local Optimization*, and *Environment Information Collection*. When PACKET_IN messages arrive at the controller, module *Runtime* retrieves packet fields, runs programmer-defined programs, and logs network state dependencies. Module *Global Optimization* is to calculate routing decisions for the whole network and to perform global optimizations (such as to choose the shortest routing path). Module *Local Optimization* is to calculate routing decisions for specific network switch and to perform optimizations such as utilizing wildcards in flow rules for rule set compression. The whole system consists of a single instance of *Global Optimization*. In contrast, the system may have multiple instances of *Local Optimization*, each of which is assigned to a switch in network. Module *Environment Information Collection* is to collect network information such as network topology and the status of network devices. Another important role of *Environment Information Collection* module is to notify other modules by invoking callback functions, when the environment information changes. The remaining of this chapter introduces Maple++'s key functions one-by-one, from "programmer-defined" high-level programs to rule sets generated for switches.

3.1. Algorithmic Policy and Northbound API of Maple++. The northbound application programming interface (API) of Maple++ is based on the *algorithmic policy* presented in Maple [8], which allows an SDN programmer to specify how an incoming packet is processed and how the packet should be forwarded, by providing a general function. For example, *onPacket* in Figure 1 is such a function and is invoked for each OpenFlow PACKET_IN message. Function *onPacket* takes one parameter: the header of the packet. Within the body of *onPacket*, programmers can define local variables and calculate forwarding decisions by using familiar algorithms and data structures. Routing decisions may depend on global variables (for example, *recognizedHost* in Figure 1) and network environment context (for example, network topology for calculating shortest path). These data are stored in data stores in module *Environment Information Collection*, which is in charge of keeping the data in data stores up-to-date and notifying other modules if they have registered to some portions of the data. In Maple++, each global data structure is a wrapper of the original data structure in addition to a callback function. The callback function is used to register current forwarding decision to the data store. The return value of function *onPacket* is a forwarding path, which specifies how the packet should be forwarded.

3.2. High-Level Program to Global Forwarding Tree. Each time when a packet arrives at the controller, Maple++ runtime invokes "programmer-defined" programs and generates a forwarding decision (such as DROP, BROADCAST, or a forwarding path). At the same time, Maple++

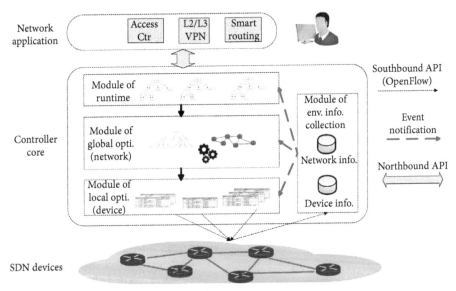

FIGURE 2: Maple++ system components.

runtime records the essence of the decision dependencies: packet fields accessed (source and destination MAC addresses and Ethernet type in the example program in Figure 1), global variables, and environment context accessed (network topology to make forwarding decisions). We refer to one such record as a *global forwarding decision*.

The record of forwarding decision is essence because Maple++ runtime can utilize it to generate switch forwarding rules which prevents subsequent packets of the same flow from unnecessarily being sent to the controller. This can substantially save bandwidth between the controller and switches. For example, assume one execution of *onPacket* is as follows: (1) the program reads the source MAC address of the packet, (2) the result is 00:00:00:00:00:01 (henceforth :01 for concreteness), (3) the program then reads the destination MAC address of the packet, (4) the result is 00:00:00:00:00:11 (henceforth :11 for concreteness), and (5) the program calculates and decides to drop the packet because the access switch of this host is not in the white list *recognizedHost*. Maple++ runtime then inserts a flow rule with the matching fields being source and destination MAC addresses (srcMAC == :01 && dstMAC == :11) and the action being DROP. Then, we can infer that if the program is again given an arbitrary packet with source and destination MAC addresses being :01 and :11, respectively, the program will similarly choose to drop the packet. And as a result, we can reuse the forwarding decision of the first packet, by inserting a flow rule in switches.

Forwarding decisions are organized as a tree in Maple++ runtime. Suppose the *onPacket* program runs for a while, and packets of five different flows have arrived. In one of these decisions, the MAC address of the arriving packet is :01, and hence the program returns the forwarding decision *DROP*. In the second trace, the MAC address of the arriving packet is :02, which is in the *protectedAP*, and hence the program returns a secure path between the source and destination switches as forwarding decision. Similarly, assume the subsequent three packets have the same source

MAC address, :03 but have different destination MAC addresses (:11, :12, and :13, respectively), Maple++ runtime will generate three different traces, one for each of the packets. Maple++ maintains these decisions by organizing them as a tree shown in Figure 3. We refer to the tree as *forwarding tree*. In this figure, an ellipse represents a matching field and a rectangle an action. The label of an arrow represents the value of the matching field. It is worth noting that an "if" statement in high-level program generates an ellipse node with two branches, one positive and another negative.

3.3. Global Forwarding Tree to Switch's Forwarding Tree.
The global forwarding tree is maintained by the *Global Optimization* module and is used to calculate forwarding decisions for the whole network. And as a result, its forwarding decision (for example, shortest path) is a list of (switch ID, port number) pairs. To generate flow tables for a specific switch, Maple++ needs to know the specific forwarding decisions for each switch (for example, output port numbers).

Fortunately, the forwarding decisions for a specific switch can be organized as a tree, which is part of the global forwarding tree, with the leaves being forwarding decisions for the switch. We refer to the forwarding tree for a specific switch as *local forwarding tree*. For example, global forwarding tree shown in Figure 3 will be translated to a local forwarding tree for switch *A* (Figure 4), if *port 1* of switch *A* is connected to the secure path, *port 2* of switch *A* is connected to the shortest path, and hosts with MAC addresses :01 and :02 attach to other switches. For each switch, there is a corresponding local forwarding tree in Maple++.

Local forwarding tree is generated and maintained by module *Local Optimization*. A straightforward strategy to generate a local forwarding tree for a specific switch is as follows: (1) copying the global forwarding tree, (2) replacing the actions by the switch-specific forwarding decisions, (3) traversing the local forwarding tree and deleting branches

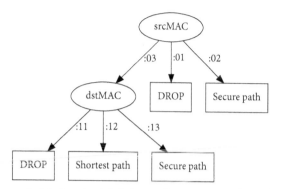

FIGURE 3: Maple++'s global forwarding tree consisting of five forwarding decisions.

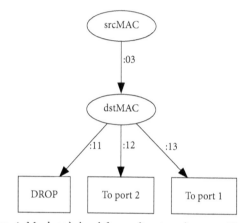

FIGURE 4: Maple++'s local forwarding tree for a specific switch.

that do not involve the switch, (4) and then monitoring global forwarding tree and updating the local forwarding tree accordingly.

It is worth noting that the architecture of local forwarding tree is not necessarily fixed. In other words, the tree in Figure 4 can choose srcMAC, dstMAC, or any other field of the packet as the root of the tree, only if Maple++ can generate the same forwarding rule set for the switch. In practice, the architecture of a local forwarding tree depends on the flow table pipeline design of the switch.

3.4. Compressing Forwarding Tree. One drawback of *reactive programming* is that the rule set generated may suffer explosion issue, which can be demonstrated by the size of forwarding trees. Figure 5 shows the redundancies in a forwarding tree and the potential rule set explosion. In worst case, node *srcMAC* has 2^{48} children (2^{48} MAC addresses), each of which has $2^{48} - 1$ children (leaves), resulting in a tree with a total number of $2^{96} + 1$ nodes.

To address the redundancy issue, Maple++ adopts a novel compression algorithm to dramatically reduce the size of forwarding tree. Specifically, as shown in Figure 5, many siblings of nodes srcMAC and dstMAC are redundant in the sense that their parents can refer to the same child and cut the others. For example, routing decision for MAC address pair (:01, :11) and routing decision for MAC address pair

(:01, :13) are the same, and hence these two branches can be merged (Figure 6(a)). Similarly, routing decision for MAC address pair (:01, *) and routing decision for MAC address pair (:03, *) can be merged because they have the same children set (Figure 6(b)).

The basic idea to compress a forwarding tree is to perform a depth-first tree traversal. The algorithm starts from the root of the tree and then recursively checks each child. Whenever the algorithm reaches a node, it first checks if any two children of this node are the same and merges redundant children by keeping one child and removing others.

Pseudocode of the compression algorithm is shown in Algorithm 1. The algorithm starts by setting the value of field *compressed* of every node in the tree. Then the algorithm starts from the root and invokes function *Compress()* (Line 4), which performs a depth-first tree traversal. Each time when a leaf is reached, the algorithm sets the *compressed* field and returns (Lines 7–9). Otherwise, *Compress()* iterates each child of the current node (Line 11). If any child, denoted as *child_t1* in the algorithm, has not been compressed (Line 12), *Compress()* first compresses this child (Line 13). Otherwise, the algorithm checks if there are any other children which (1) have been compressed and (2) has the same children set as child *child_t1* does (Line 16). If the algorithm finds any such a child *child_t2*, *Compress()* performs compression by (1) instructing *child_t2* to point to *child_t1* and then (2) deleting the node that was pointed to by *child_t2* (Lines 17-18). Finally, *Compress()* sets the *compressed* field of the current node and then returns. Algorithm *Compress()* basically performs a depth-first tree traversal and compresses the size of tree by turning a tree into a DAG. Another benefit of performing *Compress()* on forwarding tree is that it is much more easier to map the resulting DAG to a flow table pipeline (detailed in subsequent subsections).

3.5. Generating Flow Tables from Compressed Forwarding Tree. Given a compressed forwarding tree, now we can generate flow tables for switches with flow table pipeline design. This consists of two steps: *setting up an appropriate pipeline* and *generating flow rules*.

The basic idea of setting up flow table pipeline is that the compressed forwarding tree can be divided into multiple branches, each of which can be mapped to a dedicated flow table to avoid rule set explosion in a single flow table. If a branch is too large to fit for a single flow table, then we can divide it and map its branches to multiple flow tables. In an ideal case, given the compressed forwarding tree, each node of the tree can be mapped to a dedicated flow table. Edges between different nodes can be represented by the *JUMP* instructions between different flow tables. Besides, we use *metadata* (a 64-bit long variable in OpenFlow 1.3) to pass information from one flow table to its subsequent tables.

For example, Figure 7 shows how we can map the compressed forwarding tree shown in Figure 6 to multiple flow tables. Specifically, the root of the tree (node srcMAC) can be mapped to a dedicated flow table, *Table-0*. Since the root has two branches (node pointed to by edges labeled as

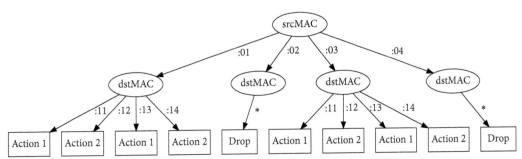

FIGURE 5: Redundancies in forwarding tree and the potential rule set explosion. In worst case, the tree consists of 2^{48} dstMAC nodes, each of which has $2^{48} - 1$ leaves.

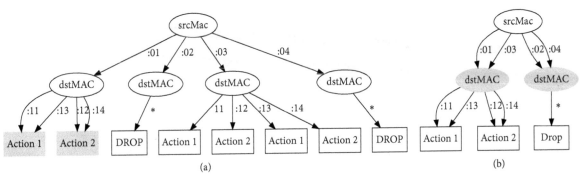

FIGURE 6: Compressing forwarding tree. (a) Compression of the leftmost subtree of forwarding tree. (b) Recursive compression of the the forwarding tree. Compression happens at nodes in blue color. The compressed forwarding tree is a DAG.

```
        Parameters: ft: Forwarding Tree
(1)  Procedure CompressFT(ft)
(2)     for node in ft:
(3)         node.compressed = false; /* Initialization. */
(4)     Compress(ft.root);
(5)     return;
(6)  def Compress(node): /* A depth-first tree traversal. */
(7)     if type(node) == Leaf: /* Check if node is a leaf. */
(8)         node.compressed = true;
(9)     return
(10)    else:
(11)        for child_t1 in node.children: /* Find a child. */
(12)           if child_t1.compressed == false:
(13)              Compress(child_t1); /* Recursively compress the child. */
(14)           return;
(15)        for child_t2 in (node.children-child_t1): /* Find a child that is the same as child_t1. */
(16)           if child_t2.compressed and child_t1 == child_t2:
(17)              child_t2 points to the same node of child_t1; /* Remove redundancies. */
(18)              node.children.delete(child_t2);
(19)        node.compressed = true;
(20)    return
```

ALGORITHM 1: Algorithm to recursively compress forwarding tree.

:01 and :03 and node pointed to by edges labeled as :02 and :04), we can map nodes of dstMAC to *Table-1* and *Table-2*, respectively. Similarly, children of the left dstMAC node can be mapped to a dedicated table, *Table-ACTION*. It is worth noting that, to save the number of tables; Maple++ may map a few nodes to one flow table. For example, in Figure 7, all of the leaves are mapped to a dedicated flow table, *Table-ACTION*.

Map compressed forwarding tree (DAG) to flow table pipeline is shown in Algorithm 2. It starts from the root of

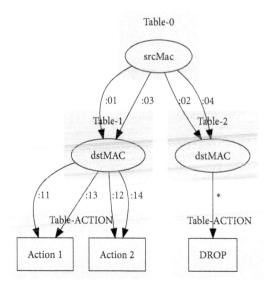

FIGURE 7: Mapping compressed forwarding tree (DAG) to flow table pipeline.

---

(1) // global variable
(2) *tableID*: global variable to record the maximum tableID in pipeline.
(3) Procedure GenerateFT(ft)
(4)   tableID = 0; /* Initialization. */
(5)   GenerateSingleFT(ft.root, ∅); /* Allocate a flow table, and generate flow rules for *node*. */
(6) **def** *GenerateSingleFT(node, metadata)*:
(7)   **if** *type(node)* == *Leaf*: /* Check if node is a leaf. */
(8)   match = metadata;
(9)   priority = 0; /* Emit a rule for this leaf. The rule matches on the register values in metadata and is inserted in a specific flow table, *table-ACTION*. */
(10)   emitRule (table-ACTION, match, priority, node.action);
(11)   **return** *table-ACTION*;
(12)   **else** /* *childrenGroup* is the set of edges pointing to the same child node in compressed forwarding tree, and *childrenGroup. groupID* is a unique integer number. */
(13)   **for** *childrenGroup in getChildrenGroup(node)*:
(14)   tableID_t = tableID;
(15)   tableID = tableID + 1; /* Save the matching condition on metadata. */
(16)   metadata += "$reg_{tableID}$ = *childrenGroup.groupID*"; /* Generate flow table for this child node. *childTableID* is the child node's flow tableID. */
(17)   childTableID = GenerateSingleFT(childrenGroup.node, metadata);
(18)   **for** *edge in childrenGroup*:
(19)   match = (node.field: edge.value);
(20)   priority = 0;
(21)   action += goto childTableID; /* For each edge pointing to the child node, add a flow rule jumping to child node's flow table. */
(22)   emitRule(tableID_t, match, priority, action);
(23)   **return** *tableID_t*;

ALGORITHM 2: Algorithm to map compressed forwarding tree (DAG) to flow table pipeline.

the tree (Line 5) and then traversals the forwarding tree and generates flow tables for each node by invoking function *GenerateSingleFT()*. For each nonleaf node (Lines 13–23), *GenerateSingleFT()* iterates each *childrenGroup* (Line 13), which is the set of edges pointing to the same child node in the compressed forwarding tree. For example, for the forwarding tree in Figure 7, edges ":01" and ":03" belong to the same *childrenGroup*. In addition to edge set, *childrenGroup* has two other fields: *node* and *groupID*. For each *childrenGroup*, Maple++ allocates a dedicated flow table for it and generates flow tables for this node by invoking *GenerateSingleFT()* (Line 17). And then, for each edge in the *childrenGroup*, Maple++ inserts a flow rule in the current flow table. The flow rule matches on the field of current node and jumps to the flow table of the child node (Line 22). For each leaf (Line 7), a flow rule is inserted into flow table *table-ACTION* (Line 10). The matching field is the accumulated register values stored in *metadata*.

Generated flow table pipeline and rule sets are shown in Table 1. For concreteness, we omit the field *ingress port* in the matching field. Each table corresponds to a node in the compressed forwarding tree and matches on a single field of the packet. Each entry of the table corresponds to an egress edge from the node. Suppose a packet with source and destination MAC address pair (00:00:00:00:00:01, 00:00:00:00:00:11) arrives at the switch, the algorithm first walks through *Table-0*. Then, Algorithm 1 sets the value of *reg0* to 1 in *metadata* which will be passed to subsequent flow tables, and (2) jumps to flow table *Table-1*. Flow table *Table-1* (1) matches on the destination MAC address of the packet, (2) sets the value of *reg1* in metadata to 1, and then (3) jumps to flow table *Table-ACTION*. *Table-ACTION* matches on the *metadata* of the packet.

3.6. Handle Network Events. In SDN programming, it is still quite challenging to correctly and efficiently handle state dependencies. Take code in Figure 1 as an example. Suppose the access switch of host *A* was not in *protectedAP*, and hence packets that were sent to or received from host *A* were forwarded to the shortest path. Then, one manager manually adds the switch to *protectedAP* for some security reasons. Merely forcing subsequent flows to route through secure paths is far from enough because rules that were inserted into the switch before the manager adding the switch to *protectedAP* also need to be removed.

Typically, there are two approaches in handling state dependencies. (1) A naive approach is to simply flush flow tables by removing all of the rules installed whenever network state changes. This approach is intuitive and easy to implement. However, it is inefficient because it probably causes false-positive issues and leads to unnecessary re-executions to generate flow rules. (2) Another approach is to provide subscription APIs to programmers to allow them to enable state dependent programming. For example, whenever a program accesses environment data (for example, network topology or global variables), it needs to register to the data store. Then, whenever the data changes, system runtime will rerun the program and update retired flow rules automatically. Since the program can register to a very specific portion of the data accessed, this approach can accurately remove affected flow rules without touching others. This approach is efficient. However, it is hard to use because it is the programmers' responsibility to handle the complexity of identifying dependent data and subscribing to data store.

Based on the two existing approaches, Maple++ makes a trade-off between efficiency and easy-to-use features by utilizing a programmer-oblivious subscription/notification strategy. Specifically, Maple++ runtime adopts a normal subscription/notification strategy. Based on that, Maple++ provides (1) wrapper data structures which include original data structures in addition to implicit subscription functions

and (2) wrapper function calls which include original function calls and implicit subscription functions. As a result, in Maple++, programmers use wrapper functions and data structures to program without subscribing to data store. It is the Maple++ runtime's responsibility to automatically register generated flow rules to the data accessed. At the same time, module *Environment Information Collection* is in charge of receiving network events, classifying them, and notifying different modules to rerun and to update retired flow rules.

4. Experiments

In this section, we demonstrate that Maple++ improves end-to-end performance and programming experience over existing SDN controllers by (1) generating compact forwarding rules for the state-of-the-art switches with flow table pipeline designs and (2) updating retired forwarding rules automatically. Maple++ is currently implemented as a component of Ryu [12]. We chose Ryu because it is component-based and open source. It is worth noting that Maple++ can also be implemented on top of other controllers. Our implementation of Maple++ consists of 1100 lines of Python code. For components such as OpenFlow 1.3 implementation, Maple++ reuses the implementation in Ryu.

4.1. Experiment Setup. We run controllers on a Dell R730 server. The server is equipped with two Intel Xeon E5-2609 processors, each of which consists of 8 CPU cores running at maximum speed of 1.7 GHz. Each CPU core has one 32 kB L1 data cache, one 32 kB L1 instruction cache, and a 256 kB L2 cache. All of the 8 cores on the same die share one L3 cache of 20 MB. The two processors are connected through two QPI links of 6.4 GT/s. The server uses 128 GB DDR4 memory. The server runs an Ubuntu 16.04 system with 64-bit Linux kernel version 4.4.0.

For comparison experiments (Sections 4.2 and 4.3), we evaluate all controllers by using Open vSwitch (OVS) with OpenFlow version 1.3.4. For experiments to measure Maple++'s performance (Section 4.4), we use two HP ProCurve 5412zl switches.

4.2. Effect of Utilizing Flow Table Pipelines. In this subsection, we compare the rule set generated by Maple++ against those generated by other controllers to highlight the effect of utilizing state-of-the-art flow table pipeline designs in switches. We chose four widely used controllers, including OpenDaylight (ODL), Floodlight, Maple, and POX. ODL and Floodlight are industry-developed open-source controllers that form the basis of commercial systems, while Maple and POX are academic systems.

We run SDN program *secure-or-shortest-forwarding* (shown in Figure 1) on every controller. We choose this program because it is straightforward and can be implemented on every controller with minor modifications. In experiments, we perform an all-to-all ping among the hosts.

TABLE 1: Flow table corresponding to forwarding tree shown in Figure 7.

	Pri	Match	Action
Table-0	0	srcMac = :01	reg0 = 1; goto Table-1;
	0	srcMac = :03	reg0 = 1; goto Table-1;
	0	srcMac = :02	reg0 = 2; goto Table-2;
	0	srcMac = :04	reg0 = 2; goto Table-2;
	0	Otherwise	Punt
Table-1	0	dstMac = :11	reg1 = 1; goto Table-ACTION;
	0	dstMac = :13	reg1 = 1; goto Table-ACTION;
	0	dstMac = :12	reg1 = 2; goto Table-ACTION;
	0	dstMac = :14	reg1 = 2; goto Table-ACTION;
	0	Otherwise	Punt
Table-2	0	Otherwise	reg2 = 1; goto Table-ACTION
Table-ACTION	0	reg0 == 1 && reg1 == 1;	Action1
	0	reg0 == 1 && reg1 == 2;	Action2
	0	reg0 == 2 && reg2 == 1;	Drop
	0	Otherwise	Punt

We then record the round-trip time (RTT) of each ping and then count OpenFlow rules installed in the switch.

Table 2 lists the number of hosts simulated (column *# Hosts*), number of flow tables used (column *# Tables Used*), number of rules generated (column *# Rules*), and median ping RTT (column *Med. RTT(ms)*) for each controller. The number of hosts is fixed to 80, which is adequate to simulate the use case of a small enterprise network. We observe that when 80 hosts are used, Maple++ generates only 162 rules, which is 29–116 times smaller than the rules generated by other controllers.

The rule compression in Maple++ is due to the utilization of hardware flow table pipeline. Column *# Tables Used* shows that Maple++ utilizes up to 12 hardware flow tables to build a sophisticated pipeline, which fundamentally prevents rule set explosion. Theoretically, Maple++ generates approximately $2 * H$ rules. In contrast, each other controller generates approximately H^2 rules.

Column *Med. RTT* presents the round-trip time of each controller. It is worth noting that the median RTT of Maple++ does not improve in this experiment because only 80 hosts are simulated, and hence the generated rule sets can reside in hardware flow tables even if a single flow table is used. However, as the number of hosts increases, rule sets generated by other controllers may explode and hence must be evicted from the hardware flow tables frequently, resulting in an extremely large RTT. We demonstrate this in the next experiment.

To highlight the benefit of flow table pipelining in avoiding flow table explosion, we compare Maple++ with other controllers by varying the number of hosts in the network. Since Maple, ODL, and POX all have similar trends as Floodlight, we only show the results of Floodlight and Maple++ in Figure 8 for concreteness. Notice that the scale of the horizontal axis of Figure 8 is logarithmic. Figure 8 shows that, as the number of hosts in the system increases linearly, the number of flow rules generated by Maple++ also increases linearly from about 40 to 462 as the number of hosts increases from 20 to 320. In contrast, the number of rules generated by Floodlight reaches 100,000, which is too large to be deployed in a real switch. It is worth noting that, in this experiment, we use Open vSwitch which is software-based and hence its capacity is "unlimited." For production hardware, however, the size of flow tables is limited. For example, the HP 5612zl switch can only support 1,500 hardware rules and 64,000 rules in total. That means if a programmer wants to achieve a good performance, the number of OpenFlow rules generated by the controller must be less than 1.5 K. Otherwise, the forwarding performance of the switch deteriorates sharply.

4.3. Fast Repair of System State Changes. We now evaluate the effectiveness of Maple++ in recovering from system state changes. Specifically, this experiment focuses on network failure, which is unexpected, critical, and hard to handle. We evaluate controllers using three topologies: "Linear," "Square," and "FatTree" [16]. The Linear topology consists of 4 switches. The Square topology is a small cyclic topology with 4 switches. The FatTree topology consists of 20 switches and two hosts per edge switch, with $k = 4$.

In the experiment, we remove one link from the network to simulate a link failure. We then measure the time to complete pings between all hosts. For Maple++, once the *Environment Information Collection* model receives the link failure message, it immediately notifies Maple++ runtime system which in turn reruns "programmer-defined" functions registered to data store. In contrast, for other controllers, programmers need to implement a function which is responsible for cleaning up retired rules and installing new ones. Besides, for ODL and POX, all of the forwarding rules must be manually removed because there is no way to identify the affected flow rules. Since Maple has the similar trend as Floodlight, we only show the results of Floodlight. Similarly, since ODL has the similar trend as POX, we only show the results of POX.

Figure 9 shows that Maple++ provides substantial improvement in the recovery from link failures in all topologies. Specifically, the mean time to complete an all-to-all ping after a link failure in Maple++ is 0.72 seconds, 1.55

TABLE 2: End-to-end performance comparison and number of rules generated for SDN program secure-or-shortest-forwarding.

Controller	# hosts	# tables used	# rules	Med. RTT (ms)
Maple [8]	80	1	5120	3.1
POX [13]	80	1	18827	8.0
Floodlight [14]	80	1	5332	3.0
OpenDaylight [15]	80	1	4692	1.7
Maple++	80	12	162	2.2

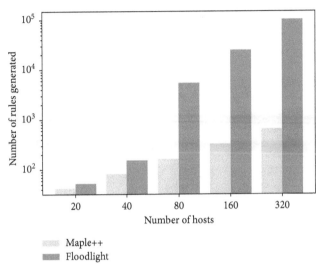

FIGURE 8: Total number of OpenFlow rules generated (horizontal axis is logarithmic.).

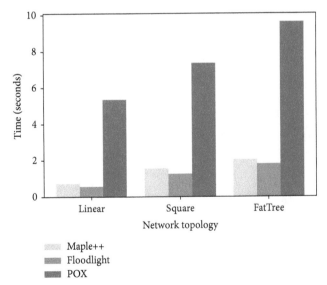

FIGURE 9: Time to repair all-to-all connectively after a link failure.

seconds, and 2.03 seconds, for the three topologies. The result is competitive to Floodlight and is much better than controllers based on POX and ODL. POX and ODL perform poor because they flush the flow table upon receiving the link failure message, which causes false-positive issues and forces the controller to recompute for every flow rules. It is worth noting that the reason Maple++ does not perform better than Floodlight is that Maple++ has to update multiple flow tables due to its flow table pipeline design. This bottleneck can be removed by allowing Maple++ to recompute and update multiple flow tables in parallel. We left this optimization as a future work.

4.4. Maple++ in Real Network. In this subsection, we deploy Maple++ in a real network, show the flow tables generated, and discuss lessons we have learned. A simplified topology of this network is shown in Figure 10. The local network consists of two normal switches (*Switch 1* and *Switch 3*) and two HP 5012zl OpenFlow switches (*Switch 2* and *Switch 4*). All of the four switches are connected through 1 Gbps links. The link between *Switch 2* and *Switch 4* and the link between *Switch 1* and *Switch 4* are secure paths. However other links are not secure because it may exist as malicious switches in between these links. We assume *Switch 1* is in the *secureAP* list, while other switches are not. Each switch is connected by two hosts. For example, *Switch 1* connects to two hosts, *Host 1* and *Host 2*. The IP addresses of these two hosts are "10.0.0.1" and "10.0.0.2," respectively. To simplify the specification, we assume the MAC addresses of *Host 1* and *Host 2* are "00:00:00:00:00:01" (shorted as :01) and "00:00:00:00:00:02" (shorted as :02), respectively. Besides, we assume that the MAC addresses of hosts with green check mark are in the *recognizedHost*. Packets from other hosts should be dropped.

To demonstrate how Maple++ works, we deploy the *secure-or-shortest-forwarding* program shown in Figure 1 and choose *Switch 2* as an example. For concreteness, we omit the field *ingress point* in the matching field. Initially, the flow tables of this switch are empty. Then, the first time when *Host 3* wants to connect to *Host 6*, a PACKET_IN message is sent from the switch to the controller, which in turn invokes the *secure-or-shortest-forwarding* program and then inserts a rule into the switch to instruct the switch to block subsequent packets because *Host 6* has not been recognized. Similarly, the first time when *Host 3* and *Host 5* want to connect to each other, the controller invokes the *secure-or-shortest-forwarding* program and then inserts rules to switch 2 and switch 3 to allow connections to go through the shortest path. In contrast, if *Host 3* wants to connect to *Host 1*, the routing path must be *Switch 2 <−> Switch 4 <−> Switch 1* because *Switch 1* is in the *secureAP*, and hence all connections involving hosts behind *Switch 1* must be routed through the secure path.

The flow tables produced by Maple++ for *Switch 2* are shown in Table 3. Table 3 shows that Maple++ utilizes four flow tables in *Switch 2*. Specifically, *Table-0* is used to match on source MAC address. For each host in the network, a flow

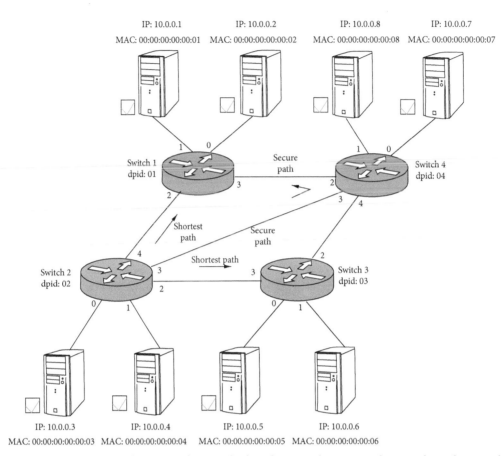

FIGURE 10: Topology of the testbed network. Hosts with green checkmarks are in the *recognizedHost*, and *switch 1* is in the *secureAP list*.

TABLE 3: Flow table pipeline and forwarding rules generated by Maple++ for Switch 2. For concreteness, MAC address 00:00:00:00:00:xx is represented as :xx in the table.

	Pri	Match	Action
Table-0	0	srcMac = (:03-:04)	reg0 = 1; goto Table-1
	0	srcMac = (:01-:02)	reg0 = 2; goto Table-2
	0	srcMac = (:05-:08)	reg0 = 2; goto Table-2
	0	Otherwise	Punt
Table-1	0	dstMac = (:01-:02)	reg1 = 1; goto Table-ACTION
	0	dstMac = :03	reg1 = 2; goto Table-ACTION
	0	dstMac = :04	reg1 = 3; goto Table-ACTION
	0	dstMac = :05	reg1 = 4; goto Table-ACTION
	0	dstMac = :06	reg1 = 5; goto Table-ACTION
	0	dstMac = (:07-:08)	reg1 = 6; goto Table-ACTION
	0	Otherwise	Punt
Table-2	0	dstMac = :03	reg2 = 1; goto Table-ACTION
	0	dstMac = :04	reg2 = 2; goto Table-ACTION
	0	Otherwise	Punt
Table-ACTION	0	reg0 == 1 && reg1 == 1	To port 3 (secure path)
	0	reg0 == 1 && reg1 == 2	To port 0
	0	reg0 == 1 && reg1 == 3	To port 1
	0	reg0 == 1 && reg1 == 4	To port 2 (shortest path)
	0	reg0 == 1 && reg1 == 5	DROP
	0	reg0 == 1 && reg1 == 6	To port 2 (shortest path)
	0	reg0 == 2 && reg2 == 1	To port 0
	0	reg0 == 2 && reg2 == 2	To port 1
	0	Otherwise	Punt

rule is added into *Table-0*. In practice, after compressing the forwarding tree, a flow rule can correspond to a group of MAC addresses. For example, the first flow rule in *Table-0* can match packets from both *Host 3* and *Host 4*. The first rule instructs the switch to set the value of *reg0* to 1 in *metadata* and then jumps to *Table-1* to process the destination MAC addresses of incoming packets. The second rule instructs the switch to set the value of *reg0* to 2 in *metadata* and then jumps to *Table-1*. Similarly, *Table-1* checks the destination MAC address of the packet, logs the routing decision on *metadata* by setting the value of field *reg1*, and then jumps to *Table-ACTION*. *Table-ACTION* checks the values in *metadata* and then takes actions.

Table 3 shows that the size of *Table-0*, *Table-1*, and *Table-2* increases linearly with the number of hosts in the network. The size of *Table-ACTION* increases linearly with the number of policies defined by programmers, which is typically a constant number. Overall, the number of rules generated by Maple++ is linear, which makes Maple++ a practical SDN controller by preventing rule set explosion.

5. Related Work

The importance of flow table pipelining has motivated researchers to provide corresponding high-level programming languages. For example, in [17], a typed programming language called Concurrent NetCore is proposed to specify flow tables. P4 [6] and POF [7] provide forwarding models with configurable flow table pipeline and programmable parsers. Jose et al. [6] study algorithms for mapping flow table designs to particular target switches [18, 19]. These languages, however, require programmers to explicitly specify low-level details of flow tables.

Another type of high-level programming is *reactive programming* [8, 20] which allows a controller to automatically identify switch configuration, generate flow tables, and populate flow rules. Maple [8] is a classic implementation of *reactive programming*. However, Maple is designed for switches with single flow table. Maple++ is an extension of Maple and supports flow table pipelining switches by addressing inherent issues in Maple.

Another trend in supporting heterogeneous switches is by providing a uniform API to controllers. For example, MACSAD [21, 22] aims at hiding data plane programming complexity by using P4 programming language while keeping the flexible data plane portability. TableVisor [23, 24], by providing a transparent proxy layer, allows pipeline processing and enables the extension of hardware flow table sizes using multiple hardware switches. These works focus on the switch side, whereas Maple++ focuses on the programming language.

6. Conclusion and Future Work

This paper explores an efficient and programmer-friendly SDN programming framework for state-of-the-art switches with flow table pipeline designs. We present novel techniques to compress the rule sets and to map them to flow table pipelines and show that the generated rule sets are highly compact on a variety of benchmarks using both simulated and real network workloads. This work can be optimized, for example, by utilizing priority numbers in generating rules.

Conflicts of Interest

The authors declare that there are no conflicts of interest regarding the publication of this article.

Acknowledgments

The authors are grateful to anonymous reviewers whose valuable comments helped to improve the quality of this paper. This work was supported in part by the National Natural Science Foundation of China under Grant No. 61602264, China Post-Doctoral Science Foundation under Grant No. 2017M611882, and Primary Research and Development Plan of Jiangsu Province under Grant No. BE2017743.

References

[1] B. Heller, S. Seetharaman, P. Mahadevan et al., "Elastictree: saving energy in data center networks," in *Proceedings of NSDI*, vol. 10, pp. 249–264, San Jose, CA, USA, April 2010.

[2] S. Jain, A. Kumar, S. Mandal et al., "B4: experience with a globally-deployed software defined wan," *ACM SIGCOMM Computer Communication Review*, vol. 43, no. 4, pp. 3–14, 2013.

[3] A. K. Nayak, A. Reimers, N. Feamster, and R. Clark, "Resonance: dynamic access control for enterprise networks," in *Proceedings of the 1st ACM workshop on Research on enterprise networking*, pp. 11–18, ACM, Barcelona, Spain, August 2009.

[4] R. Wang, D. Butnariu, and J. Rexford, "Openflow-based server load balancing gone wild," *China Communications*, vol. 11, no. 12, pp. 72–82, 2011.

[5] J. Reich, C. Monsanto, N. Foster, J. Rexford, and D. Walker, "Modular sdn programming with pyretic," Technical Report of USENIX, Berkeley, CA, USA, 2013.

[6] L. Jose, L. Yan, G. Varghese, and N. McKeown, "Compiling packet programs to reconfigurable switches," in *Proceedings of NSDI*, pp. 103–115, Oakland, CA, USA, May 2015.

[7] H. Song, "Protocol-oblivious forwarding: unleash the power of sdn through a future-proof forwarding plane," in *Proceedings of the Second ACM SIGCOMM Workshop on Hot Topics in Software Defined Networking, ser. HotSDN '13*, pp. 127–132, ACM, Hong Kong, China, August 2013.

[8] A. Voellmy, J. Wang, Y. R. Yang, B. Ford, and P. Hudak, "Maple: simplifying sdn programming using algorithmic policies," in *Proceedings of the ACM SIGCOMM 2013 Conference on SIGCOMM, ser. SIGCOMM'13*, pp. 87–98, ACM, Hong Kong, China, August 2013.

[9] A. Voellmy, S. Chen, X. Wang, and Y. R. Yang, "Magellan: generating multi-table datapath from datapath oblivious algorithmic sdn policies," in *Proceedings of the 2016 conference on ACM SIGCOMM 2016 Conference*, pp. 593-594, ACM, Florianopolis, Brazil, August 2016.

[10] A. Sivaraman, A. Cheung, M. Budiu et al., "Packet transactions: high-level programming for line-rate switches," in *Proceedings of the 2016 ACM SIGCOMM Conference*, pp. 15–28, ACM, Florianopolis, Brazil, August 2016.

[11] B. Limited, *Openflow Data Plane Abstraction (OF-DPA, Version 2)*, 2015, https://docs.broadcom.com/docs/12378911.

[12] Ryu SDN Controller, 2018, https://osrg.github.io/ryu/.

[13] POX SDN Controller, 2018, https://github.com/noxrepo/pox.

[14] Floodlight OpenFlow Controller, 2018, http://floodlight. openflowhub.org/.

[15] OpenDaylight, 2018, http://www.opendaylight.org.

[16] M. Al-Fares, A. Loukissas, and A. Vahdat, "A scalable, commodity data center network architecture," in *Proceedings of the ACM SIGCOMM 2008 Conference on Data Communication, ser. SIGCOMM'08*, pp. 63–74, ACM, Seattle, WA, USA, August 2008.

[17] C. Schlesinger, M. Greenberg, and D. Walker, "Concurrent netcore: from policies to pipelines," in *Proceedings of the 19th ACM SIGPLAN International Conference on Functional Programming, ser. ICFP'14*, pp. 11–24, ACM, Gothenburg, Sweden, September 2014.

[18] P. Bosshart, G. Gibb, H.-S. Kim et al., "Forwarding metamorphosis: fast programmable match-action processing in hardware for sdn," in *Proceedings of the ACM SIGCOMM 2013 Conference on SIGCOMM, ser. SIGCOMM'13*, pp. 99–110, ACM, Hong Kong, China, August 2013.

[19] R. Ozdag, *Intel Ethernet Switch FM6000 Series—Software Defined Networking*, 2016, http://www.intel.com/content/ dam/www/public/us/en/documents/white-papers/ethernet-switch-fm6000-sdn-paper.pdf.

[20] C. He and X. Feng, "Pomp: protocol oblivious sdn programming with automatic multi-table pipelining," in *Proceedings of the IEEE INFOCOM 2018-IEEE Conference on Computer Communications*, pp. 998–1006, IEEE, Honolulu, HI, USA, April 2018.

[21] P. G. Patra, C. E. Rothenberg, and G. Pongrácz, "Macsad: multi-architecture compiler system for abstract dataplanes (aka partnering p4 with odp)," in *Proceedings of the 2016 ACM SIGCOMM Conference*, pp. 623-624, ACM, Florianópolis, Brazil, August 2016.

[22] P. G. K. Patra, F. E. R. Cesen, J. S. Mejia et al., "Towards a sweet spot of dataplane programmability, portability and performance: on the scalability of multi-architecture P4 pipelines," *IEEE Journal on Selected Areas in Communications*, vol. 36, no. 6, pp. 3–14, 2018.

[23] S. Geissler, S. Herrnleben, R. Bauer, S. Gebert, T. Zinner, and M. Jarschel, "Tablevisor 2.0: towards full-featured, scalable and hardware-independent multi table processing," in *Proceedings of the IEEE Conference on Network Softwarization (NetSoft)*, pp. 1–8, Bologna, Italy, July 2017.

[24] S. Geissler and T. Zinner, "Tablevisor 2.0: hardware-independent multi table processing," in *Proceedings of the KuVS-Fachgespräch Fog Computing 2018*, p. 33, Darmstadt, Germany, March 2018.

8

Using Coarrays to Parallelize Legacy Fortran Applications: Strategy and Case Study

Hari Radhakrishnan,[1] Damian W. I. Rouson,[2] Karla Morris,[3] Sameer Shende,[4] and Stavros C. Kassinos[5]

[1]EXA High Performance Computing, 1087 Nicosia, Cyprus
[2]Stanford University, Stanford, CA 94305, USA
[3]Sandia National Laboratories, Livermore, CA 94550, USA
[4]University of Oregon, Eugene, OR 97403, USA
[5]Computational Sciences Laboratory (UCY-CompSci), University of Cyprus, 1678 Nicosia, Cyprus

Correspondence should be addressed to Damian W. I. Rouson; damian@rouson.net

Academic Editor: Jeffrey C. Carver

This paper summarizes a strategy for parallelizing a legacy Fortran 77 program using the object-oriented (OO) and coarray features that entered Fortran in the 2003 and 2008 standards, respectively. OO programming (OOP) facilitates the construction of an extensible suite of model-verification and performance tests that drive the development. Coarray parallel programming facilitates a rapid evolution from a serial application to a parallel application capable of running on multicore processors and many-core accelerators in shared and distributed memory. We delineate 17 code modernization steps used to refactor and parallelize the program and study the resulting performance. Our initial studies were done using the Intel Fortran compiler on a 32-core shared memory server. Scaling behavior was very poor, and profile analysis using TAU showed that the bottleneck in the performance was due to our implementation of a collective, sequential summation procedure. We were able to improve the scalability and achieve nearly linear speedup by replacing the sequential summation with a parallel, binary tree algorithm. We also tested the Cray compiler, which provides its own collective summation procedure. Intel provides no collective reductions. With Cray, the program shows linear speedup even in distributed-memory execution. We anticipate similar results with other compilers once they support the new collective procedures proposed for Fortran 2015.

1. Introduction

Background. Legacy software is old software that serves a useful purpose. In high-performance computing (HPC), a code becomes "old" when it no longer effectively exploits current hardware. With the proliferation of multicore processors and many-core accelerators, one might reasonably label any serial code as "legacy software." The software that has proved its utility over many years, however, typically has earned the trust of its user community.

Any successful strategy for modernizing legacy codes must honor that trust. This paper presents two strategies for parallelizing a legacy Fortran code while bolstering trust

in the result: (1) a test-driven approach that verifies the numerical results and the performance relative to the original code and (2) an evolutionary approach that leaves much of the original code intact while offering a clear path to execution on multicore and many-core architectures in shared and distributed memory.

The literature on modernizing legacy Fortran codes focuses on programmability issues such as increasing type safety and modularization while reducing data dependancies via encapsulation and information hiding. Achee and Carver [1] examined object extraction, which involves identifying candidate objects by analyzing the data flow in Fortran 77 code. They define a cohesion metric that they use to group global variables and parameters. They then extracted methods from the source code. In a 1500-line code, for example, they extract 26 candidate objects.

Norton and Decyk [2], on the other hand, focused on wrapping legacy Fortran with more modern interfaces. They then wrap the modernized interfaces inside an object/abstraction layer. They outline a step-by-step process that ensures standards compliance, eliminates undesirable features, creates interfaces, adds new capabilities, and then groups related abstractions into classes and components. Examples of undesirable features include **common** blocks, which potentially facilitate global data-sharing and aliasing of variable names and types. In Fortran, giving procedures explicit interfaces facilitates compiler checks on argument type, kind, and rank. New capabilities they introduced included dynamic memory allocation.

Greenough and Worth [3] surveyed tools that enhance software quality by helping to detect errors and to highlight poor practices. The appendices of their report provide extensive summaries of the tools available from eight vendors with a very wide range of capabilities. A sample of these capabilities includes memory leak detection, automatic vectorization and parallelization, dependency analysis, call-graph generation, and static (compile-time) as well as dynamic (run-time) correctness checking.

Each of the aforementioned studies explored how to update codes to the Fortran 90/95 standards. None of the studies explored subsequent standards and most did not emphasize performance improvement as a main goal. One recent study, however, applied automated code transformations in preparation for possible shared-memory, loop-level parallelization with OpenMP [4]. We are aware of no published studies on employing the Fortran 2008 coarray parallel programming to refactor a serial Fortran 77 application. Such a refactoring for parallelization purposes is the central aim of the current paper.

Case Study: PRM. Most commercial software models for turbulent flow in engineering devices solve the Reynolds-averaged Navier-Stokes (RANS) partial differential equations. Deriving these equations involves decomposing the fluid velocity field, $\mathbf{u}$, into a mean part, $\overline{\mathbf{u}}$, and a fluctuating part, $\mathbf{u}'$:

$$\mathbf{u} \equiv \overline{\mathbf{u}} + \mathbf{u}'. \tag{1}$$

Substituting (1) into a momentum balance and then averaging over an ensemble of turbulent flows yield the following RANS equation:

$$\rho \overline{u_j} \frac{\partial \overline{u_i}}{\partial x_j} = \rho \overline{f_i} + \frac{\partial}{\partial x_j}\left[-\overline{p}\delta_{ij} + \mu\left(\frac{\partial \overline{u_i}}{\partial x_j} + \frac{\partial \overline{u_j}}{\partial x_i} \right) - \rho\overline{u_i' u_j'} \right], \tag{2}$$

where μ is the fluid's dynamic viscosity; ρ is the fluid's density; t is the time coordinate; u_i and u_j are the ith and jth cartesian components of $\mathbf{u}$; and x_i and x_j are the ith and jth cartesian components of the spatial coordinate $\mathbf{x}$.

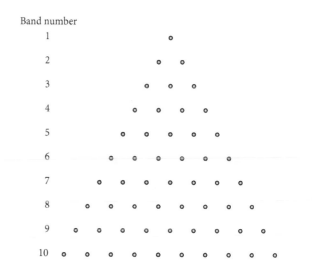

FIGURE 1: Distribution of particles in bands in one octant.

The term $-\rho\overline{u_i' u_j'}$ in (2) is called the Reynolds stress tensor. Its presence poses the chief difficulty at the heart of Reynolds-averaged turbulence modeling; closing the RANS equations requires postulating relations between the Reynolds stress and other terms appearing in the RANS equations, typically the velocity gradient $\partial \overline{u_j}/\partial x_i$ and scalars representing the turbulence scale. Doing so in the most common ways works well for predicting turbulent flows in which the statistics of $\mathbf{u}'$ stay in near-equilibrium with the flow deformations applied via gradients in $\overline{\mathbf{u}}$. Traditional RANS models work less well for flows undergoing deformations so rapid that the fluctuating field responds solely to the deformation without time for the nonlinear interactions with itself that are the hallmark of fluid turbulence. The Particle Representation Model (PRM) [5, 6] addresses this shortcoming. Given sufficient computing resources, a software implementation of the PRM can exactly predict the response of the fluctuating velocity field to rapid deformations.

A proprietary in-house software implementation of the PRM was developed initially at Stanford University, and development continued at the University of Cyprus. The PRM uses a set of hypothetical particles over a unit hemisphere surface. The particles are distributed on each octant of the hemisphere in bands, as shown in Figure 1 for ten bands. The total number of particles is given by

$$N_{\text{particles}} = \underbrace{4}_{\text{Number of octants in hemisphere}}$$

$$\times \underbrace{\frac{N_{\text{bands}} \times (N_{\text{bands}} + 1)}{2}}_{\text{Number of particles in one octant}} \tag{3}$$

$$= 2 \times N_{\text{bands}} \times (N_{\text{bands}} + 1).$$

So, the computational time scales quadratically with the number of bands used.

Each particle has a set of assigned properties that describe the characteristics of an idealized flow. Assigned particle properties include vector quantities such as velocity and

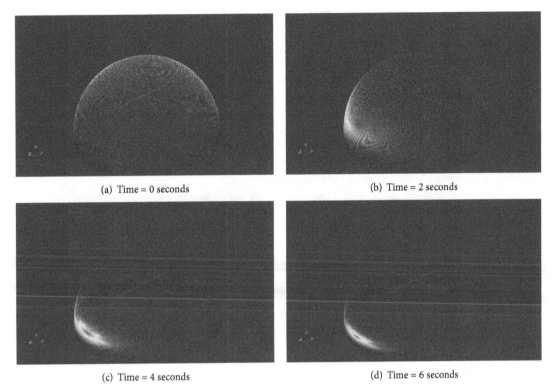

(a) Time = 0 seconds

(b) Time = 2 seconds

(c) Time = 4 seconds

(d) Time = 6 seconds

FIGURE 2: Results of a PRM computation. The particles are colored based on their initial location. The applied flow condition, shear flow along the y-direction, causes the uniformly distributed particles to aggregate along that axis.

orientation as well as scalar quantities such as pressure. Thus, each particle can be thought of as representing the dynamics of a hypothetical one-dimensional (1D), one-component (1C) flow. Tracking a sufficiently large number of particles and then averaging the properties of all the particles (as shown in Figure 2), that is, all the possible flows considered, yield a representation of the 3D behavior in an actual flowing fluid.

Historically, a key disadvantage of the PRM has been costly execution times because a very large number of particles are needed to accurately capture the physics of the flow. Parallelization can reduce this cost significantly. Previous attempts to develop a parallel implementation of the PRM using MPI were abandoned because the development, validation, and verification times did not justify the gains. Coarrays allowed us to parallelize the software with minimal invasiveness and the OO test suite facilitated a continuous build-and-test cycle that reduced the development time.

2. Methodology

2.1. Modernization Strategy. Test-Driven Development (TDD) grew out of the Extreme Programming movement of the 1990s, although the basic concepts date as far back as the NASA space program in the 1960s. TDD iterates quickly toward software solutions by first writing tests that specify what the working software must do and then writing only a sufficient amount of application code in order to pass the test. In the current context, TDD serves the purpose of ensuring that our refactoring exercise preserves the expected results for representative production runs.

Table 1 lists 17 steps employed in refactoring and parallelizing the serial implementation of the PRM. They have been broken down into groups that addressed various facets of the refactoring process. The open-source CTest framework that is part of CMake was used for building the tests. Our first step, therefore, was to construct a CMake infrastructure that we used for automated building and testing and to set up a code repository for version control and coordination.

The next six steps address Fortran 77 features that have been declared obsolete in more recent standards or have been deprecated in the Fortran literature. We did not replace **continue** statements with **end do** statements as these did not affect the functionality of the code.

The next two steps were crucial in setting up the build testing infrastructure. We automated the initialization by replacing the keyboard inputs with default values. The next step was to construct extensible tests based on these default values, which are described in Section 3.

The next three steps expose optimization opportunities to the compiler. One exploits Fortran's array syntax. Two exploit Fortran's facility for explicitly declaring a procedure to be "**pure**," that is, free of side effects, including input/output, modifying arguments, halting execution, or modifying non-local state. Other steps address type safety and memory management.

Array syntax gives the compiler a high-level view of operations on arrays in ways the compiler can exploit with various optimizations, including vectorization. The ability to communicate functional purity to compilers also enables numerous compiler optimizations, including parallelism.

TABLE 1: Modernization steps: horizontal lines indicate partial ordering.

Step	Details
1	Set up automated builds via CMake[1] and version control via Git[2].
2	Convert fixed- to free-source format via "convert.f90" by Metcalf[3].
3	Replace **goto** with **do while** for main loop termination.
4	Enforce type/kind/rank consistency of arguments and return values by wrapping all procedures in a **module**.
5	Eliminate implicit typing.
6	Replace **data** statements with **parameter** statements.
7	Replace write-access to **common** blocks with module variables.
8	Replace keyboard input with default initializations.
9	Set up automated, extensible tests for accuracy and performance via OOP and CTest[1].
10	Make all procedures outside of the main program **pure.**
11	Eliminate actual/dummy array shape inconsistencies by passing array subsections to assumed-shape arrays.
12	Replace static memory allocation with dynamic allocation.
13	Replace loops with array assignments.
14	Expose greater parallelism by unrolling the nested loops in the particle set-up.
15	Balance the work distribution by spreading particles across images during set-up.
16	Exploit a Fortran 2015 collective procedure to gather statistics.
17	Study and tune performance with TAU[4].

[1]http://www.cmake.org/.
[2]http://git-scm.com/.
[3]ftp://ftp.numerical.rl.ac.uk/pub/MandR/convert.f90.
[4]http://tau.uoregon.edu/.

The final steps directly address parallelism and optimization. One unrolls a loop to provide for more fine-grained data distribution. The other exploits the co_sum intrinsic collective procedure that is expected to be part of Fortran 2015 and is already supported by the Cray Fortran compiler. (With the Intel compiler, we write our own co_sum procedure.) The final step involves performance analysis using the Tuning and Analysis Utilities [7].

3. Extensible OO Test Suite

At every step, we ran a suite of accuracy tests to verify that the results of a representative simulation did not deviate from the serial code's results by more than 50 parts per million (ppm). We also ran a performance test to ensure that the single-image runtime of the parallel code did not exceed the serial code's runtime by more than 20%. (We allowed for some increase with the expectation that significant speedup would result from running multiple images.)

Our accuracy tests examine tensor statistics that are calculated using the PRM. In order to establish a uniform protocol for running tests, we defined an abstract base tensor class as shown in Listing 1.

The base class provided the bindings for comparing tensor statistics, displaying test results to the user, and exception handling. Specific tests take the form of three child classes, reynolds_stress, dimensionality, and circulicity, that extend the tensor class and thereby inherit a responsibility to implement the tensor's deferred bindings compute_results and expected_results. The class diagram is shown in Figure 3. The tests then take the form

if (.**not**. stess_tensor%verify_result (when)) &
    error stop 'Test_failed.'

where stress_tensor is an instance of one of the three child classes shown in Figure 3 that extend tensor; "when" is an integer time stamp; **error stop** halts all images and prints the shown string to standard error; and verify_result is the **pure** function shown in Listing 1 that invokes the two aforementioned deferred bindings to compare the computed results to the expected results.

4. Coarray Parallelization

Modern HPC software must be executed on multicore processors or many-core accelerators in shared or distributed memory. Fortran provides for such flexibility by defining a partitioned global address space (PGAS) without referencing how to map coarray code onto a particular architecture. Coarray Fortran is based on the Single Program Multiple Data (SPMD) model, and each replication of the program is called an image [8]. Fortran 2008 compilers map these images to an underlying transport network of the compiler's choice. For example, the Intel compiler uses MPI for the transport network whereas the Cray compiler uses a dedicated transport layer.

A coarray declaration of the form

real, **allocatable** :: a (:, :, :) [:]

facilitates indexing into the variable "a" along three regular dimensions and one codimension so

a (1, 1, 1) = a (1, 1, 1) [2]

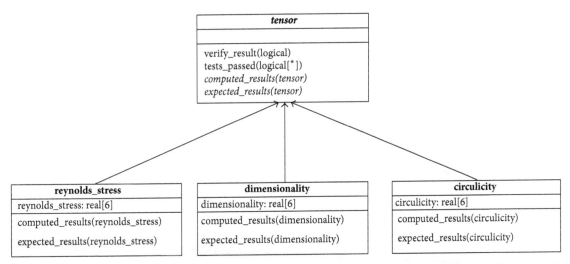

FIGURE 3: Class diagram of the testing framework. The deferred bindings are shown in italics, and the abstract class is shown in bold italics.

```
module abstract_tensor_class
  type, abstract :: tensor
  contains
    procedure(return_computed_results), deferred :: &
      computed_results
    procedure(return_expected_results), deferred :: &
      expected_results
    procedure :: verify_result
  end type
  abstract interface
    pure function return_computed_results(this) &
      result(computed_values)
      import :: tensor
      class(tensor), intent(in) :: this
      real, allocatable :: computed_values(:)
    end function
    ! return_expected_results interface omitted
  end abstract interface
contains
  pure function verify_result(this) &
    result(all_tests_passed)
    class(tensor), intent(in) :: this
    logical :: all_tests_passed
    all_tests_passed = all(tests_passed( &
      this%computed_results(), this%expected_results()))
  end function
end module
```

LISTING 1: Base tensor class.

```
l = 0 ! Global particle number
do k = 1, nb ! Loop over the bands
  do m = 1, k ! Loop over the particles in band
    ! First octant
    l = l + 1
    ! Do some computations
    ! Second octant
    l = l + 1
    ! Do some computations
    ! Third octant
    l = l + 1
    ! Do some computations
    ! Fourth octant
    l = l + 1
    ! Do some computations
  end do
end do
```

LISTING 2: Legacy particle loop.

necessary, adding coindices facilitated the construction of collective procedures to compute statistics.

In the legacy version, the computations of the particle properties were done using two nested loops, as shown in Listing 2.

Distributing the particles across the images and executing the computations inside these loops can speed up the execution time. This can be achieved in two ways.

Method 1 works with the particles directly, splitting them as evenly as possible across all the images, allowing image boundaries to occur in the middle of a band. This distribution is shown in Figure 4(a). To achieve this distribution, the two nested do loops are replaced by one loop over the particles, and the indices for the two original loops are computed from the global particle number, as shown in Listing 3. However in this case, the code becomes complex and sensitive to precision.

copies the first element of image 2 to the first element of whatever image executes this line. The ability to omit the coindex on the left-hand side (LHS) played a pivotal role in refactoring the serial code with minimal work; although we added codimensions to existing variables' declarations, subsequent accesses to those variables remained unmodified except where communication across images is desired. When

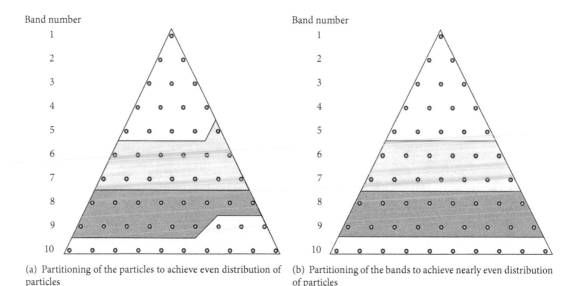

(a) Partitioning of the particles to achieve even distribution of particles

(b) Partitioning of the bands to achieve nearly even distribution of particles

FIGURE 4: Two different partitioning schemes were tried for load balancing.

```
! Loop over the particles
do l = my_first_particle, my_last_particle, 4
    k = nint(sqrt(real(l) * 0.5))
    m = (l − (1 + 2 * k * (k − 1) − 4))/4
        ! First octant
        ! Do some computations
        ! Second octant
        ! Do some computations
        ! Third octant
        ! Do some computations
        ! Fourth octant
        ! Do some computations
end do
```

LISTING 3: Parallel loop by splitting particles.

Method 2 works with the bands, splitting them across the images to make the particle distribution as even as possible. This partitioning is shown in Figure 4(b). Method 2, as shown in Listing 4, requires fewer changes to the original code shown in Listing 2 but is suboptimal in load balancing.

5. Results

5.1. Source Code Impact. We applied our strategy to two serial software implementations of the PRM. For one version, the resulting code was 10% longer than the original: 639 lines versus 580 lines with no test suite. In the second version, the code expanded 40% from 903 lines to 1260 lines, not including new input/output (I/O) code and the test code described in Section 3. The test and I/O code occupied additional 569 lines.

5.2. Ease of Use: Coarrays versus MPI. The ability to drop the coindex from the notation, as explained in Section 4, was a big

```
! Loop over the bands
do k = my_first_band, my_last_band
        ! Global number
        ! of last particle in (k − 1) band
        l = k ** 2 + (k − 1) ** 2 − 1
        ! Loop over the particles in band
    do m = 1, k
        ! First octant
        l = l + 1
        ! Do some computations
        ! Second octant
        l = l + 1
        ! Do some computations
        ! Third octant
        l = l + 1
        ! Do some computations
        ! Fourth octant
        l = l + 1
        ! Do some computations
    end do
end do
```

LISTING 4: Parallel loop by splitting bands.

help in parallelizing the program without making significant changes to the source code. A lot of the bookkeeping is handled behind the scenes by the compiler making it possible to make the parallelization more abstract but also easier to follow. For example, Listing 5 shows the MPI calls necessary to gather the local arrays into a global array on all the processors.

The equivalent calls using the coarray syntax is the listing shown in Listing 6.

Reducing the complexity of the code also reduces the chances of bugs in the code. In the legacy code, the arrays

```
integer :: my_rank, num_procs
integer, allocatable, dimension(:) :: &
    my_first, my_last, counts, displs
call mpi_comm_size(MPI_COMM_WORLD, num_procs, ierr)
call mpi_comm_rank(MPI_COMM_WORLD, my_rank, ierr)
allocate(my_first(num_procs), my_last(num_procs), &
    counts(num_procs), displs(num_procs))
my_first(my_rank + 1) = lbound(sn, 2)
my_last(my_rank + 1) = ubound(sn, 2)
call mpi_allgather(MPI_IN_PLACE, 1, MPI_INTEGER, &
    my_first, 1, MPI_INTEGER, MPI_COMM_WORLD, ierr)
call mpi_allgather(MPI_IN_PLACE, 1, MPI_INTEGER, &
    my_last, 1, MPI_INTEGER, MPI_COMM_WORLD, ierr)
do i = 1, num_procs
    displs(i) = my_first(i) − 1
    counts(i) = my_last(i) − my_first(i) + 1
end do
call mpi_allgatherv(sn, 5 * counts(my_rank + 1), &
    MPI_DOUBLE_PRECISION, sn_global, 5 * counts, &
    5 * displs, MPI_DOUBLE_PRECISION, MPI_COMM_WORLD, ierr)
call mpi_allgatherv(cr, 5 * counts(my_rank + 1), &
    MPI_DOUBLE_PRECISION, cr_global, 5 * counts, &
    5 * displs, MPI_DOUBLE_PRECISION, MPI_COMM_WORLD, ierr)
```

LISTING 5: Using MPI_ALLGATHER to collect local arrays into a global array.

```
integer :: my_first[*], my_last[*]
my_first = lbound(sn, 2)
my_last = ubound(sn, 2)
do l = 1, num_images()
    cr_global(:, my_first[l]:my_last[l]) = cr(:,:)[l]
    sn_global(:, my_first[l]:my_last[l]) = sn(:,:)[l]
end do
```

LISTING 6: Coarray method of gathering arrays.

sn and *cr* carried the information about the state of the particles. By using the coarray syntax and dropping the coindex, we were able to reuse all the original algorithms that implemented the core logic of the PRM. This made it significantly easier to ensure that the refactoring did not alter the results of the model. The main changes were to add codimensions to the *sn* and *cr* declarations and update them when needed, as shown in Listing 6.

5.3. Scalability. We intend for PRM to serve as an alternative to turbulence models used in routine engineering design of fluid devices. There is no significant difference in the PRM results when more than 1024 bands (approximately 2.1 million particles) are used to represent the flow state so this was chosen as the upper limit of the size of our data set. Most engineers and designers run simulations on desktop computers. As such, the upper bound on what is commonly available is roughly 32 to 48 cores on two or four central processing units (CPUs) plus additional cores on one or more accelerators. We also looked at the scaling performance of parallel implementation of the PRM using Cray hardware and Fortran compiler which has excellent support for distributed-memory execution of coarray programs.

Figure 5 shows the speedup obtained for 200 and 400 bands with the Intel Fortran compiler using the two particle-distribution schemes described in the Coarray Parallelization section. The runs were done using up to 32 cores on the "fat" nodes of ACISS (http://aciss-computing.uoregon.edu/). Each node has four Intel X7560 2.27 GHz 8-core CPUs and 384 GB of DDR3 memory. We see that the speedup was very poor when the number of processors was increased.

We used TAU [7] to profile the parallel runs to understand the bottlenecks during execution. Figure 6 shows the TAU plot for the runtime share for the dominant procedures using different number of images. Figure 7 shows the runtimes for the different functions on the different images. The heights of the columns show the runtime for different functions on the individual cores. There is no significant difference in the heights of the columns proving that the load balancing is very good across the images. We achieved this by mainly using the one-sided communication protocols of CAF as shown in Listing 6 and restricting the sync statements to the collective procedures as shown in Listings 7 and 8. Looking at the runtimes in Figure 6, we identified the chief bottlenecks to be the two collective co_sum procedures which sum values across a coarray by sequentially polling each image for its portion of the coarray. The time required for this procedure

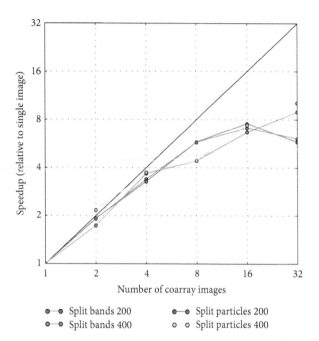

FIGURE 5: Speedup obtained with sequential co_sum implementation using multiple images on a single server.

```
subroutine vector_co_sum_parallel(vector)
  real(rkind), intent(inout) :: vector(:)[*]
  real(rkind), allocatable :: temp(:)
  integer image, step
  allocate (temp, mold = vector)
  step = 2
  do while (step/2 <= num_images())
    sync all
    if (this_image() + step/2 <= num_images()) then
      temp = vector + vector[this_image() + step/2]
    else
      temp = vector
    end if
    sync all
    vector = temp
    step = step * 2
  end do
  sync all
  if (this_image()/ = 1) vector = vector[1]
  sync all
end subroutine
```

LISTING 8: Optimized collective sum routine.

```
subroutine vector_co_sum_serial(vector)
  real(rkind), intent(inout) :: vector(:)[*]
  integer image
  sync all
  if (this_image() == 1) then
    do image = 2, num_images()
      vector(:)[1] = vector(:)[1] + vector(:)[image]
    end do
  end if
  sync all
  if (this_image()/ = 1) vector(:) = vector(:)[1]
  sync all
end subroutine
```

LISTING 7: Unoptimized collective sum routine.

is $O(N_{\text{images}})$. The unoptimized co_sum routine for adding a vector across all images is shown in Listing 7. There is an equivalent subroutine for summing a matrix also.

Designing an optimal co_sum algorithm is a platform-dependent exercise best left to compilers. The Fortran standards committee is working on a co_sum intrinsic procedure that will likely become part of Fortran 2015. But to improve the parallel performance of the program, we rewrote the collective co_sum procedures using a binomial tree algorithm that is $O(\log N_{\text{images}})$ in time. The optimized version of the co_sum version is shown in Listing 8.

The speedup obtained with the optimized co_sum routine is shown in Figure 8. We see that the scaling performance of the program becomes nearly linear with the implementation of the optimized co_sum routine. We also see that the scaling

efficiency increases when the problem size is increased. This indicates that the poor scaling at smaller problem sizes is due to communication and synchronization [9].

The TAU profile analysis of the runs using different number of images is shown in Figure 9. While there is a small increase in the co_sum computation time when increasing the number of images, it is significantly lower than increase in time for the unoptimized version.

To fully understand the impact of the co_sum routines, we also benchmarked the program using the Cray compiler and hardware. Cray has native support for the co_sum directive in the compiler. Cray also uses its own communication library on Cray hardware instead of building on top of MPI as is done by the Intel compiler. As we can see in Figure 10, the parallel code showed very good strong scaling on the Cray hardware up to 128 images for the problem sizes that we tested.

We also looked at the TAU profiles of the parallel code on the Cray hardware, shown in Figure 11. The profile analysis shows that the time is spent mainly in the time advancement loop when the native co_sum implementation is used.

We hope that, with the development and implementation of intrinsic co_sum routines as part of the 2015 Fortran standard, the Intel compiler will also improve its strong scaling performance with larger number of images. Table 2 shows the raw runtimes for the different runs using 128 bands whose TAU profiles have been shown in Figures 6, 9, and 11. The runtimes for one to four images are very close but they quickly diverge as we increase the number of images due to the impact of the collective procedures.

Table 3 shows the weak scaling performance of the program using the optimized co_sum procedures using the Intel compiler. The number of particles as shown in Figure 1 scales as the square of the number of bands. Therefore, when

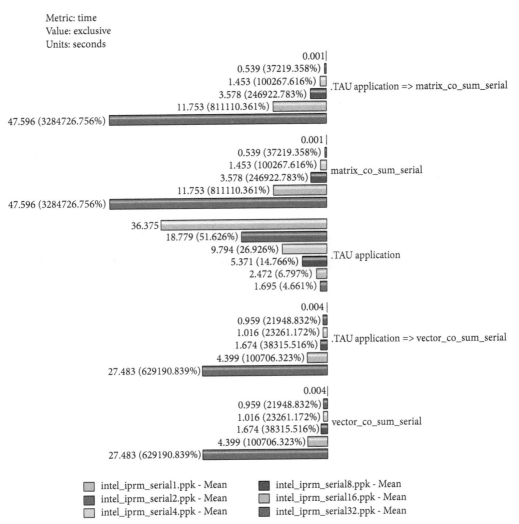

Metric: time
Value: exclusive
Units: seconds

0.001|
0.539 (37219.358%)
1.453 (100267.616%)
3.578 (246922.783%)   .TAU application => matrix_co_sum_serial
11.753 (811110.361%)
47.596 (3284726.756%)

0.001|
0.539 (37219.358%)
1.453 (100267.616%)
3.578 (246922.783%)   matrix_co_sum_serial
11.753 (811110.361%)
47.596 (3284726.756%)

36.375
18.779 (51.626%)
9.794 (26.926%)
5.371 (14.766%)   .TAU application
2.472 (6.797%)
1.695 (4.661%)

0.004|
0.959 (21948.832%)
1.016 (23261.172%)
1.674 (38315.516%)   .TAU application => vector_co_sum_serial
4.399 (100706.323%)
27.483 (629190.839%)

0.004|
0.959 (21948.832%)
1.016 (23261.172%)
1.674 (38315.516%)   vector_co_sum_serial
4.399 (100706.323%)
27.483 (629190.839%)

□ intel_iprm_serial1.ppk - Mean	■ intel_iprm_serial8.ppk - Mean
■ intel_iprm_serial2.ppk - Mean	□ intel_iprm_serial16.ppk - Mean
□ intel_iprm_serial4.ppk - Mean	■ intel_iprm_serial32.ppk - Mean

FIGURE 6: TAU profiling analysis of function runtimes when using the unoptimized co_sum routines with 1, 2, 4, 8, 16, and 32 images. The *TAU application* is the main program wrapped by TAU for profiling, and *.TAU application =>* refers to functions wrapped by TAU. This notation is also seen in Figures 7 and 9.

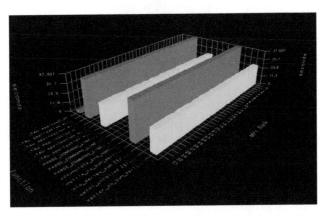

FIGURE 7: TAU analysis of load balancing and bottlenecks for the parallel code using 32 images.

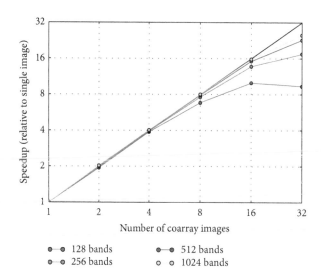

FIGURE 8: Speedup obtained with parallel co_sum implementation using multiple images on a single server.

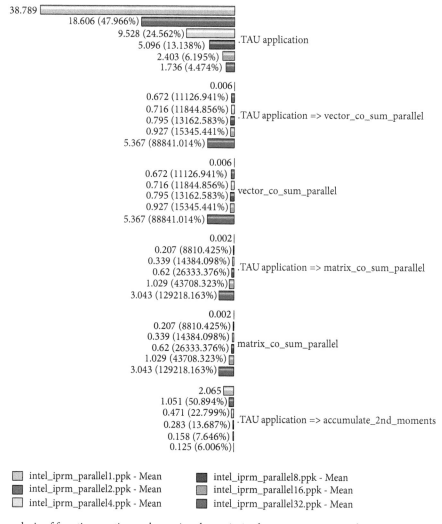

FIGURE 9: TAU profiling analysis of function runtimes when using the optimized co_sum routines with 1, 2, 4, 8, 16, and 32 images.

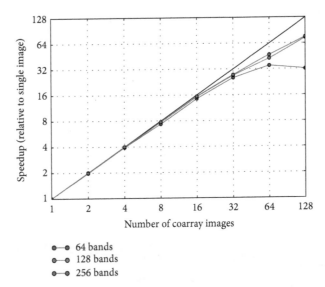

FIGURE 10: Speedup obtained with parallel co_sum implementation using multiple images on a distributed-memory Cray cluster.

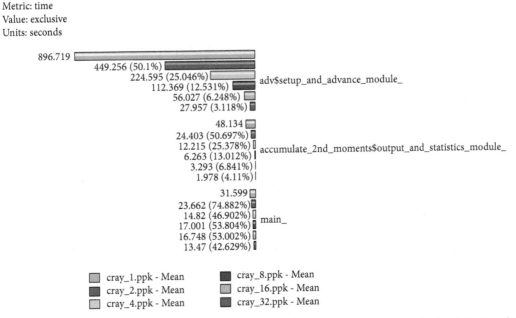

FIGURE 11: TAU profiling analysis of function runtimes when using the Cray native co_sum routines with 1, 2, 4, 8, 16, and 32 images.

doubling the number of bands, the number of processors must be quadrupled to have the same execution time. The scaling efficiency for the larger problem drops because of memory requirements; the objects fit in the heap and must be swapped out as needed, increasing the execution time.

6. Conclusions and Future Work

We demonstrated a strategy for parallelizing legacy Fortran 77 codes using Fortran 2008 coarrays. The strategy starts with constructing extensible tests using Fortran's OOP features. The tests check for regressions in accuracy and performance. In the PRM case study, our strategy expanded two Fortran 77 codes by 10% and 40%, exclusive of the test and I/O infrastructure. The most significant code revision involved unrolling two nested loops that distribute particles across images. The resulting parallel code achieves even load balancing but poor scaling. TAU identified the chief bottleneck as a sequential summation scheme.

Based on these preliminary results, we rewrote our co_sum procedure, and the speedup showed marked improvement. We also benchmarked the native co_sum implementation available in the Cray compiler. Our results show that the natively supported collective procedures show the best scaling performance even when using distributed memory. We hope that future native support for collective

TABLE 2: Runtime in seconds for parallel using 128 bands, and different collective sum routines.

	Number of Images					
	1	2	4	8	16	32
Intel Serial co_sum	35.55	19.80	11.69	9.73	18.71	66.82
Intel Parallel co_sum	37.30	19.33	10.00	6.17	4.62	5.41
Cray Native co_sum	46.71	23.68	11.88	6.06	3.06	1.73

TABLE 3: Weak scaling performance of coarray version.

Number of images	Number of bands	Number of particles	Particles per image	Time in seconds	Runtime per particle	Efficiency
1	128	33024	33024	44.279	1.34×10^{-3}	1.000
4	256	131584	32896	44.953	1.37×10^{-3}	0.978
16	512	525312	32832	49.400	1.50×10^{-3}	0.893
2	256	131584	65792	101.03	1.54×10^{-3}	1.000
8	512	525312	65664	102.11	1.56×10^{-3}	0.987
32	1024	2099200	65600	129.75	1.98×10^{-3}	0.777

procedures in Fortran 2015 by all the compilers will bring such performance to all platforms.

Conflict of Interests

The authors declare that there is no conflict of interests regarding the publication of this paper.

Acknowledgments

The initial code refactoring was performed at the University of Cyprus with funding from the European Commission Marie Curie ToK-DEV grant (Contract MTKD-CT-2004-014199). Part of this work was also supported by the Cyprus Research Promotion Foundation's Framework Programme for Research, Technological Development and Innovation 2009-2010 (ΔΕΣΜΗ 2009-2010) under Grant ΤΠΕ/ΠΛΗΡΟ/0609(ΒΕ)/11. This work used resources of the National Energy Research Scientific Computing Center, which is supported by the Office of Science of the U.S. Department of Energy under Contract no. DE-AC02-05CH11231. This work also used hardware resources from the ACISS cluster at the University of Oregon acquired by a Major Research Instrumentation grant from the National Science Foundation, Office of Cyber Infrastructure, "MRI-R2: Acquisition of an Applied Computational Instrument for Scientific Synthesis (ACISS)," Grant no. OCI-0960354. This research was also supported by Sandia National Laboratories a multiprogram laboratory operated by Sandia Corporation, a Lockheed Martin Company, for the National Nuclear Security Administration under Contract DE-AC04-94-AL85000. Portions of the Sandia contribution to this work were funded by the New Mexico Small Business Administration and the Office of Naval Research.

References

[1] B. L. Achee and D. L. Carver, "Creating object-oriented designs from legacy FORTRAN code," *Journal of Systems and Software*, vol. 39, no. 2, pp. 179–194, 1997.

[2] C. D. Norton and V. K. Decyk, "Modernizing Fortran 77 legacy codes," *NASA Tech Briefs*, vol. 27, no. 9, p. 72, 2003.

[3] C. Greenough and D. J. Worth, "The transformation of legacy software: some tools and processes," Tech. Rep. TR-2004-012, Council for the Central Laboratory of the Research Councils, Rutherford Appleton Laboratories, Oxfordshire, UK, 2004.

[4] F. G. Tinetti and M. Méndez, "Fortran Legacy software: source code update and possible parallelisation issues," *ACM SIGPLAN Fortran Forum*, vol. 31, no. 1, pp. 5–22, 2012.

[5] S. C. Kassinos and W. C. Reynolds, "A particle representation model for the deformation of homogeneous turbulence," in *Annual Research Briefs*, pp. 31–61, Center for Turbulence Research, Stanford University, Stanford, Calif, USA, 1996.

[6] S. C. Kassinos and E. Akylas, "Advances in particle representation modeling of homogeneous turbulence. from the linear PRM version to the interacting viscoelastic IPRM," in *New Approaches in Modeling Multiphase Flows and Dispersion in Turbulence, Fractal Methods and Synthetic Turbulence*, F. Nicolleau, C. Cambon, J.-M. Redondo, J. Vassilicos, M. Reeks, and A. Nowakowski, Eds., vol. 18 of *ERCOFTAC Series*, pp. 81–101, Springer, Dordrecht, The Netherlands, 2012.

[7] S. S. Shende and A. D. Malony, "The TAU parallel performance system," *International Journal of High Performance Computing Applications*, vol. 20, no. 2, pp. 287–311, 2006.

[8] M. Metcalf, J. K. Reid, and M. Cohen, *Modern Fortran Explained*, Oxford University Press, 2011.

[9] H. Radhakrishnan, D. W. I. Rouson, K. Morris, S. Shende, and S. C. Kassinos, "Test-driven coarray parallelization of a legacy Fortran application," in *Proceedings of the 1st International Workshop on Software Engineering for High Performance Computing in Computational Science and Engineering*, pp. 33–40, ACM, November 2013.

9

MPI to Coarray Fortran: Experiences with a CFD Solver for Unstructured Meshes

Anuj Sharma and Irene Moulitsas

School of Aerospace, Transport and Manufacturing (SATM), Cranfield University, Cranfield, Bedfordshire MK43 0AL, UK

Correspondence should be addressed to Anuj Sharma; a.sharma@cranfield.ac.uk

Academic Editor: Can Özturan

High-resolution numerical methods and unstructured meshes are required in many applications of Computational Fluid Dynamics (CFD). These methods are quite computationally expensive and hence benefit from being parallelized. Message Passing Interface (MPI) has been utilized traditionally as a parallelization strategy. However, the inherent complexity of MPI contributes further to the existing complexity of the CFD scientific codes. The Partitioned Global Address Space (PGAS) parallelization paradigm was introduced in an attempt to improve the clarity of the parallel implementation. We present our experiences of converting an unstructured high-resolution compressible Navier-Stokes CFD solver from MPI to PGAS Coarray Fortran. We present the challenges, methodology, and performance measurements of our approach using Coarray Fortran. With the Cray compiler, we observe Coarray Fortran as a viable alternative to MPI. We are hopeful that Intel and open-source implementations could be utilized in the future.

1. Introduction

1.1. Motivation. While it is the dominant communication paradigm, Message Passing Interface (MPI) has received its share of criticism in the High-Performance Computing (HPC) community. It provides a complex interface to parallel programming, which is mostly underutilised by researchers whose primary skill is not software development. Maintenance and modernization of parallel codes written with MPI also require more person-hours and associated funding costs compared to the serial counterpart [1].

In parallel programming, details of communication strategies should not overbear the researchers, to avoid shifting their focus from the core research objective. Unfortunately, it has been observed that hardware advancements do not come hand in hand with better performances. Scientific codes utilizing the MPI paradigm have to be modified in order to achieve the best possible performance gains. With the goal of Exascale computing, both the underlying hardware and the software tools available should support the scientific numerical codes so that they are efficiently adaptable to future computing platforms. Discussing the efficiency of a scientific code is a twofold matter and it should involve both the effort put during the development or reengineering phase, as well as the performance gains observed later.

Recently, Partitioned Global Address Space (PGAS) based parallel programming languages have been gaining popularity. Several languages such as Unified Parallel C (UPC), Coarray Fortran, Fortress, Chapel, and X10 are based on the PGAS paradigm. In comparison to many of its competitors, Coarray Fortran is relatively mature and has undergone considerable research [2]. It provides a natural syntax to Fortran programmers and generates a lucid code.

1.2. Related Work. Coarray Fortran was originally a small syntactic extension (F−) to the Fortran programming language, which enabled parallel programming. It is now part of the Fortran programming language since the adoption of the Fortran 2008 standards. Some features, such as collective intrinsic routines, teams, and error handling of failed images, were left out in Fortran 2008 standards. With the acceptance of the technical specification document, they will become standard in Fortran 2015 [3].

Like other PGAS languages, Coarray Fortran provides language constructs equivalent to one-sided communication during run-time. This feature improves productivity and could also harness the communication features of the underlying hardware. Some studies have been performed to quantify the effort and performance of such PGAS languages, most notably in the PRACE-PP (Partnership for Advanced Computing in Europe-Preparatory Phase) project. It involved the development of three benchmark cases by different researchers and collecting the feedback of development time (effort) and performance [2]. While Chapel and X10 were found to be immature, UPC and Coarray Fortran were recommended due to their performance, low development time, and relative maturity.

Coarray Fortran is today supported by Cray with extended features and by Intel with compatibility with Fortran standards [4]. Open-source compilers are also in different development stages, such as the GCC compiler (OpenCoarrays [5]) and OpenUH [6].

Over the years many benchmark studies have been performed [7–12] to investigate the performance of Coarray Fortran in comparison to MPI. In [7] Numrich et al. suggest MPI has high bandwidth, but high latency for messages. In contrast, Coarray Fortran has low bandwidth and low latency for messages. This behavior is dependent upon support for remote direct access, by the underlying hardware architecture. The overall performance comparison of MPI and Coarray Fortran is murky with contradicting results, such as, for example, by [7, 8]. The contradiction in the better performance could be attributed to the different communication requirements of various scientific codes. Other studies have focused on individual aspects of parallel programming, that is, memory layout [9], use of derived data types [9], buffered/unbuffered data transfer [10], object-oriented programming [13], and collective communication constructs [11]. One-sided communication with Coarray Fortran has also shown promising result for heterogeneous load balancing on the Intel Xeon Phi architecture [14].

1.3. Objective.
Computational Fluid Dynamics (CFD) studies of complex flows in a wide range of applications certainly benefit from parallelization due to the high computational costs of the numerical methods employed. Recent performance studies in the literature have only focused on numerical codes with structured meshes. These codes have natural, geometry driven, grid partitioning, and regular communication patterns. In many scientific domains, where complex geometries are involved, unstructured meshes are the norm. These meshes lead to nonintuitive mesh partitionings, have greater load imbalances, and suffer from nonregular communication patterns. When higher-order numerical schemes are required, the complexity of the communication patterns and associated data structures increases even more. In our study, we present our experience of converting a scientific numerical CFD code with unstructured meshes and higher-order numerical schemes from MPI to Coarray Fortran for parallel communication.

```
Real :: i(5), j(5)[*], k(5)[4,*], l[*]
real, codimension[*] :: m
```

LISTING 1: Coarray declaration.

2. Overview

2.1. Coarray Fortran.
Coarray Fortran is based on the Single Program Multiple Data (SPMD) model of parallel programming [15, 16]. A set of independent instances of the program, called *images*, executes simultaneously on different processors. The number of *images* can be chosen at compile or run-time and has a unique index (1 to number-of-processors). Fortran standards provide two intrinsic functions - this_image() and num_images() to retrieve the *image* index and the total number of *images*, respectively.

2.1.1. Coarrays.
A *coarray* is similar to an array in Fortran, that is, a collection of data objects, with an exception that it can be accessed by other *images* as well. In comparison, a regular array is private to the parent *image*. *Coarrays* are declared using an additional trailing subscript in square brackets, [], referred as *codimensions*. A *coarray* has *corank*, *coshape*, and *cobounds* similar to corresponding terms for an array. Intrinsic functions to find lower and upper cobounds are lcobound, ucobound. Examples for different types of valid *coarray* declaration are shown in Listing 1. While i is not a *coarray*; j, k, l, and m are *coarrays*. j and k are *coarray* of an array (with 5 elements). l and m are scalar *coarrays*. The upper *cobound* of the last *codimension* for a *coarray* is always defined as *, whose value is dependent upon the number of *images* specified during execution. In Listing 1, the upper *cobound* of j, l, and m would be equal to number of images, while the upper *cobound* of k would be equal to num_image()/4.

2.1.2. Allocatable Coarrays.
An allocatable *coarray* could be used to define the *codimensions* at run-time (see Listing 2). *Cobounds* must be specified, and upper *cobound* should be *. Deallocate statement is similar to that of an allocatable array in Fortran language. To declare an allocatable *coarray*, the code in Listing 2 can be used.

Also, the same allocate statement should be executed by all *images* (same *bounds* and *cobounds*); thus *coarrays* cannot have different sizes for different *images*. This limitation is not significant if the data arrays that are used for communication are of equal length on all the images, such as in structured mesh applications. With unstructured meshes and especially with higher-order numerical schemes such as WENO (Weighted Essentially Nonoscillatory), the length of communication array varies widely. To overcome this limitation, derived data types could be used as shown in Listing 3.

2.1.3. Communication: Push versus Pull.
Data is remotely accessed using *codimensions* without the conventional *send*

```
real, allocatable :: o[:,:]
...
allocate(o) !Not allowed - coubounds should be specified
allocate(o[2,3]) ! Not allowed - upper cobound should be *
allocate(o[2,*]) ! Allowed
...
deallocate(o)
```

LISTING 2: Coarray declaration of an allocatable coarray.

```
type CoData
  integer :: myrank
  real, allocatable :: sol(:)
end type
...
type (CoData), allocatable :: Image[:]
...
allocate(Image[*]) !Allocate derived data type for all
    images
...
allocate( Image%sol(storeSize) ) !storeSize could have
    different values on all images
...
deallocate(Image)
```

LISTING 3: Coarray declaration of an allocatable, derived data object coarray.

and *receive* messages used in MPI. To copy data from another *image* using a *coarray*, either *pull* or *push* approach can be used. In the *pull* approach, data is received from another *image*. That is, to copy from the next *image*, one could use Listing 4.

Note that a *coarray* reference without [] indicates a reference to the variable in the current *image*. Similarly, to *push* some data to the next *image*, one may use Listing 5.

Similarly, for an allocatable, derived data type *coarray*, one may use the Listing 6 to *push* data to the next *image*. Usually, the choice between push and pull approach is based on the algorithm used.

2.1.4. Synchronization. As the *images* run asynchronously, care must be taken to maintain correct execution order by specifying explicit synchronization statements. All the participant *images* must execute this statement before any *image* can proceed forward. Synchronization statements are `sync all` (to synchronize all *images*) and `sync images` (for selective synchronization). Implicit synchronization takes place during allocation and deallocation of allocatable *coarrays*.

2.2. CFD Solver. Our CFD solver is an unstructured mesh, finite volume Navier-Stokes solver for compressible flows, supporting mixed element meshes. In certain situations, the compressible nature of the fluid results in shock waves, with a sharp interface between regions of distinct properties such as density and pressure. These flows are commonly encountered in aerospace applications. To avoid prediction of a diffused interface and to predict the shock strength accurately using a CFD solver, higher-order numerical schemes are essential [17].

In a cell-centered finite volume solver, such as ours, the cell volume averaged solution (with either conserved or characteristic variable) is stored at the center of the cells in the mesh. If these cell-averaged values are used for the intercell flux calculations in the iterative solver to determine the solution at next time step or iteration, then first-order spatial accuracy is achieved. For greater accuracy, conservative and higher-order reconstruction polynomial is used. The neighboring cells which are used for calculating the reconstruction polynomial define the zone of influence and are collectively known as the stencil. The order of accuracy of the reconstruction is dependent upon the size of the stencil, while the reconstruction provides greater accuracy in the regions with smooth solutions; near sharp discontinuities such polynomials are inherently oscillatory [18–20].

In the traditional Total Variation Diminishing (TVD) schemes, the oscillatory nature of the polynomial near a discontinuity is kept under control by using slope or flux limiters. Thus, resulting schemes, such as MUSCL scheme (Monotonic Upstream-Centered Scheme for Conservation Laws), have higher-order accuracy in the region with smooth

```
if( this_image().ne. num_images() ) then
  j(:) = j(:)[this_image()+1]
end if
```

LISTING 4: Coarray communication: pull approach.

```
if( this_image().ne. num_images() ) then
  j(:)[this_image()+1] = j(:)
end if
```

LISTING 5: Coarray communication: push approach.

solutions while accuracy is lowered in regions with sharp or discontinuous solution.

The WENO scheme aims to provide higher-order accuracy throughout the domain by using multiple reconstruction polynomials with solution adaptive nonlinear weighting. The WENO scheme uses one central stencil and several directional stencils to construct the reconstruction polynomial. Higher weighting is given to smoother reconstruction polynomial among the directional stencils, and the highest weighting is given to the central stencil. The nonlinear weights are thus solution adaptive.

Details of the implementation of the CFD solver are provided in [19]. The MPI version of the solver has been used in previous studies for solving Euler equations [18] and compressible Navier-Stokes equations [19].

3. Conversion to Coarray Fortran

The MPI version of the code uses different derived data types to store the values of the solution variables and the associated mesh data. Since the code uses unstructured meshes and the WENO scheme, it has inherent load imbalance due to stencils of varying lengths. To accommodate the imbalanced memory storage, derived data type *coarrays* with allocatable components are essential; according to the Fortran 2008 standard, *coarrays* of standard data types must have the same size on all the *images*.

For simplicity, a generic naming scheme in the following text to explain the modifications required in the code to incorporate communication with Coarray Fortran.

Let us say, in an *image* or a process, the child data (i.e., the allocatable array) which should be sent is SendData and the parent data (i.e., the allocatable array of derived data type) holding many such SendData is SendArray. Similarly, let the array names for the receiving child data and parent data type be ReceiveData and ReceiveArray.

In the MPI version, every process has its SendArray and ReceiveArray which also hold the process numbers to which the data is to be sent, and from which process the data is to be received. The memory location at which data is to be sent is not stored in the sending process. In the combined

send receive MPI subroutine, MPI_SendRecv, a process sends data as a message which is received by another process, which decides where the data is to be saved (see Figure 1).

In the MPI version, respective SendData is sent to all the receivers among all the processes. When this data is received, the received data is stored in ReceiveData by all the receiving processes.

3.1. Construction of Communication Array. To incorporate the Coarray Fortran communication, with minimal changes to the original data structure and to avoid any additional memory copies before and after communication, an additional communication array was created.

Since push communication was needed in the Coarray Fortran version as well, the location of the ReceiveData in ReceiveArray should be known to the sender. To store this location, an additional array was created, referenced in the code as CommArr *, where * denotes a number specified to set different variable apart. For this discussion, let us give it a generic name, CommArr, and call it as communication array.

An initialization subroutine is called once before the communication subroutine to find the ReceiveData location for a receiving image. This information is stored in every sender image. Communication with Coarray Fortran becomes simpler once the CommArr is set up. A sender image now directly transfers data to a receiver image's memory using Coarray Fortran syntax (see Figure 2).

3.2. Working of the Communication Array. CommArr provides connectivity between the SendArray of the sender image and ReceiveArray of the receiving images. Along with other data, SendArray also stores the index of the receiving image. Thus, it also serves as an input for the CommArr array, which stores the position at which receive image has allocated memory for receiving the data. Since Fortran 2008 standard requires same coarray bounds, CommArr has an upper bound equal to the number of processes, and empty values in CommArr are filled with −1.

Figure 3 explains the working of communication array using two examples shown by solid and dashed lines. In the first example, *Image* 1 needs to send data to *Images* 2, 3, and

```
if( this_image().ne. num_images() ) then
    Image[this_image()+1]%sol(:) = Image%sol(:)
end if
```

LISTING 6: Coarray communication: push approach with a derived data type coarray.

4. While sending data to *Image* 3, *Image* 1 uses `CommArr`. At location 3, `CommArr` of *Image* 1 stores 1. This is the location at which data need to be sent to the receiving *Image* 3. In the second example, *Image* 3 sends data to *Image* 4. `CommArr` of *Image* 3 store 2 at position 4. 2 is the position at which the receiving *Image* 4 will receive the data.

4. Tests

4.1. Physical Case. A 2D, external flow, test case was chosen for validation and performance measurements. In this test case, air flow over RAE2822 aerofoil in steady, turbulent conditions was modeled in the transonic regime. The computational domain boundaries were fixed 300 chord lengths away, and an unstructured mixed mesh was created which contained quadrilaterals in the boundary layer near the aerofoil and triangular element away from it. The resultant mesh had 52378 cells, 39120 quadrilateral cells, and 13258 triangular cells. The free-stream conditions at the inlet correspond to *Case 6* in the experimental results from literature [21].

$$Re = 6.5 \times 10^6;$$

$$M = 0.725; \tag{1}$$

$$\alpha = 2.92.$$

Here, Re is the Reynolds number, M is the Mach number, and α is the angle of attack. The free-stream conditions in the original literature [21] are not corrected for the wind tunnel effects. Including the wind tunnel effect results in the following free-stream conditions [22].

$$Re = 6.5 \times 10^6;$$

$$M = 0.729; \tag{2}$$

$$\alpha = 2.31.$$

Subsonic boundary conditions were employed on the outer domain, while no-slip boundary conditions were employed on the aerofoil.

The third-order WENO scheme, denoted as WENO-3, was used for achieving higher-order accuracy. For the WENO-3 scheme, the central and the directional stencils for a triangular mesh element are shown in Figure 4. The zone of influence from the four stencils is shown in Figure 5. This zone of influence is considerably larger than the traditional second-order numerical schemes, which contributes toward the computational and communication costs.

4.2. Hardware and Compiler. Two HPC facilities were used in our study, ASTRAL and ARCHER. ASTRAL is an SGI, Intel processor based, cluster owned by Cranfield University. ARCHER, the UK's national supercomputing facility, is a Cray XC30 system.

ASTRAL has 80 physical compute nodes. Each compute node has two 8-core E5-2260 series processor and 8 GB RAM per core (i.e., 128 GB per node). Hyperthreading is disabled. A 34 TB parallel file storage system (Panasas) is connected to all the nodes. Infiniband QDR connectivity exists among all nodes and to the storage appliance. The operating system is Suse Linux 11.2.

ARCHER has a total of 4920 compute nodes. Each standard compute node (4544 nodes out of the total 4920 nodes) contains two 12-core E5-2697 v2 (Ivy Bridge) series processors and a total of 64 GB RAM per node. Each processor can support two hyperthreads, but they were not used. The compute nodes are connected with a parallel Lustre filesystem. The Cray Aries interconnect links all the compute nodes. A stripped-down version of the CLE, Compute Node Linux (CNL), is run on the compute nodes to reduce the memory footprint and overheads of the full OS.

Intel Fortran compiler 15.0.3 and Intel MPI version 5.0 Update 3 were used on ASTRAL and Cray compiling environment 8.3.3 was used on ARCHER.

The compiler flags used on ASTRAL were `-i4 -r8 -O2 -fp-model source`.

The compiler flags used on ARCHER were `-s interger32 -s real64 -e0 -ea -eQ -ez -hzero -eh -eZ`.

5. Results

5.1. Clarity. Coarray Fortran uses a simpler and user-friendly syntax, which results in a cleaner code in comparison to MPI.

To demonstrate the clarity obtained with the Coarray Fortran, we have presented one communication subroutine from our code in Listing 7 (MPI) and Listing 8 (Coarray Fortran). For simplicity, only the source code for the communication is shown.

This subroutine is used for communicating the reconstructed, boundary extrapolated values of each Gaussian quadrature point of the neighboring halo cells. The derived data type (`iexboundhir` and `iexboundhis`) used for the communication has the following declaration shown in Listing 9.

The resultant code is also much easier to understand, while preserving the functionality.

```fortran
            subroutine exhboundhigher( n, iexchanger, iexchanges,
          iexboundhir, iexboundhis, itestcase, numberofpoints2,
          isize )
        ...
          if (itestcase .eq. 4) then
            do i=0, isize-1
              if (i .ne. n) then
                do k=1, indl
                  if (iexboundhir(k)%procid .eq. i) then
                    do j=1, tndl
                      if (iexboundhir(k)%procid .eq. iexboundhis(j)
                          %procid) then
                      call mpi_sendrecv( iexboundhis(j)%facesol
                          (1:iexchanges(j)%muchtheyneed(1), 1:1,
                          1:numberofpoints2, 1:5), &
                          iexchanges(j)%muchtheyneed(1)*1*
                              numberofpoints2*5,
                              mpi_double_precision, iexboundhis(j)%
                              procid, n, &
                          iexboundhir(k)%facesol(1:iexchanger(k)%
                              muchineed(1), 1:1, 1:numberofpoints2,
                              1:5), &
                          iexchanger(k)%muchineed(1)*1*
                              numberofpoints2*5,
                              mpi_double_precision, iexboundhir(k)%
                              procid, &
                          iexboundhir(k)%procid, icommunicator,
                              status, ierror )
                      call mpi_sendrecv( iexboundhis(j)%facesolv
                          (1:iexchanges(j)%muchtheyneed(1), 1:1,
                          1:numberofpoints2, 1:8), &
                          iexchanges(j)%muchtheyneed(1)*1*
                              numberofpoints2*8,
                              mpi_double_precision, iexboundhis(j)%
                              procid, n, &
                          iexboundhir(k)%facesolv(1:iexchanger(k)%
                              muchineed(1), 1:1, 1:numberofpoints2,
                              1:8), &
                          iexchanger(k)%muchineed(1)*1*
                              numberofpoints2*8,
                              mpi_double_precision, iexboundhir(k)%
                              procid, &
                          iexboundhir(k)%procid, icommunicator,
                              status, ierror )
                      end if
                    end do
                  end if
                end do
              end if
            end do
          end if
        ...
        end subroutine exhboundhigher
```

LISTING 7: exhboundhigher subroutine from the MPI version of the code. Note that only the code responsible for communication is shown.

```
                  subroutine exhboundhigher ( n, iexchanger, iexchanges,
                      iexboundhir, iexboundhis, itestcase, numberofpoints2,
                      isize )
                      ...
                  if (itestcase .eq. 4) then
                      do i=1, tndl
                        ! add +1 since coarray images are mpi ranks+1
                        j = iexchanges(i)%procid + 1
                        iexboundhir(CommArr1(j))[j]%facesol(:,:,:,:) =
                          iexboundhis(i)%facesol(:,:,:,:)
                      end do
                      do i=1, tndl
                        ! add +1 since coarray images are mpi ranks+1
                        j = iexchanges(i)%procid + 1
                        iexboundhir(CommArr1(j))[j]%facesolv(:,:,:,:) =
                          iexboundhis(i)%facesolv(:,:,:,:)
                      end do
                  end if
                  sync all
                      ...
                  end subroutine exhboundhigher
```

LISTING 8: exhboundhigher subroutine from the Coarray Fortran version of the code. Note that only the code responsible for communication is shown.

```
            type exchange_boundhi
              integer :: procid, fast
              integer :: howmany
              real, allocatable, dimension(:,:,:,:) :: facesol, quadp,
                  vert
              real, allocatable, dimension(:,:,:) :: wquad, angles
              real, allocatable, dimension(:,:) :: triap, normals
              real, allocatable, dimension(:,:,:,:) :: facesolv
            end type exchange_boundhi
```

LISTING 9: Derived data type of iexboundhir and iexboundhis variables in the code.

5.2. Validation.

To validate the numerical predictions from the CFD code the experimental measurements [21] and CFD predictions [22] from the literature were used. This comparison was made for both the version of the code, with MPI communication and with Coarray Fortran communication.

The pressure coefficient profile over the aerofoil for the WENO-3 scheme along with the reference results is shown in Figure 6. The pressure coefficient is negative on the top surface of the aerofoil. It corresponds to the pressure less than the free-stream pressure. Pressure coefficient was calculated using

$$C_p = \frac{p - p_\infty}{(1/2)\,\rho_\infty V_\infty^2}, \tag{3}$$

where C_p is the pressure coefficient, p is pressure, ρ is the fluid density, V is the velocity, and subscript ∞ represents free-stream values.

The sharp dip in pressure coefficient, near $x/c = 0.55$ (x is the distance over the aerofoil and c is the chord), represents the shockwave (i.e., sudden change in the value of pressure and density). It can also be seen in Figure 7, which shows the Mach number contours over the aerofoil obtained with the WENO-3 scheme. Mach number 1 represents a shock wave.

It can be observed that the predictions with the WENO-3 scheme are more accurate in predicting the shock location, compared to the WIND code. The WIND code uses second-order finite difference scheme; thus greater errors may be expected. The MPI and Coarray Fortran version of our code provides the same predictions, which reassures that errors were not introduced during the conversion process.

5.3. Performance.

To compare the performance of MPI and Coarray Fortran communication in the code, the validation test case was run for 1000 iterations. These tests were performed on ASTRAL (Intel compiler) and ARCHER (Cray compiler), and the elapsed time was measured for the iterative calculations excluding any initialization and savefile outputs.

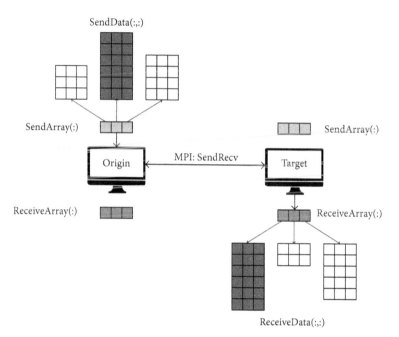

Figure 1: Schematic of data exchange process using MPI.

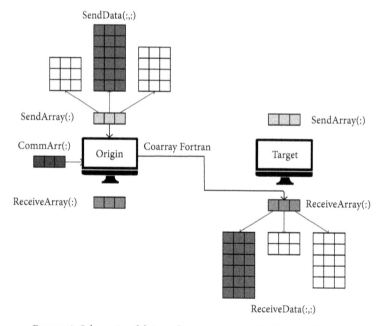

Figure 2: Schematic of data exchange process using Coarray Fortran.

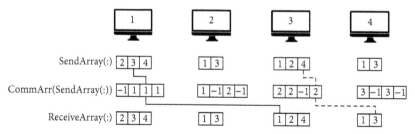

Figure 3: Working of CommArr in the Coarray Fortran version of the code.

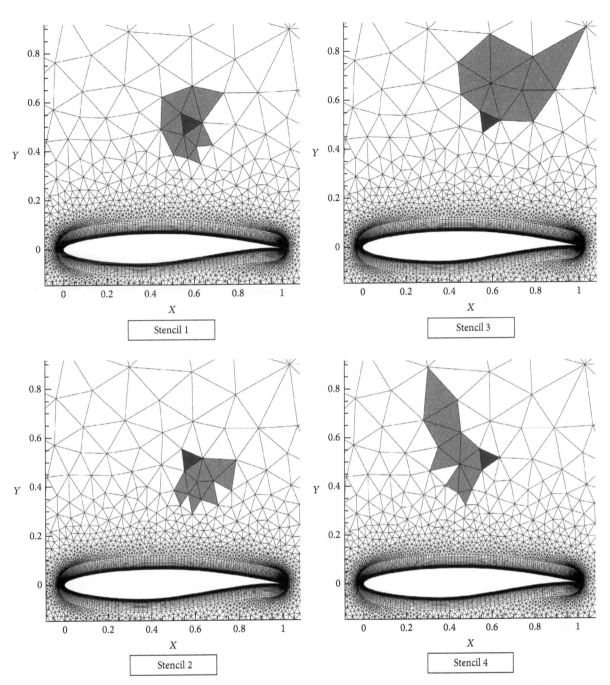

FIGURE 4: Central (stencil 1) and directional stencils (stencil 2, stencil 3, and stencil 4) for a triangular mesh element.

Since the most time-consuming part of the simulation is the iterative solver, the initialization and savefile output time can be neglected.

Figure 8 shows the execution time measured for MPI and Coarray Fortran version of the solver on ASTRAL (Intel compiler) and ARCHER (Cray compiler). On ASTRAL the data points correspond to $N = 8, 16$ (one-node), 32, 64, and 128 cores. On ARCHER the data points correspond to $N = 12, 24$ (one-node), 48, 96, 192, and 384 cores.

On ASTRAL with the Intel compiler, the Coarray Fortran version of the code is slower than MPI. Since the Coarray

Fortran implementation of Intel is based on MPI-3 remote memory access calls, it is subject to overheads over MPI. These overheads are so big that any performance gains—by replacing the blocking send and receive commands in the MPI version to nonblocking remote access calls in the Coarray Fortran version—are wiped out. An interesting result to note is that a sudden performance degradation occurs when communication takes place among *images* in multiple nodes.

Haveraaen et al. [23] observed that, even for large messages, the Intel compiler was performing element-wise transfer when Coarray Fortran was used for communication.

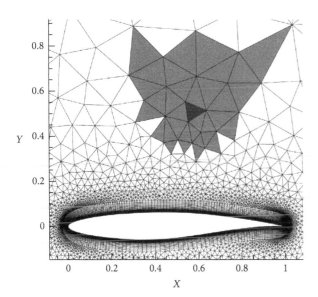

FIGURE 5: Combined stencil for the triangular mesh element.

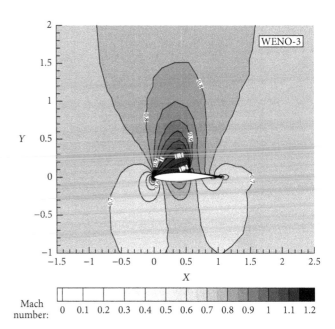

FIGURE 7: Mach number contour over the RAE 2822 airfoil.

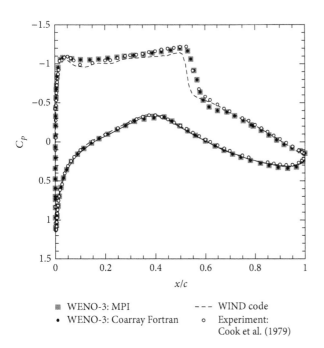

FIGURE 6: Pressure coefficient over the RAE 2822 airfoil surface for the code compared with experimental and CFD results from literature. Note: some points in CFD results are omitted for clarity.

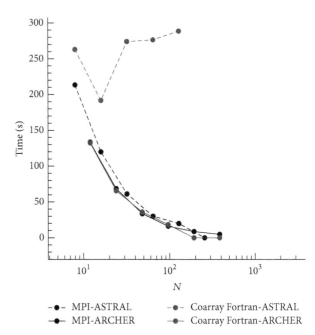

FIGURE 8: Performance results for the solver.

Their observation was based on the analysis of the assembly code of their program. Using Trace analysis, we also observed that the majority of communication time in each process is spent between *MPI_Win_lock* and *MPI_Win_unlock* calls, when internode communication is invoked. Thus, it could be concluded that the implementation of the Intel compiler is quite inefficient, with possible bugs that greatly reduce the performance when parallelization is performed using Coarray Fortran.

In contrast, on ARCHER with the Cray compiler, the performance of Coarray Fortran version of the code is mostly similar (till 96 cores) or in some cases (192 and 384 cores) better than the MPI version. Also, the execution time is lower on ARCHER due to the faster architecture compared to ASTRAL. For shorter messages, Coarray Fortran has lower overheads compared to MPI; this translated into the better performance when higher cores were used with the Coarray Fortran version. Also, the extraredirection due to the communication array did not adversely affect the results in comparison to the other gains.

Open-source compilers such as GCC (with OpenCoarrays) and OpenUH have been used in other benchmark studies to demonstrate the performance of their Coarray Fortran implementation in comparison to the MPI implementations. During our study, we found that the code featured in Listing 8 is not supported by the open-source implementations.

6. Conclusions

Coarray Fortran provides a simpler and a more productive alternative to MPI for parallelization. With minimal code modifications, even codes with unstructured meshes can be parallelized with Coarray Fortran. The increased readability of the resultant code enhances the productivity. Based on the performance and the level of current development, we found the Cray compiler to be suitable for development with Coarray Fortran. The performance with Cray compiler was similar or better than MPI in the tests. With Intel compiler, significant performance degradation was observed, especially on internode communication. It may be attributed to the inefficient implementation and possible bugs. While commercial compilers support all the features of Coarrays Fortran specified in the Fortran 2008 standard, some limitations still exist with the open-source implementations, such as OpenCoarrays (GCC) and OpenUH. We are hopeful that these limitations will be resolved soon in future versions.

Conflicts of Interest

The authors declare that there are no conflicts of interest regarding the publication of this paper.

Acknowledgments

This work used the ARCHER UK National Supercomputing Service (http://www.archer.ac.uk). The authors also thank Dr. Panagiotis Tsoutsanis and Dr. Antonios Foivos Antoniadis from Cranfield University for their insightful discussions.

References

[1] L. Hochstein, J. Carver, F. Shull et al., "Parallel programmer productivity: a case study of novice parallel programmers," in *Proceedings of the ACM/IEEE 2005 Supercomputing Conference, SC'05*, usa, November 2005.

[2] I. Christadler, G. Erbacci, and A. D. Simpson, "Performance and productivity of new programming languages," in *Facing the Multicore - Challenge II*, vol. 7174 of *Lecture Notes in Computer Science*, pp. 24–35, Springer Berlin Heidelberg, Berlin, Germany, 2012.

[3] J. Reid, "Additional coarray features in Fortran," in *Proceedings of the 7th International Conference on PGAS Programming Models*, M. Weiland, A. Jackson, N. Johnson, and M. Fortran, Eds., 104 pages, The University of Edinburgh, Edinburgh, UK, 2013.

[4] I. Chivers and J. Sleightholme, "Compiler support for the Fortran 2003 and 2008 standards revision 20," *ACM SIGPLAN Fortran Forum*, vol. 35, no. 3, pp. 29–50, 2016.

[5] A. Fanfarillo, T. Burnus, S. Filippone, V. Cardellini, D. Nagle, and D. W. I. Rouson, "OpenCoarrays: open-source transport layers supporting coarray Fortran compilers," in *Proceedings of the 8th International Conference on Partitioned Global Address Space Programming Models (PGAS '14)*, Eugene, Ore, USA, October 2014.

[6] D. Eachempati, H. J. Jun, and B. Chapman, "An open-source compiler and runtime implementation for Coarray Fortran," in *Proceedings of the 4th Conference on Partitioned Global Address Space (PGAS) Programming Models, PGAS'10*, New York, NY, USA, October 2010.

[7] R. W. Numrich, J. Reid, and K. Kim, "Writing a multigrid solver using co-array fortran," in *Applied Parallel Computing Large Scale Scientific and Industrial Problems*, vol. 1541 of *Lecture Notes in Computer Science*, pp. 390–399, Springer Berlin Heidelberg, Berlin, Germany, 1998.

[8] R. Barrett, "Co-array Fortran experiences with finite differencing methods," in *Proceedings of the The 48th Cray User Group meeting*, Italy, Lugano, Italy, 2006.

[9] M. Hasert, H. Klimach, and S. Roller, "CAF versus MPI - Applicability of Coarray Fortran to a Flow Solver," in *Recent Advances in the Message Passing Interface*, vol. 6960 of *Lecture Notes in Computer Science*, pp. 228–236, Springer Berlin Heidelberg, Berlin, Germany, 2011.

[10] A. I. Stone, J. M. Dennis, and M. M. Strout, "Evaluating Coarray Fortran with the CGPOP Miniapp," in *Proceedings of the Fifth Conference on Partitioned Global Address Space Programming Models (PGAS)*, 2011.

[11] A. Shterenlikht, "Fortran coarray library for 3D cellular automata microstructure simulation," in *Proceedings of the 7th International Conference on PGAS Programming Models*, 2013.

[12] D. Henty, "Performance of Fortran Coarrays on the Cray XE6," in *Proceedings of the Cray User Group*, 2012.

[13] R. W. Numrich, "A Parallel Numerical Library for Co-array Fortran," in *Proceedings of the International Conference on Parallel Processing and Applied Mathematics*, Springer Berlin Heidelberg, 2005.

[14] V. Cardellini, A. Fanfarillo, and S. Filippone, "Heterogeneous CAF-based load balancing on Intel Xeon Phi," in *Proceedings of the 30th IEEE International Parallel and Distributed Processing Symposium Workshops, IPDPSW 2016*, pp. 702–711, Chicago, Ill, USA, May 2016.

[15] R. W. Numrich and J. Reid, "Co-array Fortran for parallel programming," *ACM SIGPLAN Fortran Forum*, vol. 17, no. 2, pp. 1–31, 1998.

[16] R. W. Numrich, *Coarray Fortran*, Springer, Boston, Mich, USA, 2011.

[17] J. A. Ekaterinaris, "High-order accurate, low numerical diffusion methods for aerodynamics," *Progress in Aerospace Sciences*, vol. 41, no. 3-4, pp. 192–300, 2005.

[18] P. Tsoutsanis, V. A. Titarev, and D. Drikakis, "WENO schemes on arbitrary mixed-element unstructured meshes in three space dimensions," *Journal of Computational Physics*, vol. 230, no. 4, pp. 1585–1601, 2011.

[19] P. Tsoutsanis, A. F. Antoniadis, and D. Drikakis, "WENO schemes on arbitrary unstructured meshes for laminar, transitional and turbulent flows," *Journal of Computational Physics*, vol. 256, pp. 254–276, 2014.

[20] V. A. Titarev and E. F. Toro, "Finite-volume WENO schemes for three-dimensional conservation laws," *Journal of Computational Physics*, vol. 201, no. 1, pp. 238–260, 2004.

[21] P. H. Cook, M. C. P. Firmin, and M. A. McDonald, "Aerofoil RAE 2822: pressure distributions, and boundary layer and wake measurements," Tech. Rep., Advisory Group For Aerospace Research And Development (AGARD), 1979.

[22] J. W. Slater, J. C. Dudek, and K. E. Tatum, The NPARC alliance verification and validation archive, (2000).URL https://www.grc.nasa.gov/www/wind/valid/archive.html.

[23] M. Haveraaen, K. Morris, D. Rouson, H. Radhakrishnan, and C. Carson, "High-Performance Design Patterns for Modern Fortran," *Scientific Programming*, vol. 2015, Article ID 942059, 14 pages, 2015.

10

Optimized Data Transfers Based on the OpenCL Event Management Mechanism

Hiroyuki Takizawa,[1] **Shoichi Hirasawa,**[1] **Makoto Sugawara,**[2] **Isaac Gelado,**[3]
Hiroaki Kobayashi,[2] **and Wen-mei W. Hwu**[4]

[1]*Tohoku University/JST CREST, Sendai, Miyagi 980-8579, Japan*
[2]*Tohoku University, Sendai, Miyagi 980-8578, Japan*
[3]*NVIDIA Research, Santa Clara, CA 95050, USA*
[4]*The University of Illinois at Urbana-Champaign, Urbana, IL 61801, USA*

Correspondence should be addressed to Hiroyuki Takizawa; takizawa@cc.tohoku.ac.jp

Academic Editor: Sunita Chandrasekaran

In standard OpenCL programming, hosts are supposed to control their compute devices. Since compute devices are dedicated to kernel computation, only hosts can execute several kinds of data transfers such as internode communication and file access. These data transfers require one host to simultaneously play two or more roles due to the need for collaboration between the host and devices. The codes for such data transfers are likely to be system-specific, resulting in low portability. This paper proposes an OpenCL extension that incorporates such data transfers into the OpenCL event management mechanism. Unlike the current OpenCL standard, the main thread running on the host is not blocked to serialize dependent operations. Hence, an application can easily use the opportunities to overlap parallel activities of hosts and compute devices. In addition, the implementation details of data transfers are hidden behind the extension, and application programmers can use the optimized data transfers without any tricky programming techniques. The evaluation results show that the proposed extension can use the optimized data transfer implementation and thereby increase the sustained data transfer performance by about 18% for a real application accessing a big data file.

1. Introduction

Today, many high-performance computing (HPC) systems are equipped with graphics processing units (GPUs) serving as data-parallel accelerators in addition to conventional general-purpose processors (CPUs). For such a heterogeneous HPC system, application programmers need to manage the system heterogeneity while exploiting the parallelism involved in their applications. For the rest of the paper, we will follow the OpenCL terminology and refer to the CPUs as *hosts* and data-parallel accelerators as *compute devices*.

One difficulty in programming such a heterogeneous system is that a programmer has to take the responsibility for appointing the right processors to the right tasks. In the current OpenCL standard, only the host can perform some of tasks because the compute device is dedicated to kernel computation. For example, only the host can access files and communicate with other nodes. To write the computation results of a kernel into a file, the results have to be first transferred from the device memory to the host memory after the kernel execution, and then the host writes the results to the file.

From the viewpoint of programmers, accelerator programming models such as CUDA [1] and OpenCL [2] are used for data transfers between the device memory and the host memory, MPI [3] is used for internode data communication, and file functions of each programming language, such as `fprintf` and `fscanf` in the C programming, are used for the file I/O. Hence, these three categories of data transfers are described with different programming models. Some data transfers done by different programming models could be dependent; a certain data transfer can be done only after its preceding data transfer. *In order to enforce such dependence*, one popular way is to block the host thread until the preceding data transfer has finished. This kind of blocking often inhibits overlapping parallel activities of the host and the device and exposes the data transfer latencies to the total execution time. One may create a dedicated host thread for synchronizing the dependent data transfers. However, such multithreading will further increase the programming complexity. Consequently, the application performance strongly depends on the programming skills and craftsmanship of the developers.

Another difficulty is that there is no standard way to coding those data transfers even for common data transfer patterns. Since application programmers are supposed to appropriately combine those data transfers for fully exploiting the potential of a heterogeneous HPC system, the code is often specialized for a particular system. For example, one compute device may be capable of directly accessing a file, and another may not. In this case, the file access code for the former device would be totally different from that for the latter one. Therefore, the code for data transfers is likely to be system-specific and some abstractions are required to achieve functional portability as well as performance portability. Although OpenCL has been designed for programming various compute devices, it provides interfaces only for data transfers between the host memory and the device memory, but not for the other kinds of data transfers.

To overcome the above difficulties, we need a "bridging" programming model that provides a standard way for coding data transfers among various memory spaces and storages of a heterogeneous parallel system in a unified fashion. In this paper, we focus on OpenCL as the accelerator programming model for high code portability and propose an OpenCL extension for abstraction of data transfers, though the idea could be trivially extrapolated to other GPU programming models such as CUDA. The proposed OpenCL extension named *clDataTransfer* provides an illusion that the compute devices are transferring data directly to files or other nodes. This paper focuses especially on internode communication and file access as typical data transfers that need collaboration of hosts and devices. The extension offers some OpenCL commands and functions for the data transfers. The internode communication and file access commands are executed in the same manner as the other OpenCL commands, and hence the OpenCL programming model is naturally extended so as to seamlessly access file data and also to improve the MPI interoperability.

The clDataTransfer extension provides a portable, standardized way to programming of internode communications and file accesses from/to the device memory. Although MPI and file functions are used internally to perform those data transfers with help of the hosts, those internal behaviors are invisible to application programmers; it can thereby hide the system-aware optimized implementations behind function calls. Hence, we can also expect that the clDataTransfer extension improves the performance portability of OpenCL applications across different system types, scales, and generations.

The rest of this paper is organized as follows. Section 2 briefly reviews the related work. Section 3 discusses the difficulties in joint programming of OpenCL, MPI, and the standard I/O package of the C library, so-called *Stdio*. Then, Section 4 proposes clDataTransfer, which is an OpenCL extension for the collaboration with MPI and Stdio. Section 5 discusses the performance impact of clDataTransfer through some evaluation results. Finally, Section 6 gives concluding remarks and our future work.

2. Related Work

In the OpenCL programming model, a CPU works as a *host* that manages one or more *compute devices* such as GPUs. To manage the interaction between the host and devices, OpenCL provides various resources that are instantiated as OpenCL objects such as contexts, command queues, memory objects, and event objects. A unique *handle* is given to every object and is used to access the resource. A context is a container of various resources and is analogous to a CPU process. A command queue is used to interact with its corresponding compute device; a host enqueues a command to have its compute device execute a task. A memory object represents a memory chunk accessible from hosts and devices. An event object is bound with a command in the command queue to represent the status of the command and is used to block the execution of other commands. Hence, it is used to describe the dependency among commands. Moreover, multiple events can be combined to an event list to express several previous commands.

For example, `clEnqueueReadBuffer` is a typical OpenCL function for enqueuing a command, which transfers data from the device memory to the host memory. The function signature is as in Algorithm 1.

OpenCL command enqueuing functions take three arguments for event management: the number of events in the waiting list (`numevts`), the initial address of the waiting list (`wlist`), and the address to which the event object of the enqueued command is passed (`evtret`). The enqueued command is able to be executed when all the preceding commands associated with the event objects in the waiting list have been completed.

In joint programming of MPI and OpenCL, a programmer needs to consider not only host-device communication using OpenCL but also internode communication using MPI. So far, some researchers have presented several MPI extensions to GPUs to ease the joint programming of MPI and CUDA/OpenCL. We will refer to these approaches as *GPU-aware MPI implementations*. Lawlor has proposed cudaMPI [4] that provides an MPI-like interface for communication between remote GPUs. MPI-ACC [5] uses the `MPI_Datatype` argument to indicate that the memory buffer passed to an MPI function is located in the device memory. MVAPICH2-GPU [6] assumes Unified Virtual Addressing (UVA), which provides a single memory space for host and device memories, and checks if the memory buffer passed to an MPI function is in the device memory. Then, MVAPICH2-GPU internally uses different implementations depending on whether the memory buffer is in the device memory or the host memory. Stuart et al. have discussed

```
cl_int
clEnqueueReadBuffer( cl_command_queue cmd,   /* command queue */
                     cl_mem buf,             /* memory buffer */
                     cl_bool blocking,       / blocking */
                     size_t offset,          /* offset */
                     size_t size,            /* buffer size */
                     void* hbuf,             /* buffer pointer */
                     cl_uint numevts,        /* the number of events in the list */
                     cl_event* wlist,        /* event list */
                     cl_evett* evtret )      /* event object of event object */
```

ALGORITHM 1

various design options of MPI extension to support accelerators [7]. Gelado et al. proposed GMAC that provides a single memory space shared by a CPU and a GPU and hence allows MPI functions to access device memory data [8]. Those extensions allow an application to use a GPU memory buffer as the end point of MPI communication; the extended MPI implementations enable using MPI functions for internode communication from/to GPU memory buffers by internally using data transfer functions of CUDA/OpenCL.

By using GPU-aware MPI extensions, application developers do not need to explicitly describe the host-device data transfers such as clEnqueueWriteBuffer and clEnqueueReadBuffer. As with clDataTransfer, these extensions do not require tricky programming techniques to achieve efficient data transfers, because they hide the optimized implementations behind the MPI function calls.

In GPU-aware MPI extensions, all internode communications are still managed by the host thread visible to application developers. For example, if the data obtained by executing a kernel are needed by other nodes, the host thread needs to wait for the kernel execution completion in order to serialize the kernel execution and the MPI communication; the host thread is blocked until the kernel execution is completed.

Furthermore, MPI extension to OpenCL is not straightforward, as Aji et al. discussed in [5]. To keep OpenCL data transfers transparent to MPI application programs, the MPI implementation must acquire valid command queues in some way. Aji et al. assume that an MPI process mostly uses only one command queue and its handle is thus cached by the MPI implementation to be used in subsequent communications, even though this assumption could be incorrect. Even if the cached command queue is available for subsequent communications, there may exist a more appropriate command queue for the communications. clDataTransfer allows application programmers to specify the best command queue for communication. It should be emphasized that GPU-aware MPI extensions and clDataTransfer are mutually beneficial rather than conflicting. For example, although this work has implemented pipelined data transfers using standard MPI functions, it is possible for clDataTransfer to use MPI extensions for its implementation.

Stuart and Owens have proposed DCGN [9]. As with clDataTransfer, DCGN provides an illusion that GPUs communicate without any help of their hosts. Unlike clDataTransfer, DCGN provides internode communication API

functions that are called from GPU kernels. When the API is called by a kernel running on a GPU, the kernel sets regions of device memory that are monitored by a CPU thread. Then, the CPU thread reads necessary data from the device memory and thus handles the communication requests from the GPU. Accordingly, DCGN allows a kernel to initiate internode communication. However, the requirement for host to monitor the device memory incurs a nonnegligible runtime overhead. On the other hand, in clDataTransfer, internode communication requests are represented as OpenCL commands. Hence, the host initiates the commands and the clDataTransfer implementation can rely on the OpenCL event management mechanism to synchronize with the commands.

An OpenCL memory object in the same context is shared by multiple devices. The OpenCL memory consistency model implicitly ensures that the contents of a memory object visible to the devices are the same only at their synchronization points. Once a device updates a memory object shared by multiple devices, the new memory content is implicitly copied to the memory of every device in the same context. Some OpenCL implementations [10] support creating a context shared by multiple devices across different nodes and thereby attain data sharing among remote devices while conforming the OpenCL specifications. However, in this approach, multiple devices sharing one context can have only a single memory space; they cannot have different memory contents even if some of the contents are not needed by all nodes. As a result, the contents could unnecessarily be duplicated to the device memory of every node, increasing the aggregated memory usage and also internode communications for the duplication.

GPU computing is employed not only for conventional HPC applications but also for data-intensive applications, for example, [11, 12], in which the data sizes are large and hence are stored in files. As only hosts can access the data stored in files, GPU computing requires additional data transfers between hosts and GPUs. Nonetheless, GPUs are effective to accelerate the kernel execution and reduce the total execution time in practical data-intensive applications. Overlapping the kernel execution with various data transfers such as file accesses and host-device data transfers is a key technique to reduce the data transfer latencies and obviously has common code patterns. However, as far as we know, there is no standard way to develop this pattern in a manner that is reusable in other applications. As recent and future

```
(1) cl_command_queue cmd;
(2) cl_kernel kern;
(3) cl_event evt;
(4)
(5) for(int i(0);i<N;++i){
(6)     // (1) computation on a device
(7)     clEnqueueNDRangeKernel(cmd,kern,...,0,NULL,&evt);
(8)
(9)     // (2) read the result from device to host
(10)    clEnqueueReadBuffer(cmd,...,1,&evt,NULL);
(11)    clFinish(cmd); // the host thread is blocked
(12)
(13)    // (3) exchange data with other nodes
(14)    MPI_Sendrecv(...); // blocking function call
(15)
(16)    // (4) write the received data to device memory
(17)    clEnqueueWriteBuffer(cmd,...);
(18) }
```

LISTING 1: A simple pseudocode combining OpenCL and MPI.

HPC systems have hierarchical storage subsystems, high-speed local storages using nonvolatile memories will be available. In those cases, the overlapping would become more significant because host-device data transfer overheads increase relatively to the file access overhead.

3. Difficulties in Joint Programming

This section discusses some difficulties in joint programming of OpenCL and other libraries, such as MPI, which are called by host threads. Listing 1 shows a simple code of the joint programming of MPI and OpenCL. In this code, a command to execute a kernel is first enqueued by invoking clEnqueueNDRangeKernel. Another command to read the kernel execution result is then enqueued by clEnqueueReadBuffer. Using the event object of the first command, evt, the execution of the second command is blocked until the first command is completed. The second command enqueued by clEnqueueReadBuffer can be either blocking or nonblocking. The function call is non-blocking if the third argument is CL_FALSE; otherwise it is blocking. If it is nonblocking, we have to use a synchronization function such as clFinish to make sure that the data have already been transferred from device memory to host memory in advance of calling MPI_Sendrecv. In this naive implementation, the data exchange with other nodes must be performed after the data transfer from device memory to host memory; those data transfers must be serialized. Similarly, MPI_Sendrecv and clEnqueueWriteBuffer must be serialized. Therefore, kernel execution and all data transfers are serialized, which results in a long communication time exposed to the total execution time. In addition, the host thread is blocked whenever MPI and OpenCL operations are serialized. Although Listing 1 shows an example of joint programming of MPI and OpenCL, the same difficulties arise when combining OpenCL and Stdio (or any other file access programming interfaces).

To make matters worse, there is no standard way for the joint programming. Even for simple point-to-point communication between two remote devices, we can consider at least the following three implementations. One is the naive implementation as shown in Listing 1. In the implementation, host memory buffers should be page-locked (pinned) for efficient data transfers (although the OpenCL standard does not provide any specific means to allocate pinned host memory buffers, most vendors rely on the usage of clEnqueueMapBuffer to provide programmers with pinned host memory buffers). This can be also a point to make different vendors require different implementations to exploit pinned memory. Another implementation is to map device memory objects to host memory addresses by using clEnqueueMapBuffer and then to invoke MPI functions to transfer data from/to the addresses. After the MPI communication, clEnqueueUnmapMemObject is invoked to unmap the device memory objects. The other implementation is to overlap host-device data transfers with internode data transfers. In this implementation, data of a device memory object are divided into data blocks of a fixed size, called a *pipeline block size*, and host-device data transfers of each block are overlapped with internode data transfers of other blocks in a pipelining fashion [6]. In this paper, the three aforementioned implementations are referred to as *pinned*, *mapped*, and *pipelined* data transfers. Among those implementations, the best one changes depending on several factors such as the message size, device types, device vendors, and device generations. Also in the cases of overlapping host-device data transfers with file accesses there are many implementation options and parameters due to the variety of file access speeds in a hierarchical storage subsystem. Accordingly, an application developer might need to implement multiple versions to optimize data transfers

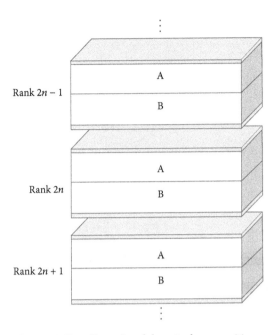

Rank 2n − 1

A

B

Rank 2n

A

B

Rank 2n + 1

A

B

FIGURE 1: One-dimensional domain decomposition.

for performance portability of an application program across various systems.

Another common approach to hide the communication overhead is to overlap the data transfers and computation through double buffering [11, 13]. To this end, the computation is usually divided into two stages. While executing the first stage computation, the first stage data transfer is performed to prepare for the second stage computation. If the computation and data transfer are inside a loop, the second stage data transfer for the first stage computation of the next iteration is performed during the second stage computation of the current iteration.

In OpenCL programming, this overlapping optimization can be achieved using two in-order execution command queues. Listing 2 shows a simplified version of the Himeno benchmark code described in [13], which is originally written in CUDA and MPI. In the code, `jacobi_kernel_*` functions in Lines (9), (18), (28), and (35) invoke kernels using the command queue `cmd1` to update the memory object specified by the second argument. The code assumes one-dimensional domain decomposition, in which each decomposed domain is further halved into upper and lower portions, A and B. Figure 1 illustrates the domain decomposition assumed by the code. The top plane of A and the bottom plane of B are halo regions that have to be updated every iteration by exchanging data with neighboring nodes. Hence, if the MPI rank of a process is an even number, during calculating A, the process updates the halo region included in B. Then, it calculates B during exchanging data for updating the halo of A. On the other hand, if the MPI rank of a process is an odd number, the process first calculates B during updating the halo of A. Then, it calculates A during exchanging data for updating the halo of B. As a result, the communication time is not exposed to the total execution time as shown in Figure 2(a) unless the communication time exceeds the computation time.

As the number of MPI processes increases, the computation time becomes shorter because the domain processed by each GPU becomes smaller. However, the second stage communication cannot start even if the first stage computation is completed earlier and hence the data are ready for the second stage communication as shown in Figure 2(b). This is because the host thread is often blocked and tied up in the first stage communication in order to serialize the MPI and OpenCL operations.

Since the code in Listing 2 is simple, there are some workaround techniques to solve this problem. However, in the case where more advanced optimization techniques such as pipelining are applied to the data transfers, the host thread is stalled more frequently to timely synchronize MPI and OpenCL operations in multiple parallel activities of an application. In general, there are at least three parallel activities in an application: host computation, device computation, and nonblocking MPI communication. If there are dependent operations of MPI and OpenCL, the host thread is usually blocked to serialize the operations, which inhibits overlapping of the parallel activities. Also, host thread blocking is often used even in a serial application if the host thread needs to load data from a file, send them to the device memory, and retrieve the computation results from the device memory. Multithread programming or complex asynchronous I/O APIs would be required to properly manage those parallel activities. In this way, an application code becomes more complicated and system-specific, resulting in low code readability, maintainability, and portability. This motivates us to design a bridging programming model that can explicitly describe the dependencies among MPI, OpenCL, and file access operations in order to initiate data transfers without any help of the host thread.

4. An OpenCL Extension for Collaboration with MPI and Stdio

This paper proposes *clDataTransfer*, an OpenCL extension to facilitate and standardize the joint programming of MPI, Stdio, and OpenCL. The key idea of this extension is to use OpenCL commands for internode data transfers, file accesses, and data transfers between hosts and local devices.

The major advantages of clDataTransfer are summarized as follows.

(1) Performance portability: the implementation details of internode data transfers and file accesses are hidden behind extended commands and can be used via a simple programming interface similar to the standard OpenCL interface.

(2) Event management: a host thread is not responsible for serializing internode communications, file operations, and host-device communications. Instead, an event object is used to block the subsequent commands until the preceding command is completed.

```
(1)  cl_command_queue cmd1, cmd2;
(2)  cl_mem p_new, p_old, p_tmp;
(3)
(4)  for(int i(0);i<N;++i){
(5)    //swap pointers
(6)    p_tmp = p_new; p_new = p_old; p_old = p_tmp;
(7)    if( rank%2 == 0)  {
(8)      // the upper portion is calculated
(9)      jacobi_kernel_even_A(cmd1,p_new,...);
(10)     // the bottom plane is updated
(11)     MPI_Irecv(...);
(12)     clEnqueueReadBuffer(cmd2,p_old,CL_FALSE,...);
(13)     clFinish(cmd2);   // blocking
(14)     MPI_Send(...);    // blocking
(15)     MPI_Wait(...);    // blocking
(16)     clEnqueueWriteBuffer(cmd2,p_old,CL_FALSE,...);
(17)     // the lower portion is calculated
(18)     jacobi_kernel_even_B(cmd2,p_new,...);
(19)     // the top plane is updated
(20)     MPI_Irecv(...);
(21)     clEnqueueReadBuffer(cmd1,p_new,CL_FALSE,...);
(22)     clFinish(cmd1);   // blocking
(23)     MPI_Send(...);    // blocking
(24)     MPI_Wait(...);    // blocking
(25)     clEnqueueWriteBuffer(cmd1,p_new,CL_FALSE,...);
(26)   }
(27)   else {
(28)     jacobi_kernel_odd_B(cmd1,p_new,...);
(29)     MPI_Irecv(...);
(30)     clEnqueueReadBuffer(cmd2,p_old,CL_FALSE,...);
(31)     clFinish(cmd2);   // blocking
(32)     MPI_Send(...);    // blocking
(33)     MPI_Wait(...);    // blocking
(34)     clEnqueueWriteBuffer(cmd2,p_old,CL_FALSE,...);
(35)     jacobi_kernel_odd_A(cmd2,p_new,...);
(36)     MPI_Irecv(...);
(37)     clEnqueueReadBuffer(cmd1,p_new,CL_FALSE,...);
(38)     clFinish(cmd1);   // blocking
(39)     MPI_Send(...);    // blocking MPI_Wait (...);  // blocking
(40)     clEnqueueWriteBuffer(cmd1,p_new,CL_FALSE,...);
(41)   } clFinish(cmd1);clFinish(cmd2);  /* error calculation */
(42)}
```

LISTING 2: A Himeno benchmark code with overlapping communication and computation.

(3) Collaboration for latency hiding: clDataTransfer can collaborate with MPI and Stdio in order to hide data transfer latencies in a pipelining fashion.

By encapsulating file accesses into OpenCL commands, the clDataTransfer extension offers two file access commands: clEnqueueReadBufferToStdioFile and clEnqueueWriteBufferFromStdioFile. clEnqueueReadBufferToStdioFile reads data from a device memory buffer and writes the data to a file, and clEnqueueWriteBufferFromStdioFile reads data from a file and writes the data to a device memory buffer. The function signatures are as in Algorithm 2.

Similarly, the clDataTransfer extension offers clEnqueueSendBuffer and clEnqueueRecvBuffer, which enqueue commands of transferring data from and to a device memory buffer, respectively. These clDataTransfer functions are direct counterparts of MPI_Send and MPI_Recv [3] and hence take the same arguments of rank, tag, and communicator as those two MPI functions. For example, the function signature of clEnqueueRecvBuffer is as in Algorithm 3.

When one MPI process invokes those functions for sending a command to a device, the device becomes a *communicator device* for one MPI communication and works as if it communicates instead of the host thread. The data sent to the MPI rank are received by the communicator device,

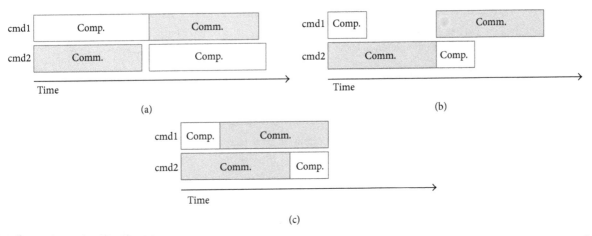

FIGURE 2: Overlapping communications and computations. (a) The communication time is overlapped with the computation time. (b) The computation time is too short to hide the communication time. Since joint programming of OpenCL and MPI cannot express the dependency between the first communication and the second computation, the host thread is blocked to execute them in a correct order. (c) The second communication can potentially start earlier because the host thread is not blocked.

```
cl_int clEnqueueReadBufferToStdioFile(
                cl_command_queue cmd, /* command queue */
                cl_mem mem,   /* memory buffer to be read */
                cl_bool blk,  /* blocking function call     */
                size_t off,   /* offset */
                size_t bsz,   /* buffer size */
                FILE* fp,     /* file pointer */
                cl_uint nev,  /* the number of events in the list */
                const cl_event* evl, /* event list */
                cl_event* evt) /* event object of the function call */
cl_int clEnqueueWriteBufferFromStdioFile(
                cl_command_queue cmd, /* command queue */
                cl_mem mem,   /* memory buffer to be written */
                cl_bool blk,  /* blocking function call     */
                size_t off,   /* offset */
                size_t bsz,   /* buffer size */
                FILE* fp,     /* file pointer */
                cl_uint nev,  /* the number of events in the list */
                const cl_event* evl, /* event list */
                cl_event* evt) /* event object of the function call */
```

ALGORITHM 2

```
cl_int
clEnqueueRecvBuffer(cl_command_queue cmd, /* command queue */
                cl_mem buf, /* memory buffer to receive data */
                cl_bool blocking, /* blocking function call */
                size_t offset,  /* offset */
                size_t size,    /* buffer size */
                int src,        /* sender's rank */
                int tag,        /* tag */
                MPI_Comm comm,  /* communicator */
                cl_uint numevts, /* the number of events in the list */
                const cl_event* wlist, /* event list */
                cl_event* evtret ) /* event object of the function call */
```

ALGORITHM 3

```
(1) if( rank == 0 ){
(2)     clEnqueueSendBuffer(cmd, buf, CL_TRUE, off, sz, 1,...);
(3) }
(4) else if(rank == 1){
(5)     clEnqueueRecvBuffer(cmd, buf, CL_TRUE, off, sz, 0,...);
(6) }
```

LISTING 3: A code with the OpenCL extension for device-to-device communication.

and the received data are stored in the memory space of the communicator device, that is, buf. The MPI rank of the sender is given to the function, and the sender could be either the host thread or the communicator device associated with the MPI rank.

In the case where both the sender and the receiver submit internode communication commands to their devices, those devices communicate with each other. Listing 3 shows a simple example of communication between remote devices. In this code, the communicator device of rank 0 sends the data of a memory buffer object to the communicator device of rank 1 without explicitly calling any MPI functions. Accordingly, devices appear to communicate with remote devices without help of their host threads. The implementation details of internode communication by combining MPI and OpenCL are hidden behind the OpenCL command execution. Hence, the application can use optimized implementations of efficient data transfers without using tricky programming techniques. If one MPI process needs to use multiple communicator devices, a unique tag is given to each MPI communication to specify which communicator device handles it.

4.1. Event Management. The clDataTransfer extension allows a programmer to use event objects in order to express the dependency among internode communication commands, storage file access commands, and other OpenCL commands. If a data transfer command provided by clDataTransfer needs the result of its preceding command, the programmer can get the event object of the preceding command and use it to block the execution of the data transfer command. This ensures that the data transfer is performed after the preceding command is completed. In this way, data transfer commands of clDataTransfer are incorporated into the OpenCL execution model in a natural manner. Accordingly, function calls of MPI and Stdio are encapsulated in OpenCL commands whose dependencies with other OpenCL commands are accurately enforced by the command queues. Unlike the conventional joint programming of MPI, Stdio, and OpenCL, the host thread does not need to wait for the preceding command completion. After enqueuing the commands by nonblocking function calls, the host thread immediately becomes available for other computations and data transfers; an application programmer can consider as if a device is able to work independently from the host thread. In due time, the OpenCL runtime will release the clDataTransfer command for timely execution of the MPI functions as shown in Figure 2(c),

even though the two communications may or may not be performed concurrently.

Using the clDataTransfer extension, the code in Listing 2 can be simply rewritten as the code in Listing 4. This is an example that demonstrates simplification of common patterns in joint programming of OpenCL and other programming models. In this particular case, the clDataTransfer extension can halve the number of code lines for describing the same computation as the joint programming of OpenCL and MPI. Since there are dependencies among the enqueued commands, they are expressed by using event objects bound with the commands. In Listing 2, the second stage computations, jacobi_even_A and jacobi_odd_B, are blocked using event objects of the first communication, e[1]. The second stage communications are blocked using the event object of the first stage computation, e[0]. On the other hand, in Listing 4, the dependencies among the function calls are managed by the OpenCL event management mechanism, and the host thread is thus freed from controlling the computation and communication. In the code, clEnqueueSendrecvBuffer enqueues an OpenCL command for exchanging data between two MPI processes by internally invoking MPI_Sendrecv under control of the OpenCL event management. Therefore, the host thread is just waiting at the end of the iteration by calling clFinish.

4.2. Interoperability with Existing MPI Functions. In clDataTransfer, an MPI process uses clDataTransfer commands for transferring data from/to a device memory buffer. If an MPI process needs to transfer data from/to a host memory buffer, clDataTransfer allows the MPI process to use standard MPI functions such as MPI_Isend and MPI_Irecv to communicate with remote devices as well as remote hosts. Listing 5 shows that the MPI process of rank 0 receives data from a remote device managed by the MPI process of rank 1. A special MPI_Datatype value, MPI_CL_MEM, is given to the third argument of MPI_Irecv in order to express that the sender is supposed to be a communicator device and the data are in the device memory. If MPI_CL_MEM is given, the sender and receiver collaborate for efficient data transfers between host and device memories. A similar approach of using MPI_Datatype can be seen in [5], even though they extend only MPI but not OpenCL.

As shown in Listing 5, nonblocking MPI functions can be used for internode communication from/to a host memory buffer. Hence, the data need to be received

```
(1) cl_command_queue cmd1, cmd2;
(2) cl_mem p_new, p_old, p_tmp;
(3) cl_event e[2];
(4)
(5) for(int i(0);i<N;++i){
(6)   p_tmp = p_new; p_new = p_old; p_old = p_tmp;
(7)   if( rank%2 == 0) {
(8)     jacobi_kernel_even_A(cmd1,p_new...0,NULL,&e[0]);
(9)     clEnqueueSendrecvBuffer(cmd2,p_old,...0,NULL,&e[1]);
(10)    jacobi_kernel_even_B(cmd2,p_new...1,&e[1],NULL);
(11)    clEnqueueSendrecvBuffer(cmd1,p_new,...1,&e[0],NULL);
(12)  }
(13)  else {
(14)    jacobi_kernel_odd_B(cmd2,p_new...0,NULL,&e[0]);
(15)    clEnqueueSendrecvBuffer(cmd1,p_old,...0,NULL,&e[1]);
(16)    jacobi_kernel_odd_A(cmd1,p_new...1,&e[1],NULL);
(17)    clEnqueueSendrecvBuffer(cmd2,p_new,...1,&e[0],NULL);
(18)  }
(19)  clFinish(cmd1);clFinish(cmd2);
(20)  /* error calculation */
(21)}
```

LISTING 4: A Himeno benchmark code with the proposed OpenCL extension.

```
(1) cl_context ctx;
(2) MPI_Request req;
(3) cl_event evt[2];
(4)
(5) if( rank == 0 ){
(6)   /* receiving data from a remote device */
(7)   MPI_Irecv(recvbuf, bufsz, MPI_CL_MEM, 1, 0, MPI_COMM_WORLD,&req);
(8)   /* creating an event object of MPI_Irecv */
(9)   evt[0] = clCreateEventFromMPIRequest(ctx,&req,NULL);
(10)  /* executing a kernel during the data transfer */
(11)  clEnqueueNDRangeKernel(..., &evt[1]);
(12)
(13)  /* executing this after the computation and communication */
(14)  clEnqueueWriteBuffer(cmd, buf, ..., 2, evt, NULL);
(15)}
(16)else if(rank == 1){
(17)  /* send data to a remote host */
(18)  clEnqueueSendBuffer(cmd, buf, CL_TRUE, 0, bufsz, 0,...);
(19)}
```

LISTING 5: A code with the OpenCL extension for host-to-device communication.

before clEnqueueWriteBuffer in lines (14) is executed to write the data to the device memory of rank 0. In addition, a kernel in line (11) is executed during the internode communication. To express the dependency among nonblocking MPI function calls and OpenCL commands, the clDataTransfer extension offers a function to create an OpenCL event object that corresponds to MPI_Request of a nonblocking MPI function call. Using the event object, another OpenCL command can be executed after the nonblocking MPI function is completed; the dependence between an MPI operation and an OpenCL operation is properly enforced without host intervention. In Listing 5, the event object is used to ensure that MPI_Irecv is completed before writing data to a device memory buffer.

The MPI interoperability is very important because many applications have already been developed in such a way that CPUs manage all internode communications via MPI function calls. Considering the importance, the clDataTransfer extension is not designed as a standalone communication library but an OpenCL extension for interoperation with

TABLE 1: System specifications.

System	Masamune	Cichlid	RICC
CPU	Intel Xeon E5-2670	Intel Core i7 930	Intel Xeon 5570
GPU	GeForce GTX TITAN	Tesla C2070	Tesla C1060
NIC	GbE 1000BASE-T	GbE 1000BASE-T	InfiniBand DDR
OS	CentOS 6.4	CentOS 6.0	RHEL 5.3
Compiler	GCC-4.4.7	GCC-4.4.4	Intel Compiler 11.1
GPU Driver	319.37	290.10	295.41
OpenCL	OpenCL1.1 (CUDA5.5)	OpenCL1.1 (CUDA4.1.1)	OpenCL1.1 (CUDA 4.2.9)
MPI	Open MPI 1.5.4	Open MPI 1.6.0	Open MPI 1.6.1
Storage	SSD (Intel 910 400 GB)	NFS	NFS

MPI. With the interoperability, legacy applications can be ported incrementally to heterogeneous computing systems by gradually replacing the MPI function calls with the clData-Transfer extension. This does not mean that all internode communications should be replaced with the clDataTransfer extension. We argue that both MPI and OpenCL need to be extended for their efficient interoperation.

Although the clDataTransfer extension offers internode peer-to-peer communications among remote hosts and devices, it does not currently offer any collective communications. This is because the function calls of MPI collective communications are blocking and no OpenCL extension is required to describe the dependability among the collective communications and OpenCL commands. If optimized collective communications for device memory objects are required, we can hide the implementation details in MPI collective communication functions, rather than developing a set of special collective communication functions for device memory objects. As the MPI-3.0 standard will support nonblocking collective communications, some synchronization mechanisms between the nonblocking collective communications and OpenCL commands might be required in the future. In this case, it will be effective to further extend OpenCL to use its event management mechanism for the synchronization.

5. Evaluation and Discussions

In this section, the performance impact of the proposed extension is discussed by showing the effects of hiding the host-device data transfer latency and the performance improvement. In this work, a GPU program of the Smith Waterman algorithm [11] is first used to evaluate the performance gain by overlapping host-device data transfers with file accesses. Then, the Himeno benchmark [13] and the nanopowder growth simulation [14] are adopted for the evaluation of MPI interoperability, which is improved by the proposed extension.

Three systems called Masamune, Cichlid, and RICC are used for the following evaluation. Masamune is a single node PC with Intel Xeon E5-2670 CPU running at 2.60 GHz and one NVIDIA GeForce GTX TITAN GPU. Cichlid is a small PC cluster system of four nodes, each of which contains one Intel Core i7 930 CPU running at 2.8 GHz and one NVIDIA Tesla C2070 GPU. The nodes are connected via the Gigabit

Ethernet network. On the other hand, in the multipurpose PC cluster of RIKEN Integrated Cluster of Clusters (RICC), 100 compute nodes are connected via an InfiniBand DDR network. Each of the compute nodes has two Intel Xeon 5570 CPUs and one NVIDIA Tesla C1060 GPU. The system specifications are summarized in Table 1.

5.1. Implementation. In this work, we have implemented the clDataTransfer extension on top of NVIDIA's OpenCL and Open MPI [15] as shown in Table 1. As most of currently available OpenCL implementations are proprietary, the clDataTransfer extension is designed so that it can be implemented on top of a proprietary OpenCL implementation. In the implementation, we have to consider at least three points. One point is how to implement clDataTransfer commands that mimic standard OpenCL commands. Another is how to implement nonblocking function calls. The other is how to implement pipelined data transfers.

To implement clDataTransfer commands whose execution is managed by the OpenCL event management system, user event objects are internally used to create event objects of those additional commands provided by the clDataTransfer extension. Since there are several different behaviors between standard event objects and user event objects, the runtime of the clDataTransfer extension has been developed so that user event objects of additional commands can mimic event objects of standard OpenCL commands. A simplified pseudocode of a clDataTransfer function is shown in Listing 6. When the function is executed, from the viewpoint of application programmers, the clDataTransfer runtime appears to work as follows. A user event object whose execution status is CL_SUBMITTED is first created when a clDataTransfer command is enqueued. Then, the clDataTransfer runtime automatically changes the execution status to CL_COMPLETE when the command is completed. This allows other commands to wait for the completion of a clDataTransfer command by using its user event object. Therefore, application programmers can use the event object of a clDataTransfer command in the same way as that of a standard OpenCL command.

The clDataTransfer function in Listing 6 can be invoked in either blocking or nonblocking mode. To invoke a clData-Transfer function without blocking the host thread, the clDataTransfer runtime internally spawns another thread dedicated to data transfers. Since most existing OpenCL

```
(1) cl_int clDataTransferFunc( ...,
(2)                              cl_uint numevts,    /* the number of events in the list */
(3)                              cl_event* wlist,    /* event list */
(4)                              cl_evett* evtret )  /* event object of event object */
(5) {
(6)    /* create a new user event object whose status is CL_SUBMITTED */
(7)    *evtret = clCreateUserEvent(...);
(8)
(9)    if( non_blocking = CL_TRUE)
(10)      pthread_create(...,cldtThreadFunc,...);
(11)   else
(12)      cldtThreadFunc(...);
(13)
(14)   return CL_SUCCESS;
(15) }
(16)
(17) /* numevt, wlist, and evtret are passed from the caller */
(18) void* cldtThreadFunc(void* p)
(19) {
(20)   clWaitForEvent(numevt, wlist);
(21)
(22)   /* pipelined data transfer */
(23)
(24)   clSetUserEventStatus(*evtret, CL_COMPLETE);
(25)   return NULL;
(26) }
```

LISTING 6: A simple pseudocode of a clDataTransfer function.

implementations are already spawning a CPU thread to support callbacks, the same thread can technically be used to handle the clDataTransfer function calls. Thus, no additional thread would be needed if clDataTransfer is implemented by OpenCL vendors.

As the clDataTransfer implementation needs to call MPI and file access functions from the host thread and the dedicated thread, their underlying implementations are assumed to be thread-safe. File access functions are generally thread-safe. On the other hand, in MPI, MPI_Init_thread should work with MPI_THREAD_MULTIPLE. To make Open MPI work correctly for InfiniBand in a multithreaded environment, IP over InfiniBand (IPoIB) is used for performance evaluation on RICC.

In our current implementation, pipelined data transfers are implemented by ourselves by reference to some papers on GPU-aware MPI implementations [5, 6] and encapsulated in clDataTransfer commands as shown in Listing 6. So far, wrapper functions of file I/O functions and some major MPI functions such as MPI_Send and MPI_Recv have been developed so that those functions can perform pipelined data transfers of overlapping host-device communication with internode communication when MPI_CL_MEM is given as the MPI_Datatype parameter.

5.2. Evaluation of File Access Performance

5.2.1. Evaluation of Sustained Data Transfer Bandwidths.
The sustained bandwidths of data transfers from files to device memory buffers are evaluated to show that clEnqueueWriteBufferFromStdioFile can reduce the data transfer time compared to conventional serialized data transfers. To evaluate the sustained bandwidths with different storage's bandwidths, the solid state drive (SSD) and the hard disk drive (HDD) of Masamune are used as the local storages, and a shared file system of NFS is used as the global storage and accessed from Cichlid.

First, we evaluate how much the clDataTransfer extension can improve the sustained bandwidth. In the case of using clEnqueueWriteBufferFromStdioFile, data are read from a file and then sent to a device memory buffer. The bandwidth of a storage is lower than that of the data transfer between the host and the device via the PCI-express bus. Hence, the sustained bandwidth of the data transfer is limited by the storage bandwidth. Since clEnqueueWrite-BufferFromSdtioFile enables the host-device data transfer to be overlapped with the file read, it can reduce the data transfer time and hence achieve a higher sustained bandwidth than the sequential execution of those two data transfers.

Figure 3 shows the sustained bandwidths obtained with changing the data size and the pipeline buffer size. The vertical axis shows the sustained bandwidth, and the horizontal axis is the data size. In the figure, *Serial* means the data transfer time in the case of not hiding the host-device data transfer latency and *N*-pipe means the data transfer time of the pipelined implementation with an *N*-byte pipeline buffer. By hiding the latency more, the data transfer time approaches to the file read time, which is *FileRead* in the figure. These

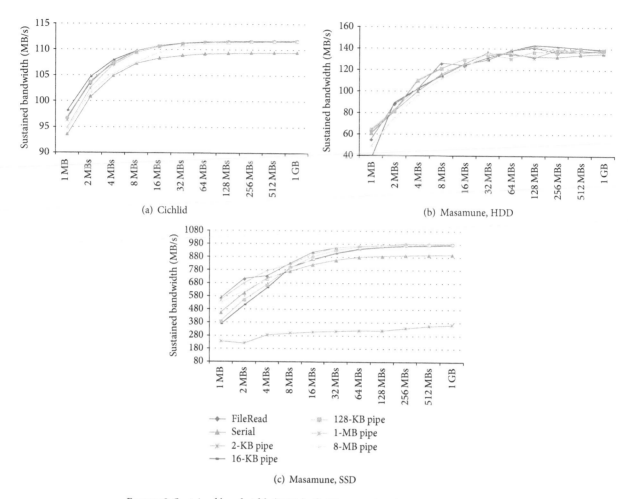

(a) Cichlid

(b) Masamune, HDD

(c) Masamune, SSD

FIGURE 3: Sustained bandwidth (MB/s) of `clEnqueueReadBufferToStdioFile`.

results indicate that the clDataTransfer extension can hide the host-device data transfer latency and hence the sustained performance of the data transfer from a file to a device memory buffer is almost comparable to the sustained bandwidth of just reading a file, that is, FileRead. A programmer can use the optimized data transfer implementation by just enqueuing a clDataTransfer command.

In the case of reading from the HDD of Masamune, the file read time varies widely as shown in Figure 3. This is likely due to the bandwidth of the disk and the behaviors of the read-ahead thread in the OS kernel. As a result, the performance gain is unseen. The FileRead performance is sometimes even lower than that of `clEnqueueWriteBufferFromStdioFile` because of the intrinsic measurement accuracy.

5.2.2. Evaluation with the Smith Waterman Algorithm. In this work, a CUDA program of the Smith Waterman algorithm [11] is ported to OpenCL. Then, the performance of the OpenCL version is evaluated to show that clDataTransfer can hide the host-device data transfer latency of a real application by overlapping it with the file access latency. In the Smith Waterman program, the data transfer time can be overlapped with the computation time. However, the data transfer time

is still partially exposed to the total execution time if the computation time is shorter than the data transfer time. The exposed data transfer time depends on the problem size. Therefore, in this evaluation, the overlap of computation and data transfer is disabled, and the fully exposed data transfer time is evaluated to clearly show the effect of overlapping the host-device data transfer latency with the file access latency.

The OpenCL program repeatedly reads the data in files to host memory buffers and sends them to device memory buffers. Suppose that `d_db` and `h_db` are handles of a device memory buffer and a host memory buffer, respectively. Their buffer size is `readsz`, and the file pointer is `fp`. Then, the original code has the following code pattern:

```
fread(h_db, readsz, 1, fp);
clEnqueueWriteBuffer(cmd,
d_db, CL_TRUE, 0, readsz, h_db, 0, NULL, NULL);
```

The above pattern is replaced with an additional OpenCL command enqueued by

```
clEnqueueWriteBufferFromStdioFile
(cmd, d_db, CL_TRUE, 0, readsz, fp, 0,
NULL, NULL);
```

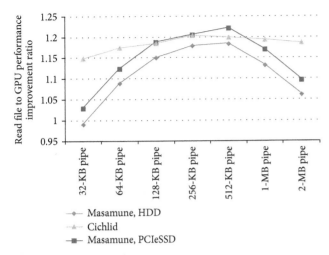

FIGURE 4: The improvement ratio of data transfer performance for the Smith Waterman algorithm.

The results of evaluating the data transfer time with changing the pipeline buffer size are shown in Figure 4. Here, the data transfer time is the total time of data transfers from a database file to a device memory buffer. These results indicate that the clDataTransfer extension can reduce the data transfer time if the pipeline buffer size is appropriately configured. The performance improvement of the clDataTransfer extension decreases if the pipeline buffer size is too small due to the runtime overhead of the pipeline implementation. It also decreases if the pipeline buffer size is too large compared to the data size, because pipelining with a too large buffer does not benefit from overlapping of data transfers. Accordingly, the optimal pipeline buffer size depends not only on the storage performance but also on the data size to be transferred from a file to a device memory buffer. The pipeline buffer size has to be dynamically adjusted because the data size is usually determined at runtime. Figure 4 discusses the effect of changing the pipeline buffer size on performance. Since the clDataTransfer extension hides the implementation details of data transfers, it is technically possible to employ empirical parameter tuning or autotuning for automatically finding the optimal pipeline buffer size, as in MVAPICH2-GPU's CUDA support.

In the Smith Waterman program, the data size to be read from a file ranges from 511 bytes to 4 Mbytes and hence is relatively small. The sustained bandwidths of both the file read and the host-device data transfer become lower for the transfer of a small data chunk. If the program is used for large input data, we believe that the performance improvement by clDataTransfer would become more remarkable as indicated in Figure 3.

5.3. Evaluation of Internode Communication Performance

5.3.1. Point-to-Point Communication Performance. One advantage of the clDataTransfer extension over conventional joint programming of MPI and OpenCL is that the clDataTransfer extension can hide the implementation details of system-aware optimization for efficient data transfers.

Figure 5 shows the difference in sustained bandwidth among pinned, mapped, and pipelined implementations described in Section 3. In the figure, "pipelined(N)" indicates the results of pipelined data transfers with the pipeline buffer size of N Mbytes. The evaluation results in Figure 5(a) show that the performance difference among the three implementations is small in the Cichlid system. This is because their sustained bandwidths are limited by the bandwidth of the GbE interconnect network. The time for host-device communication is much shorter than that of internode communication, and hence the pipelined implementation hardly improves the sustained bandwidth. On the other hand, in Figure 5(b), there is a big difference in sustained bandwidth among the three implementations. Moreover, the sustained bandwidth of the pipelined implementation changes with the pipeline buffer size. Pipelining with a relatively small pipeline buffer is the most efficient when the message size is small because the pipeline buffer size needs to be smaller than the message size. On the other hand, a large pipeline buffer leads to a higher sustained bandwidth for large messages because the sustained bandwidth of sending each pipeline buffer usually increases with the pipeline buffer size. Accordingly, the optimal pipeline buffer size changes depending at least on the message size.

From the above results, it is obvious that system-aware optimizations are often required by multinode GPU applications to achieve a high performance, and hence some abstractions of internode data transfers are necessary for high performance-portability. For example, on RICC, the pinned data transfer is always faster than the mapped one, while the mapped data transfer is faster for small messages on Cichlid due to the short latency of the implementation. The clDataTransfer extension provides interfaces that abstract internode data transfers and thereby allows an application programmer to use optimized data transfers without tricky programming techniques. An automatic selection mechanism of the data transfer implementations can be adopted behind the interfaces. The current implementation of the clDataTransfer runtime can use either the pinned or the mapped data transfer for small messages, and the pipelined data transfer can be performed for large messages. The pipelined data transfer can also be implemented using either the pinned or the mapped data transfer. In the following evaluation, the mapped and pinned data transfers are used for Cichlid and RICC, respectively. Of course, other optimized data transfers can be incorporated into the runtime and available to application programs without changing their codes, which results in high performance-portability across system types, scales, and probably generations.

5.3.2. Evaluation with the Himeno Benchmark. The performance impact of using the clDataTransfer extension is first evaluated by comparing the sustained performances of three implementations for the Himeno benchmark. One implementation is called the hand-optimized implementation presented in [13]. The hand-optimized implementation uses pinned data transfers for exchanging halo data of about 750 Kbytes. Another is called the serial implementation that is almost the same as the hand-optimized implementation

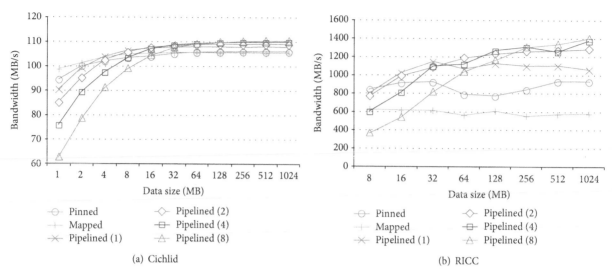

FIGURE 5: Sustained bandwidth of peer-to-peer communication.

but all the computations and communications are serialized. The performance of the serial implementation is supposed to be the lowest. The other is the implementation using the clDataTransfer extension, called the clDataTransfer implementation.

Figure 6 shows the sustained performances of the three implementations for the Himeno benchmark with M-size data. Since the hand-optimized implementation is well designed for overlapping the computations and communications, it can always achieve a higher performance than the serial implementation; the average speedup ratios are 51.2% and 15.2% for Cichlid and RICC, respectively. The performance of the clDataTransfer implementation is almost always comparable to that of the hand-optimized implementation because the communication times of both the hand-optimized and the clDataTransfer implementations are not exposed to their total execution times. Accordingly, the clDataTransfer extension allows an application programmer to easily overlap the communication and computation by simply sending internode communication commands to devices and utilizing OpenCL event objects to enforce the dependencies among OpenCL commands.

The results in Figure 6(a) are obtained using Cichlid whose network performance is low compared to the computation performance. The ratio of the computation time to the communication time in the serial implementation is also shown in the figure. Only in the case of Cichlid with four nodes, the ratio of the computation to the communication is less than one, and hence the communication time cannot completely be overlapped with the computation time when pinned data transfers are used for communication. In this case, the performance of the hand-optimized implementation is clearly lower than the clDataTransfer implementation. The main reason of the performance difference is that the mapped data transfer behind the clDataTransfer implementation is faster than the pinned data transfers. These results clearly show the importance of system-dependent optimizations for

highly efficient data transfers. As the programming model of the clDataTransfer extension encapsulates the data transfers, an application programmer does not need to know the implementation details and can automatically use the optimized implementation from a simply written code such as shown in Listing 4.

5.3.3. Evaluation with a Practical Application. The performance impact of the clDataTransfer extension is further discussed by taking the nanopowder growth simulation [14] as an example of real applications. The simulation code has been developed for numerical analysis of the entire growth process of binary alloy nanopowders in thermal plasma synthesis. Although various phenomena are considered to simulate the nanopowder growth process, about 90% of the total execution time of the original code is spent for simulating the process of coagulation among nanoparticles.

In the following evaluation, the clDataTransfer extension is applied to a parallel version of the simulation code, in which only the coagulation routine is parallelized using MPI, and its kernel loop is further accelerated using OpenCL. The other phenomena such as nucleation and condensation are computed by one host thread, and the coefficient data of about 42 Mbytes required by the coagulation routine are distributed from the host thread to each node at every simulation step. For the simulation code, two versions have been implemented to clarify the effect of using the optimized data transfers provided by the clDataTransfer extension. One is the baseline implementation that just uses `MPI_Isend` and `MPI_Recv` for coefficient data distribution. The other is the clDataTransfer implementation, which uses `MPI_Isend` with `MPI_CL_MEM` to send the coefficients in host memory buffers and `clEnqueueRecvBuffer` to receive them.

Figure 7 shows the results to compare the performances of the two implementations on RICC. Unlike the Himeno benchmark, the communication overheads are obviously

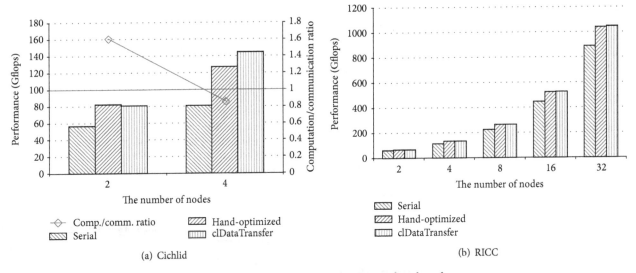

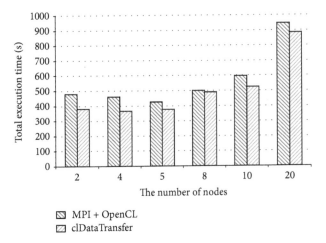

FIGURE 6: The performance for the Himeno benchmark.

FIGURE 7: The execution time of the nanopowder growth simulation (700 simulation steps).

exposed to the total execution time of this simulation program. Due to the decomposition method for MPI parallelization, the number of nodes must be a divisor of 40. Because of the poor parallelism, the performance degrades when the number of nodes increases beyond 8.

As shown in Figure 7, the clDataTransfer outperforms the baseline implementation because it can exploit an optimized implementation that overlaps the host-device communication with the internode communication in a pipelined fashion for sufficiently large messages. Accordingly, these results indicate that a higher performance can be achieved by appropriately interoperating MPI and OpenCL, and the clDataTransfer enables us to express the interoperation in a simple and effective way.

In the above evaluation, by just replacing the combination of `MPI_Recv` and `clEnqueueWriteBuffer` with `clEnqueueRecvBuffer`, the pipeline data transfer is used for the communication and leads to a higher sustained bandwidth.

Hence, the results also suggest that application programmers can incrementally improve their MPI programs so as to use the clDataTransfer extension. This is very important because most of existing applications have been developed using MPI.

6. Conclusions

This paper has proposed an OpenCL extension, clDataTransfer, to allow OpenCL to perform data transfers that need collaboration between hosts and compute devices. In the clDataTransfer extension, additional OpenCL commands are defined for encapsulating common programming patterns in data transfers from/to the device memory, such as internode communications and file accesses. The additional commands are executed in the same way as the other OpenCL commands. Using OpenCL event objects, we can express the dependency among both conventional and additional commands. Therefore, data transfers indicated by the additional commands are incorporated into the OpenCL execution model in a natural manner.

As data transfers are abstracted as OpenCL commands, the implementation details of the data transfers are hidden from application codes. Hence, clDataTransfer will be able to exploit new features of the latest devices without any user code change. As a result, clDataTransfer would allow today's applications to benefit from hardware improvements without making any code change or even without recompiling the application. That is, clDataTransfer can improve not only the performance but also the performance portabilities across system types, scales, and generations.

The performance evaluation results clearly show that clDataTransfer can achieve efficient data transfers while hiding the complicated implementation details, resulting in higher performance and scalability. Moreover, using the clDataTransfer extension, the host thread of an application is not blocked to serialize dependent operations of data transfers. As a result, the clDataTransfer extension allows an application programmer to easily use the opportunities to overlap communications and storage accesses with computations.

Although this work focuses on OpenCL, we believe that the idea itself could be applicable to other programming models such as CUDA. In the future, we will further improve the extension so that it can support other kinds of tasks that need help of host threads, such as system calls.

Conflict of Interests

The authors declare that there is no conflict of interests regarding the publication of this paper.

Acknowledgments

The authors would like to thank Professor Mayasa Shigeta and Professor Fumihiko Ino of Osaka University for allowing them to use their simulation codes in the performance evaluation. The authors would also like to thank the RIKEN Integrated Cluster of Clusters (RICC) at RIKEN for the user supports and the computer resources used for the performance evaluation. This research is partially supported by JST CREST "An Evolutionary Approach to Construction of a Software Development Environment for Massively-Parallel Heterogeneous Systems" and Grants-in-Aid for Scientific Research (B) nos. 25280041 and 25280012. The work is also partly supported by DoE Vancouver Project (DE-SC0005515).

References

[1] D. B. Kirk and W. W. Hwu, *Programming Massively Parallel Processors: A Hands-on Approach*, Morgan Kaufmann Publishers, 2007.

[2] B. Gaster, L. Howes, D. R. Kaeli, P. Mistry, and D. Schaa, *Heterogeneous Computing with OpenCL*, Morgan Kaufmann, Boston, Mass, USA, 2011.

[3] W. Gropp, E. Lusk, and A. Skjellum, *Using MPI: Portable Parallel Programming with the Message Passing Interface*, The MIT Press, 1999.

[4] O. S. Lawlor, "Message passing for GPGPU clusters: cudaMPI," in *Proceedings of the IEEE International Conference on Cluster Comptuing and Workshops (CLUSTER '09)*, pp. 1–8, 2009.

[5] A. M. Aji, J. Dinan, D. Buntinas et al., "MPI-ACC: An integrated and extensible approach to data movement in accelerator-based systems," in *Proceedings of the 14th IEEE International Conference on High Performance Computing and Communications (HPCC '12)*, pp. 647–654, Liverpool, UK, June 2012.

[6] H. Wang, S. Potluri, M. Luo, A. K. Singh, S. Sur, and D. K. Panda, "MVAPICH2-GPU: optimized GPU to GPU communication for InfiniBand clusters," *Computer Science: Research and Development*, vol. 26, no. 3-4, pp. 257–266, 2011.

[7] J. A. Stuart, P. Balaji, and J. D. Owens, "Extending MPI to accelerators," in *Proceedings of the 1st Workshop on Architectures and Systems for Big Data (ASBD '11)*, pp. 19–23, 2011.

[8] I. Gelado, J. Cabezas, N. Navarro, J. E. Stone, S. Patel, and W.-M. W. Hwu, "An asymmetric distributed shared memory model for heterogeneous parallel systems," in *Proceedings of the 15th International Conference on Architectural Support for Programming Languages and Operating Systems (ASPLOS '10)*, pp. 347–358, March 2010.

[9] J. A. Stuart and J. D. Owens, "Message passing on data-parallel architectures," in *Proceedings of the 23rd IEEE International Parallel and Distributed Processing Symposium (IPDPS '09)*, pp. 1–12, May 2009.

[10] A. Barak, T. Ben-Nun, E. Levy, and A. Shiloh, "A package for OpenCL based heterogeneous computing on clusters with many GPU devices," in *Proceedings of the IEEE International Conference on Cluster Computing Workshops and Posters*, pp. 1–7, September 2010.

[11] Y. Munekawa, F. Ino, and K. Hagihara, "Design and implementation of the Smith-Waterman algorithm on the CUDA-compatible GPU," in *Proceedings of the 8th IEEE International Conference on BioInformatics and BioEngineering (BIBE '08)*, pp. 1–6, October 2008.

[12] A. Krizhevsky, I. Sutskever, and G. E. Hinton, "ImageNet classification with deep convolutional neural networks," in *Advances in Neural Information Processing Systems*, vol. 25, pp. 1097–1105, 2012.

[13] E. H. Phillips and M. Fatica, "Implementing the Himeno benchmark with CUDA on GPU clusters," in *Proceedings of the 24th IEEE International Parallel and Distributed Processing Symposium (IPDPS '10)*, pp. 1–10, April 2010.

[14] M. Shigeta and T. Watanabe, "Growth model of binary alloy nanopowders for thermal plasma synthesis," *Journal of Applied Physics*, vol. 108, no. 4, Article ID 043306, 2010.

[15] The Open MPI Project, "Open MPI: open source high performance computing," http://www.open-mpi.org/.

11

Automated Design Space Exploration with Aspen

Kyle L. Spafford and Jeffrey S. Vetter

Oak Ridge National Laboratory, One Bethel Valley Road, Building 5100, MS-6173 Oak Ridge, TN 37831-6173, USA

Correspondence should be addressed to Jeffrey S. Vetter; vetter@computer.org

Academic Editor: Roman Wyrzykowski

Architects and applications scientists often use performance models to explore a multidimensional design space of architectural characteristics, algorithm designs, and application parameters. With traditional performance modeling tools, these explorations forced users to first develop a performance model and then repeatedly evaluate and analyze the model manually. These manual investigations proved laborious and error prone. More importantly, the complexity of this traditional process often forced users to simplify their investigations. To address this challenge of design space exploration, we extend our Aspen (Abstract Scalable Performance Engineering Notation) language with three new language constructs: user-defined resources, parameter ranges, and a collection of costs in the abstract machine model. Then, we use these constructs to enable automated design space exploration via a nonlinear optimization solver. We show how four interesting classes of design space exploration scenarios can be derived from Aspen models and formulated as pure nonlinear programs. The analysis tools are demonstrated using examples based on Aspen models for a three-dimensional Fast Fourier Transform, the CoMD molecular dynamics proxy application, and the DARPA Streaming Sensor Challenge Problem. Our results show that this approach can compose and solve arbitrary performance modeling questions quickly and rigorously when compared to the traditional manual approach.

1. Introduction

The design of next generation Exascale computer architectures as well as their future applications is complex, uncertain, and intertwined. Not surprisingly, modeling and simulation play an important role during these early design stages as neither the architectures nor the applications yet exist in any substantive form. Consequently, relevant performance models need to describe a complex, multidimensional design space of algorithms, application parameters, and architectural characteristics. Traditional performance modeling tools made this process difficult and resulted in a tendency to use simpler, less accurate models.

In our earlier work, we designed Aspen (Abstract Scalable Performance Engineering Notation) [1], a domain specific language for structured analytical performance modeling, to allow scientists to construct, evaluate, verify, compose, and share models of their applications. Aspen specifies a formal language and methodology that allows modelers to quickly generate representations of their applications as well as abstract machine models. In addition, Aspen includes a suite of analysis tools that consume these models to produce a variety of estimates for computation, communication, data structure sizes, algorithm characteristics, and bounds on expected runtime. Aspen can generate all of these estimates without application source code or low-level architectural information like Register Transfer Level (RTL). This ability to cope with high levels of uncertainty distinguishes Aspen from simulators, emulators, and other trace-driven approaches.

In fact, Aspen (and analytical modeling in general) is particularly useful at an early time horizon in the codesign process where the space of possible application parameters, algorithms, and architectures is too large to search with computationally intensive methods (e.g., cycle-accurate simulation) [2]. With this much uncertainty, application developers tend to identify important ranges of application parameters, rather than discrete values. Similarly, hardware architects may have identified a range of possible computational capabilities, but the machine characteristics have not been finalized. For example, feasible clock ranges may be dictated by the feature size and known well in advance of fabrication. Finding optima within these ranges transforms a typical performance modeling projection into an optimization problem.

1.1. Key Contributions. To address this challenge of design space exploration, we have extended our Aspen language and environment with expressive semantics for characterizing flexible design spaces rather than single models. Specifically, we add three new language constructs to Aspen: user-defined resources, parameter ranges, and a collection of costs in the abstract machine model. Then, we use these constructs to enable automated design space exploration via a nonlinear optimization solver. The solver uses these ranges (along with other constraints) to evaluate the Aspen performance models and evaluate a user-defined objective function for each point in the design space. As we will show, this automated process can allow thousands of model evaluations quickly and with minor regard to the performance model complexity.

The key contributions of this paper are as follows:

(1) a description of Aspen's syntax and semantics for specifying resources, parameter ranges, and costs in the abstract machine model;

(2) a formal problem description for four types of optimization problems derived from Aspen models;

(3) a description of new Aspen analysis tools which consume Aspen models and explore the design space with a standard nonlinear optimization solver;

(4) a demonstration of these new capabilities on existing Aspen models for 3DFFT, CoMD, and the Streaming Sensor Challenge Problem [3].

1.2. Related Work. In the space of analytical models, Aspen's approach to the abstract machine model is conceptually in between pure analytical models and semiempirical power-performance models based on direct measurement. Examples of the former include BSP [4] and Log P variants [5, 6] that focus strictly on algorithmic bounds. Examples of the latter include models based on performance counters or measurements [7–12] including proposed counters such as the leading loads counter [13]. Aspen is distinguished from these works in that it is capable of modeling machines and applications in more detail than the pure analytical models while obviating the requirement of the semiempirical approaches for an instrumented execution environment. Other related approaches are trace-driven and use linear programming for power-performance exploration, especially for searching the configuration space of dynamic voltage and frequency scaling [14, 15] or making decisions under explicit hardware power bounds [16].

On the application side, our goals for the use of Aspen and the 3DFFT model are directly related to the Exascale feasibility and projection studies of Gahvari and Gropp [17], Bhatele et al. [18], and Czechowski et al. [19].

In terms of design space exploration itself, an automated approach is a well-studied topic. Hardware-focused studies are also common, although they typically focus on reconfigurable architectures [20–22], particularly in well-constrained compiler-based planning or system on a chip (SoC) designs [23–26].

Several works focus on the theoretical aspects of exploring design spaces. Peixoto and Jacome examine metrics for the high-level design of such systems [27]. There are also works focusing on the abstractions [28] and algorithms for the search [29], environments where source code is available and modifiable [30], and specialized approaches for multilevel memory hierarchies [30]. In general, these works have similar goals and overall function to DSE in Aspen, but they consider very different machine models (usually with much more certainty and detail than the Aspen AMM).

2. Aspen Overview

While a more detailed description of Aspen has been published elsewhere [1], we briefly provide an overview and illustrate its use on an example model for a 1D Fast Fourier Transform (FFT). Aspen's domain specific language (DSL) approach to analytical performance modeling provides several advantages. For instance, Aspen's `control` construct helps to fully capture control flow and preserves more algorithmic information than traditional frameworks like BSP [4] and Log P variants [5, 6]. Similarly, the abstract machine model is more expressive than frameworks that reduce machine specifications to a small set of parameters.

The formal language specification forces scientists to construct models that can be syntactically checked and consumed by analysis tools; this formal specification also facilitates collaboration between domain experts and computer scientists. Aspen has also been defined to include the concept of modularity, so that it is easy to compose, reuse, and extend performance models.

Furthermore, this specification allows scientists to include application specific parameters in their model definitions, which would otherwise be difficult to infer. With this feature, Aspen can help answering application-specific questions such as how does parallelism vary with the number of atoms? And, this type of approach also allows inverse questions to be asked, such as, given a machine, what application problem can be solved within the system constraints?

Aspen is complementary to other performance prediction techniques including simulation [31, 32], emulation, or measurement on early hardware prototypes. Compared to these techniques, Aspen's analytical model is machine-independent, has fewer prerequisites (e.g., machine descriptions, source code), and decreased computational requirements. This positions Aspen as an especially useful tool during the early phases in the modeling lifecycle, with continuing use as a high-level tool to guide detailed studies with simulators. Hence, the primary goal of Aspen is to facilitate algorithmic and architectural exploration early and often.

2.1. Example: FFT. The FFT is a common scientific kernel and plays an important role in the image formation phase of SSCP [3], explored further in Section 5. Fortunately, FFT is also a well-studied algorithm, and tight bounds on the number of operations in an FFT are known.

```
(1) kernel 1DFFT {
(2)   exposes parallelism [n]
(3)   requires flops [5 * log2(n)] as dp, complex, simd
(4)   requires loads [a * max(1, log(n)/log(Z)) * wordSize] from
      fftVolume
(5) }
```

LISTING 1: Aspen kernel for 1D FFT.

```
(1) param n = 1 .. 100 // Basic Syntax
(2) param n = 100 in 10 .. 1000 // Default Value
```

LISTING 2: Syntax for an Aspen range.

For an n-element Cooley-Tukey style 1D FFT [33], the required number of floating point operations is bounded by $\mathcal{O}(5n \log_2 n)$, with some implementations requiring only 80% of this upper bound [34]. The number of cache misses has also been bounded for any FFT in the I/O complexity literature (on any two-level memory hierarchy which meets the tall cache assumption [35]) as $\Theta(1 + (n/L)(1 + \log_Z n))$, where L is the cache line size in words and Z is the cache capacity in words. For sufficiently large n, the number of cache misses, N_m, approaches $N_m = An \max(\log_Z n, 1)$, where A is a constant [19, 35] which translates the upper bound to an explicit count. Using the same variable names, these bounds roughly translate to two Aspen kernel clauses, as shown in Listing 1.

The listing also highlights the use of Aspen traits to add semantic information to specialize the flops, indicating that they are double precision, complex, and amenable to execution on SIMD FP units. The trait on the second clause specifies that the memory traffic in this kernel is from the fftVolume data structure.

The other variable, a, is a constant that arises from the nature of characterizing requirements by asymptotic bounds (e.g., $\mathcal{O}()$) [35]. Due to the complexity in modeling the memory hierarchy (e.g., from multilevel cache hierarchies, replacement policies) this type of constant is frequently measured using performance counters on an existing implementation of the algorithm to calibrate the model. It is a particularly common approach for characterizing memory traffic, even in the case of much simpler kernels, like matrix multiplication [36].

3. Modeling Methodology

In order to facilitate the evaluation of optimization problems, Aspen has been extended with three new language constructs to increase expressiveness.

3.1. User-Defined Resources. Prior work [1] with Aspen constrained modelers to a small set of predefined quantities of interest: flops, loads, stores, and messages. Since then, requests for modeling more exotic resources like system calls, allocation/deallocation, and more detailed modeling of system data paths (PCIe, QPI) have necessitated a more flexible system.

The first addition to Aspen is the ability for custom resources to be defined at arbitrary points in the abstract machine model (AMM) hierarchy. For instance, integer operations can be defined at the core level and access to a center-wide, shared filesystem could be defined at the machine level. Resources may also define custom traits with optional arguments. All new definitions, however, must provide an expression for how the resource maps to time and how the traits commutatively modify or replace the base expression (the mapping when no traits are present). An example of the new syntax is shown in Listing 3. Note that the new conflict statement describes the sets of resources that cannot overlap.

Furthermore, the AMM's assumptions of a completely connected socket topology and linear contention [1] are unchanged and apply equally to user-defined resources.

3.2. Ranges. The next construct is the range, illustrated in Listing 2. The range or interval is a familiar concept to programmers, has implementations in most modern languages, and is fairly easy to express and reason about.

More precisely, a *range* in Aspen is a closed, inclusive, connected, and optimal set of real numbers, S. A range that is *closed and inclusive* indicates that the interval contains lower and upper bounds a and b such that $a \leq x \leq b$, $\forall x, a, b \in S$, and $\forall S \in \mathbb{R}$. *Optimal*, in this case, means that range should be as narrow as possible. Aspen also allows for the specification of an explicit default value. This default value provides a convenient way for modelers to encode the "common case." When left unspecified, the lower bound is

```
(1)  core snbCore {
(2)
(3)    resource flops(number) [number / snbIssue ]
(4)      // Traits
(5)      with dp [base * 2],
(6)        // Optional Trait Argument
(7)        simd(width) [base / min(width, snbSIMDWidth)],
(8)        fmad [base / 2]
(9)      // Per-resource, per-core dynamic power
(10)     dynamic power [ (tdp - snbIdlePower) / snbNumCores ]
(11)
(12)   resource intops(number) [ number / snbIssue ]
(13)     dynamic power [ (intMaxPower - snbIdlePower) / snbNumCores ]
(14)
(15)   resource aesops(number) [ number / snbIssue ]
(16)     dynamic power [ (aesMaxPower - snbIdlePower) / snbNumCores ]
(17)
(18)   conflict (flops, intops, aesops)
(19)
(20)   // Shared static power cost
(21)   static power [ snbIdlePower ]
(22) }
```

LISTING 3: Aspen core model with static and dynamic costs.

used (by convention) in single analyses which do not consider ranges.

3.3. Including Costs in the Abstract Machine Model.
The second extension to Aspen includes the incorporation of several new types of costs into the abstract machine model: rack space, die area, static power, dynamic power, and component price. Each type of cost has rules for which components of the AMM hierarchy are applicable. However, all of these costs are optional. The only required cost is the specification of the time it takes to process a given resource.

Available rack space, the simplest cost, is specified at the machine level and associated costs are defined per node in standard units.

Total available die area is provided at the socket level and area costs are listed explicitly for all core, cache, and memory components. This allows, for instance, exploration of the tradeoff between die area spent on cache and the number of cores.

Static power costs are specified by providing each component of the AMM hierarchy with an idle wattage. Dynamic power is similarly specified at each point in the hierarchy, but it is also split by resource. That is, for a given component, performing different operations may result in different dynamic power requirements. A trivial example of this difference is an AMM where the cost of a floating point operation exceeds the cost of an integer operation.

Consider the example shown in Listing 3, where an AMM model for an Intel Sandy Bridge processor distinguishes between the power costs of a standard integer operation and the execution of the new advanced encryption instruction

set. While this example may seem somewhat contrived with existing hardware, its inclusion as a feature is important in future-proofing Aspen against the general trend towards more specialized instructions and fixed-function units that may vary widely in energy consumption.

These power costs also allow specifying constraints for maximum instantaneous power draw (i.e., highest wattage) and total energy consumption. Maximum power draw for an application is computed as the sum of all AMM component static costs and the largest of the sums of dynamic costs for each kernel:

$$W_{\max} = \overbrace{\sum_i^{\mathbb{M}} W_{i_{\text{idle}}}}^{\text{static}} + \overbrace{\max_j^{\mathbb{K}} \left(\sum_k^{\mathbb{R}_j} W_{k_{\text{dyn}}} \right)}^{\text{dynamic}}, \qquad (1)$$

where $\mathbb{M}$ is the set of all components in the AMM, W_i is the idle power draw of component i, $\mathbb{K}$ is the set of all kernels in the application model, $\mathbb{R}_j$ is the set of all resources required by kernel j, and $W_{k_{\text{dyn}}}$ is the dynamic power cost of resource k. In the absence of an application model, the maximum power draw is given by upper bound as the sum of static costs and the dynamic costs of all nonconflicting resources.

Similar to Aspen's other assumptions, these power calculations represent a simplified model which neglects several physical factors including cooling costs and transitions between component idle/peak states.

The Aspen tools already include the capability to produce bounds on predicted runtime by kernel clause [1], and the total energy cost of an application model is hence computed by the following:

$$C_{\text{energy}} = \overbrace{(W_{\text{idle}} \times r_{\text{total}})}^{\text{static}} + \overbrace{\sum_{i}^{\mathbb{K}} \left(\text{calls}_i * \sum_{j}^{\mathbb{C}} \left(r_j \times W_j \right) \right)}^{\text{dynamic}}, \quad (2)$$

where W_{idle} is the total system idle power, r_{total} is the total runtime, $\mathbb{K}$ is the set of all application kernels, calls_i indicates the number of calls to kernel i, $\mathbb{C}$ is the set of all clauses in kernel i, r_j is the runtime bound on clause j, and W_j is the dynamic power cost of the resource associated with clause j.

4. Nonlinear Optimization Solver

Using these new ranges and costs, a variety of optimization problems can be derived from Aspen models. These optimization problems have the following form.

(i) $f(\vec{x})$ is an objective function which must be maximized or minimized such as runtime, energy consumed, or problem size.

(ii) $\vec{x} = x_1, x_2, \ldots, x_n$ is a vector of decision variables with upper and lower bounds, sometimes called free variables. These bounds are typically derived from a range construct. Some examples include the number of nodes, problem sizes, and clock frequencies. The number of decision variables is known as the *dimensionality* of the problem.

(iii) $h_i(\vec{x}) = 0, i \in 1, \ldots, p$, is a set of p equality constraints, which are arbitrary functions of the decision variables that must be equal to zero.

(iv) $g_i(\vec{x}) \leq 0, i \in 1, \ldots, m$, is a set of m inequality constraints, which are functions on the decision variables that must be less than or equal to zero.

The difficulty of these optimization problems depends on several factors. In the best case, the constraint functions and the objective function are linear, and all of the decision variables are reals. This results in a traditional linear programming problem which can be trivially solved given the relatively low number of decision variables derived from an Aspen model.

If, however, some decision variables are integers, the problem is a mixed integer-linear program and is NP-complete. Similarly, difficulty is increased if the objective function or any of the constraint functions is nonlinear (i.e., nonlinear programming). And, if the objective function is not differentiable, a large class of efficient gradient-based methods cannot be used.

The current set of Aspen optimization tools relaxes all integer variables such that the typically generated optimization problem is a completely bounded, pure nonlinear program where the objective function may not be differentiable. An example of a relaxed integer variable might be the number of nodes (which, in practice, is easy to round to the nearest integer after optimization).

Since the objective or constraints may be complex, derived expressions (e.g., projected runtime, energy costs, and operation counts), these functions may be nonlinear and nondifferentiable. Hence, all optimization problems are solved using a gradient-free improved stochastic ranking evolution strategy (ISRES) [37] algorithm from the NLopt package [38].

Because no feasible point may be known *a priori*, these are considered global (as opposed to local) optimization problems. Establishing the criteria for termination is not always straightforward. However, due to the relatively low dimensionality (ISRES scales to thousands of variables) of Aspen-generated problems, we select NLopt's time-based stopping criterion with a threshold of a few seconds.

An interesting facet of this approach is that a user can constrain any combination of the parameters, leaving the objective function to include the remaining parameters. For example, in the Machine Planner scenario, the user defines the application model and constraints, general parameters of time to solution or power, and they use the design space exploration to search for the best combination of machine parameters. In another example, the Problem Size Planner, the user defines the machine parameters, constrains the same general parameters of time to solution or power, and then maximizes the application input problem that can be solved with that configuration.

5. Design Space Exploration

Combined with the existing analysis tools, the new range and cost constructs enable the formulation of a vast number of optimization problems for design space exploration. Combinations of the number and type of Aspen models involved, the portions of those models that are fixed or free variables, the goal (maximization or minimization), objective function, and additional constraints rapidly grow out of control. To constrain this otherwise unwieldy variety, the tool interface for design space exploration is centered on four common scenarios, summarized in Table 1.

5.1. Implementation Overview. The implementation of the tools, however, enables roughly the same workflow for each of the four scenario types, as depicted in the process diagram in Figure 1. This workflow has two main phases, problem formulation and optimization.

First, depending on the scenario, one of the Aspen optimization tools is run. This tool consumes one or more Aspen model files as input and collects the relevant ranges from the model into the vector of decision variables, $\vec{x}$. Additional constraints such as time, energy, space, capacity, or price are specified via command line option. Also specified via the command line are nonstandard objective functions, which may include one or more parameters, derived capabilities, or weighted combinations of parameters and capabilities.

Based on these inputs, the Aspen optimization tools generate a single C++ code file that drives NLopt's standard API. This generated code preserves the semantics of the original Aspen models such that variable names are consistent and

TABLE 1: Comparison of Aspen scenarios for design space exploration.

Name	Application model	AMM	Constraints	Objectives
Parameter tuner	Single, free	None	Param ranges	Minimize op counts, data sizes
Problem size planner	Single, free	Single, fixed	Param ranges, energy budget, and time limit	Maximize App params
Machine planner	Single, fixed	Single, free	Param ranges, energy budget, and time limit	Minimize AMM params
AMM architect	None	Multiple, free	Param ranges, power budget, and price	Maximize capability, minimize costs

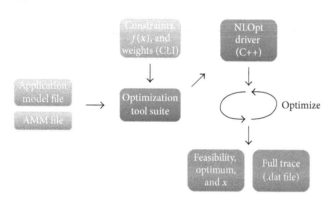

FIGURE 1: Process diagram of the design exploration workflow. CLI indicates inputs specified via command line options to the four problem formulation tools. $f(\vec{x})$ refers to the objective function and $\vec{x}$ is the vector of decision variables.

the code is amenable to inspection and modification for special use cases.

In the optimization phase, the generated C++ code is compiled and run. This code prints the value of the objective function at the optimum as well as the values of all of the decision variables. Or, in the case of unfeasible problems, it indicates that no optimum was found. It optionally generates a trace file that contains all the values of $\vec{x}$ and $f(\vec{x})$ for each evaluation of the objective function for postprocessing and visualization.

5.2. DSE Scenarios. In the following sections, we provide an overview of each scenario (and Aspen tool) in more detail and provide some pertinent example analyses. Note that, for these examples, we use relatively straightforward objective functions and only a handful of decision variables, but Aspen can handle problems of arbitrary complexity and dimensionality (given a reasonable solution timeframe).

5.2.1. Parameter Tuner. The first optimization tool addresses application models with tunable parameters that have a significant impact on performance. While this is generally applicable to application-specific parameters, our motivating use case is a tiling factor. This type of factor (equivalent to blocking and chunking factors for our purposes) is quite

common due to data-parallel decomposition and cache-blocking techniques.

As a motivating example, we consider the DARPA UHPC Streaming Sensor Challenge Problem (SSCP) [3]. In this challenge problem, dynamic sensor data are converted to an image and pushed through a multistep, data-parallel analysis pipeline. The image is split into tiles according to a tiling factor, `tf`, which specifies how many tiles to use in each dimension. The two primary phases of the pipeline are digital spotlighting and backprojection.

The `tf` factor has a particularly interesting effect on total floating point operation count. Digital spotlighting kernels tend to require less work with smaller tiling factors (largely due to a requirement for fewer FFTs) while backprojection is more efficient at larger tiling factors. Choosing poor `tf` results in a potential for substantial unnecessary work (and, consequently, poor performance and low energy efficiency).

In order to characterize this tradeoff with the Paramater Tuner, the Aspen model for SSCP encodes the tiling factor as a range:

```
param tf = 32 in 16 .. 64
```

Combined with a command line argument for the resource of interest (e.g., flops, memory capacity), the Parameter Tuner generates a minimization problem with one bounded decision variable (`tf`) and an objective function that computes the total number of that resource required by the kernels in SSCP.

Prior to this work, Aspen had the capability to plot resource requirements in terms of one or two variables [1]. Figure 2 depicts a standard resource plot annotated with a tick for the first 250 points where the objective function was evaluated, with the minimum found at $7.009e + 13$ total flops at a `tf` of 34.

We note two observations concerning Figure 2. First, each objective function evaluation is consistent with the analytically computed total flop count, indicating consistency across different Aspen tools. Second, the linear relaxation of `tf` (an integer) introduces some minor inefficiency, as the objective function is evaluated multiple times for equivalent values.

5.2.2. Problem Size Planner. The second optimization tool is focused on the exploration of what problems are feasible to solve on a machine given a set of constraints. These

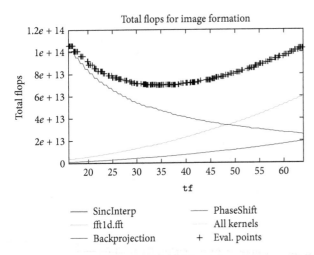

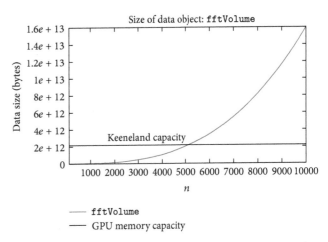

FIGURE 2: A characterization of the total number of flops required for SSCP image formation by kernel. Each black tick indicates a single evaluation of the objective function by the nonlinear optimizer as it is executed.

FIGURE 3: This chart shows the growth in the `fftVolume` data structure as a function of n relative to the memory capacity constraint (GPU physical memory on Keeneland).

constraints can consist of time, power, energy, and/or capacity limits. In addition to traditional runtime and allocation planning, searching this design space can help provide an application-specific perspective on the benefits of obtaining new hardware by comparing results across different machine models.

To motivate this tool, we consider a model for a 3DFFT [1] and want to answer the question of what is the largest 3DFFT we can solve such that

(i) the `fftVolume` data structure fits into the aggregate memory of the GPUs on the NSF Keeneland system [39];

(ii) it has an estimated runtime of less than ten seconds;

(iii) it has an estimated total energy consumption of no more than five megajoules.

Our optimization problem, then, is a maximization problem of dimensionality one where the single decision variable (and objective function) is n, the dimension of the 3DFFT volume. Furthermore, each of the three requirement statements above corresponds to a single inequality constraint. Figures 3, 4, and 5 show how the requirements for the 3DFFT scale with n.

This energy calculation is based on a simple power model where the dynamic power requirement of the GPU is the manufacturer's stated thermal design point (250 W) when performing floating point operations or memory transfers, and the static/idle power is that measured using the NVIDIA system management interface (30 W). Transitions between states are assumed to be instantaneous and without cost. While simple, this model approximates the race-to-idle behavior. In future work, this model could be improved by measuring power draw for each resource using a synthetic benchmark (e.g., only flops, only loads/stores, and only MPI messages).

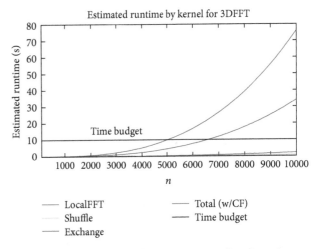

FIGURE 4: This chart shows the increase in predicted runtime as a function of the dimension of the volume n and its relation to the specified constraint of five seconds. In addition to overall runtime (CF = control flow), runtime per invocation of each kernel is also shown.

5.2.3. Machine Planner. The third interface for formulating optimization problems with Aspen models is the Machine Planner. In contrast to the first two tools, the Machine Planner fixes the application model and focuses on identifying application-specific targets for machine capabilities. In other words, it explores what minimum level of performance the machine must attain to complete a workload within a set amount of time, energy, and/or other constraints.

This scenario is typically a minimization problem over parameters in the abstract machine model. As an illustrative example, we consider a model for the CoMD molecular dynamics proxy application and the Keeneland AMM. Specifically, we want to find the minimum clock frequencies for a Fermi GPU's cores and memory that are required to complete a thousand iterations of CoMD's embedded atom

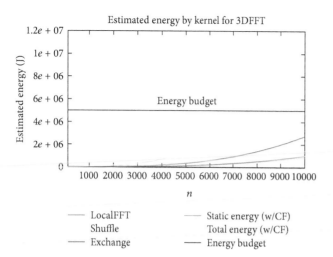

Figure 5: This chart shows the relationship between n and overall energy consumption, relative to the constraint of five megajoules. In addition to overall and per-kernel dynamic consumption, static costs for Keeneland are also shown.

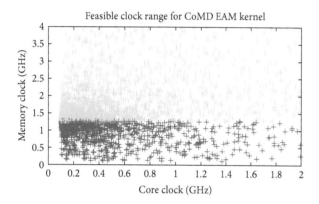

Figure 6: This figure shows the feasible core and memory clock ranges for computing one thousand iterations of the CoMD EAM force kernel on a Fermi GPU within one second. Green markers indicate evaluation points that satisfy the constraints and red markers indicate infeasible clock settings.

method (EAM) force kernel for just over a million atoms (1048576) in one second.

The parameter hierarchy in Listing 4 shows how the effective memory bandwidth is computed as a derived parameter from the clock rate that incorporates aspects of the GDDR5 architecture including the interface width and the measured overheads associated with using ECC. GDDR5's quad pumping, transferring a word on the rising and falling edge of two clocks, is accounted for within the gddr5Clock parameter, although this could be broken out into a separate parameter. Furthermore, eccPenalty accounts for overheads and sustained is based on measurements from the SHOC benchmark suite [40] that accounts for the difference between maximum sustained and peak bandwidth.

Figure 6 shows the feasible range for both clocks and provides two insights. First, the EAM kernel is strongly memory-bound and is feasible at the lowest point in the core clock range. And second, the increased concentration of evaluation points toward the computed optimum ($1e + 08, 1.27e + 09$) shows NLopt converging on the solution.

5.2.4. AMM Architect. The fourth tool is the AMM Architect which focuses on application-independent analyses. It primarily facilitates solving two types of problems—capacity planning under constraints and optimizing within a bounded projection for future performance targets (similar to the projections from the Echelon project [41] and DARPA Exascale Study [42]). These scenarios are typically maximization problems, where the objective function is some machine capability like peak flops, bandwidth, or capacity.

As an example calculation, we consider a sample problem which maximizes the floating-point capability for a Keeneland-like architecture under the following constraints:

(1) space and power budget of 42 U (one rack) and 18 KW, respectively,

(2) minimum double precision FP capability of 50 TF,

(3) minimum aggregate FP capability to memory bandwidth ratio of 3 : 1 flops : bytes.

The decision variables correspond to all the ranges in the machine model including the number of nodes, number of sockets (1–4) and GPUs per node (1–8), and all the clock frequencies (CPU core, DDR3 memory, GPU core, and GDDR5 memory).

After running the AMM Architect, we discover that this problem has no feasible solution. This problem was chosen to highlight one of the limitations of the optimization-based approach: when there is no feasible solution for a multiconstraint problem, determining why the solution is not feasible or how "close" to feasibility the best point is requires nontrivial postprocessing. In practice, however, this can usually be overcome by iteratively relaxing the constraints.

6. Conclusions

Most scientists that use performance modeling are seeking to understand systems or optimize specific configurations, rather than generating a single forward performance projection. Likewise, many of the performance modeling scenarios facilitated by Aspen are concerned with the exploration of a multidimensional design space. The addition of user-defined resources, parameter ranges, and AMM costs substantially increases Aspen's flexibility and helps facilitate more complex modeling workflows. The ability to specify static and dynamic energy costs is especially important for models that describe extreme-scale or energy-constrained environments.

With these new costs, the vast array of potential optimization problems can be unwieldy. Aspen attempts to streamline problem formulation by constraining the interface to four specific scenarios. While these tools do not address all potential problems of interest (and we anticipate that expert users will modify these tools and generate their own scenarios), they do automate the process for common performance modeling tasks.

```
(1) // Effective clock (includes quad-pump)
(2) param gddr5Clock = 3.7 * giga in 100 * mega .. 4 * giga
(3) param gddr5Width = 48
(4) param eccPenalty = 0.88
(5) param sustained = 0.852// measured
(6) param gddr5BW = gddr5Clock * gddr5Width * eccPenalty * sustained
```

LISTING 4: Aspen parameters for GDDR5 bandwidth.

6.1. Future Work. In the course of this work, we have identified two major challenges that require further study. First, complex models, especially those with high dimensionality, will require additional techniques to effectively visualize the design space. While some visualizations geared towards multidimensional data exist (e.g., parallel coordinates), visualizing ten or more dimensions is a common problem in scientific visualization. The current optimization tools write out a data file that contains each evaluation of the objective function, and the search space can be visualized a few dimensions per plot.

Another challenge for generating optimization problems involves specifying weights for complex objective functions. Directly adding weights to Aspen parameter definitions proved cumbersome and failed to address objective functions with nonparameter, derived quantities. Instead, the current tools require explicit command-line options for these weights.

Conflict of Interests

The authors declare that there is no conflict of interests regarding the publication of this paper.

Acknowledgments

This research is sponsored by the Office of Advanced Scientific Computing Research in the U.S. Department of Energy and DARPA Contract HR0011-10-9-0008. The paper has been authored by Oak Ridge National Laboratory, which is managed by UT-Battelle, LLC under Contract DE-AC05-00OR22725 to the U.S. Government. Accordingly, the U.S. Government retains a nonexclusive, royalty-free license to publish or reproduce the published form of this contribution, or allow others to do so, for U.S. Government purposes.

References

[1] K. L. Spafford and J. S. Vetter, "Aspen: a domain specific language for performance modeling," in *Proceedings of the 24th International Conference for High Performance Computing, Networking, Storage and Analysis (SC '12)*, pp. 1–11, IEEE, Salt Lake City, Utah, USA, November 2012.

[2] J. J. Yi, L. Eeckhout, D. J. Lilja, B. Calder, L. K. John, and J. E. Smith, "The future of simulation: a field of dreams?" *Computer*, vol. 39, no. 11, pp. 22–29, 2006.

[3] D. Campbell, D. Cook, and B. Mulvaney, "A streaming sensor challenge problem for ubiquitous high performance computing," in *Proceedings of 15th Annual Workshop on High Performance Embedded Computing (HPEC '11)*, November 2011.

[4] L. G. Valiant, "Bridging model for parallel computation," *Communications of the ACM*, vol. 33, no. 8, pp. 103–111, 1990.

[5] A. Alexandrov, M. F. Ionescu, K. E. Schauser, and C. Scheiman, "LogGP: incorporating long messages into the LogP model," in *Proceedings of the 7th Annual ACM Symposium on Parallel Algorithms and Architectures (SPAA '95)*, pp. 95–105, July 1995.

[6] D. Culler, R. Karp, D. Patterson et al., "LogP: Towards a realistic model of parallel computation," in *Proceedings of the 4th ACM SIGPLAN Symposium on Principles & Practice of Parallel Programming*, pp. 1–12, May 1993.

[7] M. Curtis-Maury, J. Dzierwa, C. D. Antonopoulos, and D. S. Nikolopoulos, "Online power-performance adaptation of multithreaded programs using hardware event-based prediction," in *Proceedings of the 20th Annual International Conference on Supercomputing (ICS '06)*, pp. 157–166, Association for Computing Machinery, July 2006.

[8] S.-J. Lee, H.-K. Lee, and P.-C. Yew, "Runtime performance projection model for dynamic power management," in *Advances in Computer Systems Architecture*, vol. 4697 of *Lecture Notes in Computer Science*, pp. 186–197, Springer, Berlin, Germany, 2007.

[9] D. Snowdon, G. Van Der Linden, S. Petters, and G. Heiser, "Accurate runtime prediction of performance degradation under frequency scaling," in *Proceedings of the Workshop on Operating Systems Platforms for Embedded Real-Time Applications*, 2007.

[10] S. Song and K. W. Cameron, "System-level power-performance efficiency modeling for emergent GPU architectures," in *Proceedings of the 21st International Conference on Parallel Architectures and Compilation Techniques (PACT '12)*, pp. 473–474, ACM, September 2012.

[11] S. Song, M. Grove, and K. W. Cameron, "An iso-energy-efficient approach to scalable system power-performance optimization," in *Proceedings of the IEEE International Conference on Cluster Computing (CLUSTER '11)*, pp. 262–271, September 2011.

[12] S. Song, C.-Y. Su, R. Ge, A. Vishnu, and K. W. Cameron, "Iso-energy-efficiency: an approach to power-constrained parallel computation," in *Proceedings of the 25th IEEE International Parallel and Distributed Processing Symposium (IPDPS '11)*, pp. 128–139, IEEE, May 2011.

[13] B. Rountree, D. K. Lowenthal, M. Schulz, and B. R. De Supinski, "Practical performance prediction under dynamic Voltage frequency scaling," in *Proceedings of the International Green Computing Conference (IGCC '11)*, July 2011.

[14] B. Rountree, D. K. Lowenthal, S. Funk, V. W. Freeh, B. R. de Supinski, and M. Schulz, "Bounding energy consumption in

large-scale MPI programs," in *Proceedings of the ACM/IEEE Conference on Supercomputing (SC '07)*, pp. 49:1–49:9, ACM, November 2007.

[15] B. Rountree, D. K. Lowenthal, B. R. de Supinski, M. Schulz, V. W. Freeh, and T. Bletsch, "Adagio: making DVS practical for complex HPC applications," in *Proceedings of the 23rd International Conference on Supercomputing (ICS '09)*, pp. 460–469, ACM, Newport Beach, Calif, USA, June 2009.

[16] B. Rountree, D. H. Ahn, B. R. de Supinski, D. K. Lowenthal, and M. Schulz, "Beyond DVFS: a first look at performance under a hardware-enforced power bound," in *Proceedings of the IEEE 26th International Parallel and Distributed Processing Symposium Workshops (IPDPSW '12)*, pp. 947–953, Shanghai, China, May 2012.

[17] H. Gahvari and W. Gropp, "An introductory exascale feasibility study for FFTs and multigrid," in *Proceedings of the IEEE International Parallel and Distributed Processing Symposium (IPDPS '10)*, pp. 1–9, IEEE, Atlanta, Ga, USA, April 2010.

[18] A. Bhatele, P. Jetley, H. Gahvari, L. Wesolowski, W. D. Gropp, and L. Kalé, "Architectural constraints to attain 1 exaflop/s for three scientific application classes," in *Proceedings of the IEEE International Parallel and Distributed Processing Symposium (IPDPS '11)*, pp. 80–91, IEEE, Anchorage, Alaska, USA, May 2011.

[19] K. Czechowski, C. Battaglino, C. McClanahan, K. Iyer, P.-K. Yeung, and R. Vuduc, "On the communication complexity of 3D FFT and its implications for exascale," in *Proceedings of the 26th ACM International Conference on Supercomputing (ICS '12)*, pp. 205–214, June 2012.

[20] K. S. Chatha and R. Vemuri, "An iterative algorithm for hardware-software partitioning, hardware design space exploration and scheduling," *Design Automation for Embedded Systems*, vol. 5, no. 3, pp. 281–293, 2000.

[21] E. Sotiriades and A. Dollas, "Design space exploration for the BLAST algorithm implementation," in *Proceedings of the 15th Annual IEEE Symposium on Field-Programmable Custom Computing Machines (FCCM '07)*, pp. 323–325, April 2007.

[22] A. Stammermann, L. Kruse, W. Nebel et al., "System level optimization and design space exploration for low power," in *Proceedings of the 14th International Symposium on System Synthesis (ISSS '01)*, pp. 142–146, ACM, October 2001.

[23] J. Keinert, M. Streubuhr, T. Schlichter et al., "SystemCoDesigner an automatic ESL synthesis approach by design space exploration and behavioral synthesis for streaming applications," *ACM Transactions on Design Automation of Electronic Systems*, vol. 14, no. 1, article 1, 2009.

[24] K. Lahiri, A. Raghunathan, and S. Dey, "Efficient exploration of the SoC communication architecture design space," in *Proceedings of the IEEE/ACM International Conference on Computer Aided Design (ICCAD '00)*, pp. 424–430, IEEE, Piscataway, NJ, USA, 2000.

[25] K. Lahiri, A. Raghunathan, and S. Dey, "Design space exploration for optimizing on-chip communication architectures," *IEEE Transactions on Computer-Aided Design of Integrated Circuits and Systems*, vol. 23, no. 6, pp. 952–961, 2004.

[26] M. Palesi and T. Givargis, "Multi-objective design space exploration using genetic algorithms," in *Proceedings of the 10th International Symposium on Hardware/Software Codesign (CODES '02)*, pp. 67–72, May 2002.

[27] H. P. Peixoto and M. F. Jacome, "Algorithm and architecture-level design space exploration using hierarchical data flows," in *Proceedings of the IEEE International Conference on Application-Specific Systems, Architectures and Processors (ASAP '97)*, pp. 272–282, July 1997.

[28] P. Mishra, N. Dutt, and A. Nicolau, "Functional abstraction driven design space exploration of heterogeneous programmable architectures," in *Proceedings of the 14th International Symposium on System Synthesis (ISSS '01)*, pp. 256–261, ACM, New York, NY, USA, October 2001.

[29] I. Karkowski and H. Corporaal, "Design space exploration algorithm for heterogeneous multi-processor embedded system design," in *Proceedings of the 35th Annual Design Automation Conference (DAC '98)*, pp. 82–87, San Francisco, Calif, USA, June 1998.

[30] R. Szymanek, F. Catthoor, and K. Kuchcinski, "Time-energy design space exploration for multi-layer memory architectures," in *Proceedings of the Design, Automation and Test in Europe Conference and Exhibition*, vol. 1, pp. 318–323, February 2004.

[31] C. L. Janssen, H. Adalsteinsson, and J. P. Kenny, "Using simulation to design extremescale applications and architectures: programming model exploration," *ACM SIGMETRICS Performance Evaluation Review*, vol. 38, no. 4, pp. 4–8, 2011.

[32] A. F. Rodrigues, K. S. Hemmert, B. W. Barrett et al., "The structural simulation toolkit," *ACM SIGMETRICS Performance Evaluation Review*, vol. 38, no. 4, pp. 37–42, 2011.

[33] J. W. Cooley and J. W. Tukey, "An algorithm for the machine calculation of complex Fourier series," *Mathematics of Computation*, vol. 19, no. 90, pp. 297–301, 1965.

[34] S. G. Johnson and M. Frigo, "A modified split-radix FFT with fewer arithmetic operations," *IEEE Transactions on Signal Processing*, vol. 55, no. 1, pp. 111–119, 2007.

[35] M. Frigo, C. E. Leiserson, H. Prokop, and S. Ramachandran, "Cache-oblivious algorithms," in *Proceedings of the IEEE 40th Annual Conference on Foundations of Computer Science*, pp. 285–297, October 1999.

[36] T. Hoeer, W. Gropp, W. Kramer, and M. Snir, "Performance modeling for systematic performance tuning," in *Proceedings of the State of the Practice Reports (SC '11)*, pp. 6:1–6:12, 2011.

[37] T. P. Runarsson and X. Yao, "Search biases in constrained evolutionary optimization," *IEEE Transactions on Systems, Man and Cybernetics Part C: Applications and Reviews*, vol. 35, no. 2, pp. 233–243, 2005.

[38] S. Johnson, "The NLopt nonlinear optimization package," http://ab-initio.mit.edu/nlopt.

[39] J. S. Vetter, R. Glassbrook, J. Dongarra et al., "Keeneland: bringing heterogeneous GPU computing to the computational science community," *Computing in Science and Engineering*, vol. 13, no. 5, pp. 90–95, 2011.

[40] A. Danalis, G. Marin, C. McCurdy et al., "The scalable heterogeneous computing (SHOC) benchmark suite," in *Proceedings of the 3rd Workshop on General-Purpose Computation on Graphics Processing Units (GPGPU '10)*, pp. 63–74, ACM, March 2010.

[41] S. W. Keckler, W. J. Dally, B. Khailany, M. Garland, and D. Glasco, "GPUs and the future of parallel computing," *IEEE Micro*, vol. 31, no. 5, pp. 7–17, 2011.

[42] P. Kogge, K. Bergman, S. Borkar et al., "Exascale computing study: technology challenges in achieving exascale systems," Tech. Rep., DARPA Information Processing Techniques Office, 2008.

12

Graph Drawing and Analysis Library and its Domain-Specific Language for Graphs' Layout Specifications

Renata Vaderna ⓘ, **Željko Vuković, Igor Dejanović, and Gordana Milosavljević** ⓘ

Faculty of Technical Sciences, University of Novi Sad, Trg Dositeja Obradovića 6, Novi Sad, Serbia

Correspondence should be addressed to Gordana Milosavljević; grist@uns.ac.rs

Academic Editor: Basilio B. Fraguela

This paper presents a graph drawing and analysis library written in Java called GRAD and its domain-specific language for simplifying the process of laying out graphs. One of GRAD's main goals is to provide completely automated ways of selecting and configuring a drawing algorithm, based either on the properties of a graph or on a user's input conforming to the domain-specific language. In order to verify the quality of GRAD's main features a user study was conducted. The participants were asked to grade diagrams visualized and laid out using different modeling tools, including one relying on GRAD, which received the best overall scores.

1. Introduction

Every graph, informally defined as a set of vertices and edges between them, can be drawn in a number of different ways [1]. Strictly theoretically speaking, it is only important that each vertex is mapped to a point on the plane and each edge to a curve between the appropriate two vertices. However, the arrangement of these elements directly impacts the graph's readability, understandability, and usability [1–5], that is, how clearly a viewer can understand the visualized information. An example of two different drawings of the same abstract graph is shown in Figure 1. Relationships between vertices of the graph are, for example, more evident in Figure 1(a).

Every diagram consisting of connected elements can be seen as a graph, UML class, activity, use case, business processes, and so on. In addition to conforming to some formal notation, diagrams can be created in accordance with their secondary notation. Secondary notation is defined as a set of visual cues which are not a part of a formal one [6]. In the graphical context, these cues are used to improve the readability of a formal notation and include the color of certain elements of the diagram and its layout. The study conducted by Schrepfer et al. discusses the impact of the secondary notation on the level of understanding of a business process model. It singles out the layout as the most important factor, determining how well both novices and experts perform while analyzing such models [7]. Similarly, the study by Purchase et al. focuses on the importance of different layout aesthetics in the domain of UML diagrams [8].

Bear the mentioned in mind, it is not surprising that many modeling tools (MagicDraw (http://www.nomagic.com/products/magicdraw.html), PowerDesigner (http://powerdesigner.de/en/), and Papyrus (https://eclipse.org/papyrus/)) and graphical modeling workbenches (Graphical Modeling Framework (GMF) (http://www.eclipse.org/modeling/gmp/), Sirius (http://www.eclipse.org/sirius/)) strive to offer the possibility of automatically laying out created diagrams in an aesthetically pleasing way. Such feature is particularly important in situations when a model created with some other tool is imported and visualized in the given one. In those cases, graphical elements are created and, preferably, laid out automatically. Furthermore, GMF and Sirius provide a way of expanding the set of available layout algorithms with new ones [9].

Developers of various new graphical editors as well as users of the existing ones looking to enhance their layout feature could, therefore, be interested in implementing one or more graph drawing algorithms. While there are types of layout techniques whose comprehension is not overly challenging, namely, circular, tree, and force-directed [10], implementing more sophisticated ones requires a significant

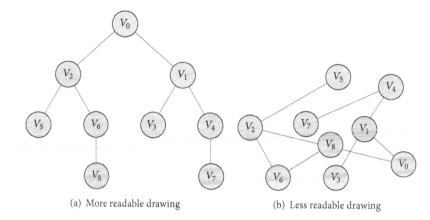

(a) More readable drawing   (b) Less readable drawing

FIGURE 1: Two drawings of the same abstract graph.

knowledge of graph theory. The reason lays in the fact that such approaches often rely on complex graph analysis algorithms, such as decomposition of a graph into k-connected components, planarity testing and planar embedding, and finding graph's automorphisms [11–14]. For that reason, most developers are forced to use existing implementations of analysis algorithms, thus easing their own development of graph drawing algorithms or of already implemented layout algorithms.

There are several existing libraries focusing on the field of graph drawing. In this paper, however, emphasis is put on open-source solutions written in Java. Three such libraries can be singled out, due to offering the greatest number of stable implementations of layout algorithms: JUNG framework (http://jung.sourceforge.net), JGraphX (https://github.com/jgraph/jgraphx), and prefuse (http://prefuse.org). While all of them provide at least one implementation of a complex layout algorithm which can be applied on any graph, there are still some notable classes of such algorithms the libraries do not cover: straight-line, orthogonal, and symmetric above all. It can also be noted that none of the libraries have an impressive collection of analysis algorithms, only offering relatively basic ones, like depth-first search and Dijkstra's shortest path [16]. The mentioned shortcomings of available solution inspired the development of our new open-source graph analysis and drawing library (GRAD) (https://www.gradlibrary.net).

On top of offering a wide arrange of graph analysis algorithms, as well as implementations of layout algorithms belonging to classes omitted by other Java libraries, GRAD provides

(i) an easy way of calling its layout algorithms and retrieving the results,

(ii) two means of automatic selection and configuration of an appropriate layout algorithm, neither of which is supported by the other solutions:

    (1) based on the properties of the graph,

    (2) in accordance with the user's desires expressed through a domain-specific language.

Automation of the process of selection of an algorithm was motivated by the fact that not every user of a graphical editor can be expected to have a prior knowledge of graph drawing theory. Without it, a user would not know what to expect when calling a certain algorithm and how to configure its parameters to get the desired result. The first method analyzes the graph and singles out an algorithm based on the existence or absence of certain properties (like planarity, if the graph is a tree or not, etc.). However, a drawing produced as a result of application of a mathematically determined algorithm might not be in accordance with a user's personal preferences. This was the inspiration behind the development of GRAD's second automatic selection option. Using a domain-specific language (a computer language specialized to a particular domain [17]), the users can specify aesthetic criteria that the drawing should conform to. It should be mentioned that since the mid-1990s, several studies trying to measure the effectiveness of different aesthetic criteria have been conducted [3, 18–21]. However, with most of them focusing on some specific types of graphs, there is still much work to be done in this field. This fact also influenced the decision to leave the users the choice of aesthetic criteria, as opposed to automatically giving priority to one over the others.

There are two main reasons why a domain-specific language (DSL) would be the most suitable solution to the problem of letting the users choose the aesthetic criteria:

(1) GRAD is a library meant to be used by graph (diagram) editors. Unlike a graphical configuration tool, the language can be used by any project being developed in Java, regardless of which framework it uses, if it is a web or a desktop application and so on.

(2) DSLs can support more complex specifications, like the usage of the logical and/or/not operators.

In order to verify that the diagrams automatically laid out by GRAD are aesthetically pleasing and that the library is simple to use, a user study was conducted. The participants were software engineers who were firstly tasked with grading diagrams laid out using GRAD, as well as those whose elements were positioned by commercial tools

(PowerDesigner and MagicDraw) and a well-known open-source Papyrus tool. The participants were also asked to evaluate the intuitiveness of GRAD's code samples, as well as those of three other libraries. The goal of the study was to confirm that

(1) GRAD's capabilities of automatically laying out diagrams are better than of industry-leading tools,

(2) it is easier to write code for configuring and executing a layout algorithm when using GRAD than when using a different graph analysis and drawing Java library.

Certain aspects of the GRAD library have already been published [22–24]. Previous work focuses on the overview of the implemented layout algorithms, integration with existing graphical editors while also presenting difficulties faced when using other libraries, and challenges of laying out UML diagrams in particular. This paper will, therefore, put emphasis on the process of automatically choosing a suitable algorithm and the domain-specific language. Furthermore, an example of the library's usage and the evaluation of some of its most important features will also be presented.

The rest of the paper is structured as follows. Section 2 gives an overview of the basic graph theory definitions. Section 3 lists some other libraries and DSLs dealing with graphs. It also presents the layout aesthetic criteria and mentions the most popular classes of layout algorithms. Section 4 presents the GRAD library and the DSL, while Section 5 shows an example of the library's usage and describes the conducted user study and its results in more detail. Finally, Section 6 concludes the paper and outlines future work.

2. Basic Graph Theory and Graph Drawing Concepts

A graph (V, E) is an ordered pair consisting of a finite set V of vertices and a finite set E of edges, that is, pairs (u, v) of vertices [25]. If each edge is an unordered (ordered) pair of vertices, the graph is undirected (directed). An edge (u, v) is a self-loop if $u = v$. A graph is simple if it does not contain neither more than one edge between the same two vertices (multiedges) nor self-loops.

A path is a sequence of distinct vertices, $v_1, v_2, \ldots, v_k$, with $k \geq 2$, together with the edges $(v_1, v_2), \ldots, (v_{k-1}, v_k)$. A cycle is a sequence of distinct vertices $v_1, v_2, \ldots, v_k$, with $k \geq 2$, together with the edges $(v_1, v_2), \ldots, (v_{k-1}, v_k), (v_k, v_1)$. A graph is said to be connected if there is a path from any vertex to any other vertex in the graph. A biconnected graph is a connected graph which has no vertices whose removal would disconnect it. Generally, a graph is k-connected if a set of $k - 1$ vertices whose removal disconnects it does not exist. So, a connected graph is 1-connected, a biconnected graph is 2-connected, and so on [26]. Graphs which contain at least one cycle are called cyclic graphs, while the ones that do not are known as acyclic.

A tree is a connected acyclic graph having no more than one path between a pair of vertices. A rooted tree is a tree with one distinguished vertex called the root. A forest is a disjoint union of trees.

A drawing Γ of a graph G maps each vertex v to a distinct point $\Gamma(v)$ of the plane and each edge (u, v) to a simple open curve $\Gamma(u, v)$ with endpoints $\Gamma(u)$ and $\Gamma(v)$ [25]. A drawing is planar if no two distinct edges intersect except, possibly, at common endpoints. A graph is planar if it admits a planar drawing.

A bend along an edge e of Γ is a common point between two consecutive straight-line segments that form e. Formally, if every edge of Γ has at most b bends, Γ is a b-bend drawing of G. A 0-bend drawing is also called a straight-line drawing.

The crossing number of a graph is defined as the minimum possible number of edge crossings with which the graph can be drawn [27]. An edge crossing is a point on the plane where two edges intersect. Having this in mind, a planar graph can be defined as a graph whose crossing number is zero.

Finally, the process of automatically creating a drawing of a graph from the underlying graph structure is called automatic graph layout [28].

3. Related Work

In this section an overview of existing Java graph analysis and visualization libraries as well as domain-specific languages focusing on graphs will be given. Furthermore, the most important aesthetic criteria and classes of graph drawing algorithms will be presented.

3.1. Graph Drawing and Analysis Libraries and DSLs. There are quite a few Java libraries for graph analysis and visualization. Since our focus is on open-source solutions, JUNG framework, and JGraphX and prefuse can be singled out as the most notable libraries of the mentioned kind. All of them offer several complex graph layout algorithms, primarily focusing on tree drawing and force-directed methods, with JGraphX also offering a good implementation of a hierarchical algorithm. However, none of the libraries implement more complex graph analysis algorithms, which are needed for automatic detection of the suitable layout method. Additionally, they heavily focus on visualization, with their main goal revolving around generating fully functional graphical editors. This means that simply calling one of the graph layout algorithms they provide from a separately developed graphical editor is often too complicated. A detailed overview of the libraries and the difficulties of integrating them with existing editors can be found in [22] and [24], respectively. The rest of this section will therefore focus on presenting other domain-specific languages concerned with graphs, the most famous of which is Graphviz's (http://www.graphviz.org) DOT language [29].

DOT is a domain-specific language (DSL) for defining directed and undirected graphs. A description of a graph in the DOT language consists of naming all of the vertices it should contain and stating which of them are connected. The strength of this language lays in the fact that over 150 attributes of a graph and its elements can be customized: color, shape and label of each vertex and edge, the style of an arrowhead at an edge's end, the graph's margin, and font just to name a few. Among the numerous adjustable properties,

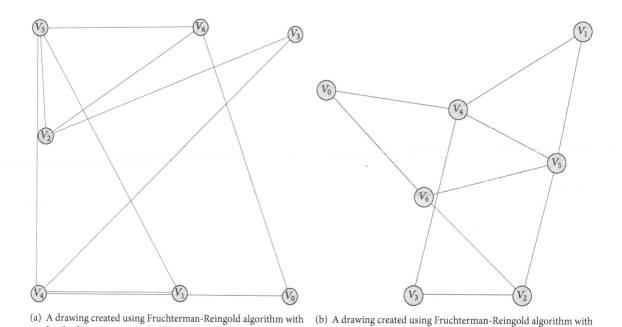

(a) A drawing created using Fruchterman-Reingold algorithm with randomly chosen parameters' values

(b) A drawing created using Fruchterman-Reingold algorithm with carefully chosen parameters' values

FIGURE 2: Two drawings of the same abstract graph created using Fruchterman-Reingold algorithm with different parameters' values.

there are also a few which focus on the graph's layout and characteristics of the resulting drawing. For example, it is possible to define how and if overlaps should be removed, the preferred lengths and representation of edges and the proximity of vertices. The edges can be drawn as splines, straight lines, or polylines.

Once a graph has been described, one of Graphviz's layout tools needs to be invoked. Each of these tools is an implementation of one or more layout algorithms. Currently, Graphviz offers the following algorithms of the mention type: hierarchical, layered, spring, radial, and circular. Some of the parameters of these algorithms, such as the spring constant or the repulsive force used in an extended Fruchterman-Reingold force-directed model [30], are also a part of the DOT language and can be embedded in the graph's description.

Bear in mind that it can be noted that DOT is a sophisticated language for describing a structure of a graph and a variety of its properties, making it possible to visualize almost any type of diagram. However, the focus of this research is not creation of a graph and customization of the appearance of its element using a domain-specific language, but providing a way of specifying characteristics of its layout without knowing anything about graph drawing algorithms. DOT does not excel at this task. The first issue is the necessity to manually pick one of the available layout algorithms by calling the appropriate Graphviz's tool. This could cause a problem to an inexperienced user with no knowledge of graph drawing theory, who might not be familiar with spring, layered, and radial layout methods. He or she would probably struggle to determine which one to use in order to achieve the best result. Furthermore, while the DOT language does enable configuration of certain aspects of the layout process,

that requires setting parameters of the chosen algorithm. Doing so properly, so that the resulting drawing is more aesthetically pleasing compared to one which would be generated using default parameters' values and can only be accomplished by the more knowledgeable users. For example, wrongly configuring a force-directed algorithm can lead to a drawing where the graph's vertices either are very far away from each other or are almost overlapping. A demonstration of the importance of proper configuration of the algorithms is shown in Figure 2, where the algorithm of Fruchterman and Reingold was applied twice, firstly with random values of the parameters (Figure 2(a)) and later with carefully chosen ones (Figure 2(b)).

GRAD's DSL, on the other hand, offers additional alternatives to specifying how a graph should be laid out and not just manual selection and configuration of an algorithm.

The DOT language is not the only DSL supporting specification of a graph's layout in some way. An example is a domain-specific language for visualizing software dependencies as graphs, called Graph [31]. In this context, graph vertices represent software elements, while edges are interpreted as dependencies between two entities. The Graph language is an internal DSL built in Pharo (http://pharo.org), which is a pure object-oriented language supported with an integrated development environment.

Graph allows its users to define vertices and edges of a graph, along with their properties such as shape and color. Furthermore, this DSL enables the definition of how a graph should be laid out and supports a number of well-known layout algorithms (force-directed, circular, and tree). It takes into consideration the fact that applying the same algorithm on all parts of a graph might not be the optimal approach. So, the DSL makes it possible to define a partitioning or a

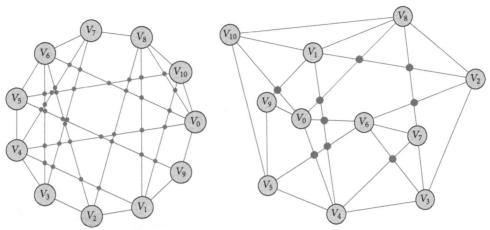

(a) A drawing of a graph with a large number of edge crossings

(b) A drawing of a graph with a small number of edge crossings

FIGURE 3: Two drawings of the same abstract graph with different numbers of edge crossings.

subgraph to which a particular algorithm will be applied. Additionally, it allows selection of several layout algorithms to be applied in succession. However, it is always necessary to name and possibly configure the layout algorithms that will be used. There are no alternatives which a user not familiar with them could use.

Furthermore, there are a large number of projects for building and analyzing graphs that do not cover the problem of specifying how they should be laid out. One such example is a small language for simplifying the input of graph data in graph theory based Java programs [32]. It allows the users to specify vertices, edges, and their weights. This description is later meant to be used in implemented graph theory algorithms. Moreover, a domain-specific language called Green-Marl [33] can also be mentioned. This language was designed in order to ease implementation of graph analysis algorithms. It translates high-level algorithmic description into an efficient implementation in general purpose programming languages, for example, C++.

Summarily, most DSLs dealing with graphs in some way focus either on their complete definition and customization of various visual properties or on their analysis. To the best of our knowledge, there is no domain-specific language whose main purpose is to offer a more descriptive way of specifying how a graphs should be laid out and automatic selection, configuration, and execution of the appropriate algorithm. The first two mentioned DSLs touch upon the subject of a graph's layout. However, the users have to pick one of the available algorithms directly. In addition to this, their configuration is done by naming one or more parameters and providing the desired values. The other mentioned DSLs do not even cover the problem of laying out elements of a graph, as they focus on implementation of graph analysis algorithms. GRAD already contains such implementations and they are automatically used in the process of determining the most suitable layout algorithm.

3.2. Graph Layout Algorithms and Aesthetics. A single graph can be drawn in a countless number of ways. Strictly

theoretically speaking, all that is important is which vertices are connected. However, in practice the positions of a graph's vertices and edges within the drawing directly affect its readability and understandability [1–5]. So, a wide set of aesthetic principles believed to improve these aspects of a drawing has been proposed. Different designers of layout algorithms often focus on different criteria, believing that optimization of these measurable aesthetics produces nice graph drawings. This section presents the most common aesthetic criteria [3, 5, 28] and the most important classes of graph drawing algorithms [34].

3.2.1. Graph Aesthetics. The upcoming paragraphs describe the aesthetics which many graph drawing algorithms strive to achieve. These criteria are also at the core of the DSL presented in this paper, since they are intuitive on one hand and closely linked to layout algorithms on the other.

Minimization of the number of edge crossings is widely regarded as one of the most important aesthetic criteria. Readability of a two-dimensional graph layout is considered to be strongly dependent on this number. This was verified by several conducted studies [18, 28]. Bearing in mind that the main information given by an abstract graph is whether two vertices are connected by an edge, it is obvious that reducing the number of crossings significantly increases the readability [35].

In Figure 3 two drawings of the same graphs are shown. The drawing in Figure 3(a) has a large number of edge crossings (over 30), while the one in Figure 3(b) has notably less (only 9). The crossings are marked with red dots. This aesthetic criterion strongly favours drawing Figure 3(b), which is, undoubtedly, far more readable.

Maximization of minimum angles is an aesthetic criterion which states that the minimum angle between edges extending from a vertex should be maximized [19, 36]. Purchase et al. explain that the best possible result is achieved when all graph vertices have equal angles between all incident edges [37]. In Figure 4 two drawings of the same simple abstract graph are shown. The drawing in Figure 4(a) has maximized

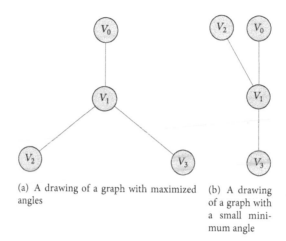

(a) A drawing of a graph with maximized angles

(b) A drawing of a graph with a small minimum angle

FIGURE 4: Two drawings of the same abstract graph with significantly different values of the minimum angle between edges.

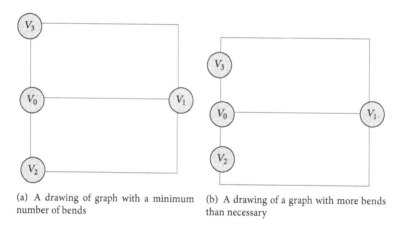

(a) A drawing of graph with a minimum number of bends

(b) A drawing of a graph with more bends than necessary

FIGURE 5: Two drawings of the same abstract graph, one with the minimum number of bends and one with a nonoptimal embedding.

angles at its center vertex, thus completely conforming to this aesthetic criterion. The other one, shown in Figure 4(b), has a small minimum angle.

Number of bends is a criterion which points out minimization of the number of bends as being important to the overall graph readability, especially in areas such as VLSI (very-large-scale integration) circuit layout, architectural design, and transportation problems [38]. Figure 5 contains two drawings of the same graph, where the one shown in Figure 5(a) has the minimum number of bends, whereas the one in Figure 5(b) has more bends than necessary, thus being less aesthetically pleasing according to the current criterion.

Uniform flow criterion names the flow of directed edges as something to pay attention to when creating a drawing of a graph. Generally, the direction of edges should be consistent [37]. A demonstration of this criterion is shown in Figure 6, consisting of two drawings of the same abstract graph. The drawing shown in Figure 6(a) has consistent flow and is more understandable than the drawing shown Figure 6(b), which has inconsistent flow.

Orthogonality aesthetic criterion claims that nodes and edges should be fixed to an orthogonal grid [38, 39]. So, the concept of orthogonality can be separated into two [37]:

(i) edges and edge segments should follow the lines of an imaginary Cartesian grid;

(ii) vertices and bend points should make maximal use of an imaginary Cartesian grid.

In other words, segments of the edges should not deviate much from an orthogonal angle and vertices and bend points should be fixed to intersections on an imaginary unit grid, thus making maximal use of the grid area.

Symmetry is an aesthetic criterion that clearly reveals the structure and properties of a graph [12]. Knowing that every drawing of a graph has a trivial symmetry, it can be noted that this criterion enforces creating drawings of graphs with a nontrivial one, or, more ambitiously, with multiple symmetries. Figure 7 shows two drawings of the same graph, where the first one (shown in Figure 7(a)) has 8 nontrivial symmetries, and the other one (shown in Figure 7(b)) has only one. The drawing in Figure 7(a), on the other hand, also has 5 edge crossings, while the other drawing is planar. Still, most people prefer the drawing shown in Figure 7(a), which demonstrates importance of this criterion [40].

Symmetries of a drawing of a graph G are related to its automorphisms. An automorphism of a graph G is a

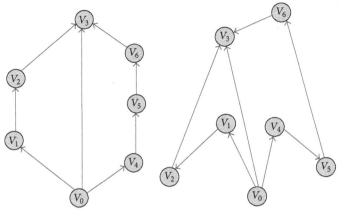

(a) A drawing of a graph with consistent flow

(b) A drawing of a graph with inconsistent flow

FIGURE 6: Two drawings of the same abstract graph, one with consistent flow and one with inconsistent.

mapping from its vertices back to those vertices such that the resulting graph is isomorphic with G [41]. An automorphism is geometric if there is a drawing which displays it.

In addition to previously described criteria, the authors of layout algorithms have also proposed the following ones [28]:

(i) Node distribution: nodes should be distributed evenly within a bounding box.

(ii) Edge lengths: edge lengths should not be neither too short nor too long.

(iii) Edge variation: edge lengths should be similar.

3.2.2. Graph Layout Algorithms. There are a large number of different graph drawing algorithms, with the oldest ones dating back to the 1950s. However, the field is still evolving, with new algorithms still being developed and old ones enhanced. These algorithms are often valued based on their computational efficiency and the extent to which they conform to one of more aesthetic criteria [28]. Some of the algorithms can be applied to every graph, while others require presence of certain features. This section will give an overview of the most popular classes of graph layout algorithms, with the emphasis being put on aesthetic criterion or criteria they focus on as well as the restrictions concerning their applications, if there are any.

Tree drawing algorithms are designed to produce nicely looking drawings of trees. These algorithms are often the best choice when hierarchical information should be conveyed. Tree drawing is among the best studied areas of graph drawing.

Some of the algorithms belonging to this class can only be used on binary trees (trees in which each vertex has at most two children) and others can be used on general trees as well. Depending on the algorithm of choice, the resulting tree can conform to a number of aesthetic criteria: planarity, orthogonality, symmetry, flow, similar lengths of edges, node distribution, and minimization of the number of bends. Furthermore, application of most of the available algorithms results in drawings which display more than one

of the desirable properties; for example, they are planar and symmetric and have edges of similar lengths. A detailed overview of various approaches to drawing trees can be found in [42].

Straight-line drawing algorithms represent a class of graph drawing algorithms where edges can only contain straight-line segments. There are several types of these algorithms, which, in addition to focusing on the mentioned property also try to achieve goals set by one or more other aesthetic criteria. These include planar, polyline, convex, orthogonal, and rectangular drawings. Planar straight-line drawing algorithms rely on the fact that if a drawing can be drawn planar using edges of arbitrary shapes, they can also be drawn planar using just straight-line segments [11]. Moreover, planar straight-line drawing algorithms often accentuate the size of the angles and strive to produce convex, orthogonal, or polyline drawings. Convex drawings are defined as drawings where all faces are drawn as convex polygons. Orthogonal drawings only use horizontal and vertical line segments for edges and are, therefore, often quite visually pleasing. A more specific type of orthogonal drawings is rectangular drawings, which also make sure that each face is drawn as a rectangle [13]. It can easily be concluded that orthogonal drawings can only be constructed for graphs which do not contain a vertex with more than four edges entering and leaving it (its degree is four at most). Polyline drawings are more general and do not have this limitation. They directly focus on not allowing sizes of the angles to be smaller than some fixed threshold.

Hierarchical drawing algorithms can be used to draw directed graphs (or digraphs) which represent hierarchies [43]. Vertices represent entities and edges relationships between them. These algorithms produce drawings with consistent direction of edges, in accordance with one of the previously described aesthetic criteria.

Circular drawing algorithms are a class of graph drawing algorithms that partition the graph into clusters and place each node of each cluster onto the circumference of an embedding circle [44].

Symmetric graph drawing algorithms aim to draw a graph with nontrivial symmetry, or, more ambitiously, with as

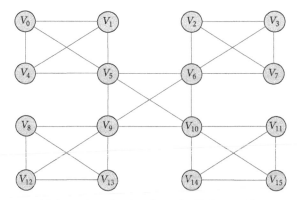

(a) A nonplanar drawing of a graph with 8 symmetries

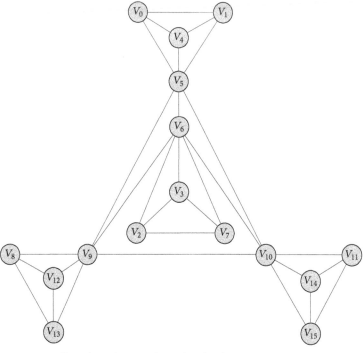

(b) A planar drawing of a graph with only an axial symmetry

FIGURE 7: Two drawings of the same abstract graph, with one having more symmetries and the other one being planar with not as many symmetries.

much symmetry as possible. In other words, these algorithms construct drawings of graphs with regard to the aesthetic criterion of the same name. Some of the algorithms require an automorphism of the graph to be passed and then proceed to construct a drawing which displays it. The more advanced ones, on the other hand, firstly find the largest automorphisms group or even the maximal planar group of this kind [12]. However, a need to manually specify an automorphism to be displayed could also arise, so both types of symmetric algorithms have their significance.

Force-directed algorithms are among the most important and most flexible graph drawing algorithms due to the fact that they can be used to lay out all simple undirected graphs. They only need the information contained within the structure of the graph itself [45]. Graphs drawn with these algorithms tend to be aesthetically pleasing, exhibit symmetries, and often produce crossing-free layouts for planar graphs. So, while they might not be able to guarantee that conditions set by the desired aesthetic criterion will be completely met, they can be used to produce drawings that satisfy a larger number of these criteria to some extent. For example, there is no guarantee that all drawings of planar graphs will necessarily be planar, but they will have a small number of edge crossings. There are many force-driven algorithms, with Tutte's 1963 barycentric method [46] being considered to be the first one. The most popular ones include the spring layout method of Eades [47], Kamada-Kawai [40], and Fruchterman-Reingold [30] methods.

4. GRAD and Its DSL for Graph Layout Description

This section presents our graph analysis and drawing library, GRAD, and describes its domain-specific language for specifying graph layouts. The language is supposed to be used by both users knowledgeable in graph drawing theory and those who lack such experience, so it features several ways of defining how a graph should be laid out. The most complex of them enables full configuration of the layout process, while the simplest ones only require the users to name certain characteristics of the resulting drawing, based on which the best algorithm is automatically selected and configured. More precisely, one of the available algorithms whose resulting drawings exhibit the greatest number of the mentioned characteristics is chosen. Automatic detection of the preferable algorithm would not be possible without GRAD's implementations of graph analysis algorithms. Therefore, the GRAD library will be described in more detail before the DSL itself is presented.

4.1. Graph Drawing and Analysis Library (GRAD). GRAD is an open-source graph drawing and analysis library written in Java aiming to provide

(1) a large number of algorithms from graph and graph drawing theory,

(2) automatic selection, configuration, and execution of a layout algorithm based on the properties of a graph or a user's descriptive input,

(3) simple integration with existing graphical editors.

GRAD ports the best implementations of layout algorithms from other open-source graph drawing and analysis libraries, JUNG framework, JGraphX, and prefuse, and adds several original ones. GRAD's layout algorithms include both those which were specifically designed with a certain type of graphs in mind, for example, biconnected planar, and those which can be applied to any graph, generating drawings conforming to one or more aesthetic criteria. Overall, GRAD includes the following layout algorithms:

(i) several tree drawing, ranging from the standard level-based approaches, to those creating radial tree drawings,

(ii) the majority of the well-known force-directed algorithms (Kamada-Kawai, Fruchterman-Reingold, spring, organic [48], and a so-called ISOM layout based on Meyer's self-organizing graph methods [49]),

(iii) one hierarchical algorithm [50],

(iv) a symmetric layout algorithm, based on the work of Carr and Kocay [51],

(v) a straight-line drawing algorithm based on Tutte's theorem [46].

(vi) Chiba's convex straight-line drawing algorithm [52],

(vii) a circular drawing algorithm with the optional optimization of the number of edge crossings [53],

(viii) a simple layout algorithm which places a certain number of vertices in one row before continuing to the next one, called box layout.

TABLE 1: Times the algorithms need to lay out randomly generated graphs with 1000 vertices and 2000 edges.

Algorithm	Time [ms]
Spring	724
Fruchterman-Reingold	689
Kamada-Kawai	5232
ISOM	461
Fast-organic	9584
Organic	90273
Hierarchical	56100
Symmetric	523
Circular	419
Box	114

TABLE 2: Times the algorithms need to lay out trees with 1000 vertices.

Algorithm	Time [ms]
Level-based tree	60
Radial tree	52
Compact tree	140
Balloon tree	158
Node-link tree	461
Hierarchical	621

Furthermore, an orthogonal layout algorithm based on visibility representations [54] is currently in development. The last five algorithms are GRAD's original implementations. To the best of our knowledge, some of them (symmetric, Chiba's, optimized circular algorithms) have not been implemented in Java before. Some examples of drawings of graphs created using GRAD's layout algorithms are shown in Figure 8. More examples are available at [55] (GRAD's official site). A more detailed overview of the algorithms can be found in [22]. The examples were created using GRAD's simple graphical editor (https://github.com/renatav/GraphDrawing/tree/master/GraphEditor), developed in order to support familiarization and experimentation with the available algorithms.

In addition to being judged based on the extent to which they conform to one or more aesthetic criteria, layout algorithms are rated in accordance with their computational efficiency, that is, the quantity of resources they need in order to compute their results, positions of graph's elements. In Tables 1 and 2 times certain implementations which need to lay out bigger graphs are presented. The graphs used in the tests had 1000 vertices and twice as many edges. Algorithms only meant to be performed on smaller graphs, like Tutte's embedding, and which can only be applied to very specific graphs, like Chibba's algorithm, were omitted.

Hu developed highly effective force-directed algorithms and concluded that a graph of similar size to the ones used in the previously mentioned tests can be laid out in under 1 second [56]. Some of the algorithms offered by GRAD live up to that standard, while also producing understandable drawings. The ISOM algorithm is the best example. It is

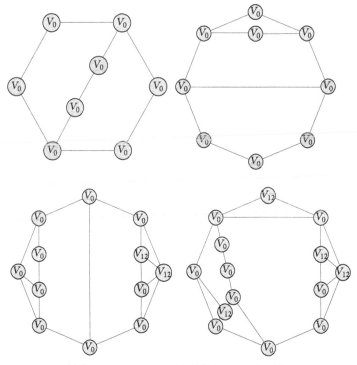

(a) Drawings generated using Chiba's convex algorithm

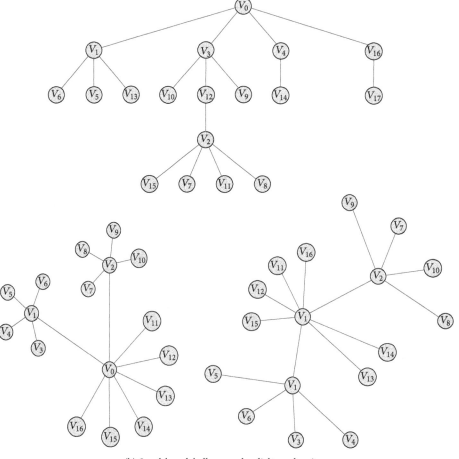

(b) Level-based, balloon, and radial tree drawings

FIGURE 8: Continued.

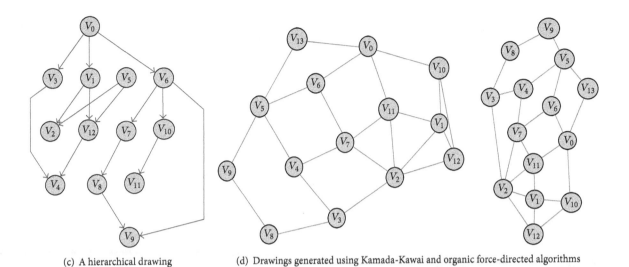

(c) A hierarchical drawing   (d) Drawings generated using Kamada-Kawai and organic force-directed algorithms

FIGURE 8: Examples of drawing of graphs created using GRAD's layout algorithms.

also evident that all tree methods are very efficient. The hierarchical one performs poorly when used to lay out a general graph, while being much faster if the graph is actually a hierarchy.

Moreover, GRAD also performs some postprocessing, thus enhancing the results produced by the algorithms. Since very few of the algorithms route loops and multiple edges, GRAD detects them and recalculates their positions in order to avoid overlapping of edges and correctly show those which connect one vertex to itself. Additionally, some of the algorithms take into consideration the sizes of the vertices, but not all. Therefore, GRAD can also slightly move the vertices after an algorithm has been performed in order to prevent their overlapping. It should be mentioned that GRAD's original implementations take into account the sizes of a graph's vertices.

In addition to providing the mentioned layout algorithms, GRAD implements many concerned with graph analysis, traversal, decomposition, and so on. Most notable of them are the following:

(i) Dijkstra's shortest path [16],

(ii) checking connectivity, biconnectivity, and triconnectivity of a graph,

(iii) finding simple cycles of a directed or an undirected graph,

(iv) Fraysseix-Mendez [57], Boyer-Myrvold [58], and PQ-tree [59] planarity testing,

(v) finding a planar embedding of a graph,

(vi) Hopcroft-Tarjan division of graph into triconnected components [60], which is considered to be one of the most difficult algorithms to implement,

(vii) Fialko and Mutzel's 5/3 approximation algorithm for the planar augmentation problem [61],

(viii) McKay's canonical graph labeling algorithm (nauty) for finding permutations [62].

Graph analysis algorithms are of great significance to the field of graph drawing, with some of them being the core of different layout algorithms. For example, implementation of Chiba's convex drawing algorithm includes planarity and triconnectivity checking and splitting the graph into triconnected components, while the orthogonal algorithm based on visibility representations requires finding a planar embedding. GRAD's analysis algorithms can also be used by other developers interested in implementing additional layout algorithms.

Furthermore, the analysis algorithms can be used to check if a particular drawing algorithm can be applied to a given graph. Although there exist layout algorithms that can be applied to any type of graphs, using an algorithm which primarily focuses on graphs such as the given one is usually a far better solution. For example, if a graph is a tree, it should be laid out using a tree drawing algorithm and not using a hierarchical or force-directed one. This fact is the basis of the automatic detection of the best drawing algorithm and therefore of the implementation of some of the library's most important features. Additionally, algorithms like planar augmentation can transform a graph into a suitable one prior to execution of a layout algorithm. For instance, some edges can be added to make a graph biconnected, seeing that many algorithms require that property.

Finally, it can be mentioned that GRAD's algorithms can directly be used to lay out elements of any diagram. In fact, the ease of calling any of the library's algorithms from a separately developed graphical editor is one of its main goals. If that is possible, the editor's classes corresponding to graph vertices and edges should implement GRAD's `Vertex` and `Edge` interfaces, thus specifying information needed by the algorithms, sizes of the vertices and origins and destinations of the edges. If for whatever reason this requirement cannot be satisfied, GRAD provides two classes (`GraphVertex` and `GraphEdge`) which already implement the mentioned interfaces. If a GRAD's vertex is then created for each of the editor's vertices and a GRAD's edge for each of its edges, any of our library's algorithms can be called. A more thorough explanation can be found in [23].

The library is currently being used in our Kroki mockup tool's (http://www.kroki-mde.net) lightweight UML diagram editor to lay out models sometimes containing over 600 classes.

4.2. Graph Layout DSL.

The development of DSLs consists of the following phases: decision, analysis, design, implementation, testing, deployment, and maintenance [17, 63, 64]. This section will present a DSL for specifying how a graph should be laid out and describe each of its development phases.

4.2.1. Decision.

The decision phase focuses on the question if developing a DSL is worthwhile or not. In other words, benefits of the new language can justify time and effort which needs to be put into its development. There are three main reasons why a positive answer was given to these questions in case of GRAD's DSL language:

(1) One of GRAD's main goals is to provide a generic way of its integration with any graphical editor. This can be accomplished by using a DSL, as discussed in Section 1. Additionally, the DSL can offer end-users of such an editor, who might be neither programmers nor knowledgeable in graph theory, the possibility of descriptively specifying how a diagram's layout should look like. That is, which features (e.g., orthogonality, symmetry, and uniform flow) should the layout exhibit and which are not desired. This option could save the mentioned users a lot of time and effort, as they would not have to experiment with configuring and calling different algorithms in order to lay out a diagram in accordance with their personal preferences. The developers of the graphical editors would only need to provide a regular input component, where the users would enter text conforming to the DSL.

(2) Although any of GRAD's layout algorithms can be configured and called directly by a developer using this library, a DSL can provide a way of achieving the same result in fewer lines of code (compare Listing 9 with 10 or Listing 11 with Listing 12). Additionally, studies showed that when using a DSL, developers are more accurate and more efficient in program comprehension than when using a GPL [65].

(3) Modern libraries and languages provide programmers with tools which make developing their own external DSL (DSL which is parsed independently of the host purpose language [66]) within their reach [67]. One such example is textX [68], a metalanguage for DSL specification, with whose help a new textual language can quickly be created.

4.2.2. Domain Analysis.

Detailed domain analysis precedes design and implementation of a DSL [64]. Its goal is to define domain of focus, collect necessary domain information, and optionally create a domain model. More often than not, domain analysis is done informally [69], which was also the case during development of GRAD's DSL. The domains of particular interest to the mentioned language include graph drawing, which was introduced in Section 3.2, as well as GRAD's layout API, presented in [23] and GRAD's official site [55].

4.2.3. Design.

Language design consists of the definition of constructs and language semantics [64]. Approaches to DSL design can be characterized along two orthogonal dimensions: the relationship between the DSL and existing languages and the formal nature of the design description [17].

The first dimension refers to construction of the language, either by basing it on an existing one or by creating it from the beginning. GRAD's DSL was built from scratch using textX. Although recent studies show that using an embedded (internal) DSL (one based on an existing language) can be made easier for nonprogramming users if the IDE (integrated development environment) is properly customized [70], external DSLs, which have no commonalities with existing languages (and therefore less syntactic noise), are generally regarded as more intuitive to the domain users. GRAD's DSL is an external domain-specific language, as it should also offer the option of being used by end-users of graphical editors looking to lay out their diagrams. Furthermore, many Java programmers prefer to configure certain elements of the applications they are developing through external files (e.g., JSON, YAML, and properties), pointing out code readability as the main advantage of this approach. An external DSL can significantly improve understandability of code for configuring and executing a layout algorithm, in addition to making it a lot shorter.

The second dimension incorporates formal or informal design of the language, that is, its syntax and semantics. Although building a DSL often seems intuitive, it is important to evaluate its usability systematically, and not just in the final stage of its development [71]. While no formal framework was used to achieve this, it can be noted that the members of our Kroki mockup tool's development team (http://www.kroki-mde.net/people/), who are also among the target end-users of this language, were involved in its design, by evaluating intuitiveness of the grammar and potential usefulness of different concepts.

Syntax specification of GRAD DSL's was done using the textX metalanguage, whose main features include the possibility of defining both language concrete syntax and its metamodel using a single description [68]. The description consists of rules, which are the basic building blocks of the textX metalanguage. The base rules of the DSL are shown in code Listing 1, while the complete specification can be found in [72]. The language was designed in such a way that the users could get the feeling of directly issuing orders to the application. So, the rules are meant to feel like sentences if written without skipping the optional words. If, however, a user is primarily interested in minimizing the length of the input, all parts of the rules followed by the ? symbol can be omitted.

The `LayoutGraph` rule defines how to trigger the process of laying out the a graph. That is accomplished by typing the

```
LayoutGraph: 'lay' 'out' 'graph' LayoutEnum;
LayoutEnum: LayoutAlgorithm | LayoutStyle | AestheticCriteria |
    AestheticCriteriaMath;
LayoutStyle: 'using'? 'style' LayoutStyleEnum;
LayoutStyleEnum: 'automatic' | 'circular' | 'tree' | 'hierarchical' | '
    symmetric' | 'general';
AestheticCriteria: ('conforming' 'to')? 'criteria' (AestheticCriterion
    ',')+;
LayoutAlgorithm: 'using'? 'algorithm' LayoutAlgorithmEnum;
AestheticCriteion: EdgeCrossings | MinimumAngles | MinimumBands;
LayoutAlgorithmEnum: TreeAlgorithm | StraightLineAlgorithm |
    HierarchicalAlgorithm;
```

LISTING 1: Base rules of the graph layout DSL.

```
MinimumBands: ('minimization' 'of')? 'edge' 'crossings';
```

LISTING 2: An example of a rule corresponding to an aesthetic criterion.

words lay out graph, with any number of spaces between them, followed by the input conforming to one of the four available layout methods. Those include

(i) directly naming a layout algorithm and optionally setting its parameters,

(ii) naming the general style of the layout (hierarchy, circular, symmetric, etc.), including the possibility of stating that the layout process should be done automatically,

(iii) naming aesthetic criteria that the drawing should conform to (minimization of edge crossings, maximization of minimum angles, uniform flow, etc.) in the order of importance,

(iv) writing expressions using logical operators and aesthetic criteria, thus being able to state that, for example, a certain criterion should not be present in the resulting drawing, while two others both should and so on.

The rule LayoutAlgorithm corresponds to the firstly mentioned method of specifying how to lay out a graph. This rule references other ones, all of which represent a layout algorithm that can be used. If an algorithm has configurable parameters, they can be specified as well. This is, however, optional and it is assumed that the default values will be set if the user does not provide them. Not all algorithms were listed, due to their number.

The rule LayoutStyle represents the second method, which is the easiest one to use, as it is only necessary to select the overall style of the layout. LayoutStyleEnum represents a choice of these styles.

AestheticCriterion enables the third method of layout specification. It references other rules, where each of them corresponds to one of the aesthetic criteria described

in Section 3.2.1. The repetition is achieved through usage of symbol +, which defines that one or more criteria must be listed. Since there are many such rules, only one will be presented, and it can be seen in code Listing 2.

In this rule, the sequence of two words, minimization of, is completely optional.

The most complex of the definitions is rule AestheticCriteriaMath, shown in code Listing 3. It introduces logical operators into the language, respecting their mathematical priorities. There is no limit to the length of the expression.

The choice to base this and the previous approach on the aesthetic criteria was inspired by the fact that they are descriptive and self-explanatory but also closely related to the layout algorithms. As mentioned before, these algorithms tend to strongly focus on producing drawings conforming to one or more aesthetic criteria.

Code Listing 4 shows a few examples of inputs conforming to GRAD's DSL incorporating everything previously mentioned.

The DSL also supports specification of how one or more subgraphs of the whole graph should be laid out. Since the rules through which that is accomplished are very similar to the ones shown in Listing 1, they were omitted from the overview of the grammar.

Semantics of a language can be specified formally, using attribute grammars, denotational semantics, rewrite systems, or abstract state machines, but also informally, usually using a natural language with optional program examples [17, 64]. GRAD's DSL is a simple language, with a very high level of abstraction, whose programs are transformed into complex Java code which relies on GRAD's layout API. As a result, the semantics of the language can most effectively be explained using the second mentioned method. Firstly, the meanings of the main rules of the language will be clarified via Table 3. Secondly, one example of how an input conforming to the

```
AestheticCriteriaMath: CriteriaExpression;
CriteriaFactor: 'not'? (AestheticCriteion | ('(' CriteriaExpression ')')
    );
CriteriaTerm: CriteriaFactor CriteriaAndFactor*;
CriteriaAndFactor: 'and' CriteriaFactor;
CriteriaExpression: CriteriaTerm CriteriaOrTerm*;
CriteriaOrTerm: 'or' CriteriaTerm;
```

LISTING 3: Language rules for the support of logical operators.

```
lay out graph using style symmetric
lay out graph using algorithm Kamada-Kawai
lay out graph conforming to planarity, bends
lay out graph not(planarity and flow) or symmetry
```

LISTING 4: Examples inputs conforming to the DSL.

```
radial tree(horizontal distance = 5, vertical distance = 20)
```

LISTING 5: An input conforming to the LayoutAlgorithm rule.

```
//select algorithm
LayoutAlgorithms algorithm = LayoutAlgorithms.RADIAL_TREE;
//set properties
GraphLayoutProperties layoutProperties = new GraphLayoutProperties();
layoutProperties.setProperty(RadialTreeProperties.X_DISTANCE,5);
layoutProperties.setProperty(RadialTreeProperties.Y_DISTANCE,20);
//initialize the layouter, assuming that vertices and edges
//are lists containing elements of the graph
Layouter<GraphVertex, GraphEdge> layouter = new Layouter<>(
                        vertices, edges, algorithm, layoutProperties);
Drawing<GraphVertex, GraphEdge> drawing = layouter.layout();
```

LISTING 6: JAVA code corresponding to the layout specification from Listing 5.

DSL is mapped onto GRAD's API calls will be given for each of the four layout specification methods.

As previously mentioned, inputs (programs) written in GRAD's DSL are transformed into Java code mostly consisting of this library's layout API calls. The upcoming code listings are pairs of DSL and resulting Java code samples. Code Listing 5 shows an example of input conforming to the LayoutAlgorithm rule, whereas the JAVA/GRAD code which should be executed is encapsulated in Listing 6. Similarly, code Listing 7 contains an example of layout specification written in accordance with the LayoutStyle rule, while Listing 8 shows the corresponding Java code. Finally, code Listings 9, 10, 11, and 12 are pairs of inputs written in the DSL, conforming to rules AestheticCriteria and AestheticCriteriaMath, respectively, and the resulting API calls.

```
lay out graph using style circular
```

LISTING 7: An input conforming to the LayoutStyle rule.

4.2.4. Implementation. Implementation is a phase in construction of DSLs when the most suitable approach of DSL development is chosen and performed. These approaches include creation of interpreters, compilers, and preprocessors to name a few [17]. GRAD's DSL uses an interpreter, which relies on textX's ability to create an object graph (model) from the input string conforming to the DSL.

While processing the grammar, textX creates the metamodel of the language. More precisely, a class is created for

TABLE 3: DSL expressions and their semantics.

DSL input	Semantics
`lay out graph using algorithm AlgorithmName (property1 = value1, property2 = value2)`	Select algorithm named AlgorithmName and set value of its property called property1 to value1, property2 to value2. Execute the selected algorithm
`lay out graph using style StyleName`	Select the best algorithm automatically. If the provided style is not automatic, limit the set of considered algorithms to those belonging to the appropriate group. If the style is circular, hierarchical, tree or symmetric, select an algorithm belonging to the group of the same name. If it is general, select a force-directed algorithm. Execute the selected algorithm
`lay out graph conforming to criteria criterion1, criterion2, criterion3`	Select a layout algorithm which can be applied to the given graph and produces drawings which exhibit characteristics favored by aesthetic criterion criterion1 and, if possible, criterion2 and criterion3. Execute the selected algorithm
`lay out graph not?(criterion1 and criterion2) or not?(criterion3 and criterion4)`	Select a layout algorithm which satisfies either criterion1 and criterion2 (or doesn't satisfy at least one of them, depending on the presence or absence of the negation operator), or criterion3 and criterion4. Execute that algorithm

```
//select the best algorithm based on properties of the graph,
//but only consider those belonging to a class specified by style
LayoutAlgorithms algorithm =
                LayoutPicker.pickAlgorithm(graph, "circular");
GraphLayoutProperties layoutProperties = DefaultGraphLayoutProperties.
                getDefaultLayoutProperties(algorithm, graph);
Layouter<GraphVertex, GraphEdge> layouter = new Layouter<>(
                vertices, edges, algorithm, layoutProperties);
Drawing<GraphVertex, GraphEdge> drawing = layouter.layout();
```

LISTING 8: JAVA code corresponding to the layout specification from Listing 8.

each rule of the grammar. This means that when a program written in the DSL is parsed and the model is created, each of the model's objects is an instance of its metamodel's class. A model of the input string from code Listing 13 generated by textX is shown in Figure 9.

Once the model is available, the interpreter performs its transformation into appropriate GRAD API calls. For example, names and properties of the algorithms are transformed into corresponding GRAD's `LayoutAlgorithms` enumeration values and entries in `GraphLayoutProperties` map. While implementing such transformations is not a complicated task and syntax and semantics of the language are fairly simple, its complexity is encapsulated in `PickAlgorithm` methods. They contain implementations of selection of an appropriate layout algorithm based on properties of the graph and the user's input. A detailed description of these procedures will be given in Section 4.3.

4.2.5. Testing and Deployment. Testing and deployment are the next phases of DSL development. As the name suggests, a DSL's evaluation is performed during the testing phase,

while deployment marks the point in time when applications constructed with the DSL are used [64]. The GRAD library and its DSL were integrated with our Kroki mockup tool [73], whereas their evaluation was performed by conducting a user study. The study showed that more participants would prefer to use the DSL to trigger the layout process than any of the other options.

4.2.6. Maintenance. Maintenance is the last phase in DSL construction, which occurs when there are new requirements. When additional layout algorithms are implemented, the DSL should be expanded to support them. This means adding new grammar rules, implementing more transformations, and enhancing the procedure described in Section 4.3, to take newly added algorithms into considerations. Due to its ability to build both a metamodel and a parser from a single grammar description, as well as its dynamic nature, textX makes iterative development of new DSLs easy.

4.3. Integration of the DSL with GRAD. The main focus of the DSL is to trigger execution of the appropriate layout

```
lay out graph conforming to planarity, symmetry, flow
```

LISTING 9: An input conforming to the LayoutCriteria rule.

```
List<AestheticCriteria> criteria = new ArrayList<AestheticCriteria>();
criteria.add(AestheticCriteria.PLANAR);
criteria.add(AestheticCriteria.SYMMETRIC);
criteria.add(AestheticCriteria.UNIFORM_FLOW);
LayoutAlgorithms algorithm = LayoutPicker.pickAlgorithm(graph, criteria)
    ;
GraphLayoutPropertieslayoutProperties = DefaultGraphLayoutProperties.
            getDefaultLayoutProperties(algorithm, graph);
Layouter<GraphVertex, GraphEdge> layouter = new Layouter<>(
            vertices, edges, algorithm, layoutProperties);
Drawing<GraphVertex, GraphEdge> drawing = layouter.layout();
```

LISTING 10: JAVA code corresponding to the layout specification from Listing 9.

```
lay out graph not(symmetry and angle) or edge crossings
```

LISTING 11: An input conforming to the AestheticCriteriaMath rule.

```
List<Pair<List<AestheticCriteria>, List<AestheticCriteria>>> orPairs =
        new ArraList<Pair<List<AestheticCriteria>,
        List<AestheticCriteria>>>();
List<AestheticCriteria> positiveCriteria =
        new ArrayList<AestheticCriteria>();
positiveCriteria.add(AestheticCriteria.MINIMAL_EDGE_CROESSES);
List<AestheticCriteria> negativeCriteria =
        new ArrayList<AestheticCriteria>();
negativeCriteria.add(AestheticCriteria.SYMMETRIC);
negativeCriteria.add(AestheticCriteria.MINIMUM_ANGLES);
orPairs.add(new Pair<List<AestheticCriteria>, List<AestheticCriteria>>(
                positiveCriteria, negativeCriteria));
LayoutAlgorithms algorithm = LayoutPicker.pickAlgorithm(graph, orPairs);
GraphLayoutPropertieslayoutProperties = DefaultGraphLayoutProperties.
        getDefaultLayoutProperties(algorithm, graph);
Layouter<GraphVertex, GraphEdge> layouter = new Layouter<>(
        vertices, edges, algorithm, layoutProperties);
Drawing<GraphVertex, GraphEdge> drawing = layouter.layout();
```

LISTING 12: JAVA code corresponding to the layout specification from Listing 11.

```
lay out graph not(symmetry and angle) or planarity or edge crossings
```

LISTING 13: An input conforming to the DSL whose model will be shown.

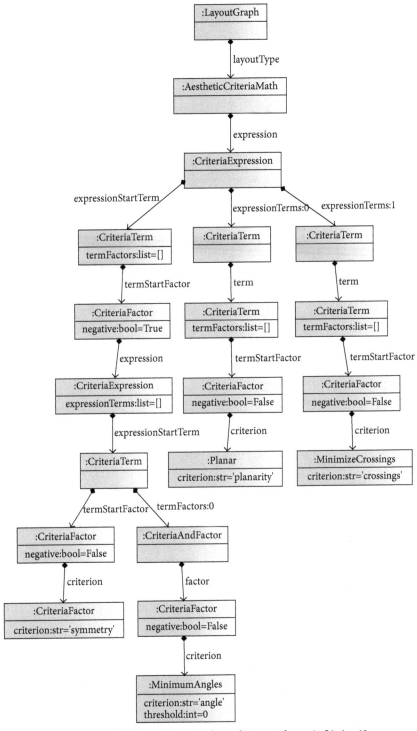

FIGURE 9: Model created by textX from the input shown in Listing 13.

algorithm or algorithms given a description conforming to it. This is why it heavily relies on the GRAD library, which contains implementations of the needed graph drawing and analysis algorithms.

Naturally, in terms of implementation, the easiest method is the one requiring the most specific input from the users, directly naming an algorithm and possibly configuring its parameters. In such a case, there is no need to analyze the graph or to take any additional steps. However, in order to achieve the desired goal using this method, a user would have to be fairly knowledgeable. Such users could also directly take advantage of one of the available implementations of the layout algorithms and completely skip the step of using the DSL. For them, the DSL is simply another alternative. Therefore, the remaining methods are much more interesting and potentially useful.

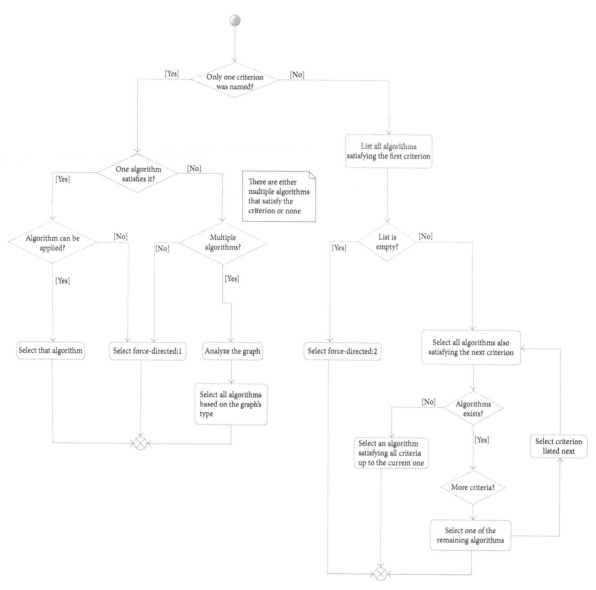

FIGURE 10: The process of selecting an algorithm based on a list of aesthetic criteria.

The first of them provides a way of defining how a graph should be laid out by naming one or more of the desirable properties of the drawing, that is, one or more aesthetic criteria, with the order in which they are listed defining their priorities. Like it was mentioned in the previous section, all graph layout algorithms (except for the most basic ones) were designed in accordance with at least one aesthetic criterion. Some, like the force-directed graph layout algorithms, tend to satisfy several criteria to some extent. However, if one specific criterion is particularly significant, these more general approaches are rarely the best choice. An algorithm focusing on that criterion will produce a drawing satisfying it to a greater extent. For example, while force-directed layout algorithms tend to produce crossing-free drawings of planar graphs, there is no guarantee. Planar straight-line drawing, on the other hand, will always do so. Similarly, force-directed algorithms tend to produce symmetric drawings, but they will almost certainly exhibit

far less symmetries than those created by a symmetric algorithm.

Tables 4 and 5 show which criteria the available algorithms conform to. The symbol ± means that the algorithm satisfies the criterion to some extent. It can be noticed that not all force-directed algorithms were taken into consideration, since the organic one, which was designed in accordance with the greatest number of aesthetic criteria, was singled out.

Having everything mentioned in mind, a process of selecting an algorithm based on the list of aesthetic criteria was designed. In order to simplify its understanding, it was visualized using an activity diagram shown in Figure 10. The selection process consists of the following rules:

(i) If only one criterion was named, an algorithm specifically designed with it in mind is sought.

    (a) If there is such algorithm and it can be applied to the given graph, it is selected. For example, if

TABLE 4: Algorithms and the more general aesthetic criteria.

Algorithm	Planarity	Flow	Symmetry	Distribution of nodes
Organic	±	−	±	+
Radial tree	+	−	±	±
Level-based tree	+	+	±	−
Balloon tree	+	−	±	−
Hierarchical	±	+	−	−
Symmetrical	−	−	+	−
Tutte	+	−	−	−
Convex	+	−	−	−
Orthogonal	+	−	−	−
Circular	±	−	−	−

TABLE 5: Algorithms and aesthetic criteria related to edges.

Algorithm	Bends	Angle	Variation	Lengths
Organic	+	−	±	±
Radial tree	+	−	+	+
Level based tree	+	−	+	+
Ballon tree	+	−	−	−
Hierarchical	±	−	−	−
Symmetrical	+	−	−	−
Tutte	+	−	−	−
Convex	+	±	−	−
Orthogonal	±	+	−	−
Circular	+	−	−	−

the only criterion is symmetry, the symmetrical one is chosen.

(b) If only one algorithm addresses that criterion, but just to some extent, it is chosen if it can be applied on the graph.

(c) If several algorithms produce drawings which conform to that criterion, properties of the graph are also taken into account. For example, if the graph is a tree and planarity is the selected criterion, a tree drawing algorithm is picked.

(d) If none of the algorithms that satisfy the criterion can be applied, the organic force-directed algorithm is selected, unless the graph has over 1000 vertices. If that, however, is the case, the ISOM algorithm is chosen instead, due to its exceptional computation efficiency.

(ii) If more than one criterion is specified, an algorithm whose results conform to the greatest number of them is sought. The order in which the criteria were listed is an important factor of the selection process; it defines their priority. Naturally, the firstly mentioned criterion has the highest priority. So, the algorithm which is to be picked should satisfy the first criterion as much as possible, which narrows down the set of possible candidates. For example, if flow, planarity, and even distribution of nodes are listed in that order and graph is not a tree, a hierarchical

algorithm will be chosen. If the order is then changed, with the criteria list being distribution of nodes, planarity, and flow, the organic algorithm will be picked. It should be noted that it is possible to specify a combination of criteria such that not all of them can be satisfied. Criteria with lower priorities are then ignored.

The second layout specification method relying on aesthetic criteria is the one allowing the usage of logical (and/or/not) operators. Its implementation is based on data provided in Tables 4 and 5. If, for example, the input corresponds to the last example seen in Listing 4, it is first checked if there is an algorithm whose drawings do not conform to neither planarity nor uniform flow criteria. As can be seen in Table 4, the symmetrical algorithm satisfies that condition and is then selected.

Finally, the last method enables the users to name a general style of the drawing, for example, hierarchical or circular, or to say that a graph should be laid out automatically. If a style was specified, the best available implementation of an algorithm belonging to the appropriate class is selected. This means that an algorithm generally producing nice drawings while also being reasonably efficient is chosen. If a graph should be laid out automatically, it is analyzed with the goal of detecting properties required by the available specialized algorithms (like planar straight-line or the tree ones). The existence of the more restrictive properties is determined first. So, if a graph is a tree (which means that it is also planar),

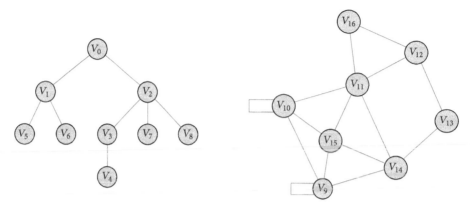

FIGURE 11: An example of an automatically laid out graph.

a tree drawing algorithm is to be chosen and not a more general planar one. If it represents a hierarchy and is not a tree, a hierarchical algorithm is selected. If the graph does not have any of the sought features, a force-directed algorithm is singled out, since members of this class can be applied to any graph. Additionally, if the given graph has over 1000 vertices, the set of possible picks is limited to more efficient implementations. An example of an automatically laid out graph, consisting of two disjoint subgraphs and containing loops is shown in Figure 11.

As it was already mentioned, GRAD strives to make integration with any graphical editor a very easy task. Making use of any of GRAD's layout methods can be by writing just a few lines of code. All that needs to be passed to GRAD in order to lay out a graph using the DSL are lists of its vertices and edges and a text that should conform to the rule's of the language. The result is then returned as a mapping from each vertex to its position and from each edge to a list of positions of its nodes. One example of GRAD's usage will be shown in the next section.

5. Example of Usage and Evaluation

The previous sections presented different aspects of the GRAD library, including the processes of automatically selecting, configuring, and applying a layout algorithm and its domain-specific language. This section will focus on showing a user study whose main goal was to verify that readability and understandability of diagrams automatically generated by a graphical editor using GRAD are on average better than of those generated by well-known commercial and open-source tools. The graphical editor which relies on GRAD and was used in the study is Kroki's lightweight UML editor.

5.1. Kroki Mockup Tool and GRAD. Kroki [73] is an open-source tool for interactive development of business applications. It supports two different notations: UML based and mockup based, implemented by its lightweight UML editor and mockup editor, respectively. Mockup editor allows the users to create forms by dragging and dropping user interface components (text fields, combo-boxes, etc.) from a palette. Every designed form is represented with a UML class in

a UML class diagram editor and vice versa. Both editors can be used interchangeably to define a single application, which means that a specification created using the mockup tool might later be opened using the UML editor. In that case, it is necessary to automatically create, link, and lay out UML classes corresponding to the forms. Additionally, Kroki supports importing models created using general purpose tools, which can be quite large and contain hundreds of elements.

Figure 12 shows an imported model opened using Kroki's UML class diagram editor and automatically laid out using GRAD. The diagram is relatively large, containing 26 classes and 40 links.

5.2. The User Study. The evaluation of the GRAD library was carried out by conducting a user study where the participants (programmers with up to 25 years of experience) were asked to rate visual attractiveness and readability of the same models laid out and visualized using different tools, as well as understandability of several code samples for triggering the process of laying out a graph. The goal of the study was to confirm that

(1) layouts of diagrams opened in a graphical editor which relies on GRAD are on average more appealing than those of diagrams laid out and visualized with leading commercial and open-source modeling tools;

(2) GRAD's layout API is easier to use and understand compared to those of the most popular Java graph analysis and drawing libraries;

(3) a large percent of developers (close to 50%) would prefer to use GRAD's external DSL when invoking a layout algorithm to any of the other methods.

5.2.1. The Evaluation Procedure. The evaluation was based on visualizing a relatively complex UML model (containing over 200 classes belonging to 31 packages) using four different tools supporting UML class diagram modeling: SAP Sybase PowerDesigner, MagicDraw, Kroki (which uses GRAD), and Papyrus. PowerDesigner and MagicDraw are industry-leading software and system modeling tools, while Papyrus is an open-source modeling environment, with increasing

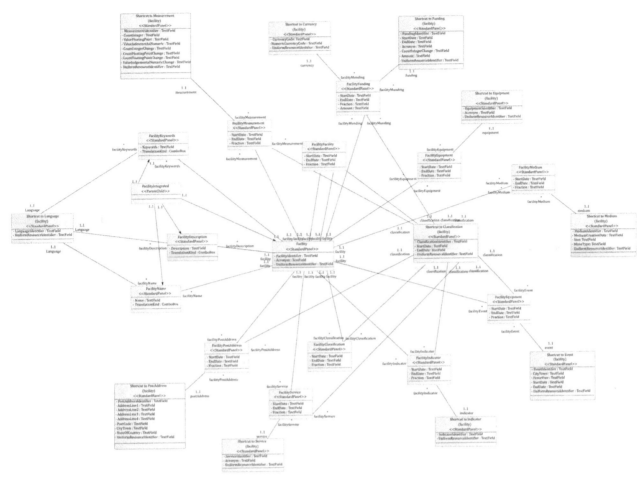

FIGURE 12: An imported model [15] opened in Kroki's UML diagram editor and automatically laid out using GRAD.

popularity. Ten of the 31 packages were selected and opened in each of the tools. PowerDesigner and Kroki automatically laid out the diagrams, while in case of MagicDraw and Papyrus the process had to be invoked manually. Both MagicDraw and Papyrus do, however, provide completely automated layout functionalities (without forcing the users to pick or configure an algorithm themselves). All properties of the diagrams' elements, except for their positions, were set to equal values for each of the tools, in order to avoid the impact of personal preferences of the participants on the results. Without being told which tool generated which diagram, the participants were shown ten sets of four diagrams (a diagram automatically laid out with each tool for every package) and were given two tasks:

(1) To grade their overall aesthetics using a 1–5 Likert scale, represented by a gradation between the choices of very poor and excellent.

(2) To try to solve a relatively simple task and rate the difficulty of doing so. These tasks included finding paths between classes, counting the number of edges connecting two classes (thus testing how well the tools handle multiple edges), counting the number of edges involving a certain class and so on. The participants

could pick an answer ranging from very difficult (1) to very easy (5).

The latter mentioned type of questions was introduced in order to compare the readability of the diagrams, since a diagram can be nice to look at, but impractical. For example, a diagram where multiple edges completely overlap could seem more aesthetically pleasing compared to one showing all such edges, while also hiding some of the important relationships between classes. While choosing the ten packages to use for the evaluation, attention was paid to selecting both smaller and simpler ones with just 5 or 6 classes and under 10 links and relatively complex ones, with over 20 classes and approximately twice as many links. As an example, Figure 13 presents one of the ten packages laid out using the four mentioned tools.

In the second phase of the study, the participants were shown five different code samples where a layout algorithm is invoked and results of its execution are retrieved. The samples included those using the mentioned JGraphX, JUNG, and prefuse libraries, while the remaining two used GRAD, one with and one without taking advantage of the DSL. All diagrams and code samples used in the study as well as more detailed results are available online [74].

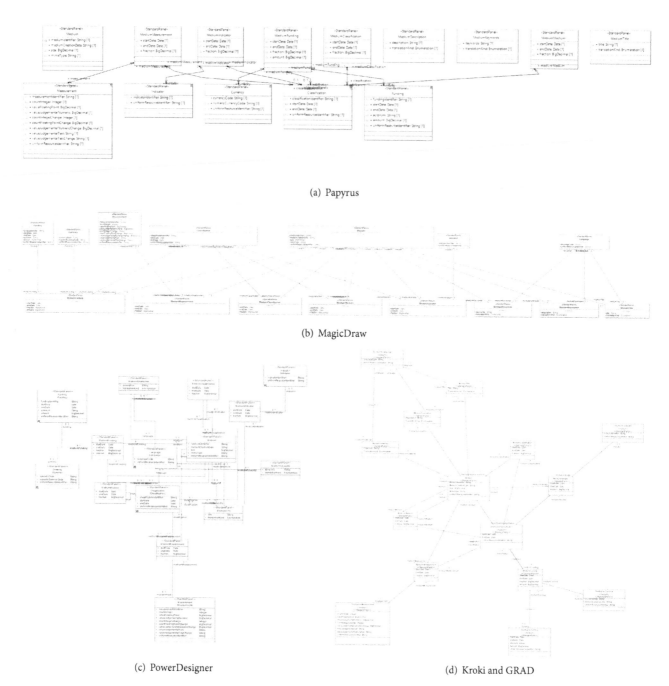

(a) Papyrus

(b) MagicDraw

(c) PowerDesigner   (d) Kroki and GRAD

FIGURE 13: The models' medium-sized package visualized using four different tools.

TABLE 6: Average values of provided answers to the background information questions.

Age	Years of programming experience in Java	Years of modelling experience
31.4	10	5.6

5.2.2. Participants. All participants, the total number of which was 31, were software engineers with some experience in UML modeling. At the start of the evaluation, they were asked to provide some general information about themselves and rate their skills in relevant fields on a scale of 1–10. The average results of these questions are shown in Tables 6 and 7.

The participants were asked if they would, if they were developing a graphical editor rather implement a layout algorithm themselves or look for existing solutions. A vast

TABLE 7: Results of the skill evaluation questionnaire.

Question	1	2	3	4	5	6	7	8	9	10	Average
How skilled you would say you are at modeling UML class diagrams?	3%	0%	0%	6%	0%	10%	16%	23%	29%	13%	7.71/10
Are you familiar with the area of graph drawing?	6%	10%	13%	6%	13%	16%	19%	13%	3%	0%	5.19/10
How would you rate your graphic design skills?	6%	6%	16%	16%	19%	10%	3%	10%	13%	0%	5.03/10

TABLE 8: Average aesthetics scores and standard deviations.

Model number	GRAD		PowerDesigner		MagicDraw		Papyrus	
	Average	SD	Average	SD	Average	SD	Average	SD
(1)	3.65	4.17	2.71	5.11	3.61	3.19	1.97	5.49
(2)	4.55	7.39	3.81	4.71	4.03	4.75	2.48	4.26
(3)	4.29	5.88	2.45	5.42	3.45	4.17	1.65	6.14
(4)	4.13	5.15	2.1	5.53	3.32	3.87	1.68	6.14
(5)	4.1	5.19	2.03	5.08	3.58	6.34	1.90	6.65
(6)	4.1	4.92	2.0	5.67	3.84	4.45	1.81	5.98
(7)	4.06	6.52	2.32	4.92	2.35	5.95	1.81	5.74
(8)	4.42	6.85	2.45	4.66	3.87	6.21	2.26	4.83
(9)	4.29	5.84	2.77	5.0	3.61	5.78	2.52	5.74
(10)	4.06	4.96	2.48	5.78	3.39	5.88	1.84	5.38

TABLE 9: Average task solving scores and standard deviations.

Model number	GRAD		PowerDesigner		MagicDraw		Papyrus	
	Average	SD	Average	SD	Average	SD	Average	SD
(1)	4.29	6.4	2.9	2.32	2.35	4.49	3.35	4.17
(2)	4.68	8.45	4.32	6.11	4.1	4.87	2.71	2.23
(3)	4.52	8.06	2.19	4.96	3.9	4.31	1.61	7.11
(4)	3.74	4.75	1.97	4.92	3.19	3.76	1.52	7.65
(5)	4.39	6.68	1.94	5.04	4.1	5.64	1.97	4.83
(6)	4.35	6.24	1.97	4.83	4.03	4.66	2.0	4.45
(7)	4.65	8.13	2.26	4.02	3.19	4.17	2.42	3.76
(8)	4.68	9.06	1.84	5.27	3.32	2.48	2.71	4.17
(9)	4.13	5.81	2.23	4.02	3.45	4.92	2.48	3.37
(10)	4.23	5.71	2.23	5.04	3.52	5.56	1.65	6.14

majority (84%) said that they would prefer to use existing implementations.

5.2.3. Results. Results of the first phase of the evaluation are shown in Tables 8 and 9. Average aesthetics scores with standard deviations can be seen in Table 8, while Table 9 contains assessments of difficulties of completing the presented tasks.

The average scores show that the participants found diagrams laid out using GRAD to be the most aesthetically pleasing. In fact, 9 out of 10 these diagrams received an average score of 4/5 or better. It can also be noted that the difference between GRAD and other tools is particularly evident in cases of larger diagrams, such as models 3, 4, 9, and 10. GRAD also received the highest scores with regard to how easy it was to solve the presented tasks.

The results of the evaluation of the ease of use of several graph drawing libraries are shown in Table 10. The participants were also asked to pick a code sample they would

prefer to use, and the percentages of those selections are shown in Table 11.

It can be noticed that GRAD's regular method of calling a layout algorithm and retrieving the results, which does not use the DSL, received the highest average score. However, GRAD's second method, where the DSL is used, was selected by 42% of participants as the method they would prefer to use. Doing so requires learning the syntax of the DSL, which explains the fact that some participants did not give it a very high grade. On the other hand, it is the shortest of all methods, which almost half of the participants appreciated.

6. Conclusion

This paper presented a domain-specific language designed for simplifying the process of laying out a graph, as well as GRAD, our library for graph analysis, and drawing containing the algorithms necessary for the DSL's implementation. To the best of our knowledge, there is no other DSL focusing

TABLE 10: Average scores and standard deviations of code intuitiveness evaluation.

JGraphX		JUNG		GRAD		prefuse		GRAD DSL	
Avg	SD	Avg	SD	Avg	SD	Avg	SD	Avg	SD
3.06	3.82	3.48	5.78	4.06	6.27	2.45	3.31	3.94	4.31

TABLE 11: Percentage of users who would prefer to use the code sample.

JGraphX	JUNG	GRAD	prefuse	GRAD DSL
6%	16%	32%	3%	42%

exclusively on graph layout and some of the algorithms implemented in GRAD have not been implemented Java before.

GRAD's domain-specific language primarily aims to help users without extensive knowledge of graph drawing theory and algorithms lay out a certain diagram in accordance with their wishes. This is accomplished through naming a general style of the drawing or listing its desirable properties (or aesthetic criteria of the drawing). Based on such specification and properties of the graph, the most appropriate layout algorithm is automatically chosen, configured, and executed. The DSL can also be used by expert users to quickly select and configure an algorithm. Furthermore, if so is desired, subgraphs can be singled out and their layouts can be defined separately.

GRAD is currently being used in our Kroki mockup tool for laying out models which sometimes contain over 600 classes. A conducted user study showed that the participants generally rated diagrams whose elements were positioned using GRAD better than diagrams laid out using commercial tools (PowerDeigner and MagicDraw) and one of the most widely used open-source solutions, Papyrus. Furthermore, the study revealed that a vast majority of participants found GRAD's code samples more intuitive compared to the alternatives, JGraphX, JUNG framework, and prefuse.

As new algorithms are added to the GRAD library, the DSL will be expanded to support them. The automatic choice of the most appropriate algorithm will be enhanced, so that it is also checked if the newly implemented algorithm is the best option in a particular situation. Algorithms whose addition is planned include one or more orthogonal, polyline, and more sophisticated symmetric ones.

Additionally, integration with the popular Sirius tool for creation of graphical editors is also among planned future enhancements.

Conflicts of Interest

The authors declare that there are no conflicts of interest regarding the publication of this paper.

References

[1] G. Di Battista, P. Eades, R. Tamassia, and I. G. Tollis, "Algorithms for drawing graphs: an annotated bibliography," *Computational Geometry. Theory and Applications*, vol. 4, no. 5, pp. 235–282, 1994.

[2] H. C. Purchase, D. Carrington, and J.-A. Allder, "Empirical evaluation of aesthetics-based graph layout," *Empirical Software Engineering*, vol. 7, no. 3, pp. 233–255, 2002.

[3] H. C. Purchase, "Effective information visualization: A study of graph drawing aesthetics and algorithms," *Interacting with Computers*, vol. 13, no. 2, pp. 147–162, 2000.

[4] R. Tamassia, G. D. Battista, and C. Batini, "Automatic Graph Drawing and Readability of Diagrams," *IEEE Transactions on Systems, Man, and Cybernetics*, vol. 18, no. 1, pp. 61–79, 1988.

[5] C. Bennett, J. Ryall, L. Spalteholz, and A. Gooch, "The aesthetics of graph visualization," in *Proceedings of the in Proceedings of the Third Eurographics conference on Computational Aesthetics in Graphics, Visualization and Imaging*, pp. 57–64, 2007.

[6] M. Petre, "Cognitive dimensions 'beyond the notation,'" *Journal of Visual Languages and Computing*, vol. 17, no. 4, pp. 292–301, 2006.

[7] M. Schrepfer, J. Wolf, J. Mendling, and H. A. Reijers, "The impact of secondary notation on process model understanding," *Lecture Notes in Business Information Processing*, vol. 39, pp. 161–175, 2009.

[8] H. Purchase, J.-A. Allder, and D. Carrington, "User preference of graph layout aesthetics: A uml study," in *in Proceedings of the 8th International Symposium on Graph Drawing*, pp. 5–18, 2000.

[9] Provide a custom arrange-all, https://www.eclipse.org/sirius/doc/developer/extensions-provide_custom-arrange-all.html.

[10] M. Narkhedel, S. Patil, and V. Inamdar, "Comparative study of various graph layout algorithms," *International Journal of Emerging Trends and Technology in Computer Science*, vol. 3, 2014.

[11] L. Vismara, *Handbook of Graph Drawing and Visualization*, ch. 6, Chapman and Hall/CRC, 2007.

[12] P. Eades and P. Mutzel, *Handbook of Graph Drawing and Visualization*, ch. 3, Chapman and Hall/CRC, 2007.

[13] T. Nishizeki and S. Rahman, *Handbook of Graph Drawing and Visualization*, ch. 10, Chapman and Hall/CRC, 2007.

[14] N. Chiba, K. Onoguchi, and T. Nishizeki, "Linear algorithms for convex drawings of planar graphs," in *Progress in Graph Theory*, vol. 173, pp. 153–173, Academic Press, Toronto, ON, 1984.

[15] Cerif, http://www.eurocris.org/cerif/introduction/.

[16] E. W. Dijkstra, "A note on two problems in connexion with graphs," *Numerische Mathematik*, vol. 1, pp. 269–271, 1959.

[17] M. Mernik, J. Heering, and A. M. Sloane, "When and how to develop domain-specific languages," *ACM Computing Surveys*, vol. 37, no. 4, pp. 316–344, 2005.

[18] H. Purchase, "Which aesthetic has the greatest effect on human understanding?" in *Graph Drawing Software*, vol. 1353 of *Lecture Notes in Computer Science*, pp. 248–261, Springer Berlin Heidelberg, Berlin, Heidelberg, 1997.

[19] M. K. Coleman and D. Stott Parker, "Aesthetics-based graph layout for human consumption," *Software: Practice and Experience*, vol. 26, no. 12, pp. 1415–1438, 1996.

[20] H. C. Purchase, J.-A. Allder, and D. Carrington, "Graph layout aesthetics in UML diagrams: user preferences," *Journal of Graph Algorithms and Applications*, vol. 6, no. 3, pp. 255–279, 2002.

[21] W. Huang, S. hee Hong, and P. Eades, "Layout effects: Comparison of sociogram drawing conventions," Tech. Rep., University of Sydney, 2005.

[22] R. Vaderna, I. Dejanovic, and G. Milosavljevic, "GRAD: A New Graph Drawing and Analysis Library," in *Proceedings of the 2016 Federated Conference on Computer Science and Information Systems, FedCSIS 2016*, pp. 1597–1602, Poland, September 2016.

[23] R. Vaderna, G. Milosavljevic', and I. Dejanovic', "Laying out graphs using graph analysis and drawing library - grad," in *in Proceedings of the 25h International Computer Science Conference ERK 2016*, vol. B, pp. 51–54, 2016.

[24] R. Vaderna, G. Milosavljvic', and I. Dejanovic', "Graph layout algorithms and libraries: Overview and improvements," in *Proceedings of the in ICIST 2015 5th International Conference on Information Society and Technology Proceedings*, pp. 55–60, 2015.

[25] M. Patrignani, *Handbook of Graph Drawing and Visualization*, ch. 1, Chapman and Hall/CRC, 2007.

[26] S. Skiena, *Implementing Discrete Mathematics: Combinatorics and Graph Theory with Mathematica*, ch. 5, Addison-Wesley Publishing Company, 1990.

[27] Graph crossing number, http://mathworld.wolfram.com/Graph-CrossingNumber.html.

[28] H. Purchase, *Evaluating Graph Drawing Aesthetics: defining and exploring a new empirical research area*, ch. 8, Idea Group Publishing, 2004.

[29] The dot language, http://www.graphviz.org/doc/info/lang.html.

[30] T. M. J. Fruchterman and E. M. Reingold, "Graph drawing by force-directed placement," *Software: Practice and Experience*, vol. 21, no. 11, pp. 1129–1164, 1991.

[31] A. Bergel, S. Maass, S. Ducasse, and T. Girba, "A domain-specific language for visualizing software dependencies as a graph," in *Proceedings of the 2nd IEEE International Working Conference on Software Visualization, VISSOFT 2014*, pp. 45–49, Canada, September 2014.

[32] Dsl based approach to input graph data in graph theory based java programs, https://sanaulla.info/2013/07/19/dsl-based-approach-to-input-graph-data-in-graph-theory-based-java-programs.

[33] S. Hong, H. Chafi, E. Sedlar, and K. Olukotun, "Green-Marl: A DSL for easy and efficient graph analysis," in *Proceedings of the 17th International Conference on Architectural Support for Programming Languages and Operating Systems, ASPLOS 2012*, pp. 349–362, UK, March 2012.

[34] R. Tamassia, Ed., *Handbook of graph drawing and visualization*, CRC Press, Boca Raton, FL, 2014.

[35] C. Buchheim, M. Chimani, C. Gutwenger et al., *Handbook of Graph Drawing and Visualization*, ch. 2, Chapman and Hall/CRC, 2007.

[36] C. Gutwenger and P. Mutzel, "Planar polyline drawings with good angular resolution," in *Proceedings of the Graph Drawing Symposium 1998*, pp. 167–182, Springer.

[37] H. C. Purchase, "Metrics for Graph Drawing Aesthetics," *Journal of Visual Languages & Computing*, vol. 13, no. 5, pp. 501–516, 2002.

[38] R. Tamassia, "On embedding a graph in the grid with the minimum number of bends," *SIAM Journal on Computing*, vol. 16, no. 3, pp. 421–444, 1987.

[39] A. Papakostas and I. G. Tollis, "Efficient orthogonal drawings of high degree graphs," *Algorithmica. An International Journal in Computer Science*, vol. 26, no. 1, pp. 100–125, 2000.

[40] T. Kamada and S. Kawai, "An algorithm for drawing general undirected graphs," *Information Processing Letters*, vol. 31, no. 1, pp. 7–15, 1989.

[41] Graph automorphism, http://mathworld.wolfram.com/GraphAutomorphism.html.

[42] A. Rusu, *Handbook of Graph Drawing and Visualization*, ch. 5, Chapman and Hall/CRC, 2007.

[43] P. Healy and N. Nikolov, *Handbook of Graph Drawing and Visualization*, ch. 13, Chapman and Hall/CRC, 2007.

[44] J. Six and I. Tollis, *Handbook of Graph Drawing and Visualization*, ch. 9, Chapman and Hall/CRC, 2007.

[45] S. Kobourov, *Handbook of Graph Drawing and Visualization*, Chapman and Hall/CRC, 2013.

[46] W. T. Tutte, "How to Draw a Graph," *Proceedings of the London Mathematical Society*, vol. 3-13, no. 1, pp. 743–767, 1963.

[47] P. Eades, "A heuristic for graph drawing," *Congressus Numerantium*, vol. 42, pp. 149–160, 1984.

[48] R. Davidson and D. Harel, "Drawing Graphs Nicely Using Simulated Annealing," *ACM Transactions on Graphics*, pp. 301–331.

[49] B. Meyer, "Self-Organizing Graphs — A Neural Network Perspective of Graph Layout," in *Graph Drawing Software*, vol. 1547 of *Lecture Notes in Computer Science*, pp. 246–262, Springer Berlin Heidelberg, Berlin, Heidelberg, 1998.

[50] K. Sugiyama, S. Tagawa, and M. Toda, "Methods for Visual Understanding of Hierarchical System Structures," *IEEE Transactions on Systems, Man, and Cybernetics*, vol. 11, no. 2, pp. 109–125, 1981.

[51] H. Carr and W. Kocay, "An algorithm for drawing a graph symmetrically," *Bulletin of the Institute of Combinatorics and Its Applications*, vol. 27, pp. 19–25, 1999.

[52] N. Chiba, T. Yamanouchi, and T. Nishizeki, *Progress in Graph Theory*, ch. 5, Academic Press, 1984.

[53] J. M. Six and I. G. Tollis, "A framework and algorithms for circular drawings of graphs," *Journal of Discrete Algorithms*, vol. 4, no. 1, pp. 25–50, 2006.

[54] R. Tamassia and I. G. Tollis, "A unified approach to visibility representations of planar graphs," *Discrete & Computational Geometry*, vol. 1, no. 1, pp. 321–341, 1986.

[55] Graph analysis and drawing library, https://www.gradlibrary.net.

[56] Y. Hu, "Efficient and high quality force-directed graph drawing," *The Mathematica Journal*, vol. 10, pp. 37–71, 2005.

[57] H. de Fraysseix and P. Ossona de Mendez, "Trémaux trees and planarity," *European Journal of Combinatorics*, vol. 33, no. 3, pp. 279–293, 2012.

[58] J. M. Boyer and W. J. Myrvold, "On the cutting edge: Simplified o(n) planarity by edge addition," *Journal of Graph Algorithms and Applications*, vol. 8, no. 3, pp. 241–273, 2004.

[59] K. S. Booth and G. S. Lueker, "Testing for the consecutive ones property, interval graphs, and graph planarity using pq-tree algorithms," *Journal of Computer and System Sciences*, vol. 13, no. 3, pp. 335–379, 1976.

[60] J. E. Hopcroft and R. E. Tarjan, "Dividing a graph into triconnected components," *SIAM Journal on Computing*, vol. 2, no. 3, pp. 135–158, 1973.

[61] S. Fialko and P. Mutzel, "A new approximation algorithm for the planar augmentation problem," in *Proceedings of the Ninth Annual ACM-SIAM Symposium on Discrete Algorithms*, pp. 260–269, Society for Industrial and Applied Mathematics, 1998.

[62] B. D. McKay, "Practical graph isomorphism," *Proceedings of the Tenth MANitoba Conference on Numerical MAThematics and COMputing, Vol. I (Winnipeg, MAN., 1980)*, vol. 30, pp. 45–87, 1981.

[63] M. Mernik, D. Hrncic, B. R. Bryant, and F. Javed, "Applications of grammatical inference in software engineering: domain specific language development," *Scientific applications of language methods*, vol. 2, pp. 421–457, 2011.

[64] I. Čeh, M. Črepinšek, T. Kosar, and M. Mernik, "Ontology driven development of domain-specific languages," *Computer Science and Information Systems*, vol. 8, no. 2, pp. 317–342, 2011.

[65] T. Kosar, M. Mernik, and J. C. Carver, "Program comprehension of domain-specific and general-purpose languages: comparison using a family of experiments," *Empirical Software Engineering*, vol. 17, no. 3, pp. 276–304, 2012.

[66] M. Fowler, *Domain Specific Languages*, Addison-Wesley Professional, 2010.

[67] W. Cazzola and E. Vacchi, "Language components for modular DSLs using traits," *Computer Languages, Systems and Structures*, vol. 45, pp. 16–34, 2016.

[68] I. Dejanović, R. Vaderna, G. Milosavljević, and Ž. Vuković, "TextX: A Python tool for Domain-Specific Languages implementation," *Knowledge-Based Systems*, vol. 115, pp. 1–4, 2017.

[69] T. Kosar, S. Bohra, and M. Mernik, "Domain-Specific Languages: A Systematic Mapping Study," *Information and Software Technology*, vol. 71, pp. 77–91, 2016.

[70] M. Nosál', J. Porubän, and M. Sulír, "Customizing host IDE for non-programming users of pure embedded DSLs: A case study," *Computer Languages, Systems and Structures*, vol. 49, pp. 101–118, 2017.

[71] A. Barišić, V. Amaral, and M. Goulão, "Usability driven DSL development with USE-ME," *Computer Languages, Systems and Structures*, 2017.

[72] Graph layout dsl, https://github.com/renatav/GraphDrawing/blob/master/GraphLayoutDSL/src/language/layout.tx.

[73] G. Milosavljevic, M. Filipovic, V. Marsenic, D. Pejakovic, and I. Dejanovic, "Kroki: A mockup-based tool for participatory development of business applications," in *Proceedings of the 12th IEEE International Conference on Intelligent Software Methodologies, Tools and Techniques, SoMeT 2013*, pp. 235–242, Hungary, September 2013.

[74] R. Vaderna, *Grad Evaluation Results, Mendeley Data*, 2017.

13

Finite Element Assembly using an Embedded Domain Specific Language

Bart Janssens,[1] **Támas Bányai,**[2] **Karim Limam,**[3] **and Walter Bosschaerts**[1]

[1]*Department of Mechanics, Royal Military Academy, Avenue de Renaissance 30, 1000 Brussels, Belgium*
[2]*von Karman Institute for Fluid Dynamics, Chaussée de Waterloo 72, 1640 Rhode-Saint-Genèse, Belgium*
[3]*LaSIE, La Rochelle University, Avenue Michel Crépeau, 17042 La Rochelle Cedex 1, France*

Correspondence should be addressed to Bart Janssens; bart@bartjanssens.org

Academic Editor: Bormin Huang

In finite element methods, numerical simulation of the problem requires the generation of a linear system based on an integral form of a problem. Using C++ meta-programming techniques, a method is developed that allows writing code that stays close to the mathematical formulation. We explain the specifics of our method, which relies on the Boost.Proto framework to simplify the evaluation of our language. Some practical examples are elaborated, together with an analysis of the performance. The abstraction overhead is quantified using benchmarks.

1. Introduction

The application of the finite element method (FEM) requires the discretization of the integral form of the partial differential equations that govern the physics, thus transforming the problem into a set of algebraic equations that can be solved numerically. In essence, the resulting numerical model only depends on the governing equations and the set of basis and test functions. From the point of view of a model developer, it would therefore be ideal to only need to specify these parameters in a concise form that closely resembles the mathematical formulation of the problem, without sacrificing computational efficiency.

The current work is part of Coolfluid 3 [1], a C++ framework intended primarily for the solution of fluid dynamics problems and available as open source under the LGPL v3 license. The system is designed around a Component class that can provide a dynamic interface through Python scripting and a GUI. Model developers will typically write a set of components to build a solver for a given set of equations, using functionality provided by our framework and external libraries. Problem-dependent settings such as the mesh, boundary conditions, and model parameters can then be controlled through Python or a GUI, though these

aspects are beyond the scope of the current paper. In this context, we provide an Embedded Domain Specific Language (EDSL) that can be used to implement finite element solver components. It uses a notation similar to the mathematical formulation of the weak form of a problem, allowing the programmer to focus on the physics rather than coding details. We assume a typical finite element workflow, where a global linear system is assembled from element matrix contributions. Our language can also describe boundary conditions and field arithmetic operations.

All language elements consist of standard C++ code, so they easily embed into the components of our framework. An extension mechanism is available, allowing any developer to implement his own language elements without touching the library code. The implementation uses the Boost.Proto [2] framework, which builds on template meta programming techniques for generating efficient code. The actual performance overhead will be quantified and compared to the global solution time for some applications.

The automatic generation of code based on an intuitive specification of the physical problem is of course a feature that is highly desirable for any numerical simulation framework. One example of previous work providing such functionality is OpenFOAM [3], a C++ library primarily intended for fluid mechanics. It allows for the easy expression of differential equations by providing an embedded tensor manipulation language, specific to finite volume discretizations. The FEniCS project [4] provides an easy and efficient method for developing finite element discretizations. The approach differs from ours in that the language is embedded into Python and compiled using a just-in-time compiler. It also offers the option of automated analytical evaluation of integrals [5]. Another example is the FEEL++ project [6], which also provides a domain specific language embedded into C++ using expression templates.

Notwithstanding the existence of all these excellent projects, we decided to implement our own framework for tight integration with the Coolfluid data structures and to support our workflow of building user-configurable components. The implementation relies on expression templates, just like FEEL++, but we use Boost.Proto to handle the expression template generation and to define a grammar for our language. This results in simpler code and has a limited impact on runtime performance, as we will show. Even though our language is not as feature-complete as the more established FEEL++ and FEniCS projects, we do believe that the easy integration of user-defined extensions into the language is a unique feature. The purpose of the current paper is to present how Proto can be used to construct a language for finite element modeling—based on a simple example building a mass matrix—and to show the capabilities and performance of the language we developed. Aspects that are new compared to previous work in the field are the use of Proto as a new way to construct the language and the possibility to add user-defined terminals to the language.

This paper is structured as follows. In Section 2 the mathematical formulation of the integral form will be laid out in order to clearly define the class of problems that is supported. Next, in Section 3 the mechanics for constructing and interpreting the EDSL are explained in detail, based on a simple application. Section 4 contains some application examples and Section 5 a performance analysis. Finally, in Section 6 we present our conclusions and suggest future work.

2. Finite Element Discretization

In this section, we introduce the notation used for finite element discretizations, starting from the Poisson problem as an example. A more generic and much more thorough introduction to the finite element method is given in, for example, [7]. Considering a domain Ω with boundary Γ, the differential equations describing the Poisson problem are

$$\nabla^2 f + g = 0 \quad \text{over } \Omega, \tag{1}$$

$$f = f_0 \quad \text{over } \Gamma. \tag{2}$$

To transform these continuous equations into a discrete problem, the unknown f is interpolated using a linear

combination of n shape functions $N(\mathbf{x})$ with the unknown coefficients f_i:

$$f \approx \sum_{i=1}^{n} N_i(\mathbf{x}) f_i = \widetilde{f}. \tag{3}$$

The shape functions depend only on the spatial coordinates $\mathbf{x}$ and to simplify the notation we will from here on just write N instead of $N(\mathbf{x})$. The shape functions have a local support and the interpolation happens on a per-element basis, so n is equal to the number of nodes in an element. The interpolation can also be written in vector form as $\widetilde{f} = \mathbf{N}_f \mathbf{f}_e$. Here, $\mathbf{N}_f$ is a row vector with the shape functions associated with unknown f and $\mathbf{f}_e$ is the column vector of the unknown coefficients for the element.

To obtain a linear system for the discrete problem, we need to multiply the equations with a weighting function and integrate over the domain. Using the Galerkin method (i.e., the weighting functions are the shape functions) as well as integrating per-element yields the following linear system for the Poisson problem, using the weak formulation here:

$$\sum_{e=1}^{n_\Omega} \underbrace{\int_{\Omega_e} \nabla \mathbf{N}_\mathbf{f}^\mathrm{T} \nabla \mathbf{N}_\mathbf{f} \mathbf{f}_e \, d\Omega_e}_{A_{ff}} = \sum_{e=1}^{n_\Omega} \underbrace{\int_{\Omega_e} \mathbf{N}_\mathbf{g}^\mathrm{T} \widetilde{g} \, d\Omega_e}_{\mathbf{a}_f}. \tag{4}$$

Due to the local support of the shape functions, the integral is written as a sum of integrals over all the elements. Each element integral results in an element matrix A_{ff} on the left hand side and an element vector $\mathbf{a}_f$ on the right hand side. Summing up the contributions of all elements that share a given node assembles a global linear system that has the total number of nodes as dimension.

The indices f are useful for problems with multiple unknowns. In this case, each unknown can be associated with its own shape function, and the element matrices and vectors are built up of blocks associated with each variable and equation.

The matrix assembly procedure is the same for all problems; only the values of the element matrices depend on the initial equation (1). This observation drives the current work: we will present a convenient language to write out the element equations and automate the steps that are common for all finite element discretizations. The code for the Poisson problem is presented in Listing 1, where lines (17) and (18) map directly to the element matrix and vector, as defined in (4), and lines (20) and (21) represent the assembly into the global system. Lines (17) and (18) form the core of our language, and the techniques for implementing this will be explained in detail in the next section. The remainder of Listing 1 will be further explained in Section 4.1.

From this simple example, the basic requirements for our language can be identified: provide access to the shape functions and their derivatives, as well as nodal values of the variables; control the evaluation of integrals; and allow the application of boundary conditions. Finally, we must be able to express the assembly into global matrices and vectors. The embedding of such a language into C++ is the main topic of the remainder of this paper.

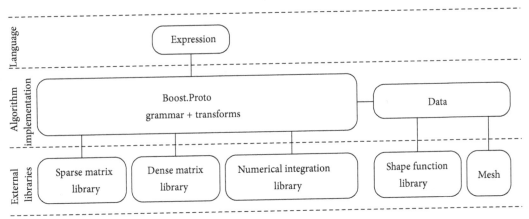

FIGURE 1: The structure of the program, showing the three different levels of the implementation.

3. Construction of the Language

Our language consists of three levels of implementation, as shown in Figure 1. The top level contains the language itself, which consists of keywords that the user combines into an expression. Because the language is embedded, only valid C++ expressions are allowed, but we can define the interpretation freely via operator overloading. This is the job of the algorithm implementation layer. Here, the language is parsed and appropriate actions—called semantic actions in language grammar terms—are linked to each part of the input. Some of the actions may result in calls to a shape function library or matrix operations, so the final layer contains all external libraries needed to execute these.

The remainder of this section will focus on each layer in more detail, using a simple stand-alone example. This allows us to easily demonstrate the techniques used in Coolfluid 3 while avoiding the need to explain the details of our mesh structure and linear algebra interface, which are beyond the scope of this paper. The example will result in a program that builds the mass matrix for a finite element problem with a single scalar variable. It is a stand-alone program that depends only on the Boost libraries and on the Eigen library [8] for matrix operations.

The mass matrix M is assembled from the outer product of the weight and shape functions; that is,

$$M = \sum_{n_\Omega} \int_{\Omega_e} \mathbf{N}^\mathrm{T}\mathbf{N}\, d\Omega_e. \tag{5}$$

The shape function has no index referring to a specific variable here, since we only consider a single, unspecified scalar variable. We want to ensure that the following code evaluates (5):

$$\text{for\_each\_element (mesh, element\_quadrature} \tag{6}$$
$$(\text{M+ = transpose (N) * N));}$$

here, for_each_element represents a generic function, taking the finite element mesh structure as first argument and a Proto expression as second argument. The expression consists here of a call to element_quadrature to evaluate

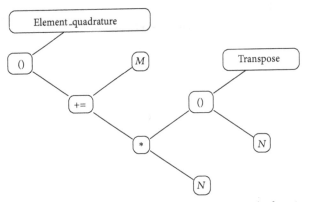

FIGURE 2: The expression tree for line (19) in Listing 2. The function call operator is denoted by ().

the integral over an element and the += operator should be interpreted as an assembly into the mass matrix M. The outer product of the shape function vectors maps directly to transpose(N)*N. In what follows, we show how we can evaluate this expression.

3.1. The Language Layer. Using the Boost.Proto [2] library, expressions are constructed from so-called "terminals." These are C++ objects that are instances of the Proto terminal class, which overloads all of the C++ operators. Combining different terminals using operators builds an expression that can be evaluated later. This expression is analogous to the expression templates used in, for example, FEEL++ [6]. Listing 2 presents a minimal program that allows compiling the expression for (5). Line (19) contains the expression, built from the terminals defined at lines (11) to (13). Because all operations are defined on a Proto terminal, the code compiles. The result of line (19) is an expression tree, retaining the concrete type of each element in the expression. This is the same kind of data structure that we encounter in any expression template library, but it is generated automatically by Proto here.

Figure 2 shows the expression tree corresponding to line (19). Leaf nodes in this tree correspond to Proto terminals.

```
(1) // The unknown function. The first template argument is a constant to distinguish each
        variable at compile time
(2) FieldVariable<0, ScalarField> f("f", solution_tag());
(3) // The source term, to be set at runtime using an initial condition
(4) FieldVariable<1, ScalarField> g("g", "source_term");
(5)
(6) // Action handling the assembly
(7) Handle<ProtoAction> assembly = create_component<ProtoAction>("Assembly");
(8) // Set the expression
(9) assembly->set_expression(elements_expression
(10) (
(11)   mesh::LagrangeP1::CellTypes(), // All first order Lagrange elements
(12)   group
(13)   (
(14)     _A = _0, _a = _0,// The element matrix and RHS vector, initialized to 0
(15)     element_quadrature // Integration over the element
(16)     (
(17)       _A(f) += transpose(nabla(f)) * nabla(f),
(18)       _a[f] += transpose(N(g))*g
(19)     ),
(20)     system_matrix += _A, // Assemble into the global linear system
(21)     system_rhs += _a
(22)   )
(23) ));
```

LISTING 1: Implementation of the assembly procedure for the Poisson problem.

```
(1) #include <boost/proto/proto.hpp>
(2)
(3) using namespace boost;
(4)
(5) // Different types to distinguish terminals at compile time
(6) struct shape_func_tag {};
(7) struct element_quadrature_tag {};
(8) struct transpose_tag {};
(9)
(10) // Some statically created terminals
(11) proto::terminal< shape_func_tag >::type const N= {};
(12) proto::terminal< element_quadrature_tag >::type const element_quadrature = {};
(13) proto::terminal< transpose_tag >::type const transpose = {};
(14)
(15) int main(void)
(16) {
(17)   double* M;
(18)   // This is a proto expression:
(19)   element_quadrature(M += transpose(N)*N);
(20)   return 0;
(21) }
```

LISTING 2: Generating expressions from Boost.Proto terminals.

Each function call operator (denoted by ()) has two child nodes: the terminal representing the function itself (e.g., transpose) and the argument to the function. The terminal that represents the function is used to link it with the correct code of the function, based on the unique type of that terminal. This implies that functions can easily be renamed by creating a new terminal of the same type. The binary operators += and * also have two children, corresponding to the left and right hand side.

So far, the expression on line (19) does nothing. The parsing and the implementation of the appropriate actions to evaluate this are the subject of the next section.

```
(1) struct fem_grammar:
(2)   // Match the following rules in order:
(3)   proto::or_
(4)   <
(5)     // Evaluate shape functions using the eval_shape_func transform
(6)     proto::when
(7)     <
(8)       proto::terminal<shape_func_tag>,
(9)       eval_shape_func(proto::_data)
(10)    >,
(11)    // Evaluate transpose expressions using eval_transpose
(12)    proto::when
(13)    <
(14)      proto::function<proto::terminal<transpose_tag>, fem_grammar >,
(15)      eval_transpose(fem_grammar(proto::_child1))
(16)    >,
(17)    // Evaluate element_quadrature using eval_element_quadrature
(18)    proto::when
(19)    <
(20)      proto::function< proto::terminal<element_quadrature_tag>, proto::plus_assign<proto::
                terminal<Eigen::MatrixXd>, fem_grammar> >,
(21)      eval_element_quadrature(proto::_value(proto::_left(proto::_child1)),
                proto::_right(proto::_child1), proto::_data)
(22)    >,
(23)    // On any other expression: perform the default C++ action
(24)    proto::_default<fem_grammar>
(25)  >
(26) {
(27) };
```

LISTING 3: Grammar capable of parsing a simple expression for interpolating coordinates using a shape function.

3.2. The Algorithm Implementation Layer. The algorithm implementation layer in Figure 1 takes care of the interpretation of expressions and the execution of the associated actions. In this section, we take a top-down approach for evaluating our example expression. To this end, we first define a class—grammar in Proto terminology—capable of parsing the expression. The class defined in Listing 3 describes the language that we use in our example expression. The grammar is defined entirely in a templated type from which fem_grammar derives. This notation is actually the embedded domain specific language provided by Proto itself for defining a grammar. The or_construct allows us to list a series of rules (each a Proto grammar in itself) that are checked in sequence. The when statement first describes what kind of syntax to expect, followed by a second argument—the semantic action—that describes how to evaluate the expression matching the when clause. In the case of terminals, we can use the type to distinguish them. The grammar can be used to check the validity of an expression at compile time, using the proto::matches metafunction, which does not evaluate the expression but simply checks if it matches a given grammar, taking into account only the when clauses. This functionality can be used to generate compilation errors that can help in finding errors in expressions, but this is not further discussed in the current work.

The main use of the grammars is the actual evaluation of the expressions. To this end, we can use fem_grammar as a C++ functor on an expression, in which case the grammar acts as a Proto "transform" (i.e., a kind of functor), evaluating the expression by executing the semantic actions embedded into the grammar. We will now describe each rule in the grammar in detail.

First, at line (6), shape function expressions are matched and evaluated. In (6), shape functions appear as the terminalN. The grammar matches this using proto::terminal with the appropriate type on line (8). The second argument in the when clause (line (9)) performs the evaluation. All the grammar code is inside template parameters, so everything is actually a type. Line (9) is then not really a function call, but the type of a function that returns something of the type eval_shape_func and takes proto::_data as argument. This function is never really defined, but Proto uses the type to call an eval_shape_func functor and pass its arguments. The argument consists of context data here—the "data" block from Figure 1—and will be discussed in detail later.

The implementation of the eval_shape_func functor is given in Listing 4. To be usable in a Proto grammar, a functor must inherit the proto::callable class. Lines (4) to (13) are used by Proto to compute the result type of the functor.

```
(1) struct eval_shape_func: proto::callable
(2) {
(3)   // C++ result_of declaration
(4)   template<typename Signature>
(5)   struct result;
(6)
(7)   // C++ result_of implementation
(8)   template<class ThisT, typename DataT>
(9)   struct result<ThisT(DataT)>
(10)  {
(11)   typedef const typename
(12)     boost::remove_reference<DataT>::type::element_t::shape_func_t& type;
(13)  };
(14)
(15)  template<typename DataT>
(16)  const typename DataT::element_t::shape_func_t& operator()(DataT& data) const
(17)  {
(18)   // Return a reference to the result, stored in data
(19)   return data.shape_func;
(20)  }
(21) };
```

LISTING 4: Functor to evaluate the shape functions.

```
(1) struct eval_transpose: proto::callable
(2) {
(3)   template<typename MatT>
(4)   Eigen::Transpose<MatT> operator()(MatT& mat) const
(5)   {
(6)     return mat.transpose();
(7)   }
(8) };
```

LISTING 5: Functor to evaluate the matrix transpose.

In C++11, it is possible to obtain this automatically, so this part of the code can be omitted. The function itself is defined on lines (15)–(20) and on line (19) we return the shape value functions, which are just cached in the context data. As will be seen later, this cached value is actually computed in the element_quadrature function.

The next grammar rule, on line (12) in Listing 3, matches and evaluates the matrix transpose. In the matching rule on line (14), it is prescribed that a function call using a terminal of type transpose_tag and with as argument an expression that matches fem_grammar is the correct form of a transpose expression. To evaluate the argument, we make a recursive call to fem_grammar itself (using _child1 to isolate the function argument in the expression) and apply the eval_transpose functor to the result. Listing 5 shows the relevant code for evaluating the transpose. It is a functor that takes any matrix type from the Eigen library [8] as argument and calls the transpose function on line (6).

The rule describing the integration over an element starts on line (18) in Listing 3. On line (20), we impose that only

expressions of the plus_assign type, that is, +=, can be used as an argument to the element_quadrature function. This expression is then picked apart on line (21) using the _left and _right Proto operations, where the value of the left hand side (an Eigen matrix representing the global system matrix), the right hand side expression, and the context data are passed to the eval_element_quadrature functor. This functor is defined in Listing 6. On line (13), the numerical integration is performed by looping over the Gauss points defined for the element. First, the shape function values and Jacobian determinant are computed and stored in the context data (lines (15) and (16)). Next, the element matrix is updated with the value of the expression at the Gauss point, multiplied with the appropriate weight and the Jacobian determinant. The expression itself is evaluated using the call:

$$\texttt{fem\_grammar}()(expr, 0, data). \qquad (7)$$

Here, our grammar is default-constructed (i.e., the first ()) and then called using three arguments: the expression, the state (0 here), and the context data. The state is similar to

```
(1)  struct eval_element_quadrature: proto::callable
(2)  {
(3)    template<typename ExprT, typename DataT>
(4)    void operator()(Eigen::MatrixXd& mat, const ExprT& expr, DataT& data) const
(5)    {
(6)      // Temporary storage for the result from the RHS
(7)      Eigen::Matrix<double, DataT::element_t::nb_nodes, DataT::element_t::nb_nodes> rhs_result
         ;
(8)      rhs_result.setZero();
(9)
(10)     // Loop over the gauss points
(11)     const typename DataT::element_t::gauss_points_t gauss_points = DataT::element_t::
             gauss_points();
(12)     const typename DataT::element_t::gauss_weights_t gauss_weights = DataT::element_t::
             gauss_weights();
(13)     for(int i = 0; i != DataT::element_t::nb_gauss_points; ++i)
(14)     {
(15)       data.shape_func = DataT::element_t::shape_function(gauss_points.row(i));
(16)       data.det_jacobian = DataT::element_t::jacobian_determinant(gauss_points.row(i), data.
             coord_mat);
(17)       rhs_result += gauss_weights[i] * data.det_jacobian * fem_grammar()(expr, 0, data);
(18)     }
(19)
(20)     // Place the result in the global matrix
(21)     for(int i = 0; i != DataT::element_t::nb_nodes; ++i)
(22)       for(int j = 0; j != DataT::element_t::nb_nodes; ++j)
(23)         mat(data.node_indices[i], data.node_indices[j]) += rhs_result(i,j);
(24)   }
(25) };
```

LISTING 6: Functor to perform numerical integration over an element and assemble the result into the global matrix.

the data, but we chose not to use it in the present work and just pass an integer. By supplying the context data, any shape function evaluations that occur in expr will use the correct value at the current Gauss point as computed on line (15). This also means that the shape function is evaluated only once, no matter how many times it occurs in the expression.

In this example, the element quadrature function also places the result in the global system matrix (i.e., M in (6)). This happens on lines (21)–(23), where the global node index for every entry in the element matrix is obtained from the context data and the corresponding global matrix entry is updated.

The final rule in the grammar (line (24) in Listing 3) is a fall-back to the default C++ behavior. It tells Proto to perform the default C++ action when none of the earlier rules are matched, recursively calling fem_grammar to interpret any subtrees. In the case of our example expression, it ensures that the matrix product is evaluated using the operators defined in the Eigen library, after evaluating the left and right operand using fem_grammar.

The definition of the context data used by the functors is given in Listing 7. It holds the knowledge about the concrete element type and the finite element mesh that we use. We are completely free to define this type as we see fit, since Proto passes it along as a template parameter. In our example, we provide storage for results such as the shape function

values and the node coordinates. The data changes for each element and is updated by the set_element function that is called by the element looping algorithm (still to be discussed). This function updates the node coordinates and the mapping between local element node index and global node index. The entire class is templated on the element type, which allows using high-performance fixed size matrices from the Eigen library.

Using predefined transforms from the Proto framework and user-defined function objects allows for the creation of grammars which can call themselves transforms recursively. This concise domain specific language describing grammars is a key feature of Proto: it makes it possible to indicate how to evaluate an expression without resorting to complicated metaprogramming techniques, resulting in code that is easier to read and maintain. The complexity of the grammar and the expressions it can parse is limited only by the time and memory available for the compilation.

To obtain a working code, we still need to implement the loop over the elements and generate the data that is used in expression evaluation. The data is templated on the concrete element type, but as can be seen from Listing 14 the mesh data lacks this information at compile-time. This is logical, since in a real application the user loads the mesh, so the software cannot know what concrete type is used at compile time. To select the element at run time, we need to

```
(1) template<typename ElementT>
(2) struct dsl_data
(3) {
(4)     // Required by Eigen to store fixed-size data
(5)     EIGEN_MAKE_ALIGNED_OPERATOR_NEW
(6)     // The concrete element type
(7)     typedef ElementT element_t;
(8)
(9)     // Construct using the mesh
(10)    dsl_data(const fem::mesh_data& d): mesh_data(d)
(11)    {
(12)    }
(13)
(14)    // Set the current element
(15)    void set_element(const int e)
(16)    {
(17)      for(int i = 0; i != element_t::nb_nodes; ++i)
(18)      {
(19)        const int node_idx = mesh_data.connectivity[e][i];
(20)        node_indices[i] = node_idx;
(21)        for(int j = 0; j != element_t::dimension; ++j)
(22)          coord_mat(i,j) = mesh_data.coordinates[node_idx][j];
(23)      }
(24)    }
(25)
(26)    // Reference to the mesh
(27)    const fem::mesh_data& mesh_data;
(28)    // Storage for the coordinates of the current element nodes
(29)    typename ElementT::coord_mat_t coord_mat;
(30)    // Global indices of the nodes of the current element
(31)    int node_indices[element_t::nb_nodes];
(32)    // Value of the last shape function computation
(33)    typename element_t::shape_func_t shape_func;
(34)    // Value of the last Jacobian determinant computation
(35)    double det_jacobian;
(36)};
```

LISTING 7: Data passed to the functors.

generate code for all the element types that are supported by the solver. In this example, we will support both 1D line elements and 2D triangle elements. The difference in the mesh data lies in the number of columns in the coordinates and connectivity tables, so we can use that to determine which mesh we are using. By checking for each supported element type if the mesh matches, we can execute the correct code at runtime. We use the MPL functor defined in Listing 8 to match the correct element type to the mesh. The functor is executed for each item in a list of allowed elements (line (37)), resulting in cleaner code than a long list of if-else statements. Once the element type check at line (13) passes, the data can be constructed and we can start the loop, updating the data for each element at line (23). The actual expression is executed using the grammar at line (24), in the same way as in the previously discussed element integration functor (Listing 6, line (17)). The expression itself remains a template parameter, allowing us to write any kind of Proto expression in a call to for_each_element and keeping all compile-time

information. Both of these properties are key advantages over a similar system that could be set up using virtual functions. By generating code for a list of predefined element types, the technique can be seen as a special case of generative programming [9], where the code to generate is defined through the MPL vector of element types.

In Coolfluid 3, the process is more complicated, since we can have different shape functions for the geometry and each variable that appears in an expression. This means we must now generate code for every possible combination of shape functions. We chose to organize the data so that each unknown that appears in an expression has its own data structure, aggregated into a global data structure for the expression. This approach makes it possible to have a unified data structure supporting expressions with an arbitrary number of variables. Another complication is the possibility to mix different element types in one mesh, for example, triangles and quadrilaterals. We solve this by organizing the mesh into sets that contain only one element type and then

```
(1) /// MPL functor to loop over elements
(2) template<typename ExprT>
(3) struct element_looper
(4) {
(5)   element_looper(const fem::mesh_data& m, const ExprT& e): mesh(m), expr(e)
(6)   {
(7)   }
(8)
(9)   template < typename ElemT >
(10)  void operator()(ElemT) const
(11)  {
(12)    // Bail out if the shape function doesn't match
(13)    if(ElemT::dimension != mesh.coordinates.shape()[1] || ElemT::nb_nodes != mesh.
           connectivity.shape()[1])
(14)      return;
(15)
(16)    // Construct helper data
(17)    dsl_data<ElemT> data(mesh);
(18)
(19)    // Evaluate for all elements
(20)    const int nb_elems = mesh.connectivity.size();
(21)    for(int i = 0; i != nb_elems; ++i)
(22)    {
(23)      data.set_element(i);
(24)      fem_grammar()(expr, 0, data);
(25)    }
(26)  }
(27)
(28)  const fem::mesh_data& mesh;
(29)  const ExprT& expr;
(30)};
(31)
(32)/// Execute the given expression for every element in the mesh
(33)template<typename ExprT>
(34)void for_each_element(const fem::mesh_data& mesh, const ExprT& expr)
(35){
(36)  // Allowed element types
(37)  typedef mpl::vector2<fem::line1d, fem::triag2d> element_types;
(38)  mpl::for_each<element_types>(element_looper<ExprT>(mesh, expr));
(39)}
```

LISTING 8: The element looping algorithm.

deal with each set in turn. The complete algorithm to create the data and loop over a set of elements of the same type is as in Algorithm 1.

At this point we might wonder what happens if we try to evaluate an expression that makes no sense (e.g., N + transpose). Unfortunately, this often results in a very long list of compiler messages (430 lines for the example), exposing Proto implementation details and long template types. In the current example, it would be easy to fix using compile-time error messages, but for a more complex language grammar this is difficult and we have not yet implemented a satisfactory error handling system. We do intend to handle some common cases, and already errors from Eigen indicating incompatible matrix expressions come

through, but they are often obscured by a great number of other errors.

3.3. *External Libraries.* The example code uses the simplest possible data structures: the mesh simply contains arrays for the coordinates and the element nodes. The shape functions are simplified to only provide the functionality needed for the examples and they also include a fixed set of Gauss points for numerical integration. Listings 13 and 14 show the code for a first order 1D line element of the Lagrange family and the mesh data structure, respectively.

In Coolfluid 3, we provide our own mesh data structure, shape function library, and numerical integration framework. For operations at the element level, the Eigen [8] library is used, since it provides highly optimized routines for small,

```
(1) template<typename T> struct user_op {};
(2) struct my_callable {};
(3) // A terminal typed using the above structs
(4) proto::terminal< user_op<my_callable>>::type const my_op={};
(5) // Can be used as a function
(6) my_op(1,2,3);
```

LISTING 9: Definition of a terminal allowing user extension.

```
(1) proto::when
(2) <
(3)   proto::function< proto::terminal< user_op<proto::_> >, proto::vararg<proto::_>>,
(4)   evaluate_user_op(proto::function< proto::_, proto::vararg<fem_grammar> >)
(5) >
```

LISTING 10: Extension of `fem_grammar` to add user-defined operations.

dense matrices. Finally, sparse matrix operations—required for the solution of the linear system arising from the element-wise assembly—are performed using the Trilinos [10] library.

3.4. User Defined Terminals. If we want to extend the language with new functionality, this currently requires modification to the grammar (Listing 3). Since this is part of the programming framework, it is not something that is supposed to be modified by the user of the language. To provide more flexibility, we allow users to define new terminals that can be used in expressions without modifying the grammar. To the best of our knowledge, this is a unique feature for this kind of embedded language. We will show here how it works, by providing an overview of how this could be added to our example code. We return to the definition of terminals, tagged using empty classes as in Listing 9. We created a terminal with the template class user_op as type. Its use as a function (line (6)) can be matched using the grammar:

    proto::function<proto::terminal< user_
    op<proto::_>>,
    proto::vararg<proto::_>>

Here, proto::_ is a wildcard that matches any type and vararg allows the function to have any number of arguments. This kind of construct is exactly what we need to make my_op a user defined terminal, though we still have to provide a way to evaluate the expression. Adding a when clause as in Listing 10 yields the code that we need to add to fem_grammar in Listing 3. This uses fem_grammar to evaluate all function arguments and then calls the evaluate_user_op functor to evaluate the call (not listed here for the sake of brevity). In evaluate_user_op, we use the template argument to user_op (my_callable here) as a functor to evaluate the operator. This allows the user to define how the terminal should be evaluated without ever

needing to touch the core grammar, by simply implementing the correct function call operator in the type that is passed to user_op.

In Coolfluid 3, this technique is used to implement specialized code for certain solvers, directly setting entries of the element matrix when analytical expressions are known. Some core functions, such as the gradient and divergence operations, are also defined this way. Listing 11 shows the implementation for the divergence operation. On line (9), we have the function call implementation, where var is expanded into the data associated with the unknown for which we want to compute the divergence. This data is then used to access the gradient matrix (line (12)), much like we computed the shape function value in our previous example (i.e., line (15) in Listing 6). The terminal is statically created on line (30), using the MakeSFOp metafunction to avoid a long Proto type name. We can easily overload the function signature using additional function call operators. This is used on line (24) to provide an alternative divergence call that does not take a mapped coordinate as an argument but evaluates the divergence at the current quadrature point instead.

3.5. Integration into a Framework. So far, we have focused on building a small language, with the for_each_element looping function as entry point. In Coolfluid 3, our EDSL is used to implement reusable solver components, so before showing the concrete examples in Section 4 we have to present a few concepts about our framework and how it interfaces with our EDSL.

Each class in Coolfluid 3 is derived from the Component base class, which offers infrastructure to set options at run time and holds an arbitrary number of child components, thus creating a tree. A particular subclass Action implements the Command pattern [11], and we derive a class from that for working with expressions, called ProtoAction. Expressions can then be added to

Require: Mesh with field data for n variables
Require: A compile-time list of m shape functions N_i that may be used
Require: An expression E
Ensure: Construction of context data of the correct type
    for all shape functions N_i **do**
      if N_i matches the geometry shape function **then**
      set geometry shape function: $N_g = N_i$
      for all variables V **do**
        for all N_j compatible with N_g **do**
        if N_j matches the variable shape function **then**
          set $N_V = N_j$
        end if
      end for
      end for
      create context data d using known N_g and N_V ($\forall V$)
      for all elements e **do**
        execute grammar (E, d)
      end for
    end if
  end for

ALGORITHM 1: Element looping algorithm.

```
(1) // Operator definition
(2) struct DivOp
(3) {
(4)   // The result is a scalar
(5)   typedef Real result_type;
(6)
(7)   // Return the divergence of unknown var, computed at mapped_coords
(8)   template<typename VarT>
(9)   Real operator()(const VarT& var, const typename VarT::MappedCoordsT& mapped_coords)
(10)  {
(11)    // Get the gradient matrix
(12)    const typename VarT::GradientT& nabla = var.nabla(mapped_coords);
(13)    Real result = 0.;
(14)    // Apply each component and return the result
(15)    for(int i = 0; i != VarT::EtypeT::dimensionality; ++i)
(16)    {
(17)      result += nabla.row(i) * var.value().col(i);
(18)    }
(19)    return result;
(20)  }
(21)
(22)  // Divergence at the current quadrature point
(23)  template<typename VarT>
(24)  Real operator()(const VarT& var);
(25)};
(26)
(27) // The terminal to use in the language
(28) // divergence(v, xi): compute the divergence at any mapped coordinate xi
(29) // divergence(v): compute the divergence at current quadrature point
(30) static MakeSFOp<DivOp>::type const divergence = {};
```

LISTING 11: Definition of the Coofluid 3 gradient operation, using a user-defined terminal.

```
(1) // Terminal that refers to the temperature
(2) FieldVariable<0, ScalarField> T("T", "temperature_field");
(3) // Create a new action, as a child component of parent
(4) Handle<ProtoAction> action = parent.create_component<ProtoAction>("Action");
(5) // Set an expression to loop over nodes
(6) action->set_expression(nodes_expression(T = 288.));
(7) // Execute the action
(8) action->execute();
```

LISTING 12: Loop over nodes, setting a temperature field.

an object tree by creating a ProtoAction and setting its expression using the set_expression function. The framework executes it transparently just like any other Action. Expressions in Coolfluid 3 can loop over either elements or nodes, using different grammars. The node expressions are primarily used for setting boundary and initial conditions and to update the solution.

We also need a way of accessing the mesh and the unknowns, which we do by making use of FieldVariable terminals. A basic action for looping over nodes could be added to a parent component as in Listing 12, in this case setting the temperature to 288 K. Here, the temperature is defined on line (2), indicating that it is stored as variable T in the field temperature_field. This seems redundant here, but fields can store more than one variable. Furthermore, the parser needs to be able to distinguish each variable at compile time, which is why each variable has a unique number in the first template argument. Each distinct variable that is used in the same expression must have a different number. The second template argument specifies whether we are dealing with a scalar or a vector. We then create the expression component and set its expression on line (6), choosing an expression that loops over nodes and simply assigns the value 288 to the temperature field here. Boundary and initial conditions are provided in a similar fashion, but there the component is parametrized on the field and variable names, so it can be reused in any solver.

3.6. Compatibility with Matrix Expression Templates. At the element level, matrix calculations are delegated to the Eigen library, which uses its own expression templates. As it turns out, such libraries cause problems when embedded into a Proto expression tree. A library like Eigen will, in the case of complex operations, create temporary matrices on the fly. When a temporary object is passed on through the functors that evaluate our expressions we return references to these temporary objects, resulting in memory errors. The problem is common to all modern matrix expression template libraries, and Iglberger et al. [12] review some cases where these temporaries might appear. To handle this issue, we preprocess the expressions using a special grammar: whenever a matrix product is found, the multiplication expression is modified to store a temporary matrix—allocated only once—that can hold the result of the multiplication. Any matrix multiplication result is then stored in the Proto expression

itself and a reference to it is returned during matrix product evaluation. The preprocessing happens by calling an additional functor in the element looping function, so the whole process is transparent to the user of the expressions and allows writing matrix arithmetic of arbitrary complexity.

4. Application Examples

In this section we work out a few examples to illustrate the mapping between the mathematical formulation and the code for different problems.

4.1. Poisson Problem. The Poisson problem was already used as introductory example in Section 2. Here, we provide some more details on the code from Listing 1 that was skipped in the introduction.

First, there is the declaration of the unknown f and the source term g on lines (2) and (4), respectively. This follows the same mechanism as in Listing 12, using a distinct number to distinguish the variables at compile time. On line (7), we create an Action component to hold the expression. Finally, the expression is set on line (9). The elements_expression function indicates that the loop will happen over the elements and is comparable to the for_each_element function in the simplified example. On line (11), the applicable element types are chosen (all elements from the first order Lagrange family here). The actual expression starts on line (12), with a call to group to combine multiple expressions into one. This is an advantage if multiple steps are required in the assembly, since they can be combined into one loop over the elements. The assembly makes use of an element matrix _A and element vector _a, which are set to zero on line (14).

An expression of the form _A(f) returns only the rows of the element matrix that refer to the equation for f (i.e., all rows in this case). If we pass a second variable as argument, the returned matrix only contains the columns that refer to it, so _A(f, f) would return a block that only contains the f contributions from the f equation (again, all rows and columns in this case). This notation is convenient in the presence of multiple variables to select only the relevant entries in an element matrix. The size of the element matrix is also determined by looking for blocks like this, so here we only use _A(f) to indicate that the element matrix contains

```
(1) /// 1D Line shape function
(2) struct line1d
(3) {
(4)   static const int nb_nodes = 2; // Number of nodes
(5)   static const int dimension = 1;
(6)
(7)   // Type of the mapped coordinates
(8)   typedef Eigen::Matrix<double, 1, dimension> coord_t;
(9)   // Type of the shape function vector
(10)  typedef Eigen::Matrix<double, 1, nb_nodes> shape_func_t;
(11)  // Type of the coordinates matrix
(12)  typedef Eigen::Matrix<double, nb_nodes, dimension> coord_mat_t;
(13)
(14)  // Compute the shape function vector at mapped coordinate c
(15)  static shape_func_t shape_function(const coord_t& c)
(16)  {
(17)    const double xi = c[0];
(18)    shape_func_t result;
(19)    result[0] = 0.5*(1.-xi);
(20)    result[1] = 0.5*(1.+xi);
(21)    return result;
(22)  }
(23)
(24)  // Compute the jacobian determinant
(25)  static double jacobian_determinant(const coord_t& mapped_coord, const coord_mat_t&
          node_coords)
(26)  {
(27)    return 0.5*(node_coords[1] -node_coords[0]);
(28)  }
(29)
(30)  static const int nb_gauss_points = 2;
(31)  // Type of the matrix with the Gauss points
(32)  typedef Eigen::Matrix<double, nb_gauss_points, 1> gauss_points_t;
(33)  // The Gauss points for the current shape function (definition omitted)
(34)  static const gauss_points_t gauss_points();
(35)  // Type for the weights
(36)  typedef Eigen::Matrix<double, nb_gauss_points, 1> gauss_weights_t;
(37)  // The Gauss weights (definition omitted)
(38)  static const gauss_weights_t gauss_weights();
(39)};
```

LISTING 13: Element type for first order line elements of the Lagrange family.

only a single equation for f. The same applies to the element right hand side vector _a using square brackets.

The element integral fills these matrices on lines (17) and (18), in a similar fashion to the simple example. The assembly into the global system is a separate step and occurs on lines (20) and (21). The system_matrix and system_rhs terminals keep track of wrapper objects for a Trilinos matrix and vector, using a generic linear solver API that is part of Coolfluid. They are initialized in a base class that provides the functionality for working with expressions and linear systems.

The code in Listing 1 builds a component that assembles the linear system. At run time, it can be combined with other components to add initial and boundary conditions and to solve the linear system, all of which can be controlled from a Python script.

4.2. Navier-Stokes Equations Using Chorin's Method. The Navier-Stokes equations for incompressible flow with velocity vector $\mathbf{u}$, pressure p, and kinematic viscosity ν are

$$\nabla \cdot \mathbf{u} = 0, \tag{8}$$

$$\frac{\partial \mathbf{u}}{\partial t} + (\mathbf{u} \cdot \nabla)\, \mathbf{u} + \frac{\nabla p}{\rho} - \nu \nabla^2 \mathbf{u} = \mathbf{0}. \tag{9}$$

We will first solve this system of equations using Chorin's method [13], since this will allow us to easily compare performance later on with the same example from the FEniCS project. Chorin proposed an iterative time stepping scheme, computing first an auxiliary velocity $\mathbf{u}^{\mathrm{aux}}$, followed by the pressure and finally the corrected velocity at the new time

```
(1) /// Unstructured mesh data
(2) struct mesh_data
(3) {
(4)    // Construct using a number of nodes and element properties
(5)    mesh_data(const int nb_nodes, const int nb_elems, const int nb_nodes_per_elem, const int
            dimension):
(6)      coordinates(boost::extents[nb_nodes][dimension]),
(7)      connectivity(boost::extents[nb_elems][nb_nodes_per_elem])
(8)    {
(9)    }
(10)
(11)   // Global coordinates array
(12)   boost::multi_array<double, 2> coordinates;
(13)   // Global connectivity array
(14)   boost::multi_array<int, 2> connectivity;
(15) };
```

LISTING 14: The mesh data structure.

step. The weak form (written again for a single element) for the $\mathbf{u}^{\text{aux}}$ equation is

$$
\left(\frac{1}{\Delta t} \underbrace{\int_{\Omega_e} \mathbf{N_u}^{\mathrm{T}} \mathbf{N_u} \mathrm{d}\Omega_e}_{T_{u_i u_i}} + \nu \underbrace{\int_{\Omega_e} \nabla \mathbf{N_u}^{\mathrm{T}} \nabla \mathbf{N_u} \mathrm{d}\Omega_e}_{A_{u_i u_i}} \right) (\mathbf{u}_e^{\text{aux}})_i
$$

$$
= \frac{1}{\Delta t} \int_{\Omega_e} \mathbf{N_u}^{\mathrm{T}} \tilde{u}_i^n \mathrm{d}\Omega_e
$$

$$
- \int_{\Omega_e} \mathbf{N_u}^{\mathrm{T}} \tilde{\mathbf{u}}^n \nabla \mathbf{N_u} (\mathbf{u}_e^n)_i \mathrm{d}\Omega_e = \mathbf{a}_{u_i}.
$$

(10)

The superscript n indicates the known solution at time step n. The index i represents the ith component of the velocity here, which is a scalar in the case of the interpolated value $\tilde{u}_i^n$ and a vector of values for each node of the element for the unknowns $(\mathbf{u}_e^{\text{aux}})_i$. This means that, for each value of i, we insert a square block with dimension equal to the number of nodes into the element matrix and a corresponding segment into the element right hand side vector. We split up the element matrix as indicated by the braces, where $T_{u_i u_i}$ indicates the block corresponding to the rows and columns of component i of the velocity. The code to build this linear system is presented in Listing 15.

To get a stable solution, we will interpolate the velocity and pressure using second and first order shape functions, respectively (the Taylor-Hood element). If we restrict the solver to triangles, we can obtain this using the typedef on line (2). The actual shape function is chosen at run time, but we enforce the use of second order for the velocity here through the third constructor argument for the velocity variable on line (6). We use separate actions for the system matrix and right hand side assembly, since in this case the matrix coefficients do not change with time, so we can run the assembly procedure only once. The definition of the element matrices A and T is provided on lines (19) and (20). The Laplacian is written exactly the same as in the Poisson

problem (Section 4.1), but a new aspect is the introduction of the index _i when indexing into the element matrix. It is automatically expanded into a loop over the number of physical dimensions, addressing the diagonal blocks of the element matrices as defined in (10). The same applies for the mass matrix on line (20), and both matrices are combined and assembled into the global system on line (22). The auxiliary_lss component provides access to the terminals related to the linear system and the time. Here, invdt returns a reference to the inverse of the time step, which is set by the user running the simulation.

In the right hand side expression on line (34), the index _i is used again, using u[_i] to get each component of the interpolated velocity vector $\tilde{\mathbf{u}}$. The last term represents the advection, and it requires access to a single component of the nodal values vector $\mathbf{u}_e$. We store the nodal values for a vector variable as a matrix, with each column corresponding to one physical component of the vector. This matrix is obtained using the nodal_values function while individual columns can be addressed using _col. The notation is a bit verbose, but if the user determines this to be a problem it is easy to introduce a user defined terminal for the advection operation.

The next step in Chorin's algorithm calculates the pressure, through the following Poisson problem:

$$
\int_{\Omega_e} \nabla \mathbf{N_u}^{\mathrm{T}} \nabla \mathbf{N_u} \mathrm{d}\Omega_e \mathbf{p}_e^{n+1} = -\frac{1}{\Delta t} \int_{\Omega_e} \mathbf{N}_p^{\mathrm{T}} (\nabla \mathbf{N}_p)_i \mathrm{d}\Omega_e (\mathbf{u}_e^{\text{aux}})_i .
$$

(11)

Listing 16 shows the code for this system, again using two assembly actions. For the right hand side assembly on line (22), we used the divergence function that was defined in Listing 11. We could also write this in terms of the nodal values matrix like this:

```
element_quadrature(_a[p]
+= transpose(N(p))
*nabla(u)[_i]*_col(nodal_values(u),_i))
```

```
(1) // Allow a mix of first and second order shape functions
(2) typedef boost::mpl::vector2<mesh::LagrangeP1::Triag2D, mesh::LagrangeP2::Triag2D>
        LagrangeP1P2;
(3) // Kinematic viscosity, as a user-configurable constant:
(4) PhysicsConstant nu("kinematic_viscosity");
(5) // The velocity
(6) FieldVariable<0, VectorField> u("u", "navier_stokes_u_velocity", "cf3.mesh.LagrangeP2");
(7) // LSSActionUnsteady links with the linear algebra backend and the time tracking
(8) Handle<LSSActionUnsteady> auxiliary_lss =
(9)   create_component<LSSActionUnsteady>("AuxiliaryLSS");
(10) // The matrix assembly
(11) Handle<ProtoAction> auxiliary_mat_assembly =
(12)   auxiliary_lss->create_component<ProtoAction>("MatrixAssembly");
(13) auxiliary_mat_assembly->set_expression(elements_expression(LagrangeP1P2(),
(14) group
(15) (
(16)   _A(u) = _0, _T(u) = _0,
(17)   element_quadrature
(18)   (
(19)     _A(u[_i], u[_i]) += transpose(nabla(u))*nabla(u),
(20)     _T(u[_i], u[_i]) += transpose(N(u))*N(u)
(21)   ),
(22)   auxiliary_lss->system_matrix += auxiliary_lss->invdt()*_T + nu*_A
(23) )));
(24)
(25) // RHS assembly
(26) Handle<ProtoAction> auxiliary_rhs_assembly =
(27)   auxiliary_lss->create_component<ProtoAction>("RHSAssembly");
(28) auxiliary_rhs_assembly->set_expression(elements_expression(LagrangeP1P2(),
(29) group
(30) (
(31)   _a[u] = _0,
(32)   element_quadrature
(33)   (
(34)     _a[u[_i]] += auxiliary_lss->invdt() * transpose(N(u))*u[_i] -
(35)                  transpose(N(u))*(u*nabla(u))*_col(nodal_values(u), _i)
(36)   ),
(37)   auxiliary_lss->system_rhs += _a
(38) )));
```

LISTING 15: Code to build the linear system for $\mathbf{u}^{\mathrm{aux}}$ in Chorin's method.

On line (23), we call the lit function on invdt. This is actually a Proto function that constructs a terminal in-place, and it is needed to delay the evaluation of the minus sign, which would otherwise be evaluated right away by C++, resulting in the storage of a copy of the negative inverse timestep at expression creation, rather than a reference to the current value.

The final step of the algorithm updates the velocity, using the gradient of the newly calculated pressure:

$$\int_{\Omega_e} \mathbf{N}_u^{\mathrm{T}} \mathbf{N}_u \mathrm{d}\Omega_e \left(\mathbf{u}_e^{n+1}\right)_i \\ = \int_{\Omega_e} \mathbf{N}_u^{\mathrm{T}} \tilde{u}_i^{\mathrm{aux}} \mathrm{d}\Omega_e - \Delta t \int_{\Omega_e} \mathbf{N}_u^{\mathrm{T}} \left(\nabla \mathbf{N}_p\right)_i \mathbf{P}_e^{n+1} \mathrm{d}\Omega_e. \quad (12)$$

The system matrix is the mass matrix, so as seen in Listing 17 we assemble it in its own action. Note the similarity here with

the stand-alone example equation (6). The gradient function on line (18) is defined using the user defined function mechanism, and just as is the case with the divergence it can be written using nodal values as well:

```
transpose(N(u))
*(u[_i] - lit(correction_lss->dt())
*(nabla(p)[_i]*nodal_values(p)))[0])
```

The implementation of Chorin's method shows how different systems can be combined to solve a problem with multiple unknowns, each interpolated using a different shape function. The coding of the assembly procedure remains concise and follows the structure of the mathematical equations.

4.3. PSPG/SUPG Stabilized Incompressible Navier-Stokes. As an alternative to the use of the Taylor-Hood element used

```
(1) // The pressure field, using the default first order shape function
(2) FieldVariable<1, ScalarField> p("Pressure", pressure_lss->solution_tag());
(3) // The linear system manager
(4) Handle<LSSActionUnsteady> pressure_lss = create_component<LSSActionUnsteady>("PressureLSS");
(5) // The assembly action
(6) Handle<ProtoAction> pressure_mat_assembly =
(7)   pressure_lss->create_component<ProtoAction>("MatrixAssembly");
(8) pressure_mat_assembly->set_expression(elements_expression(LagrangeP1(),
(9) group
(10) (
(11)   _A(p) = _0,
(12)   element_quadrature(_A(p) += transpose(nabla(p))*nabla(p)),
(13)   pressure_lss->system_matrix += _A
(14))));
(15)
(16) Handle<ProtoAction> pressure_rhs_assembly =
(17)   pressure_lss->create_component<ProtoAction>("RHSAssembly");
(18) pressure_rhs_assembly->set_expression(elements_expression(LagrangeP1P2(),
(19) group
(20) (
(21)   _a[p] = _0,
(22)   element_quadrature(_a[p] += transpose(N(p))*divergence(u)),
(23)   pressure_lss->system_rhs += -lit(pressure_lss->invdt())*_a
(24))));
```

LISTING 16: Pressure Poisson problem for Chorin's method.

in the previous example, we can use equal interpolation order for the pressure and velocity, provided that we add a stabilization term to the continuity equation. We follow the method presented in [14], which adds PSPG and SUPG stabilization, as well as a bulk-viscosity term. When using Crank-Nicolson time stepping, the method is second order accurate in both time and space. We also start from the skew symmetric momentum equation, yielding the following form to replace (9):

$$\frac{\partial \mathbf{u}}{\partial t} + (\mathbf{u} \cdot \nabla)\mathbf{u} + \frac{\mathbf{u}(\nabla \cdot \mathbf{u})}{2} + \frac{\nabla p}{\rho} - \nu\nabla^2\mathbf{u} = \mathbf{0}. \quad (13)$$

In the absence of stabilization, the discretization of the skew symmetric form preserves the kinetic energy [15]. The weak form of the equations for a single element, after discretization in time, can be written as

$$\left(\frac{1}{\Delta t}T + \theta A\right)\Delta\mathbf{x}_e = -A\mathbf{x}_e^n. \quad (14)$$

We applied a theta scheme here for the time discretization, solving for the difference between two time steps, $\Delta\mathbf{x}_e$. The vector of unknowns $\mathbf{x}_e^n$ is arranged in blocks for each unknown, that is, first the pressures for all nodes, then the velocities in the x direction, and so on. This results in a

corresponding blocked structure for the element matrices T and A, where the blocks are given by

$$A_{pu_i} = \int_{\Omega_e} \left(\left(\mathbf{N}_p + \frac{\tau_{\text{PSPG}}\tilde{\mathbf{u}}_{\text{adv}}\nabla\mathbf{N}_p}{2} \right)^T (\nabla\mathbf{N}_u)_i \right.$$
$$\left. + \tau_{\text{PSPG}}(\nabla\mathbf{N}_p)_i^T \tilde{\mathbf{u}}_{\text{adv}}\nabla\mathbf{N}_u \right) d\Omega_e,$$

$$A_{pp} = \int_{\Omega_e} \tau_{\text{PSPG}}\frac{1}{\rho}\nabla\mathbf{N}_p^T\nabla\mathbf{N}_p d\Omega_e,$$

$$A_{u_iu_j} = \int_{\Omega_e} \left(\tau_{\text{BULK}}(\nabla\mathbf{N}_u)_i + \frac{1}{2}(\tilde{\mathbf{u}}_{\text{adv}})_i (\mathbf{N}_u + \tau_{\text{SUPG}}\tilde{\mathbf{u}}_{\text{adv}}\nabla\mathbf{N}_u) \right)^T$$
$$\cdot (\nabla\mathbf{N}_u)_j d\Omega_e,$$

$$A_{u_iu_i}$$
$$= \int_{\Omega_e} \left(\nu\nabla\mathbf{N}_u^T\nabla\mathbf{N}_u + (\mathbf{N}_u + \tau_{\text{SUPG}}\tilde{\mathbf{u}}_{\text{adv}}\nabla\mathbf{N}_u)^T \tilde{\mathbf{u}}_{\text{adv}}\nabla\mathbf{N}_u \right) d\Omega_e$$
$$+ A_{u_iu_i},$$

$$A_{u_ip} = \int_{\Omega_e} \frac{1}{\rho}(\mathbf{N}_u + \tau_{\text{SUPG}}\tilde{\mathbf{u}}_{\text{adv}}\nabla\mathbf{N}_u)^T (\nabla\mathbf{N}_p)_i d\Omega_e,$$

$$T_{pu_i} = \int_{\Omega_e} \tau_{\text{PSPG}}(\nabla\mathbf{N}_p)_i^T \mathbf{N}_u d\Omega_e,$$

$$T_{u_iu_i} = \int_{\Omega_e} (\mathbf{N}_u + \tau_{\text{SUPG}}\tilde{\mathbf{u}}_{\text{adv}}\nabla\mathbf{N}_u)^T \mathbf{N}_u d\Omega_e.$$

$$(15)$$

```
(1) Handle<LSSActionUnsteady> correction_lss = create_component<LSSActionUnsteady>("
        CorrectionLSS");
(2)
(3) Handle<ProtoAction> correction_matrix_assembly = correction_lss->create_component<
        ProtoAction>("MatrixAssembly");
(4) correction_matrix_assembly->set_expression(elements_expression(LagrangeP1P2(),
(5) group
(6) (
(7)   _A(u) = _0,
(8)   element_quadrature(_A(u[_i], u[_i]) += transpose(N(u))*N(u)),
(9)   correction_lss->system_matrix += _A
(10) )));
(11)
(12) Handle<ProtoAction> correction_rhs_assembly = correction_lss->create_component<ProtoAction>(
        "RHSAssembly");
(13) correction_rhs_assembly->set_expression(elements_expression(LagrangeP1P2(),
(14) group
(15) (
(16)   _a[u] = _0,
(17)   element_quadrature(_a[u[_i]] +=
(18)     transpose(N(u))*(u[_i] -lit(correction_lss->dt()) * gradient(p)[_i])),
(19)   correction_lss->system_rhs += _a
(20) )));
```

LISTING 17: The code for the correction step in Chorin's method.

Each stabilization term is multiplied with a corresponding coefficient τ. Splitting the equation into blocks helps in managing the added complexity due to the stabilization and skew-symmetric terms. Block A_{pp}, for example, represents the pressure Laplacian that arises from the PSPG stabilization. The SUPG terms in blocks $A_{u_i u_i}$, $A_{u_i u_j}$, and $T_{u_i u_i}$ are all written as a modification to the weighting function, adding more weight to upstream nodes. The bulk viscosity and skew symmetric terms in the momentum equation fill the off-diagonal blocks, as indicated by the use of both indices i and j. Equation (14) is assembled into a single linear system using the elements expression defined in Listing 18 (showing only the part relevant to the assembly itself).

Since only one linear system is involved, the code is integrated into the framework in the same way as in Listing 1. The value of the coefficients τ depends on local element properties [16]. We calculate them using a user-defined terminal compute_tau, passing a reference to a double for each coefficient (line (7)). On line (13), we use indices _i and _j to create a nested loop over the dimension of the problem, filling all $A_{u_i u_j}$ blocks. The right hand side from (14) is built by applying the element matrix A to the current element unknowns $\mathbf{x}_e$, represented by _x. On line (22), we divide by θ to avoid the use of the θ scheme on the continuity equation, improving stability. Finally, on line (23) we write the system matrix as in the left hand side of (14).

5. Performance Analysis

In this section we discuss the results of some performance tests, using the application examples from the previous

TABLE 1: System characteristics for the performance tests.

	Poisson and Chorin	PSPG/SUPG (per node)
CPU(s)	Intel i7-2600	Two Intel Xeon E5520
RAM	16 GB	24 GB
Operating system	Fedora 18	CentOS 6.2
Compiler	GCC 4.7.2	GCC 4.8.0
Trilinos version	11.4.1	11.2.3

section. Table 1 lists our system characteristics. The PSPG/SUPG tests were run on a cluster with 28 nodes, connected using 1 Gb Ethernet. To avoid any difficulties in installing DOLFIN on the cluster, the tests comparing our results with DOLFIN were run on a separate desktop computer.

5.1. *Poisson Problem.* Our first performance test concerns the Poisson problem. The element equations (4) can easily be calculated analytically when using linear shape functions, allowing a comparison between manually coded versions, a code using a virtual function interface to the shape functions and code generated using our language. Additionally, we compare with a specialized user-defined terminal containing the manually coded version and with DOLFIN [4] from the FEniCS project. Problem (4) is completed with boundary conditions and a source term identical to the Poisson demo case from FEniCS:

$$f = -6 \quad \text{over } \Omega,$$
$$u = 1 + x^2 + 2y^2 \quad \text{over } \Gamma. \tag{16}$$

```
(1) assembly->set_expression(elements_expression
(2) (
(3)    AllElementsT(),
(4)    group
(5)    (
(6)      _A = _0, _T = _0,
(7)      compute_tau(u, nu_eff, u_ref, lit(tau_ps), lit(tau_su), lit(tau_bulk)),
(8)      element_quadrature
(9)      (
(10)       _A(p, u[_i]) += transpose(N(p) + tau_ps*u_adv*nabla(p)*0.5) * nabla(u)[_i]
(11)                     + tau_ps * transpose(nabla(p)[_i]) * u_adv*nabla(u),
(12)       _A(p, p) += tau_ps * transpose(nabla(p)) * nabla(p) / rho,
(13)       _A(u[_i], u[_j]) += transpose((tau_bulk + 1/3*nu_eff)*nabla(u)[_i]
(14)                     + 0.5*u_adv[_i]*(N(u) + tau_su*u_adv*nabla(u))) * nabla(u)[_j],
(15)       _A(u[_i], u[_i]) += nu_eff * transpose(nabla(u)) * nabla(u)
(16)                     + transpose(N(u) + tau_su*u_adv*nabla(u)) * u_adv*nabla(u),
(17)       _A(u[_i], p) += transpose(N(u) + tau_su*u_adv*nabla(u)) * nabla(p)[_i] / rho,
(18)       _T(p, u[_i]) += tau_ps * transpose(nabla(p)[_i]) * N(u),
(19)       _T(u[_i], u[_i]) += transpose(N(u) + tau_su*u_adv*nabla(u)) * N(u)
(20)      ),
(21)      system_rhs += -_A * _x,
(22)      _A(p) = _A(p) / theta,
(23)      system_matrix += invdt() * _T + theta * _A
(24) )));
```

LISTING 18: The assembly of the PSPG/SUPG stabilized incompressible Navier-Stokes equations.

TABLE 2: Linear system assembly times (wall clock time and timing relative to Manual) for the Poisson problem on the unit square, using first order triangle shape functions on a 1000×1000 grid.

	Dummy matrix		Epetra matrix	
	Wall clock (s)	Relative	Wall clock (s)	Relative
Proto	0.32	5.93	0.61	1.79
Proto specialized	0.069	1.27	0.35	1.03
Manual	0.054	1	0.34	1
Virtual	2.82	52.2	3.18	9.35
DOLFIN	0.31	5.74	1.13	3.32

When using linear shape functions, the solution for the discrete system captures the analytical solution up to machine precision at the nodes. As an illustration, the code for the specialized user-defined terminal is presented in Listing 19. The terminal `assemble_triags` can then be used to directly assemble the linear system as shown on line (41). The manually coded version uses the same algorithm, but here we also loop over elements directly, avoiding the use of Proto entirely.

We first run a test on the unit square, divided into 1000 parts in both the x and y direction. Each square cell is divided into two triangles and first order shape functions from the Lagrange family are used. Table 2 summarizes the results, with labeling as follows: "Proto" is the code usng our EDSL (see Listing 1); "Proto specialized" is the user-defined terminal from Listing 19; "Manual" is the manually coded assembly loop; "Virtual" is the code using the virtual function interface to the shape functions as it is available in Coolfluid

3; and finally "DOLFIN" is the code generated by the FEniCS project demo. All timings represent the average of 10 assembly runs. Given the large problem size, 10 runs are representative and the variation between subsequent averaged runs was less than 2%. Due to the simplicity of the Poisson problem, the insertion into the global sparse matrix structure can actually be more expensive than the evaluation of the element integrals. We run the benchmark using both the Trilinos backend (using an Epetra CRS matrix) and a "dummy" matrix—not storing any data—to properly time the assembly procedure. As seen from Table 2, the overhead of the matrix insertion is about 0.3 s in Coolfluid 3 and 0.8 s in DOLFIN, that is, at least of the order of the time it takes to compute the element matrix itself. When comparing the timings for the dummy matrix, we see that the generic Proto code—which uses second order Gauss quadrature—is more than 5 times slower than the manually coded version. The difference between the specialized and the manual versions is much smaller. Since the specialized code still uses the Proto element looping mechanism, we can conclude that its inherent overhead is small. We confirmed this by profiling the assembly with gperftools (http://gperftools.googlecode.com/), generating the call graphs shown in Figure 3. Each graph starts in the `execute` method of the relevant `Action` class. On the left, the generic Proto code is seen to be mostly inlined into the element looper, with only 15% of the time spent in calls to other functions (mostly the shape functions). The large absolute execution time (numbers next to the arrows) is due to the extra matrix operations involved in the second order quadrature. For the specialized function (middle

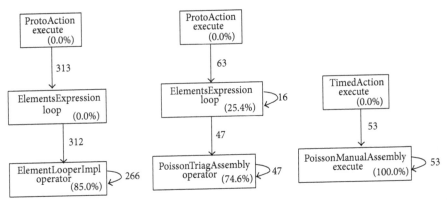

FIGURE 3: Call graphs of optimized code for the Poisson element matrix computation, from left to right: the generic Proto code, the Proto code with user-defined terminal, and the manually coded version. The percentages indicate the time spent in each function relative to the total execution time. The numbers next to the arrows indicate the absolute execution time, expressed in number of "ticks."

TABLE 3: Linear system assembly times (wall clock time and timings relative to the default Proto implementation) for the Poisson problem on the unit cube, using first order tetrahedron or hexahedron shape functions on a $100 \times 100 \times 100$ grid.

	Dummy matrix		Epetra matrix	
	Wall clock (s)	Relative	Wall clock (s)	Relative
Proto, default	3.29	1	5.51	1
Proto, hexahedra	4.60	1.40	5.65	1.03
Proto, 1st order	0.81	0.25	2.64	0.48
DOLFIN	1.22	0.37	5.05	0.92

graph), some operations related to index book-keeping are performed in the `loop` function, while the rest is executed in the user-defined `PoissonTriagAssembly` operator. Finally, in the manual version on the right, all operations are in the specific implementation of the execute function, resulting in 10 fewer ticks for the overall execution time.

The virtual function implementation performs much worse than any other method. Like Proto, it allows writing generic code for all elements but does so by using virtual function calls and dynamically allocated matrices. This makes the method much slower than the Proto code. A separate test comparing dynamically and statically sized matrices (size 4×4) from the Eigen library shows a slowdown by a factor of about 8 for dynamic matrices when running matrix-matrix and matrix-vector multiplications, reinforcing the results from Table 2.

In DOLFIN, the right hand side and the matrix are computed using separate assembly loops. The presented timing is the total time spent on assembly, divided by the number of assembles executed. For this particular case, Proto and DOLFIN result in the same performance. This is surprising, since the more advanced integration routines in DOLFIN detect here that first order quadrature is sufficient, while our Proto code assumes the worst case and applies second order integration.

The above observation leads us to perform the test in 3D, using a unit cube with 100 segments in each direction and built up of tetrahedra. We only compare the Proto and DOLFIN versions, since this code can be applied in 3D without modification. The results are shown in Table 3. The effect of the quadrature order is obvious here, with our second order quadrature being almost three times slower than the first order quadrature performed by DOLFIN. To check if this is the only effect, we temporarily forced our code to use first order quadrature, that is, using one quadrature point instead of four. The speedup is as expected, but we do emphasize that it is only obtained after modification of the integration code: we do not have a method for determining the integration order based on the terms appearing in the equations. Instead, our integration system assumes there is a mass matrix term in the equation and proceeds to choose the integration order based on the shape function. If the performance penalty is significant, as is mostly the case with simple problems, it is possible to use a user-defined terminal to override the integration method, or even to avoid numerical integration altogether.

We also include some results for hexahedral elements, where the second order quadrature is necessary. The element matrix dimension is also doubled, resulting in longer computation times for the matrix operations. We see that this is compensated here when inserting into the sparse matrix, due to the lower number of elements (each hexahedron represents 6 tetrahedra).

5.2. Chorin's Method. In Chorin's method, there are a total of 6 different assembly loops to be run: one for each system matrix, and one for each right hand side. Even though the matrices only need to be assembled once for the simulation, we present timings here for comparison purposes. Table 4 summarizes the results. We see that, except for the auxiliary matrix assembly, DOLFIN is faster every time when the "dummy" matrix is used, with a very large discrepancy for the correction matrix assembly. This is due to an optimization in DOLFIN, which recognizes the coefficients of the element matrix can easily be precomputed, avoiding quadrature. Our code does not allow this optimization to happen automatically, although it is of course possible to add a user-defined terminal. In the auxiliary matrix, the same term appears, but here it is divided by Δt, causing DOLFIN to apply quadrature.

```
(1) // Specialized code for triangles
(2) struct PoissonTriagAssembly
(3) {
(4)   typedef void result_type;
(5)   // Functor that takes: source term f, Linear system lss, element matrix and vector acc
(6)   template <typename FT, typename LSST>
(7)   void operator()(const FT& f, LSST& lss, math::LSS::BlockAccumulator& acc) const
(8)   {
(9)     typedef mesh::LagrangeP1::Triag2D ElementT;
(10)    // Get the coordinates of the element nodes
(11)    const ElementT::NodesT& nodes = f.support().nodes();
(12)
(13)    // Compute normals
(14)    ElementT::NodesT normals;
(15)    normals(0, XX) = nodes(1, YY) -nodes(2, YY);
(16)    // ...repetitive code omitted
(17)    // Jacobian determinant
(18)    const Real det_jac = normals(2, YY)*normals(1, XX) -normals(1, YY)*normals(2, XX);
(19)    const Real c = 1. / (2.*det_jac);
(20)
(21)    // Indices of the nodes of the current element
(22)    acc.neighbour_indices(f.support().element_connectivity());
(23)
(24)    for(Uint i = 0; i != 3; ++i)
(25)      for(Uint j = 0; j != 3; ++j)
(26)        acc.mat(i, j) = c * (normals(i, XX)*normals(j, XX) + normals(i, YY)*normals(j, YY));
(27)
(28)    // Get the values of the source term
(29)    const Real f0 = f.value()[0];
(30)    // ...f1 and f2
(31)    acc.rhs[0]= (2*f0 + f1 + f2);
(32)    // ...acc.rhs[1] and acc.rhs[2]
(33)    acc.rhs *= det_jac/24.;
(34)    lss.matrix().add_values(acc);
(35)    lss.rhs().add_rhs_values(acc);
(36)  }
(37) };
(38) // Create an terminal that can be used as a function in a proto expression
(39) static MakeSFOp <PoissonTriagAssembly>::type const assemble_triags = {};
(40) // Usage example:
(41) assembly->set_expression(elements_expression
(42) (
(43)   boost::mpl::vector1< mesh::LagrangeP1::Triag2D>(),
(44)   assemble_triags(f, system_matrix, m_block_accumulator)
(45) ));
```

LISTING 19: Code for the specialized user-defined terminal for the Poisson problem, valid for linear shape functions over a triangle.

The Proto-generated code is currently suboptimal for the assemblies of the right hand sides. This is due to some missed chances for matrix reuse: the advection operation in (10), for example, is calculated once for every component. While this effect is significant when we eliminate the influence of the linear system, it is much less apparent when looking at the results for Epetra matrices and vectors in the last column of Table 4. This leads us to conclude that our performance level is adequate for practical use and the element matrix and vector calculations will not be a dominant factor in the total solution time.

5.3. Channel Flow Simulation. In the last performance test, we take a look at a practical example, using the PSPG/SUPG stabilized Navier-Stokes formulation from Listing 18. The test problem is the flow between two infinite flat plates, that is, a 3D channel flow with two periodic directions. We initialize the flow using a laminar solution with centerline Reynolds number of 11250 with respect to the channel half-height. We apply periodic boundary conditions in the stream- and span-wise directions and a no-slip condition at the walls. The average timings for the first 100 timesteps (initial Courant number: 0.57) are presented in Table 5. We ran the test using

TABLE 4: Assembly times for each step in Chorin's method, compared between our Proto expressions and DOLFIN. Relative is the DOLFIN timing in multiples of the Proto timing. Wall times are in seconds.

| | Dummy matrix | | | Epetra matrix | | |
| | Proto | DOLFIN | | Proto | DOLFIN | |
	Wall	Wall	Relative	Wall	Wall	Relative
Aux. matrix	4.33	10.15	2.34	7.17	17.98	2.51
p matrix	0.28	0.19	0.67	0.53	0.75	1.42
Corr. matrix	2.38	0.22	0.09	5.23	8.09	1.55
Aux. RHS	3.12	1.17	0.375	3.18	2.32	0.73
p RHS	0.85	0.40	0.47	0.86	0.85	0.99
Corr. RHS	1.23	0.35	0.28	1.26	1.59	1.26

TABLE 5: Assembly and solution times for the coupled PSPG/SUPG stabilized Navier-Stokes equations (Listing 18) on a 3D channel flow with 128 hexahedra (tetrahedralized in the tetra cases) in each direction.

# CPU	Element	Assembly	Solution	solution/assembly
	Hexa	8.97 s	90.90 s	10.14
32	Tetra	7.69 s	73.06 s	9.51
	Tetra specialized	2.73 s	70.95 s	25.99
	Hexa	4.89 s	48.33 s	9.88
64	Tetra	4.14 s	40.59 s	9.81
	Tetra specialized	1.45 s	40.15 s	27.67
	Hexa	3.05 s	32.91 s	10.47
128	Tetra	2.58 s	54.53 s	21.13
	Tetra specialized	0.99 s	46.32 s	46.70

hexahedra and tetrahedra, where the test on tetrahedra also used a specialized code wrapped into a user-defined terminal ("Tetra specialized" in the table). The linear system was solved using the Belos Block GMRES method from Trilinos, preconditioned using ML algebraic multigrid. We tweaked the settings to obtain the fastest possible solution time. We see that the solution of the system takes about 10 times as long as its assembly using our EDSL. This shows that, even for the relatively complicated assembly expressions of (15), our language can be used to assemble the system efficiently. Any further optimization should first focus on the linear system solution before the assembly will become a bottleneck. In this context, it should be noted that the solution of the linear system does not scale as well as the assembly. This may be related to the relatively slow communication (1 Gb Ethernet) between the nodes.

The user-defined code for tetrahedra results in a further speedup factor of 2.5. In this case, the code was reused from a previous version of the solver, written only for tetrahedra. A domain specific language can also assist in developing hand-tuned code, however: using the language we can first easily specify the generic formulation and then check the element matrices of manually coded optimizations against the automatically generated matrices.

6. Conclusion and Future Work

We presented a domain specific language for the implementation of finite element solvers, embedded in C++. The language mirrors the mathematical notation faithfully, providing a clean separation between numerics and equations. Our work is set apart from other work in this area by the use of the Boost.Proto library and the possibility to implement user defined terminals. Proto uses concise grammars to describe and extend the functionality of the language, as explained in detail using the stand-alone example. The addition of user defined terminals allows using hand-optimized code when possible, while staying within the automated framework for element looping.

We also analyzed the performance, demonstrating—in our opinion—acceptable abstraction overhead when compared to manual implementations and FEniCS. A large scale test with the PSPG/SUPG method for the incompressible Navier-Stokes equations showed that assembly took up to 10 % of the linear system solution time. This makes the assembly only the second largest consumer of CPU time by a large margin. It is our opinion that the sacrifice of some speed in the assembly is acceptable in view of the reduced turnaround time for model development.

Possible directions for future development include changes to the numerical integration framework, to better deduce the required quadrature order. On a more technical level, some parts of the code could be simplified by using new features of the C++11 standard, such as variadic templates and automatic return type deduction. Better error handling can also be looked into. One final interesting possibility is the investigation of expression optimization techniques. Using grammars, it is theoretically possible to scan the expressions for recurring matrix products and calculate each product only once, for example.

Appendix

Code Download Information

All of the code used in this work is available under open source licenses. Coolfluid 3 is licensed under the LGPL version 3 and available from https://github.com/coolfluid/coolfluid3/. Most benchmarks are in the plugins/UFEM/test/demo directory. The test comparing dynamically and statically sized Eigen matrices is at test/math/ptest-eigen-vs-matrixt.cpp. The code for the stand-alone example can be found in the repository https://github.com/barche/eigen-proto/, where fem_example.cpp contains the complete running program.

We also had to adapt DOLFIN, adding a "dummy" linear algebra backend to be able to measure without any overhead from the linear system backend. This code can be found at https://bitbucket.org/barche/dolfin/.

Finally, the code for benchmarks (including FEniCS tests) used in this paper is in the repository https://github.com/barche/coolfluid3-benchmarks/.

Nomenclature

$\mathbf{a}_{u_i}$: Block of the element right hand side vector for the ith component of the vector variable $\mathbf{u}$

$A_{u_i u_j}$: Block of the element matrix corresponding to rows for the ith component of vector variable $\mathbf{u}$ and the columns of the jth component

f: Unknown in the Poisson problem

$\tilde{f}$: Value of unknown f interpolated by shape functions

$\mathbf{f}_e$: Vector of values at the element nodes for variable f

g: Source term for the Poisson problem

$\mathbf{N}_f$: Element shape function vector for variable f

n: Number of nodes in an element

n_Ω: Number of elements in the mesh

p: Pressure

t: Time

$\mathbf{u}$: Velocity vector

Γ: The problem domain boundary

ν: Kinematic viscosity

Ω: The problem domain.

Conflict of Interests

The authors declare that there is no conflict of interests regarding the publication of this paper.

Acknowledgments

The authors thank the Coolfluid 3 development team for the many hours of work and helpful discussions, without which this work would not have been possible. In particular they thank Tiago Quintino for laying out the basic framework; Willem Deconinck for the work on the mesh structure; and Quentin Gasper for the work on the GUI.

References

[1] T. Quintino, W. Deconinck, B. Janssens et al., "Cooluid 3," 2012, http://coolfluid.github.io/.

[2] E. Niebler, "Proto: a compiler construction toolkit for DSELs," in *Proceedings of the Symposium on Library-Centric Software Design (LCSD '07)*, pp. 42–51, October 2007.

[3] H. G. Weller, G. Tabor, H. Jasak, and C. Fureby, "A tensorial approach to computational continuum mechanics using object-oriented techniques," *Computers in Physics*, vol. 12, no. 6, pp. 620–631, 1998.

[4] A. Logg and G. N. Wells, "DOLFIN: automated finite element computing," *ACM Transactions on Mathematical Software*, vol. 37, no. 2, article 20, 2010.

[5] M. S. Alnæs and K.-A. Mardal, "On the efficiency of symbolic computations combined with code generation for finite element methods," *ACM Transactions on Mathematical Software*, vol. 37, no. 1, p. 1, 2010.

[6] C. Prud'homme, "A domain specific embedded language in C++ for automatic differentiation, projection, integration and variational formulations," *Scientific Programming*, vol. 14, no. 2, pp. 81–110, 2006.

[7] O. Zienkiewicz and R. Taylor, *The Finite Element Method*, Butterworth-Heinemann, Oxford, UK, 2000.

[8] G. Guennebaud, B. Jacob, M. Lenz et al., Eigen v3, 2010, http://eigen.tuxfamily.org.

[9] K. Czarnecki and U. Eisenecker, *Generative Programming: Methods, Tools, and Applications*, Addison-Wesley, Boston, Mass, USA, 2000.

[10] M. A. Heroux and J. M. Willenbring, "Trilinos users guide," Tech. Rep. SAND2003-2952, 2003.

[11] R. Johnson, R. Helm, J. Vlissides, and E. Gamma, *Design Patterns: Elements of Reusable Object-Oriented Software*, Addison-Wesley, Reading, Mass, USA, 1995.

[12] K. Iglberger, G. Hager, J. Treibig, and U. Rüde, "Expression templates revisited: a performance analysis of current methodologies," *SIAM Journal on Scientific Computing*, vol. 34, no. 2, pp. C42–C69, 2012.

[13] A. J. Chorin, "Numerical solution of the Navier-Stokes equations," *Mathematics of Computation*, vol. 22, no. 104, pp. 745–762, 1968.

[14] T. Bányai, D. Vanden Abeele, and H. Deconinck, "A fast fullycoupledsolution algorithm for the unsteady incompressible Navier-Stokes equations," in *Proceedings of the Conference on Modelling Fluid Flow (CMFF '06)*, Budapest, Hungary, 2006.

[15] T. A. Zang, "On the rotation and skew-symmetric forms for incompressible flow simulations," *Applied Numerical Mathematics*, vol. 7, no. 1, pp. 27–40, 1991.

[16] T. Tezduyar and S. Sathe, "Stabilization parameters in SUPG and PSPG formulations," *Journal of Computational and Applied Mechanics*, vol. 4, no. 1, pp. 71–88, 2003.

14

ScalaLab and GroovyLab: Comparing Scala and Groovy for Scientific Computing

Stergios Papadimitriou,[1] **Kirsten Schwark,**[2] **Seferina Mavroudi,**[3,4]
Kostas Theofilatos,[3] **and Spiridon Likothanasis**[3]

[1]*Department of Computer Engineering & Informatics, Technological Educational Institute of Kavala, 65404 Kavala, Greece*
[2]*iDashboards, 900 Tower Drive, Troy, MI 48098, USA*
[3]*Department of Computer Engineering and Informatics, University of Patras, Greece*
[4]*Technological Educational Institute of Patras, 26332 Patras, Greece*

Correspondence should be addressed to Stergios Papadimitriou; sterg@teikav.edu.gr

Academic Editor: Damian Rouson

ScalaLab and GroovyLab are both MATLAB-like environments for the Java Virtual Machine. ScalaLab is based on the Scala programming language and GroovyLab is based on the Groovy programming language. They present similar user interfaces and functionality to the user. They also share the same set of Java scientific libraries and of native code libraries. From the programmer's point of view though, they have significant differences. This paper compares some aspects of the two environments and highlights some of the strengths and weaknesses of Scala versus Groovy for scientific computing. The discussion also examines some aspects of the dilemma of using dynamic typing versus static typing for scientific programming. The performance of the Java platform is continuously improved at a fast pace. Today Java can effectively support demanding high-performance computing and scales well on multicore platforms. Thus, both systems can challenge the performance of the traditional C/C++/Fortran scientific code with an easier to use and more productive programming environment.

1. Introduction

The recently introduced ScalaLab [1] scientific programming environment for the Java Virtual Machine (JVM) leverages the statically typed Scala object-oriented/functional language [2]. It provides a MATLAB-like syntax that is used to construct scripts that are then compiled by ScalaLab for execution on the JVM.

The GroovyLab environment is based on the Groovy dynamic language for the Java platform [3]. The underlying mechanisms in GroovyLab are very different from ScalaLab, primarily due to the dynamic character of Groovy.

The Scala language supports the implementation of simple, coherent, and efficient MATLAB-like interfaces for many Java scientific libraries. These interfaces are compiled within the core of ScalaLab. The Groovy language also provides mechanisms to access easily and elegantly many Java scientific libraries, but these mechanisms are quite different from those provided by ScalaLab.

ScalaLab and GroovyLab are open source projects and can be obtained from http://code.google.com/p/scalalab/ and http://code.google.com/p/jlabgroovy/, respectively. Both ScalaLab and GroovyLab can be installed easily. The only prerequisite is the installation of the Java 8 (or newer) run-time (which is free). We supply scripts for launching these systems for all the major platforms. Also, for Linux 64 bit, and Windows 64 bit platforms, native executables (e.g., for Windows the *WinScalaLab.exe*) provide an even easier startup. The general high-level architecture of ScalaLab is depicted in Figure 1 and is described in [1]. The architecture of GroovyLab is shown in Figure 2 and is very similar to that of ScalaLab, except GroovyLab uses the Groovy programming language rather than the Scala programming language. It is also a successor of jLab that is described in [4].

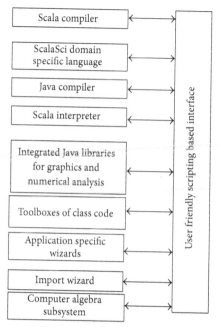

FIGURE 1: The architecture of the main software components of ScalaLab.

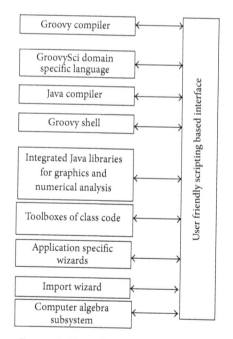

FIGURE 2: The architecture of GroovyLab.

GroovyLab is essentially a redesign of jLab that is based on the Groovy scripting language, which proves to be superior to the various scripting modes provided by jLab (j-script, JavaSci, GroovySci, compiled j-script mode). In a few words, the GroovySci scripting mode of jLab proved much superior and GroovyLab was developed by improving that mode and removing the others as somewhat redundant. Historically, ScalaLab was developed in parallel with GroovyLab as a similar environment using the powerful statically typed Scala language.

In this paper some important similarities and differences between ScalaLab and GroovyLab will be examined. The user interfaces of the two systems are similar. Also, the exploited Java scientific libraries and native code high performance libraries are the same. The major differences emerge when code is developed for these systems. They present different scripting languages for writing applications and are also very different when designing and implementing libraries.

The paper proceeds as follows: Initially the frameworks for developing matrix libraries in Scala and in Groovy will be examined (Section 2). Next the implementation of high-level mathematical operators in ScalaLab and GroovyLab is discussed (Sections 3 and 4). The functional programming abilities of the two environments are then briefly examined (Section 5). Both systems provide the user with flexible scripting environments; the main features of these environments are then compared (Section 6). Compile-time metaprogramming is a powerful feature offered both by Groovy and Scala; an example is then presented to demonstrate how compile-time metaprogramming can be used to expand the syntax of GroovyLab without any run-time performance penalties (Section 7). A few aspects of the ScalaLab and GroovyLab environments that are important for scientific computation are then presented and compared. Next performance related issues are discussed and benchmarking results are presented (Section 8). Finally, the paper concludes with remarks concerning the relative strengths and weakness of each system.

2. Matrix Design in ScalaLab and GroovyLab

In this section some main features of the Scala and Groovy languages that are used to facilitate the utilization of the Java scientific libraries are described and compared. These features are presented in the context of providing support for a MATLAB-like syntax for matrix manipulation and the utilization of underlying Java libraries to provide the implementation of the matrix functionality.

2.1. Matrices in ScalaLab. The general architecture for interfacing with Java libraries in ScalaLab is illustrated in Figure 3. Below we describe these components.

2.1.1. The Java Library. The *Java library* module in Figure 3 corresponds to the Java code of the library that performs the main numerical calculations. Some examples of the Java libraries are the EJML library (https://code.google.com/p/efficient-java-matrix-library/), the Apache Common Maths (http://commons.apache.org/proper/commons-math/), and the MTJ (Matrix toolkits for Java, https://github.com/fommil/matrix-toolkits-java). It should be noted that the Scala interpreter can also use the native Java interface of each library.

2.1.2. The Wrapper Scala Class (WSC). The *Wrapper Scala Class (WSC)* aims to provide a simpler interface to the more essential functionality of the Java library; for example, matrices A and B can be simply added as $A + B$, rather than invoking the cumbersome $A.plus(B)$. The wrapper Scala class

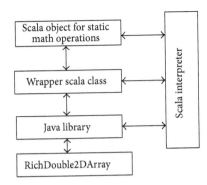

FIGURE 3: The general architecture of interfacing Java libraries in ScalaLab.

Matrix represents a one-indexed matrix and is based on the NUMAL library [5]. The wrapper class *Mat* is a zero-indexed matrix implemented in Scala. It borrows functionality from the JAMA Java package. Some other wrapper classes exist that interface the functionality of important Java libraries as, for example, the *EJML.Mat* class based on the EJML library and the Apache Common Maths library. We implement separate zero-based and one-based indexed *Matrix* classes for two reasons: (a) obtaining maximum implementation efficiency and (b) the one-indexed *Matrix* class is a wrapper for the NUMAL library routines. We feel that is rather inconvenient to mix zero and one indexing styles at the same *Matrix* class.

2.1.3. The Scala Object for Static Math Operations. The *Scala Object for Static Math Operations (SOSMOs)* provide overloaded versions of basic routines for our new Scala matrix types. For example, it provides an overloaded version of the *sin* method that accepts an instance of our *Mat* Scala class as an argument (i.e., *sin(B)* where *B* is a *Mat* instance).

Each SOSMO object implements a large set of mathematical operations. The rationale behind these objects is to facilitate the switching of the Scala interpreter to a different set of libraries. The interpreter simply needs to import the corresponding SOSMO objects in order to switch functionality.

The top-level mathematical functions for the zero-indexed matrices, for example, *rand0(int n, int m), ones0(int n)*, and so forth, return the matrix representation associated with the currently utilized library. A matrix object can refer to different matrices depending on the library. The "switching" of libraries is performed by creating a different, new Scala interpreter that imports the corresponding libraries with the aid of the specially designed SOSMOs Scala objects. For example, the *StaticMathsJAMA* object performs important initializations for the JAMA library and the *StaticMathsE-JML* utilizes the Efficient Java Matrix Library (EJML). The utilization of the JAMA library is accomplished by creating a Scala interpreter that imports the *StaticMathsJAMA* SOSMO object while for the EJML the *StaticMathsEJML* is imported. The ScalaLab user can easily switch different underlying Java libraries.

2.1.4. The RichDouble2DArray. The *RichDouble2DArray* is the "super" Matrix class of ScalaLab. It implements mathematical routines that expose the best aspects of various Java scientific computing libraries. It is however independent of any particular utilized library. By convention, utility routines that do not end in 0 or 1 return *RichDouble2DArray* objects. For example, *rand(), zeros(), ones()*, and so forth all construct *RichDouble2DArray* objects. Furthermore, the extensibility of *RichDouble2DArray* is leveraged with implicit conversions in order to provide its rich functionality to standard two-dimensional Java/Scala arrays.

2.2. Matrices in GroovyLab. The design of matrix support in GroovyLab is simpler than that in ScalaLab. Instead of providing switchable matrix interfaces to different libraries like ScalaLab, GroovyLab provides one powerful *Matrix* class that aims to combine effective numerical routines from multiple numeric libraries. In essence this *Matrix* class has many similarities in functionality to the *RichDouble2DArray* class of ScalaLab. As *RichDouble2DArray*, it provides a lot of operations, in pure Java for efficiency. Also, a set of efficient native code routines is interfaced with JNI (Java Native Interface) from the BLAS and LAPACK libraries.

The *Matrix* class of GroovyLab is a zero-indexed, two-dimensional dense matrix type that realizes much functionality of *GroovySci*. *GroovySci* is the scripting language of GroovyLab that is an extension of Groovy that provides MATLAB-like operators and syntax (corresponds to *ScalaSci* of ScalaLab). The Matrix class leverages functionality from multiple libraries such as JAMA, LAPACK, NUMAL, EJML, JBLAS, Apache Common Maths, and MTJ.

The *Matrix* class is fundamental in GroovySci because of the following.

(a) It provides a number of *mathematical operations* on the Matrix object that are implemented using a variety of Java libraries. For example, for linear system solvers, the solver from the JLAPACK library, the NUMAL library, or the JAMA library could be used.

Some libraries such as the *Apache Common Maths* library, the *JAMA* library, and the *NUMAL* library use a two-dimensional double array matrix representation. The GroovyLab *Matrix* class also uses the same underlying matrix representation; therefore their routines are readily accessible without any conversion. Some other libraries use different matrix representations. For example, JLAPACK uses a one-dimensional double array representation, in which the matrix storage layout is in column based order (i.e., Fortran like). In these cases, $O(N)$ conversion routines (where N is the number of matrix elements) are required before using the methods of these libraries. However, mathematical routines with much higher complexity than simple linear complexity (e.g., matrix factorization, Singular Value Decomposition, eigenvalue computations) benefit from such libraries. The EJML library also uses a one-dimensional "flat" matrix representation, in either row or column based order. EJML is one of the more efficient pure Java numerical libraries, one reason being the proper setup for effective caching that the one-dimensional storage representation presents.

(b) It provides many useful *static methods* that are usually overloaded to handle many different types. For example, the *sin()* method is overloaded to handle input from a Matrix, a two-dimensional double array, and a one-dimensional double array:

Matrix sin(Matrix a)

double [] [] sin(double [] [] a)

double [] sin(double [] a)

Static importation of all the static methods of the Matrix class is performed by GroovyLab before any code is executed with the GroovyShell (the component that executes Groovy scripts); therefore we can write *sin(x)*, where *x* can take many possible types, for example, *Matrix, double [][], double [], and double*. Therefore, the Matrix class provides much of the same functionality provided by the Scala Objects for Static Math Operations described in the previous section.

2.3. Sparse Matrices. ScalaLab and GroovyLab provide extensive support for sparse matrices using the Java implementation of the techniques presented in [6] (the source is supplied free from the authors). Both systems also implement classes that wrap the sparse routines with a higher level and elegant syntax. Clearly, GroovyLab exploits Groovy's facilities for building Domain Specific Languages (DSLs) and ScalaLab those of Scala. Also, the open source project *Matrix Toolkits for Java* (https://github.com/fommil/matrix-toolkits-java) offers an effective framework for handling sparse matrices with Java classes. These classes are integrated in the built-in libraries of both ScalaLab and GroovyLab and can be utilized with MATLAB-like convenience.

3. Designing High-Level Operators in ScalaLab and GroovyLab

Both Scala and Groovy provide the ability to define operators that function on operands of arbitrary types. Groovy's support for operator definition is more limited than Scala's and is restricted to a set of well-known symbolic operators.

3.1. Defining Operators in ScalaLab. ScalaLab's support for operator definition is best demonstrated with an example. The class used as an example for ScalaLab is the *EJML.Mat* class.

The *SimpleMatrix* class of the Efficient Java Matrix Library (EJML, http://code.google.com/p/efficient-java-matrix-library/) implements mathematical operations in an object-oriented way while maintaining the immutability of the operands. For example, to multiply matrix F and x the *mul* method on F can be invoked as in *F.mul(x)*. The Java-like method calls are not very elegant though. For example the matrix calculation $F P F' + Q$ is executed as *F.mult(P).mult(F.transpose()).plus(Q)* instead of the much clearer $F*P*F\sim + Q$ that is performed in ScalaLab.

The *scalaSci.EJML.Mat* (abbreviated *Mat*) class in ScalaLab wraps the EJML *SimpleMatrix* class and provides the Scala support for high-level MATLAB-like operations.

```
def apply(row: Int, col: Int) = {
    sm.get(row, col)
}
```

ALGORITHM 1

In Scala, operators on objects are implemented as *method calls*, even for primitive objects like integers (i.e., *int* type). Although operators are treated syntactically and semantically as method calls, at the code generation phase the Scala compiler treats the usual arithmetic operators on primitive types by generating direct efficient bytecode. Thus, Scala mathematical expressions have speeds similar to those of Java. Operator characters are valid method names. A familiar operator symbol (e.g., "+") can be used to define a method that implements the operator. Infix operators are implemented as methods that have a single parameter that is of the type of the second operand. For example, $a*5$ corresponds to $a.*(5)$. *Prefix* operators such as +, −, !, ∼ are implemented by prepending the word: *unary_*, to construct the corresponding method name. *Postfix* operators are implemented in Scala as methods that take no arguments. For example, implementing a method named ∼ on the Matrix class could be used to indicate Matrix transposition. So, the transpose of A would be obtained using the ∼ operator as $A\sim$.

Scala provides the *apply* method to provide support for a subscript-like operator for indexed object access that appears similar to both method invocation and array element access. For example for the *EJML.Mat* class, the apply method can be used to provide access to the *(row, col)* element of the matrix. The method is implemented, by calling the corresponding routine *get()* of the EJML library, as shown in Algorithm 1.

The method is then invoked as $M(i, j)$ to access the element of the matrix in the *i*th row and *j*th column of M. The *apply* method can also be overloaded in order to obtain a subrange of a matrix as well.

In a similar fashion, Scala provides the *update* method to support indexed object assignment. For the *EJML.Mat* class, the update method can be implemented to assign a value to a specific element of the matrix. The method is implemented as shown in Algorithm 2.

The *update* method is then invoked as $M(i, j) = 9.8$ to assign the number 9.8 to the *i*-*j*th element of M.

ScalaLab provides an implementation of the colon (:) operator, to support the MATLAB colon operator for creating vectors as the following example:

```
var t = 0::0.02::45.9
```

This expression returns a scalaSci.Vec type for *t*. To implement such syntax, *implicit conversions* are combined with the *token cells* approach [7, 8].

Methods with names ending with the ":" characters are invoked on their right operand, passing in the left operand. For example, the above expression is evaluated as (45.9.::(0.02)).::(0). Since the *Double* class does not have a :: method, it is implicitly converted to a *MATLABRangeStart* object. The *MATLABRangeStart* object retrieves the

```
def update(row: Int, col: Int, value: Double): Unit = {
    sm.set(row, col, value)
  }
```

ALGORITHM 2

```
x = rand(50, 100)
row = 5; col = 2
xr = x[1..4+row, col..4*col]   // take a range
xrb = x[(1..20).by(2), (1..30).by(3)]  // like, x(1:2:20, 1:3:30)
x[(1..40).by(5), 1..2] = 44.
```

ALGORITHM 3

receiver's value (i.e., 45.9) with its constructor and stores it as the ending value of the range. The *MATLABRangeStart* class has a method named :: that processes the increment parameter (i.e., 0.02). Finally, the method :: creates a *MATLABRangeNext* object passing itself, that is, the *MATLABRangeStart* object, as the argument. The :: method of the *MATLABRangeNext* receives as a parameter the starting value of the range (i.e., 0). Therefore, it has all the information (i.e. start, increment, end) to construct and return the vector t.

MATLAB-like indexing/assignment is implemented easily by defining overloaded versions of *apply()* that operate on vectors. For example, to evaluate the expression M(2::4::20, 3::2::100), the implicit conversions mechanism converts the arguments to vectors. The apply method is then invoked which will extract from the vector arguments the necessary start, step, and increment values.

3.2. *Defining Operators in GroovyLab.* In contrast to Scala, Groovy provides support for operator overloading only for a specific set of operator symbols. The positive side of this restriction is that we enforced to avoid unusual operator symbols, conforming to the familiar ones (e.g., "*" for multiplication, "≪" for left shift, etc.). To support operator overloading, Groovy supplies a standard mapping of operator to implementing method. For example, the "+" operator corresponds to the *plus* method. From Java only these methods can be used, but from Groovy either the operators or their corresponding methods may be used.

We provide implementations of the Groovy operator methods in pure Java code for both efficiency's sake and to use them from Java as methods. Scala operators cannot be implemented directly in Java (at least without considering the internal details of the Scala compiler) because Java does not support operators as method names. It would also be difficult to call them. In order to call the methods corresponding to Scala operators from Java, the synthetic names that the Scala compiler creates for the operators must be used, which is very inconvenient.

Operator support in Groovy is supplied by implementing the appropriate corresponding method. For example, the *plus*

method is implemented to provide the addition operator "+," the *minus method* is implemented to provide the subtraction operator "−," and the *multiply* method is implemented to provide the multiplication "*" operator. This operator method mapping approach is not as flexible as Scala's "methods as operators" approach that permits the user to define arbitrary symbols as operators. These predefined methods in Groovy can be implemented in Java and (as noted) are implemented in GroovyLab in Java for the sake of efficiency. The syntactic convenience of using the operator rather than the method is only applicable in Groovy though. For example, $x + 100$ is a valid expression in Groovy, where x is a Matrix object, but in Java matrix addition is performed using *x.plus(100)*.

Another example of Groovy's syntactic elegance is demonstrated in the implementation of matrix indexing and assignment operators. The subscript indexing operator in Groovy is overloaded by implementing the *getAt()* method and the subscript assignment operator is overloaded with the *putAt()* method. Groovy has built-in support for integer ranges via the .. operator, so the syntax 2..5 can be used to create an *IntRange* instance. The concept of a step can be implemented by defining a class named *IntRangeWithStep* that inherits from the Groovy range class *IntRange*. This class is used in GroovyLab to write elegant MATLAB-like constructs, as shown in Algorithm 3.

Since the predefined *IntRange* type does not have a *by()* method, the Groovy compiler handles 1..20 as *IntRangeWithStep*. The *by()* method stores the step argument. Finally, elements are accessed using the subscript access operator implemented with the *getAt()* method and the subscript assignment operator that is implemented by the *putAt()* method.

Similarly, the *DoubleRangeWithStep* class that extends *ObjectRange* is provided by *GroovyLab* and implements the *step()* method in order to return a vector. Thus we can write

$x = (0.5..50).step(0.01)$ as equivalent to MATLAB's 0.5:0.01:50.

After examining both Scala's and Groovy's support for operator overloading, it can be concluded that while GroovyLab's syntax is convenient it cannot provide the MATLAB-like syntax that can be implemented in ScalaLab.

3.3. Matrix Operations Performance. The performance of the basic indexing and assignment operations in GroovyLab's Matrix class when Groovy is statically compiled is similar to that of Scala's two-dimensional matrices. Other Matrix range operations are slower in GroovyLab, even though many of the submatrix operations are performed in Java. Specifically, for operations involving large submatrices the speed is about the same, but performance is about three times better in ScalaLab than in GroovyLab when many small submatrices are processed. In the latter case, the GroovyLab implementation involves much more dynamic Groovy code, rather than the faster Java code, hence the performance penalty.

4. Defining Operators for User Types: Implicit Conversions versus the Metaobject Protocol

Both Scala and Groovy provide run-time mechanisms to handle the situation where an operator is applied to a type in which there is not a specific operator that matches the argument types. Implicit conversion of argument types is supplied in Scala to address these potential type mismatches. Groovy provides metaprogramming to address these sorts of type violations.

4.1. Implicit Conversions in Scala. Returning to the matrix *Mat* class example in Scala, when the compiler detects the addition operator "+" on a *Double* object *d* that adds a *Mat* object *M*, that is, $d + M$, it encounters a type error because there is no method defined on the predefined *Double* type that adds a *Mat* instance to a *Double* (and there cannot be one since *Mat* is a user defined type). A similar error occurs when a Mat instance is added to a double array.

Scala provides implicit conversions [2, 9, 10] to address these sorts of type issues. When an operation is not defined for a type, the compiler will try to apply available implicit conversions in order to transform the type into a type for which the operation is valid.

The concept of implicit conversion is of fundamental importance in the construction of high-level mathematical operators in ScalaLab. Implicit conversion in ScalaLab is used with many classes, for example, *RichNumber, RichDouble1DArray*, and *RichDouble2DArray* classes.

For example, the *RichNumber* class is implemented to support implicit conversions in Scala related to the Double class. The RichNumber class models extended Number capabilities of accepting operations with all the relevant classes of ScalaLab, for example, with *Mat, Matrix, EJML.Mat, MTJ.Mat,* and generally whatever class we need to process.

Suppose that we have

$$var\ a = 2.0 + rand(2,2)$$

The 2 is transformed by the Scala compiler to a *RichNumber* object that defines an operation to add a Matrix and the

addition can be performed by the addition operator implementation.

Similarly, the classes *RichDouble1DArray* and *RichDouble2DArray* wrap the *Array[Double]* and *Array[Array[Double]]* Scala classes in order to support implicit type conversion for the addition and multiplication of *Array[Array[Double]]* types.

As *RichNumber* enriches simple numeric types, *RichDouble1DArray* enhances the *Array[Double]* type and *RichDouble2DArray* the *Array[Array[Double]]* type. For example, the following code is valid in Scala:

```
var a = Ones(9, 10) // an Array[Array
[Double]] filled with 1s
var b = a+10 // add the value 10 to
all the elements returning b as
RichDouble2DArray
var c = b + a*89.7 // similarly using
implicit conversions this computation
proceeds normally
```

In the next section we continue by describing the corresponding implementations of high-level mathematical operators in the context of GroovyLab. Although similar functionality as in ScalaLab can be achieved in GroovyLab, the underlying approaches are very different.

4.2. The Metaobject Protocol in Groovy. In Groovy as in many other dynamic languages, the implementation of high-level mathematical operators for the standard language types is based on the *Metaobject protocol.* The Metaobject protocol forms the basis of metaprogramming in Groovy that is used to implement dynamic method invocation [3]. This protocol is the means by which dynamic functionality can be added to classes at runtime. Dynamic behavior is added to classes and objects in Groovy using the *MetaClass* machinery.

In dynamic languages, methods can be injected into a class by adding methods to its *MetaClass*. These added methods are then available globally on instances of the class. In the case of Groovy, metaprogramming can be used to add methods, properties, constructors, and static methods to classes at runtime. New methods in Groovy can be added to both Groovy classes and Java classes. Groovy supports metaprogramming at both the class and object level.

For example, the *Number* class of the standard Groovy's library does not implement the addition operator to support adding an array to a Number instance. Metaprogramming can easily be used to define a method on the number class to support this addition operation and adding it to the MetaClass of the Number class, the Groovy Code is illustrated in Algorithm 4.

The keyword *delegate* refers to the current object, that is, the *Number* object. Also, since Groovy's bytecode is somewhat slow for numeric calculations, GroovyLab intermixes Java code to attain improved performance.

Although this mechanism is seemingly easier to implement than Scala's implicit conversions, it requires indirect

```
//  define the operation: Number + double [],
// at the MetaClass of the Number's class
Number.metaClass.plus =
      {
//  the double []  m array denotes the input parameter
  double []  m ->
// call a Java routine for the operation
      res =
   groovySci.math.LinearAlgebra.LinearAlgebra.plus(delegate, m)  // calls Java code
      res
}
```

ALGORITHM 4

method calls through the MetaClass machinery and imposes additional method invocation overhead. However, Groovy's approach is more flexible in that it supports changing which method will be executed at runtime. This flexibility is useful if implementations from different libraries are used interchangeably, for example, when it is desired to use an eigenvalue decomposition from a different library than the one supplied by default.

5. Functional Programming: Functions versus Closures

A core concept in any language that supports functional programming is the provision of functions as "first-class citizens." In object-oriented languages like Scala and Groovy functions are objects. They can be passed as arguments to other functions, be a return value from a method, and have a concise literal definition syntax. Most programming languages now support first-class functions because they vastly improve the readability and understandability of the source code by allowing behavior to be captured, assigned to variables, and passed to functions. For instance, the major new feature of Java 8 is the support of functional programming with *lambda expressions*.

5.1. Functions in Scala. Scala has the concept of both *functions* and *closures*. Functions are like static methods that do not belong to any class/object.

An example of a function definition in Scala is

$$def \ cube(x: Double) = x*x*x$$

Scala also has a literal function syntax that can be used to assign a function to a variable. For example, the function above can be declared as follows:

$$val \ cube = (x: Double) => x*x*x$$

The Function variable "cube" can be invoked as if it were the function definition above that is as in the invocation *cube(3)*.

A function in Scala that refers to a variable outside of its scope is called a *closure*. These variables from outside the scope of function are referred to as *free* variables. An example of the definition of a Scala closure is

$$val \ raiseIt = (x: Int) => Math.pow(x, power)$$

Here "power" is a free variable because it is defined outside of the scope of the function. At compile time a variable named "power" must be in the scope of the literal definition of the *raiseIt* function; otherwise a compiler error will result.

Therefore, Scala differentiates between a function and a closure based on whether or not the definition contains free variables.

5.2. Closures in Groovy. Groovy also supports "global" function definitions (i.e., functions that are not defined within a class) but these functions are simply static methods of classes imported automatically. Therefore, they do not support the functional programming style.

Groovy however provides strong support for closures that are *first-class* objects that can be passed as parameters and assigned to variables. The syntax of closure definition is different from the definition of methods; for example, a simple Groovy closure that implements the *cube* function is

$$def \ cube = \{x -> x*x*x\}$$

The closure is then invoked as expected as *cube(3)*.

5.3. Global Function Workspace. Scientific programming environments demand a *global namespace of functions*. Scala and Groovy do not have the concept of globally visible methods; every method must be contained in an object or a class. In both environments though, a global function namespace can be implemented easily with *static imports*. In Scala objects are imported since these objects encapsulate the static imports. In Groovy static imports are performed as they are in Java. Therefore, the automatic import of static methods provides the appearance of the existence of global methods. For example, the *plot* method appears to be available globally since we import it from the object *scalaSci.plot.plot*. Scala also offers the ability to define *apply* methods for the companion objects of classes. If a class implements the apply method, an instance of the class can essentially be "executed" like a function as the instance name followed by a list of arguments in parentheses. When the apply method is implemented by a class, a method does not need to be imported into the "global" namespace, it is only necessary to import the class itself. Groovy does not offer a similar ability to essentially execute

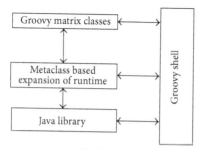

FIGURE 4: The general architecture of interfacing Java libraries in GroovyLab.

object instances, but the classic *import static* Java facility can be used to import the appropriate static methods.

6. The Scala Interpreter and the Groovy Shell

An essential component of Scala's scripting framework is the Scala interpreter. The corresponding component in the Groovy scripting framework is the GroovyShell. This section discusses and compares some aspects of these components (Figure 4).

The overall approach of the Scala interpreter is based on initially compiling the requested code. A Java classloader and Java reflection are then used to run the compiled bytecode and access its results.

In general, Scala's approach to scripting and Groovy's approach to scripting are similar. Scala's approach is more complicated than Groovy's approach though. Groovy's scripting approach is based on detecting the undeclared variables of a script. Groovy then declares them implicitly as an Object and maintains their state in a *binding structure* implemented by means of a Java hashtable. The binding scheme of Groovy is restricted to data variables and closures. It is important that although GroovyShell does not keep objects and classes, it keeps *closure* objects. Therefore, the computation workspace consists not only of data variables but also of defined code. This permits functional programming within GroovyLab.

In contrast, the scheme implemented in the Scala interpreter extracts the whole visible computation state as the interpreter's context. ScalaLab binds both data and code objects automatically to this context. Although this is more powerful it imposes difficulties in retrieving the context when we create a new Scala interpreter. In that case it is necessary to replay the commands in order to restore the environment. However, the restoration of the user environment in ScalaLab is performed fast; the user does not notice the delay of the few Scala compiler runs. Restoration of the computation context also is a somewhat rare operation.

A single compiler instance is used in the Scala's interpreter to accumulate all successfully compiled or interpreted Scala code. The interpretation of a line of code is performed by generating a new object that includes the line of code and has public members to export all variables defined by that code.

The results of the interpreted lines are extracted by using a second "result object" which imports the variables exported by the above object and then exports a single member named "result." To accommodate user expressions that are read from variables or methods defined in previous statements, "import" statements are used.

It becomes evident that an effective approach for detecting the variables that a piece of code defines is required. The Scala interpreter utilizes the Scala parser to accomplish the nontrivial task of analyzing variable visibility. The Scala parser is also utilized, in order to detect which variables are used by a code snippet. The values of these variables are then requested from previously executed code. It is unnecessary to request variables from the interpreter that do not appear in a new code snippet, since these values will not change. For example, if *prevVar* = 5.5 is not used at our new script, the interpreter does not request the value of prevVar.

At this point we should contrast the state management of the Scala interpreter with the corresponding one of the GroovyShell. GroovyShell automatically handles variable binding and therefore it is much easier to handle the state of variables in GroovyLab.

The Scala interpreter keeps a list of names of identifiers bound with a var or val declaration (*boundVarNames*) and also a list of function identifiers defined with a def declaration (*boundDefNames*). In addition we can retrieve the last text source code of the program that has been interpreted (*lastLineInterpreted*).

We keep a symbol table of the current *ScalaSci* bound variables. This task is used to graphically display the current work context to the user. We have to keep this external table synchronized with the internal variables binding that the interpreter keeps (i.e., *boundVarValNames*). The current value of each variable is retrieved from the interpreter by issuing a simple command with the name of the variable.

If an identifier is being redefined as a function then it is removed from the variable binding. This is necessary since the namespace of variables and functions in Scala is common [2] and thus the identifier is hidden by the function definition.

The corresponding task in the GroovyShell of displaying to the user the variable's workspace is much simpler; in fact it only requires a simple lookup into the hashtable binding.

The GroovyShell lacks the ability to retain imports from a previously executed script. This can be rather inconvenient in many cases, since these same import statements must be manually incorporated before executing code that depend on them. For that reason, GroovyLab implements simple import buffering that removes the tediousness of incorporating the import statements explicitly each time a script is executed in GroovyLab.

GroovyLab automatically incorporates some basic import statements into the user's scripts that extend the functionality. These imports allow the user to utilize many GroovyLab functions such as figure() and plot(). The user can also use a code buffer to retain code (both classes and script code) for the current working session.

7. Compile-Time Metaprogramming

Compile-time metaprogramming allows intervening in the compilation process and the implementation of customized structures that do not impose any run-time overhead. This is important in scientific scripting, since it opens up possibilities for implementing efficient convenient high-level structures.

Both languages support compile-time metaprogramming, Groovy with Abstract Syntax Tree (AST)—*Transformations* and Scala with *Scala Macros*. *Abstract Syntax Trees (AST)* keep a tree like representation of a program in which interior nodes represent programming constructs [11]. Scala macros have not been utilized in ScalaLab yet (actually they are used only to provide a C style *for* loop), so the discussion of compile-time metaprogramming will be limited to an exploration of Groovy's compile-time metaprogramming support.

Compile-Time Metaprogramming in Groovy. Run-time metaprogramming provides the ability to modify class and instance behavior at runtime. Groovy provides compile-time metaprogramming via *AST transformations* and *compilation customizers* to support altering the behavior of classes and objects at compile time.

AST transformations in Groovy come in two flavors: *local AST transformations* and *global AST transformations.* Local AST transformations are defined using annotations and are applied locally to a program element by annotating the element whose AST is to be altered by the AST transformation. Global AST transformations are essentially provided as services that are applied by the compiler to every class that is being compiled. Local AST annotations are more widely used than global AST transformations.

Groovy implements some predefined local AST transformations. Examples include the @Immutable AST transformation that generates code to make a class immutable and the @Log AST transformation which injects a logger into a class. Of specific interest to GroovyLab is the @*CompileStatic AST transformation.* This AST transformation is applied to Groovy code that is known not to utilize Groovy's dynamic programming capabilities. When the @CompileStatic AST transformation is applied to a method the compiler checks to see that the source code can indeed be statically compiled and bypasses Groovy's dynamic dispatch for methods that are invoked within the method implementation. This ability to bypass dynamic dispatch can have a marked impact on performance, which is of the utmost importance in scientific computing. We should note that the recent versions of the Groovy compiler automatically avoid dynamic dispatch in simple numerical loops; thus in such cases Groovy's performance is similar to Java/Scala, even without the static compilation annotation.

GroovyLab also provides the @*CompileJava AST transformation.* This transformation is applied only to methods and essentially compiles the method directly into Java bytecode. The code is compiled as it appears in the Groovy source code, so the source code of the annotated method must be valid Java and must be completely self-contained (i.e., it must essentially be a static method that contains no references to class attributes). The @CompileJava AST transformation provides the ability to execute Java code from within a GroovyLab script, both for efficiency and as a preferred choice.

Groovy also provides the ability to modify the behavior of the compiler using compilation customizers. Compilation customizers are applied by the compiler to the AST corresponding to every class that is being compiled. They differ from global AST transformations in that customizers are easier to define than global AST transformations. GroovyLab uses a compilation customizer to convert BigDecimal literals to primitive double to improve performance.

8. Performance

Groovy was initially considered a slow language; Groovy 1.5 was about 200 to 1000 times slower than Java in performing number calculations. The implementers of the language have performed impressive performance improvements in recent versions of Groovy though. A clever implementation of call-site caching in Groovy 1.6 has reduced the performance gap between Groovy and Java to Groovy being about 20–50 times slower than Java. Special handling of primitive operations as direct bytecode rather than via dynamic dispatch using the MetaObject protocol has provided significant performance gains, primarily because these optimizations can be applied at compile time. In many cases, Groovy with compiled computational loops and primitive operations runs as fast as Java code (since both emit direct bytecodes). Statically compiled Groovy, a mode of the Groovy compiler introduced with Groovy 2.0, produces statically compiled code that is as fast as Java but requires sacrificing the dynamic features of the Groovy language in the source code that is to be statically compiled. Therefore, this mode is most suitable for computationally intensive methods. Groovy 2.0 also exploits the JDK7 *invoke-dynamic* bytecode and the related framework that supports the compilation of dynamic code. However in the current release of Groovy 2.4 the invoke dynamic implementation improved a lot related to Groovy 2.0. Generally code that is compiled with Groovy's invoke dynamic support currently runs somewhat slower than the code that optimizes primitive operations. The speed difference is constantly decreased on each new Groovy release. As both the invoke dynamic support in Groovy improves and Java Virtual Machine implementations better support the invoke dynamic instruction, the static compilation and primitive optimizations features of Groovy become of less importance.

GroovyLab is designed with the goal in mind of performing fast numeric calculations. For example, all of the main mathematical operations in GroovyLab are implemented in pure Java for the sake of efficiency. The important *Matrix* class is also implemented in Java, but it implements the *GroovyObjectSupport* interface, in order to allow flexible overloaded operator syntax, for example, to use $A + B$ instead of something like the cumbersome method $A.plus(B)$ to add matrices. The Matrix class also supports many of operations that make use of the native BLAS. This is accomplished with the JBLAS library (http://mikiobraun.github.io/jblas/).

TABLE 1

	ScalaLab	MATLAB	SciLab	GroovyLab
Speed	Very fast, execution speed depends on the Java runtime, generally faster than MATLAB at script code, but slower for routines implemented as built-in with MATLAB	Very fast, especially the built-in routines which are highly optimized; overall ScalaLab and MATLAB run at comparable speeds and which one outperforms depends on the case	Much slower than ScalaLab (or MATLAB), about 20 to 100 times slower. Newer versions of SciLab, however, improved a lot; speed differences are now about 3 to 10 times	Slower than ScalaLab, about 2 to 5 times slower. However, with statically typed blocks of code, performance is at about the same level as Java/Scala
Portability	Very portable, anywhere exists installed Java 8 JRE	There exist versions for each main platform, for example, Windows, Linux, MacOS	There exist versions for each main platform, for example, Windows, Linux, MacOS	Very portable, anywhere exists installed Java 8 JRE
Open source	Yes	No	Yes	Yes
User-friendliness	Very user friendly	Very user friendly	Very user friendly	Very user friendly
Libraries/toolbox availability	All the JVM libraries	A lot of toolboxes are available, but generally not free	There exist toolboxes for basic applications but for specialized ones it is difficult to find	All the JVM libraries
Documentation	Little yet, and limited to on-line help, since even main code components are in the development process	Extensive documentation	Sufficient documentation	On-line documentation only
Flexibility of the language (i.e, syntax malleability)	The Scala language is designed to be flexible and with very malleable syntax	The syntax of MATLAB is not designed to be extensible	SciLab is not designed to be extensible	The Groovy language is dynamic and different tricks from the Scala's case can form customizable syntax
Development of large applications	Scala has a lot of novel features that can facilitate the development of large applications. ScalaLab applications can run standalone, as any Java code	The notion of MATLABPATH integrates many MATLAB scripts, something not very scalable	Similar to MATLAB, the SciLab scripts are not well suited for complex applications, but rather they fit well for rapid testing of scientific algorithms	Groovy has a full compiler that can be used to produce standalone code of a large application project
Active user development community	ScalaLab is a new project, and thus up-to-now lacks a large user base	MATLAB has a huge user base	SciLab has a large user base, however, much smaller than MATLAB's	GroovyLab is a new project, and thus up-to-now lacks a large user base

Another performance pitfall with Groovy is the preference of the Groovy compiler to perform default mathematical calculations with *BigDecimals* objects. Groovy is a flexible, extensible language that allows GroovyLab to bypass that constraint by performing a *compile-time metaprogramming* transformation. These transformations are a powerful tool to modify the AST representation of the source code that is generated during compilation, before bytecode is generated from it for execution. Since the AST modifications are performed by the compiler during compilation, there is no run-time performance penalty that results from applying the AST modifications.

In case of ScalaLab, the Scala language is statically typed and therefore Scala code can theoretically be compiled to bytecode that runs as fast as Java, sometimes a bit faster sometimes a bit slower, depending on the situation. However, for the advanced features of Scala such as pattern matching, trait inheritance, and type parameters, it is difficult to optimize

their compilation. The Scala language developers concentrate on these issues and improve the performance of the Scala compiler with each new version of the language.

Table 1 compares characteristics of *ScalaLab, MATLAB, SciLab,* and *GroovyLab*. SciLab (http://www.scilab.org/) is an open source system, similar to MATLAB.

We would note that the performance of the recent version of MATLAB (2012b) has been impressively improved, while SciLab has been improved also but not so much.

9. Benchmarking

In order to access the performance of the GroovyLab and ScalaLab platforms, a variety of mathematical computation algorithms will be examined. These will include matrix computations, Fast Fourier Transforms (FFT), eigen decomposition of a matrix, and singular value decomposition of a matrix.

$$
\begin{aligned}
&N = 2000; M = 2000 \\
&tic \\
&a = \mathrm{rand}(N, M); \\
&sm = 0.0; \\
&for\ r = 1 : N, \\
&\quad sm = 0.0; \\
&\quad for\ c = 1 : M, \\
&\qquad a(r, c) = 1.0/(r + c + 1); \\
&\qquad sm = sm + a(r, c) - 7.8 * a(r, c); \\
&\quad end \\
&end \\
&tm = toc
\end{aligned}
$$

ALGORITHM 5: Array access benchmark in MATLAB.

9.1. Matrix Computation Benchmarking. In order to access the efficiency of matrix processing in GroovyLab and ScalaLab, implementations of the MATLAB script of Algorithm 5 are used.

For the ScalaLab version of this script, ScalaLab clearly outperforms both MATLAB and SciLab. GroovyLab has similar speed when the static compilation is used. With the implementation of *optimized primitive operations* (i.e., later versions of Groovy produce fast code for arithmetic operations since they avoid the overhead of the metaobject protocol) and with the later *invoke dynamic* implementation, Groovy generally is slightly slower than Scala. The reason for the superiority of ScalaLab in terms of scripting speed is clearly the statically typed design of the Scala language that permits the emission of efficient Java bytecode.

9.2. Fast Fourier Transform Benchmark. The Fast Fourier Transform (FFT) benchmark is performed in ScalaLab using implementations of the FFT from various libraries.

Of these libraries, the Oregon DSP library provides the best performance. Close in performance to this library is the JTransforms (https://sites.google.com/site/piotrwendykier/software/jtransforms) library. Since JTransforms is multithreaded and it will accordingly perform more efficiently with more robust machines (e.g., having 8 or 32 cores, instead of only 4). The tutorial FFT implementation of the classic Numerical Recipes book [12] (with the C/C++ code translated to Java) was also observed to achieve reasonable performance in ScalaLab. Interestingly, it was observed that the Oregon DSP and JTransforms FFT routines are nearly as fast as the optimized built-in FFT of MATLAB. We should note that the reported differences in benchmarks are stable; for example, the relative differences are about the same on different computers, and individual runs show small variations at the results. Contributing to the small variability is that we perform explicitly garbage collection before any benchmark run.

9.3. Other Benchmarks. Other types of problems such as the eigen decomposition, singular value decomposition, and solution of overdetermined systems were examined for the purposes of obtaining GroovyLab and ScalaLab benchmarks. The general conclusion is that ScalaLab is faster than SciLab 5.21 by about 3 to 5 times but is slower than MATLAB 7.1 by about 2 to 3 times. It is also evident that the routines of JLAPACK for special matrix categories run orders of magnitude faster than routines for general matrices; for example, for a 1500 by 1500 band matrix with 2 bands above and 3 bands below the main diagonal, the JLAPACK's SVD routines run about 250 times faster than for a general 1500 by 1500 matrix.

Table 2 summarizes some basic performance results. We should note that often ScalaLab and GroovyLab perform equally well since they call the same Java library routines.

Recent MATLAB versions have improved impressively the performance of Matrix multiplication and of many important routines, as, for example, the SVD computation. However, both ScalaLab and GroovyLab offer the potential to issue commands to the MATLAB engine using the Java/MATLAB interface. Similarly, SciLab scripts can be executed using the Java/SciLab interface. The wiki pages of the ScalaLab and GroovyLab projects describe details and provide examples of these interfacings.

9.4. Native Code Optimizations. In order to test the JVM performance versus native code performance, an implementation of SVD is used [see http://code.google.com/p/scalalab/wiki/ScalaLabVsNativeC]. Both the Microsoft's *cl* compiler of Visual Studio on Windows 8 64-bit and the *gcc* compiler running on Linux 64-bit were used. ScalaLab is based on the Java runtime version: 1.7.0_25 and Scala 2.11 M7, and Groovy-Lab on Groovy 2.2.1. Again both ScalaLab and GroovyLab perform similarly, since they are based on the same Java code. It has been observed that ScalaLab and GroovyLab perform better than unoptimized C and are even close to optimized C code when performing matrix calculations. Table 3 shows some results.

10. Conclusions and Future Work

This paper compares some aspects of ScalaLab and Groovy-Lab, which are both environments for scientific computing that run within the Java Virtual Machine framework. It was demonstrated that both environments can effectively utilize existing Java scientific software. Both can elegantly integrate well-known Java numerical analysis libraries for basic tasks. These libraries are wrapped by either Scala objects in ScalaLab or Groovy objects in GroovyLab and their basic operations are provided to the user with a uniform MATLAB-like interface.

An extension of Scala with MATLAB-like constructs called ScalaSci is the language of ScalaLab and the corresponding language of GroovyLab is GroovySci. Both languages are effective and convenient for both writing small scripts and for developing large production-level applications.

The design of the user interface of ScalaLab and Groovy-Lab is similar. Both emphasize user friendliness and provide integrated development environment- (IDE-) like features

TABLE 2: Results of some basic benchmarks.

	ScalaLab (secs)	SciLab 5.21 (secs), SciLab 5.5	MATLAB 7.1 (secs) MATLAB 2012b	GroovyLab (secs)
Matrix multiplication with matrix sizes: **(2000, 2500) × (2500, 3000)**	0.9 secs using Native BLAS combined with Java multithreading	61.8, 5.05	13.05, 0.6	The same with ScalaLab
LU				
1000	0.3	3.13, 2.42	0.36, 0.03	The same as ScalaLab
1500	1.2	3.82, 2.1	1.18, 0.04	As ScalaLab
2000	2.9	6.42, 1.6	2.72, 0.09	As ScalaLab
inv				
1000	2.7	12.97, 1.6	1.3, 0.05	As ScalaLab
1500	7.8	13.14, 2.5	4.5, 0.15	As ScalaLab
2000	9.31	19.07, 3.2	5.9, 0.3	As ScalaLab
QR				
1000	1.03	4.3, 4.2	1.2, 0.04	As ScalaLab
1500	3.7	9.96, 9.9	4.26, 0.2	As ScalaLab
2000	9.25	19.69, 19.3	9.89, 0.3	As ScalaLab
Matrix access scripting benchmark	0.03	32.16, 32.67	10.58, 0.32	0.031 static compilation, 0.156 with primitive ops, 0.211 with invoke dynamic
FFT 100 ffts of 16384 sized signal	**Oregon DSP:** real case: 0.05, complex case: 0.095 **JTransforms:** real case: 0.07 complex case: 0.11, **Apache Common Maths:** complex case: 0.5 **Numerical Recipes (Java Translation):** real case: 0.09 complex case: 0.12	Real case: 2.32 Complex case: 4.2	Real case: 0.05 Complex case: 0.08	The Java libraries for FFT are the same as ScalaLab's

TABLE 3: SVD performance: Java versus native C code.

Matrix size	Optimized C (gcc, similar is for cl)	ScalaLab/GroovyLab	Unoptimized C (gcc, similar is for cl)
200 × 200	0.08	0.15	0.34
200 × 300	0.17	0.2	0.61
300 × 300	0.34	0.58	1.23
500 × 600	3.75	5.06	8.13
900 × 1000	35.4	51.3	53.3

such as on-line help, code completion, graphical control of the class-path, and a specialized text editor with code coloring facilities that greatly facilitate the development of scientific software.

Future work will concentrate on improving the interfaces to Java basic libraries and on incorporating smoothly other interested libraries (e.g., the parallel COLT library for basic linear algebra, the JCUDA library for supporting the CUDA massively parallel computing framework on NVIDIA graphics cards). Both ScalaLab and Groovy-Lab explore the *symja* Java Computer Algebra system (https://code.google.com/p/symja/). This system implements a wide range of Computer Algebra facilities. Further work is in progress for making work with Computer Algebra easier. This work will include providing better on-line help and code completion for these routines. These components are of the utmost importance in incorporating this rather complicated libraries into ScalaLab and GroovyLab.

Conflict of Interests

The authors declare that there is no conflict of interests regarding the publication of this paper.

References

[1] S. Papadimitriou, K. Terzidis, S. Mavroudi, and S. Likothanassis, "ScalaLab: an effective scientific programming environment for the Java Platform based on the Scala object-functional language," *IEEE Computing in Science and Engineering*, vol. 13, no. 5, Article ID 5487486, pp. 43–55, 2011.

[2] M. Odersky, L. Spoon, and B. Venners, *Programming in Scala*, Artima, 2008.

[3] D. König, A. Glover, P. King, G. Laforge, and J. Skeet, *Groovy im Einsatz*, Manning Publications, 2007.

[4] S. Papadimitriou, K. Terzidis, S. Mavroudi, and S. Likothanassis, "Scientific scripting for the java platform with jlab," *Computing in Science and Engineering*, vol. 11, no. 4, pp. 50–60, 2009.

[5] H. T. Lau, *A Numerical Library in Java for Scientists and Engineers*, Chapman & Hall/CRC, Boca Raton, Fla, USA, 2003.

[6] T. A. Davis, *Direct Methods for Sparse Linear Systems*, SIAM Publishing, Philadelphia, Pa, USA, 2006.

[7] G. Dubochet, "On Embedding domain-specific languages with user-friendly syntax," in *Proceedings of the 1st Workshop on Domain Specific Program Development*, pp. 19–22, Nantes, France, July 2006.

[8] G. Dubochet, *Embedded domain-specific languages using libraries and dynamic metaprogramming [Ph.D. thesis]*, École Polytechnique Fédérale de Lausanne, Lausanne, Switzerland, 2011.

[9] D. Wampler and A. Payne, *Programming Scala*, O'Reilly, 2009.

[10] V. Subramaniam, *Programming Scala: Tackle Multi-Core Complexity on the Java Virtual Machine*, Pragmatic Bookself, 2009.

[11] A. Aho, M. S. Lam, R. Sethi, and J. D. Ullman, *Compilers, Principles, Techniques & Tools*, Addison-Wesley, Boston, Mass, USA, 2nd edition, 2007.

[12] W. H. Press, S. A. Teukolsky, W. T. Vetterling, and B. P. Flannery, *Numerical Recipes in C: The Art of Scientific Computing.*, Cambridge University Press, Cambridge, UK, 2002.

15

A Language and Preprocessor for User-Controlled Generation of Synthetic Programs

Alton Chiu, Joseph Garvey, and Tarek S. Abdelrahman

The Edward S. Rogers Sr. Department of Electrical and Computer Engineering, University of Toronto, Toronto, ON, Canada

Correspondence should be addressed to Tarek S. Abdelrahman; tsa@eecg.toronto.edu

Academic Editor: Frank Hannig

We describe Genesis, a language for the generation of synthetic programs. The language allows users to annotate a template program to customize its code using statistical distributions and to generate program instances based on those distributions. This effectively allows users to generate programs whose characteristics vary in a statistically controlled fashion, thus improving upon existing program generators and alleviating the difficulties associated with ad hoc methods of program generation. We describe the language constructs, a prototype preprocessor for the language, and five case studies that show the ability of Genesis to express a range of programs. We evaluate the preprocessor's performance and the statistical quality of the samples it generates. We thereby show that Genesis is a useful tool that eases the expression and creation of large and diverse program sets.

1. Introduction

Large sets of programs are important in a number of areas of computer science and engineering. For example, in supervised machine learning (ML) for performance autotuning, a sufficiently large number of training programs are needed to represent the desired program space. Similarly, in compiler testing, successfully running test programs through a compiler increases confidence in its functionality and correctness. Finally, in software testing, the adequacy of the testing strategy of a program is measured by testing a large number of faulty mutant versions of the program [1]. The percentage of mutants for which errors are detected is used as a measure of the adequacy of the testing.

However, the number of real programs available for use is often limited. For compilers, it can be difficult to build up a diverse set of programs that contain enough functionality combinations and error scenarios. Similarly, benchmark suites used to evaluate performance of software and systems [2, 3] usually consist of only tens of programs and are usually too small to build sufficiently large and diverse training sets for ML models. Finally, a large number of mutant programs are needed to increase confidence in a testing strategy. Thus, *program generators* are often used to produce synthetic programs for use in such situations.

There are several existing program generators [4–6]. However, these generators suffer from limitations, in particular, the lack of user control over the generated code [4], inflexible and restrictive use cases or target languages [6–8], and difficulties with associated tools [6]. Ad hoc methods of generating large program sets, such as the use of Perl or Python scripts, also have their own limitations; the resulting scripts are difficult to write, maintain, and extend.

Thus, in this work, we design, implement, and evaluate *Genesis*, a program generation language that addresses the above shortcomings. Genesis facilitates the generation of synthetic programs in a statistically controlled fashion. It allows users to annotate a template program to identify and parameterize those segments of the program they wish to vary, the values each parameter may take, and the desired statistical distribution of these values across generated programs. The Genesis preprocessor uses the annotations to generate programs based on a template program, with the values of each parameter drawn from its corresponding distribution.

Genesis is unique in that it allows the generation of synthetic code with controlled statistical properties, which is important in some application domains. The constructs of the language provide a simple yet flexible means of varying template code. They also allow for the hierarchical composition of generated code segments. This facilitates the generation of large numbers of programs that are arbitrarily long with only a handful of constructs. It also makes it easy to create, modify, and extend existing Genesis programs. Genesis is target-language agnostic in that it can be used with template programs written in various programming languages.

The goal of this paper is to provide a detailed description of the Genesis language and to demonstrate its utility through a number of case studies of problems in which large program sets are needed. In addition, the paper provides an evaluation of the performance of the Genesis preprocessor. The paper is organized as follows. Section 2 gives an overview of Genesis with a simple example to illustrate its basic use. Section 3 gives a detailed description of the constructs of Genesis language. Section 4 describes five case studies of using Genesis. The current implementation of the Genesis preprocessor prototype is described in Section 5 and its evaluation in Section 6. Finally, Sections 7 and 8 review related work and provide some concluding remarks, respectively.

2. Overview of Genesis

The Genesis preprocessor takes two inputs: a *template program*, expressed in a standard programming language, such as C, Java, or C++, and a *Genesis program*, expressed using the Genesis language, as shown in Figure 1. The template program contains *references* to Genesis *features*, which are code snippets that are to vary across generated *instance programs*. The Genesis program defines the features using code mixed with Genesis *names*. When a feature referenced in the template program is *processed* by the preprocessor, the names in its definition are replaced by values sampled from user-specified distributions, producing an actual code snippet that replaces the feature reference. The following example helps to demonstrate this process.

```
for (int i = 0; i < n; ++i) {
        :
    t1 = x[c1*i+s1];
        :
    t2 = x[c2*i+s2];
        :

}
```

The loop in this example, extracted from a GPU kernel, makes two reads to an array, x, in each iteration. The memory access constants c_1, s_1, c_2, and s_2 affect memory performance, and it is desired to use them as features to train a machine learning model. Thus, we wish to generate a number of training programs that have different values of these constants. For the sake of this example, it is desired to uniformly distribute c_1 and c_2 over the range 1 to 4 and s_1 and s_2 over the range 0 to 7.

A Genesis program and a template program that could be used to generate such training programs are shown on the left side of Figure 1. The template program is essentially the code from the example but with the memory accesses replaced by references to the feature `mem_access`. The feature itself is defined in the Genesis program, delimited by `begin genesis` and `end genesis`, as the code snippet `x[${coef}*i+${offs}]`. The two Genesis names `coef` and `offs` are used in this code snippet. The values of `coef` and `offs` are taken from the distributions `coef_dist` and `offs_dist` as indicated by the `sample` constructs in their definitions. The distributions themselves are defined by Genesis' `distribution` construct declared in the Genesis program.

The `generate` statement in the Genesis program instructs the preprocessor to generate 15 instances of the template program. In each instance, the preprocessor processes the feature `mem_access` twice, sampling the values of each name from its respective distribution. The right side of Figure 1 shows some examples of the programs produced.

3. The Genesis Language

3.1. Design. There are several design concerns that we faced when designing Genesis. We briefly discuss some of these concerns and rationalize the decisions we made.

One important design concern in Genesis is the choice of its programming paradigm. We opt to use the imperative paradigm [9] because the domains we expect Genesis to be used in (i.e., compiler testing, automatic performance tuning, etc.) mostly employ imperative languages, such as C, C++, or OpenCL. Thus, the use of an imperative paradigm for Genesis makes it easier to adopt it in these domains. Nonetheless, fundamentally, there is no limitation preventing it from being used with functional and/or declarative target languages.

A second design concern is whether to have Genesis as a standalone language or embed it within a host language, such as C. The latter option has the advantage of providing a rich type system for Genesis variables and entities. However, it would severely limit the portability of the language. By designing Genesis as a preprocessor with simple data types, it becomes applicable to many target programming languages or even possibly nonprogramming ones (e.g., our image layering applications described in Section 4.4).

Yet another design concern in Genesis is that of variable scoping. We adopt a simple scoping scheme. Genesis variables and entities defined in a feature are *local* to that feature and can only be used within it. In contrast, Genesis variables/entities that are defined in the global section of a Genesis program (see Section 3.3 for the description of Genesis sections) are *global* and can be used anywhere in the Genesis program. Finally, variables defined within the program section of Genesis are local to the current program being generated. The choice of this scoping scheme leads to natural semantics for the sampling of variables, as discussed in Section 3.3.

Finally, an important design concern is the typing of variables. While it is possible to envision a rich type set and/or dynamic typing of variables that is common in various languages, we elect to use a simple typing scheme in which variables take one of four types: integer, float, string, or Boolean. The type of a variable is inferred from the values assigned to it. The choice of these types is driven by our initial

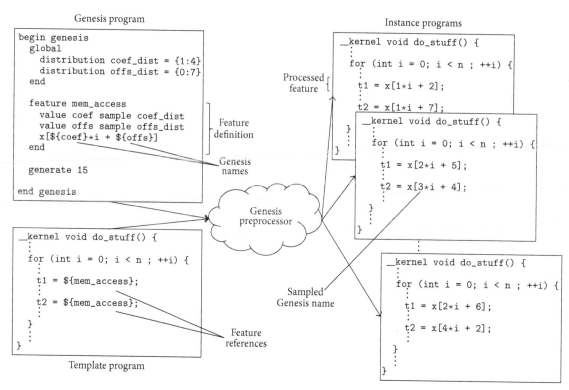

FIGURE 1: Overview of Genesis.

use studies of Genesis to generate programs for autotuning and compiler testing. These four types are found sufficient to express a large set of target programs of interest and, thus, we opt to simplify the language and limit variable types to one of the these four.

3.2. Genesis Constructs. Genesis provides several constructs for describing instance programs. Genesis constructs are designed to describe different code patterns, while keeping the Genesis program readable to the user. The appearance of a Genesis construct in a target program instructs the Genesis preprocessor to interpret it as part of a Genesis program and not to have it appear in the output instance program. Thus, these constructs must not conflict with reserved words and variables in the target program. We avoid such conflicts in two ways. First, we introduce an escape character (the backslash "\") that can be used to treat the construct as part of the target program and not as a Genesis construct. Second, Genesis constructs that conflict with common programming constructs (e.g., `if` and `for`) are named with a `gen` prefix, as will be described below.

The remainder of this section describes the Genesis constructs and illustrates them with examples. For simplicity, lines in code snippets beginning with `print` are generic print statements in some target language and are not specific to Genesis.

(i) The `distribution` construct specifies values and their corresponding probabilities. For example,

```
distribution a_dist={1{0.7};2{0.2};
4{0.1}}
```

defines a distribution named `a_dist` with values: 1, 2, and 4, each with the probability shown in the curly braces next to it. If the probabilities are omitted, a uniform distribution is used. It is also possible to define uniformly distributed ranges of values, for example,

```
distribution s_dist = {1:10}
```

By default, distributions can contain integers and strings. It is possible to use the modifier `real` to allow real distributions, as in the following example:

```
distribution s_dist = {1:10;;real}
```

This distribution, `s_dist`, allows real values between 1 and 10.

Distributions can be defined using Genesis values. For example,

```
value upperBound sample {5:10}
distribution b_dist =
{1:${upperBound}}
```

defines a distribution named `b_dist` created with a bound using `upperBound`, a previously sampled Genesis value. Distributions are set once their definition line is processed and do not change during processing. Distributions defined using Genesis values do not change if the Genesis value changes later on in processing.

(ii) The `value` construct defines a Genesis entity whose value is sampled from a distribution. Values can be propagated as constants to the instance programs or can be used in the definition of other constructs. An example of a value line is

```
value stride  sample s_dist
```

This declares the Genesis entity with the given Genesis name `stride`, whose value is sampled from the distribution `s_dist` using the `sample` construct. Thus, assuming the `s_dist` is defined above, `stride` equally likely takes a value from 1 to 10 each time it is sampled. A reference to `stride` in a feature is replaced by the sampled value when the feature is processed. The assigned distribution can also be defined inline

```
value stride  sample {1:10}
```

This distribution is functionally the same as the previous example. This allows for a simpler declaration but removes the ability for reuse of the same distribution. Instead of sampling from a distribution, a Genesis value can also enumerate one. Thus,

```
value stride2 enumerate s_dist
```

makes `stride2` take on every possible value of `s_dist`, one per instance program. A program instance that reaches an `enumerate` construct in processing is split into multiple program instances from that point onward, one for each value in the enumerated distribution. As a result, values sampled before an enumerate will be held constant across these programs, while values sampled after may differ across these programs. Alternatively, arrays can be used for multiple sampling:

```
value stride[5] sample s_dist
```

This results in 5 strides, referred to in the code as stride[0], stride[1]... up to stride[4].

Lastly, values can be set without sampling from a distribution. For example,

```
value stride=2
```

declares the Genesis entity named `stride` and sets its value to 2, equivalent to a Genesis value sampling from a distribution containing only the value 2.

(iii) The `varlist` construct defines a pool of variables for use in a processed feature and hence is a part of the instance program. Along with the `varlist` construct, the created pool of variables itself is also called a *varlist*. A varlist is analogous to a distribution as entities which can be sampled from. An example of a varlist line is

```
varlist my_vars[5]
```

This defines a pool named `my_vars` of size 5. Five variables in the target language, named `my_vars1` to `my_vars5`, can be sampled from this varlist using Genesis variables. The names of the variables in the varlist can be changed using a `name` modifier, as shown:

```
varlist my_vars[5] name(temp)
```

The given Genesis name of the varlist remains `my_vars`, and this Genesis name is used to refer to this varlist. It contains 5 variables ranging from `temp1` to `temp5`. It is possible to create a pool of variables using an existing varlist. For example,

```
varlist other_vars from my_vars
```

defines another pool of variables named `other_vars` containing all the variables in the `my_vars` varlist. This allows manipulation of two separate varlists with the same set of `my_vars` variables. Varlists can be referenced with an argument to query information from the varlist. This includes the size of the varlist (using `(size)`), the name used for the variables in the varlist (using `(name)`), and a specific variable name for a variable in a varlist (using a number). For example,

```
value stride1  sample a_dist
varlist my_vars[5] name(foo)
```

The first varlist reference outputs 5, the varlist's size. The second reference outputs `foo`, the name used in all the variables in the varlist. The third reference outputs `foo4`, the specific name of the 4th variable in the varlist.

The section in which varlists are declared indicates the reinitialization rate of the varlists. Varlists declared in the global section are created once for the entire set of programs. The size of the Varlist and state of variables are maintained between instance programs in this case. Varlists declared in the program section are reinitialized at the point of its declaration, and thus, it returns to a full varlist with all its variables for each instance program. Varlists declared in a feature are local to that feature only and are reinitialized for each processing of the feature.

(iv) The `variable` construct defines a Genesis name whose value is sampled from a varlist and is propagated as a variable name to the target program. For example,

```
variable dest  from my_vars
```

defines a Genesis entity named `dest`. Its value is sampled from the previously defined varlist named `my_vars`. For each sample, the variable used in the instance program is a variable from `my_vars1` to `my_vars5`. An occurrence of ${dest} in a feature is replaced by this variable name when the feature is processed.

(v) The `feature` construct defines a code snippet that is built up using Genesis names or possibly other features. For example,

```
feature computation
    variable dest,src1,src2 from
    my_vars
    ${dest}=${src1} * ${src2};
end
```

defines a feature named `computation` that has the code snippet `${dest} = ${src1} * ${src2};`. The `variable` construct defines three Genesis variables sampled from `my_vars`. Thus, each time the feature `computation` is processed, the variables `dest`, `src1`, and `src2` are sampled to select three variables from `my_vars1` to `my_vars5`. The sampled values replace the corresponding variable references in the code snippet.

A feature is used in the template program or in other features. A feature is processed on demand for each feature reference. The resultant feature instance is substituted into that feature reference only, and each feature reference is substituted by a newly generated feature instance.

A code snippet spanning multiple lines returned by a feature can be condensed to a single line using a `singleline` modifier before the name of the feature. Multiple references to the same feature can be compacted by using square brackets. For example,

```
${computation[5]}
```

processes computation five times and replaces this reference with the five instances. A previously sampled Genesis value can be used instead of an integer.

Features can also be stored and represented by a Genesis name. In this case, features are explicitly processed and stored, and any reference to this Genesis name causes the already processed code to be substituted similar to a Genesis value or variable. For example,

```
feature stored_comp process
computation
```

processes a computation and stores the code snippet in `stored_comp`. Thus, when a reference to `stored_comp` is found, the code snippet previously processed is substituted, without any further sampling of its values and variables. Thus, using stored features allows a user to separate processing from replacement, allowing multiple replacements as necessary from a single processing of a feature.

Features can also have arguments, passed by value. For example,

```
feature access(offset)
```

```
    my_vars1 = arr[${offset}];
end
```

defines a feature called `access`, where `offset` is passed in, and its value is substituted into the code snippet in the same manner as a Genesis name. When storing a feature, the arguments must be supplied when the feature is processed.

(vi) The `generate` construct defines how many program instances to generate. For example,

```
generate 5
```

indicates that 5 instance programs should be generated. The generate construct allows the definition of global distributions:

```
generate 5 with
    a_dist={1{0.7};2{0.1};4{0.1};
    8{0.1}}
    b_dist={1:6}
end
```

(vii) The `genmath` construct allows the evaluation of expressions and updating of previously sampled values. Consider the following example:

```
value testValue sample {1:5}
...    ${testValue}";
genmath testValue = ${testValue}+5
...    ${testValue}";
```

This samples a `testValue` value from 1 to 5. After replacing the value in the following line, it increases the value of `testValue` by 5. The `testValue` reference in the last line is then replaced by the updated value.

(viii) The `add` and `remove` constructs modify a varlist in order to affect future samplings. For example,

```
variable dest1,src1,src2 from my_vars
${dest1} = ${src1} * ${src2};
remove dest1 from my_vars
variable dest2 from my_vars
${dest2} = ${src1} * ${src2};
add dest1 to my_vars
```

prevents `dest1` and `dest2` from sampling the same variable by removing `dest1`'s sampled variable from the `my_vars` varlist before `dest2` is sampled. The `add` readds `dest1`'s sampled variable back to `my_vars` so that it can be selected by future samplings.

(ix) The `genif` construct is used for conditional generation of code snippets. Consider the following example:

```
value conditionValue sample {1:3}
```

```
genif ${conditionValue}==1

    ${computation}

end
```

The above code samples a value from 1 to 3 for `conditionValue`. If the value sampled is 1, then `computation` is processed and placed into the instance program. Otherwise, this section of the Genesis program is processed but produces no code as a result. The `genif` construct does not generate if statements in the instance program and is only used to control the flow through the preprocessor.

Using `genelsif` constructs after a `genif` statement allow for a second condition block that is only evaluated if the first `genif` statement is evaluated to be false. Also, `genelse` constructs allow a code section to be processed if all preceding `genif` and `genelsif` statements were evaluated to be false.

(x) The `genloop` construct facilitates repetitive generation. Consider the following example:

```
genloop loopvar:1:5

    ${access(${loopvar})}

end
```

This code produces 5 references to the feature `access`, each with a different value from 1 to 5 passed in as an argument. Note that this does not produce a loop in the instance program, but instead 5 consecutive versions of the code are produced when the `access` feature is processed.

The `genloop` construct can also test Boolean conditions, similar to a C while loop. Consider the following example:

```
genloop ${testValue} < 5

    genmath testValue = ${testValue}
    +1
    ⋯ ${testValue};

end
```

This repeatedly generates code snippets that reference `testValue`. During each iteration, `testValue` increases its value by one. This code stops processing when `testValue` is greater than 5 when the Boolean condition is checked at the beginning of the genloop iteration.

(xi) The `geninclude` construct allows Genesis code in another file to be used in the current Genesis program. Usually, this construct is used with premade library files provided with Genesis, which implement useful feature definitions that may be useful across multiple Genesis programs of the same target language. For example,

```
geninclude gen_c.glb
```

makes those features defined in `gen_c.glb` available, a library containing features that declare and initialize variables in C programs. For example, `varlistdeclare` is defined in `gen_c.glb`, which initializes C variables in an indicated varlist.

(xii) The `genassert` construct makes an assertion of a Boolean expression, similar to a `genif` statement. If the expression is evaluated to be true, processing of the instance program continues normally. However, if it is false, processing stops for the current instance program and the program is deleted. The preprocessor then continues processing the next instance program. For example,

```
value xCoord  sample {1:5}
value yCoord  sample {1:5}
genassert ${xCoord}*${yCoord}!=1
```

defines two Genesis values, sampled from 1 to 5. The `genassert` construct calculates the product and asserts that it is not 1 (i.e., 1 is not sampled for both values). If the product is 1, the generation of that instance program is aborted, and that program is not included in the final set of instance programs.

3.3. Genesis Processing Flow. There are three sections in a Genesis program: the *global* section, the *program* section, and the *feature definition* section. The global section contains Genesis constructs that are processed once for the entire set of generated program instances. The program section contains Genesis constructs that are processed once for every instance program. The feature definition section contains all the definitions of features. A feature is generally processed once each time the feature appears in the template program. Genesis names defined in the global and program sections can be used in any feature. However, names defined within a feature cannot be used outside that feature. This process is illustrated graphically in Figure 2.

When a Genesis program is read, the preprocessor begins with the global section, processing each statement sequentially. Once the end of the global section is reached, the generate statement is processed, creating multiple instance programs, each a copy of the template program. For each of those programs, the program section is sequentially processed. When this processing is complete, each instance program is scanned for feature references, and these features are processed as described earlier. Processing all these references results in the final, generated set of instance programs.

3.4. Genesis Sampling. The location of the declaration of a Genesis entity affects the duration for which the entity keeps its sampled value. This can be illustrated with the Genesis program shown in Program 1. In this example, `globalValue` is declared in the global section on line (3). Other Genesis values are declared in the program section on lines (7)–(9). `featureValue` is declared in a feature `varSet` on line (13). Each sampled entity is referenced inside `varSet` on lines (15)–(19), replaced with its sampled value when processed.

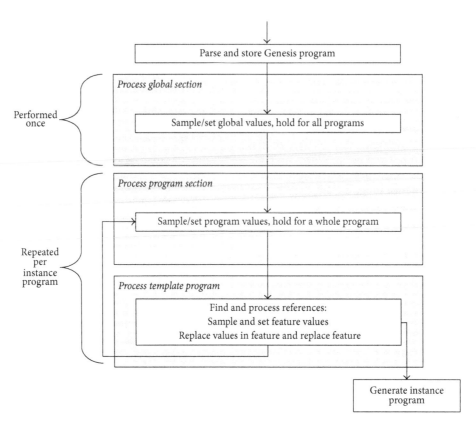

FIGURE 2: Processing flow of sections in Genesis.

With the `generate 2` statement on line (22) and the value `enumerator` in the program section on line (8) enumerated through 2 values, 4 instance programs are generated in 2 sets of 2 programs each.

Thus, the global value `globalValue` is sampled once and held constant through all 4 instance programs. Next, `setValue` is sampled once per program set. While that value is held constant, `enumerator` generates two program sets. For each value of `enumerator`, `holdValue` is sampled independently for each set. Next, while processing the template program, `featureValue` is sampled once for each feature reference to `varSet`. Thus, `featureValue` can be different in each different feature reference within the same instance program.

3.5. Using `enumerate`. The `enumerate` construct breaks away from the notion of random sampling by allowing a Genesis `value` to take on each value in a distribution exactly once, one per instance program. When `enumerate` is used in the Genesis program, the number of generated programs by a `generate <number>` construct depends on the location of the enumerated value.

Enumerated values can be placed in either the global section or the program section, both of which affect the flow of Genesis differently. Figures 3 and 4 illustrate the difference between the two using a Genesis value enumerated through 3 values and a `generate 3` statement. When a value being enumerated is in the global section, as shown in Figure 3,

the preprocessor first processes the value using `enumerate` before the `generate` construct, and the entity takes on all 3 possible values. When the global section finishes processing, the preprocessor reads the `generate` construct with each of the possible enumerated values. The preprocessor generates 3 programs with each possible value, creating a total of 9 programs. In this case, the preprocessor generates 9 total sets of programs, with each set having 1 instance program and with each enumerated value creating 3 sets.

When a value is being enumerated in the program section, as shown in Figure 4, the preprocessor processes the `generate` construct first, and the number in the `generate` statement determines the number of instance program sets to generate. For each instance program, the preprocessor processes the program section once, and thus, when the preprocessor processes the enumerated value for each instance program, it turns that instance program into a program set. Each program set contains a program for the 3 possible values in the enumeration, resulting in 3 total sets of 3 instance programs each.

Thus, the total number of programs generated is

$$N = E_G * G * E_P, \tag{1}$$

where N is the total number of programs generated, E_G is the number of enumerated values a Genesis value can take in the global section, G is the number in the generate statement, and E_P is the number of enumerated values a Genesis name can take in the program section.

```
(1)   begin genesis
(2)      global
(3)         value globalValue sample sampleDist
(4)      end
(5)
(6)      program
(7)        value setValue sample sampleDist
(8)        value enumerator enumerate enumeratorDist
(9)        value holdValue sample sampleDist
(10)     end
(11)
(12)     feature varSet
(13)        value featureValue sample sampleDist
(14)        #These will be outputted in each instance with Genesis names replaced
(15)        #SAME ALWAYS:          ${globalValue}
(16)        #SAME THROUGH SET:     ${setValue}
(17)        #ENUMERATED:           ${enumerator}
(18)        #DIFFERENT PER PROGRAM: ${holdValue}
(19)        #DIFFERENT IN PROGRAM: ${featureValue}
(20)     end
(21)
(22)     generate 2 with sampleDist = {1:100}, enumeratorDist = {1:2}
(23)   end genesis
```

PROGRAM 1: Example of sampling in Genesis sections.

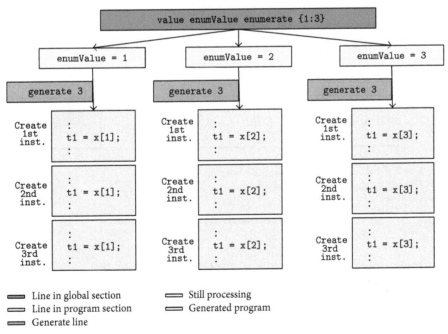

FIGURE 3: Effect of **enumerate** in global section.

Each program set need not contain the same number of programs when using enumerate. For example, for

```
distribution firstDist = {1:5}
value upperBound  sample firstDist
distribution dist2 = 1:${upperBound}
value enumValue  enumerate dist2
```

· · ·

generate 5

the number of possible values enumValue is enumerated through is unknown until upperBound is sampled. If this code is in the global section, upperBound is set once, and each enumerated value of enumValue generates 5 programs. However, if these enumerated values are put in the program

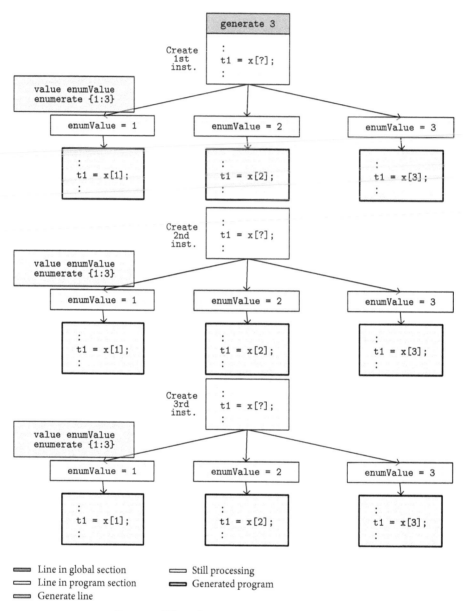

FIGURE 4: Effect of **enumerate** in program section.

section instead, 5 instance program sets are generated, with the number of programs in each set sampled independently. In these cases, the total number of programs generated is

$$N = E_{P1} + E_{P2} + \cdots + E_{Pn} \quad (n = E_G * G), \qquad (2)$$

where N is the total number of programs generated, E_G is the number of enumerated values a Genesis value can take in the global section, G is the number in the generate statement, and E_{Pi} is the number of enumerated values a Genesis value can take in the program section during the ith iteration.

One can think of the generate construct as a special case of enumerate in which the enumerated values are unused. Thus, it is possible to generate the same set of programs using only the enumerate construct. Nonetheless, we opt to keep generate as "syntactic sugar" to simplify the common case where enumerate is not necessary.

4. Case Studies

In this section, we present five case studies to show the utility of Genesis in different application domains. The case studies demonstrate the Genesis language constructs, their use to hierarchically define and compose code segments to generate a rich set of synthetic codes, and the ease by which a Genesis program can be extended to modify the manner in which the code is generated.

4.1. Image Filtering. The first case study deals with the generation of image filtering applications for training in performance autotuning on GPUs. These applications typically have two perfectly nested loops that sweep over two-dimensional images. Each element of an output image is computed as a function of a subset of the pixels in an input image. Specific image filtering applications differ in the subset and the function used to compute the output.

This case study focuses on memory performance, which is affected by the number and pattern of image accesses and the pixel computations in the loop nest. Thus, we model the body of the loop nest as one or more read *epochs* followed by a write *epoch*, where an *epoch* is a sequence of computations followed by a memory access. We wish to generate a number of such programs where the number of read epochs, the number of computations per epoch, and the pattern of memory accesses all vary.

Program 2 shows the Genesis program used for this purpose. The Genesis program defines five features. The first describes a `computation`, which samples four different variables from the varlist `temp`. The code snippet in this feature computes a value using three of the sampled variables and assigns it to the variable sampled by `dest`.

The `read_access` feature describes a memory read that samples a destination variable and three values. The three values and the loop iterators (`it0` and `it1`) determine the array element to read, which is stored in the destination variable. Similarly, the `write_access` feature describes a memory write, where a variable will be stored in a memory location determined by the loop iterators, the inner trip count, and a sampled `offset` value.

With these building blocks, an epoch feature can be described. This feature consists of a number of computations followed by a read or write access. The value `numcomps` is sampled and, using a `genloop`, references the `computation` feature `numcomps` times, after the set of computations is either a `read_access` or a `write_access` depending on the value of the `epoch_type` argument.

The template program, shown in Program 3, is a skeletal OpenCL kernel that contains the loops that sweep over the image and reference epochs, a feature containing multiple references to the epoch feature. The template program also contains two references to features that are defined in the library `gen_c.glb`: `varlistdeclare`, which initializes variables in a varlist, and `keeplive`, which touches every element in a varlist to keep it live and writes to the supplied location. The end result is the creation of 1000 instance programs, each consisting of multiple read epochs and a write epoch. Each instance program contains a variable number of epochs, number of computations in each epoch, and pattern of memory accesses.

4.2. Static Program Characteristics.

This case study is inspired by the work on cTuning with its MilepostGCC compiler [10], an autotuning compiler that extracts characteristics of a program [11, 12], and uses them with a machine learning model to tune programs for performance. Many of these characteristics come from low-level properties of a program's intermediate representation such as the number of basic blocks (BBs), the number of instructions per BB, the number of back edges, and the number of BBs with two successors. Thus, the goal of this case study is to use Genesis to generate a large number of programs with varying values of these characteristics as inputs to this tuning problem. We focus only on varying the type and number of instructions per BB, the

number of BBs, and the number of successors to each BB. For presentation purposes, each BB has a series of instructions, namely, `sum`, `copy`, or `load-from-memory`, and ends with a goto to the next BB.

Program 4 shows the Genesis program that can be used to generate 1000 instance programs from the template program shown in Program 5. The instructions that can be sampled are described in features on lines (14)–(35). The `can_be_defined` varlist keeps a list of `temp` variables that are used in the instance program and can be sampled as `dest`. The `add` and `remove` constructs in the instruction features manipulate `can_be_defined` to ensure that no dead code will be produced. The instruction sampling is performed in the `singleinsn` feature on lines (37)–(46), where a random instruction type is chosen using a sampled value and multiple `genif` statements.

The above code can be easily extended to generate a set of programs where the number of BBs with two successors will vary. The Genesis program in Program 4 is augmented with the features in Program 6. Lines (1)–(10) describe the top block with two successors. The group number is passed in as an argument and used as a label on line (2). A number of instructions are created on line (4). Lines (5)–(9) are the code that gives this block two successors, where it can branch to one of the two blocks succeeding it. The condition on line (5) can be changed depending on the application.

Lines (12)–(18) describe a block with 1 successor. It follows a similar format to the block with two successors. An additional argument is passed in to determine which of the two successor blocks is being created. Thus, no if statements are needed before the goto statement on line (17) as was needed on line (5). Lines (20)–(27) describe the new codebody feature that replaces the one in Program 4. The number of blocks with two successors is sampled. That sampled value is used as a bound to a `genloop` statement, which creates many basic block groups. In each group, the top block is created on line (23), the bottom left block is created on line (24), and the bottom right block is created on line (25).

4.3. Stencil Code Generation and Optimization.

This case study is rooted in autotuning of stencil computations on GPUs. We wish to create OpenCL kernels with a variety of stencil types and apply different optimizations, configured in different ways, to each kernel. Genesis can be used to independently accomplish each of these two goals, but what makes this example interesting is how both goals are accomplished simultaneously. In particular, changing the optimization parameters should not change the type of stencil, and, as such, while exploring a variety of optimizations, the stencil parameters must be held constant.

Stencil computations sweep through an array and for each element of that array they perform a set of reads at specific offsets from the element in question, they calculate a weighted sum of the read values, and they write the result to the corresponding element of an output array. The stencil parameters that are to be varied in this example are the number of spatial dimensions of the arrays, the number of elements in the stencil (size), how far each read

```
(1)  begin genesis
(2)
(3)     geninclude gen_c.glb
(4)
(5)     global
(6)         distribution epochdist = {1:10}
(7)         distribution numvardist = {8;16;32}
(8)         distribution compdist = {1:20}
(9)         distribution coefdist = {0:7}
(10)        distribution offsdist = {0:15}
(11)    end
(12)
(13)    program
(14)        value numepochs sample epochdist
(15)        value numvars sample numvardist
(16)        varlist temp[${numvars}]
(17)    end
(18)
(19)    feature computation
(20)        variable dest,src1,src2,src3 from temp
(21)        ${dest}  = ${src1} * ${src2} + ${src3};
(22)    end
(23)
(24)    feature read_access
(25)        variable dest from temp
(26)        value coef1,coef2 sample coefdist
(27)        value offs_r sample offsdist
(28)        ${dest}  = arr_in[${coef1} * it0 + ${coef2} * it1 + ${offs_r}];
(29)    end
(30)
(31)    feature write_access
(32)        variable src from temp
(33)        value offs_w sample offsdist
(34)        arr_out[inner_tc*it0 + it1 +${offs_w}]=${src};
(35)    end
(36)
(37)    feature epoch (epoch_type)
(38)        value numcomps sample compdist
(39)        genloop i:1:${numcomps}
(40)          ${computation}
(41)        end
(42)        genif ${epoch_type} eq "read"
(43)          ${read_access}
(44)        genelse
(45)          ${write_access}
(46)        end
(47)    end
(48)
(49)    feature epochs
(50)        genloop i:1:${numepochs}
(51)          ${epoch("read")}
(52)        end
(53)        ${epoch("write")}
(54)    end
(55)
(56)    generate 1000
(57) end genesis
```

PROGRAM 2: Genesis program for image filtering.

```
(1)    void filter(unsigned int outer_tc, unsigned int inner_tc, global float *arr_in,
               global float *arr_out, global int *result){
(2)
(3)        ${varlistDeclare(int, temp)}
(4)
(5)        for (int it0 = get_local_id(0); it0 < outer_tc; it0 += get_local_size(0)){
(6)          for (int it1 = get_local_id(1); it1 < inner_tc; it1 += get_local_size(1)){
(7)              ${epochs}
(8)          }
(9)        }
(10)
(11)       ${keepLive(*result, temp)}
(12)
(13)  }
```

PROGRAM 3: Template program for image filtering.

element can be from the center element (radius), and the weights. The optimization parameters that will be explored are the workgroup size and the number of workgroups, which control the division of work across GPU threads, as well as whether or not the kernel uses local memory, an on-chip cache that is shared across threads in a workgroup.

In the distribution definitions for this example, declared in the global section shown in Program 7, the first four distributions correspond to the properties of the stencil itself while the next five distributions relate to the optimization configurations.

The goal is to produce a variety of programs sampled from the first four distributions and to apply every combination of the values from the second set of distributions to each program. In order to do this, values taken from the first set of distributions use the sample construct, while those from the second set use the enumerate construct, as shown in the program section in Program 8. Hence, the first set of values will be kept constant in order to preserve the stencil parameters while the second set of values enumerate through all the optimization parameters.

In this way, the sampled values of dim, size, radius, and the various offsets and weights will remain constant while all combinations of the values for the other five parameters are generated. These values are then used in various features such as the reads feature shown in Program 9. The values for the offsets and weights will remain the same every time this feature is processed for a given base program, but depending on the value of use_local, a different final argument will be passed to the read feature thereby producing varying final code.

When the Genesis preprocessor is run with these inputs and, for example, a generate 5 statement, it creates 360 instance programs consisting of 5 different base programs each with 72 different configurations. An example of two of the instance programs is shown in Program 10 and 11. In this case, both instance programs are from the same base program but in Program 10 local memory was not used while in Program 11 it was. As can be seen, despite their different optimizations, the version that uses local memory performs the same stencil calculation as the version that does not, albeit with some extra indirection. Note that, in this example, for brevity, only some of the Genesis code was shown.

4.4. *Image Layering.* This case study is motivated by face detection software [13] that use machine learning techniques to detect faces in images. A large set of images with faces of different sizes, shapes, and location within an image are needed to train a machine learning model. Genesis can be used to synthetically generate such images using a set of *face images* as building blocks. A *target* synthetic image can be generated by placing a variable number of face images in the target image at different positions and with different scale. The face images can be viewed as layers on the top of one another and on the top of a background target image. Thus, based on their location, the face images can partially occlude one another as faces are layered, with the top layer being the most visible.

Program 12 shows an example Genesis program that can be used for this purpose. The example assumes that each background image is a 1024 × 1024 pixel image but makes no assumptions on the face images used to overlay. The template program has a single line with a reference to the top-level feature createImage, indicating that the entire code should vary:

${createImage}

The distributions are laid out in the global section on lines (3)–(9) of Program 12. These distributions control the number of background images, the number of faces to overlay, the filename of the face image, the locations the face images are placed on the target image, and the size of the face image. The feature definition of createImage on lines (38)–(43) contains four lines: a reference to the loadImage feature, a value numberFaces determining the number of faces to load, a reference to the overlayFace feature (using the sampled value numberFaces to indicate how often faces are overlaid), and a reference to the storeImage feature. The three features referenced are for loading an image, placing a face onto an image, and storing an image, respectively.

Loading an image as a background (feature loadImage on lines (14)–(25)) is done by first sampling a value from

```
(1)    begin genesis
(2)      global
(3)        distribution insn_type_dist = {"sum","cp","ld"}
(4)        distribution insns_dist = {1:20}
(5)        distribution bb_dist = {2:5}
(6)        distribution offs_dist = {0:7}
(7)      end
(8)
(9)      program
(10)       varlist temp[5]
(11)       varlist can_be_defined from temp
(12)     end
(13)
(14)     feature suminsn
(15)       variable src1, src2 from temp
(16)       add src1,src2 to can_be_defined
(17)       variable dest from can_be_defined
(18)       remove dest from can_be_defined
(19)       ${dest} = ${src1} + ${src2};
(20)     end
(21)
(22)     feature cpinsn
(23)       variable src from temp
(24)       add src to can_be_defined
(25)       variable dest from can_be_defined
(26)       remove dest from can_be_defined
(27)       ${dest} = ${src};
(28)     end
(29)
(30)     feature ldinsn
(31)       value offs sample offs_dist
(32)       variable dest from can_be_defined
(33)       remove dest from can_be_defined
(34)       ${dest} = arr[${offs}];
(35)     end
(36)
(37)     feature singleinsn
(38)       value insntype sample insn_type_dist
(39)       genif ${insntype} eq "sum"
(40)         ${suminsn}
(41)       genelsif ${insntype} eq "cp"
(42)         ${cpinsn}
(43)       genelsif ${insntype} eq "ld"
(44)         ${ldinsn}
(45)       end
(46)     end
(47)
(48)     feature codebody
(49)       value numblocks sample bb_dist
(50)       genloop loopvar:1:${numblocks}
(51)         T${loopvar}:
(52)         value numinsns sample insns_dist
(53)         genloop insn:1:${numinsns}
(54)           ${singleinsn}
(55)         end
(56)         genif ${loopvar}!=${numblocks}
(57)           value dest = ${loopvar}+1
(58)           ${gotoinsn(${dest})}
(59)         end
(60)       end
(61)     end
(62)
(63)     feature gotoinsn(dest)
```

PROGRAM 4: Continued.

```
(64)          goto T${dest};
(65)      end
(66)
(67)      generate 1000
(68)  end genesis
```

PROGRAM 4: Genesis program for program characteristics.

```
(1) void basic_block_code(float *arr){
(2)     ${codebody}
(3) }
```

PROGRAM 5: Template program for program characteristics.

backgroundDist. Depending on the sampled value, the filename from which the background is loaded varies. The feature overlayFace on lines (26)–(33) is referenced multiple times in storeImage. This feature samples two locations, a height value and a width value. It also samples a size multiplier and a number to indicate which face to load. These values are then placed into an abstract place command and returned and replaced in storeImage. This feature is referenced multiple times to load and place multiple layered faces.

The abstract command to store the image to file, generated by feature storeImage on lines (35)–(37), is performed at the end of the generated commands. The feature is defined as a single resultant code snippet with no references and thus is the same across all instance programs. The definition requires no sampling, showing that features do not need varying parts if so desired. When the preprocessor reads the Genesis program and template program, it generates 1000 image layering instance programs as indicated by the generate statement.

Different output filename names can be realized by modifying the storeImage to keep a global counter value and use genmath to increment it after every reference. Using a value defined in the global section counter, the modified feature storeImage looks as follows:

```
feature storeImage

    genmath counter = ${counter}+1
    load outputFile to "output${counter}
    .jpg"

end
```

4.5. Task Graphs. This case study is motivated by studies on using Dynamic Voltage and Frequency Scaling (DVFS) to conserve energy in applications [14, 15]. In many of these studies, the applications are modelled as a *task graph* in which nodes represent computations and edges represent dependence among these computations. Given a task graph, computations not on the critical path are slowed down using

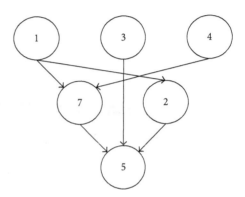

FIGURE 5: A simple MARE example. Equivalent task graph.

DVFS to save energy (e.g., [15–18]). Often, the proposed techniques are sensitive to the structure and properties of the task graph. Thus, it is desirable to have a large set of task graphs that are diverse in their topology, task execution times, and dependence to better assess a proposed technique. Genesis provides a flexible and convenient way to generate such task graphs.

We express task graphs using the MARE programming model [19], which is used to express tasks and their dependence on Qualcomm SoC platforms. A MARE program consists of tasks, each of which must be created, have its dependencies on previous tasks expressed, and then be launched. This process is demonstrated in Program 13, which provides a snippet of MARE code used to realize the task graph shown in Figure 5.

Genesis is well suited for the task of generating synthetic MARE programs as it allows a user to easily create task graphs with varying depth, width, and connectivity. Program 14 shows an excerpt from a Genesis file used to produce such programs. On lines (1) and (4), the depth of the graph and the width of each layer are sampled from user-defined distributions. On line (10), the number of fan-in for a given node is sampled from another user-defined distribution.

Genesis also makes the problem of handling task dependency simple. As a level of the graph is built, its tasks are each represented as variables that are added to the varlist this_level (line (34) of Program 14). Once an entire level has been completed, that varlist is added to two other varlists (lines (38)–(43)), one tracking all tasks and one tracking those without fan-out (as any newly created tasks have no fan-out). When a new task is created, its fan-in can be chosen among all those tasks from previous levels by simply sampling from the varlist of all tasks (line (17)). By removing the sampled task from the no-fan-in varlist at this time (line (20)), we can

```
(1)    feature basicBlockWith2Successors(groupNumber)
(2)        T${groupNumber}:
(3)        value numinsns sample insns_dist
(4)        ${singleinsn[numinsns]}
(5)        if (dest1 > 0) {
(6)            ${gotoinsn(${groupNumber}L)}
(7)        } else
(8)            ${gotoinsn(${groupNumber}R)}
(9)        }
(10)   end
(11)
(12)   feature basicBlockWith1Successor(groupNumber,type)
(13)       T${loopValue}${type}:
(14)       value numinsns sample insns_dist
(15)       ${singleinsn[numinsns]}
(16)       value dest = ${loopValue} + 1
(17)       ${gotoinsn(${dest})}
(18)   end
(19)
(20)   feature codebody
(21)       value numBlocksWith2Successors sample bb_dist
(22)       genloop loopValue:1:${numBlocksWith2Successors}
(23)           ${basicBlockWith2Successors(loopValue)}
(24)           ${basicBlockWith1Successor(loopValue,L)}
(25)           ${basicBlockWith1Successor(loopValue,R)}
(26)       end
(27)   end
```

PROGRAM 6: Genesis feature creating BBs with sampled values.

```
(1) global
(2)     distribution dim_dist = {1:2}
(3)     distribution size_dist = {1:9}
(4)     distribution radius_dist = {0:5}
(5)     distribution weight_dist = {1:3}
(6)
(7)     distribution wg_size_y_dist = {1, 4, 16}
(8)     distribution wg_size_x_dist = {1, 4, 16}
(9)     distribution num_wgs_y_dist = {8, 16}
(10)    distribution num_wgs_x_dist = {8, 16}
(11)    distribution use_local_dist = {0, 1}
(12) end
```

PROGRAM 7: Stencil code distributions.

also track which tasks have no fan-out. This allows for the creation of a join task at the end of the program which uses all remaining tasks with no fan-out to ensure the results of all tasks are used. The creation of this joining task is shown in Program 15.

5. Implementation

Genesis was implemented as a standalone preprocessor in Perl, and thus, Genesis is not limited to a specific target language. Using a scripting language such as Perl as opposed to a proper lexer and parser reduced development time while keeping the implementation flexible as the language evolved.

The preprocessor works in three phases. During the first phase of *file parsing*, the preprocessor reads a Genesis program and builds an internal representation of the constructs present. Each line is stored in a separate array based on its Genesis construct type, such as value or variable, and given a distinct ID. Each feature is stored in memory, with each Genesis line in that feature represented by the construct type and ID. The template program is also read and stored during this phase.

In the second phase of *instance generation*, the information stored is used to generate the desired number of instance programs. First, the global section is processed. Then, for each of the generated instance programs, the program section is

```
(1)    program
(2)        value dims sample dim_dist
(3)        value size sample size_dist
(4)        value radius sample radius_dist
(5)        value n_radius = -1*${radius}
(6)        distribution offset_dist = {${n_radius}:${radius}}
(7)        value y_offset[${stencil_size}]
(8)        value x_offset[${stencil_size}]
(9)        value weight[${stencil_size}]
(10)       genloop i:1:${stencil_size}
(11)           genmath y_offset[${i}] sample offset_dist
(12)           genmath x_offset[${i}] sample offset_dist
(13)           genmath weight[${i}] sample weight_dist
(14)       end
(15)
(16)       value wg_size_y enumerate wg_size_y_dist
(17)       value wg_size_x enumerate wg_size_x_dist
(18)       value num_wgs_y enumerate num_wgs_y_dist
(19)       value num_wgs_x enumerate num_wgs_x_dist
(20)       value use_local enumerate use_local_dist
(21)   end
```

PROGRAM 8: Stencil code sampling and enumeration.

```
(1)    feature reads
(2)      genloop i:1:${size}
(3)        genif ${use_local} == 1
(4)          ${read(${y_offset[${i}]},${x_offset[${i}]},${weight[${i}]},local_in)}
(5)        genelse
(6)          ${read(${y_offset[${i}]},${x_offset[${i}]},${weight[${i}]},input)}
(7)        end
(8)      end
(9)    end
(10)
(11)   feature read (y_offset,x_offset,weight,array)
(12)     temp += ${weight} * ${array}
(13)     genif ${dims} == 2
(14)       [y+${y_offset}]
(15)     end
(15)     [x+${x_offset}];
(17)   end
```

PROGRAM 9: Feature reads with offsets and weights.

processed and a copy of the template program is created. The code in each copy is scanned for any feature references as regular expressions. For each feature reference, the feature is processed and using similar regular expressions, the resulting code snippet replaces the reference. Random sampling of Genesis entities is done using the rand() function provided by Perl. Once all feature references in the template program are detected and replaced, the instance program is written to an output file in the third and final phase: *file output*. The last two phases are done iteratively to generate the set of instance programs.

The preprocessor can produce a comment block at the beginning of each generated file that includes the sampled values for each Genesis entity used to generate that instance program. Since Genesis is language agnostic, the user must provide a comment character when running Genesis to produce this comment block in each file. The preprocessor can also display statistical information, such as how often each value in a distribution is sampled for a Genesis entity across all instance programs. Using these values, the preprocessor can also output an analysis of the sampled values using Pearson's chi-squared test [20], which helps the user of Genesis determine the amount of deviation an actual set of sampled values has from its declared distribution.

In some cases, instance programs can fail to generate. For example, an instance program can fail to generate if a

```
(1)    __kernel void stencil(global double (*input), global double (*output), local double *
          local_in) {
(2)    int x_gid = get_global_id(0);
(3)    int x_lid = get_local_id(0);
(4)
(5)    int x_base = x_gid / 4 * 16;
(6)    int x_start = x_base + x_lid * 1;
(7)
(8)    for (int x_block = x_start; x_block < x_base + 16; x_block+= 4) {
(9)       int x = x_block;
(10)      double temp = 0;
(11)      temp += 1 * input[x+1];
(12)      temp += 2 * input[x+0];
(13)      output[x] = temp;
(14)   }
(15) }
```

PROGRAM 10: Example of generated stencil code. Instance program without local memory.

```
(1)    __kernel void stencil(__global double (*input), __global double (*output), __local double
          *local_in) {
(2)    int x_gid = get_global_id(0);
(3)    int x_lid = get_local_id(0);
(4)
(5)    int x_base = x_gid / 4 * 16;
(6)    int x_start = x_base + x_lid * 1;
(7)
(8)    :
(9)    //For brevity, the code that loads from global memory into local memory is omitted
(10)   :
(11)
(12)   for (int x_block = x_start; x_block < x_base + 16; x_block+=4) {
(13)      int x = x_block;
(14)      double temp = 0;
(15)      temp += 1 * local_in[x-x_base+1+2];
(16)      temp += 2 * local_in[x-x_base+0+2];
(17)      output[x] = temp;
(18)   }
(19) }
```

PROGRAM 11: Example of generated stencil code. Instance program with local memory.

user attempts to sample from an empty varlist. When this happens, the program is not generated and that program instance number is skipped. The preprocessor then continues onto the next instance program. Our Perl preprocessor implementation reports the number of programs generated, the number of program sets, and which programs failed to generate.

Our implementation provides logging information to the terminal, at various levels of verbosity, controlled by the user. Further, it reports usage errors as well as errors that cause the generation of an instance program to fail. It also reports a host of warnings [21]. The implementation allows for the user to specify a naming scheme for the instance output programs: an output filename followed by a sequence number for each instance. The current implementation prototype does not allow for the target program to be split across multiple files. However, this is not a fundamental limitation of Genesis and can be incorporated into a future release.

6. Evaluation

In this section, we describe our evaluation of Genesis. We verify the correctness of our implementation using a large number of test programs [21]. In addition, we conduct an evaluation of the performance of the Perl preprocessor using the case studies of Section 4. We also assess the statistical quality of data sampling of Genesis values to demonstrate how faithful the sampled data is to the declared distributions.

We collect the runtime and sampling data by running Genesis programs and template programs through the

```
(1)    begin genesis
(2)
(3)       global
(4)           distribution backgroundDist = {1:3}
(5)           distribution numFacesDist = {1:10}
(6)           distribution facesDist = {1:1000}
(7)           distribution locationDist = {0:1023}
(8)           distribution sizeDist = {1:10}
(9)       end
(10)
(11)      program
(12)      end
(13)
(14)      feature loadImage
(15)          value background sample backgroundDist
(16)          value background_image
(17)          genif ${background} == 1
(18)              genmath background_image = "grass.jpg"
(19)          genelsif ${background} == 2
(20)              genmath background_image = "field.jpg"
(21)          genelsif ${background} == 3
(22)              genmath background_image = "house.jpg"
(23)          end
(24)          load "${background_image}" to outputFile
(25)      end
(26)
(27)      feature overlayFace
(28)          value heightValue sample locationDist
(29)          value widthValue sample locationDist
(30)          value sizeValue sample sizeDist
(31)          value face sample facesDist
(32)          place facefile${face}.jpg at height ${heightValue} and width ${widthValue} with size
                  ${sizeValue}x
(33)      end
(34)
(35)      feature storeImage
(36)          store outputFile to "output.jpg"
(37)      end
(38)
(39)      feature createImage
(40)          ${loadImage}
(41)          value numberFaces sample numFacesDist
(42)          ${overlayFace[${numberFaces}]}
(43)          ${storeImage}
(44)      end
(45)
(46)      generate 1000
(47)    end genesis
```

PROGRAM 12: Image layering Genesis program.

preprocessor on an Intel Core i7-4930K CPU running at 3.40 GHz, with 32 GB of memory and running Perl 5.18.2.

6.1. Preprocessor Performance. We generate instance programs in powers of 10 from 10 to 100,000 using the Genesis and template programs of the case studies in Section 4 and measure the runtime of each run of the preprocessor. Each experiment is run 10 times and results are averaged. Figure 6 shows the runtime as a function of the number of generated instance programs (the number of generated instance programs for the stencil generation case study starts at 1000). The graph shows that runtime scales linearly with the number of generated instance programs in all cases. The image filtering, stencils, and program characteristics case studies contain nested genloop constructs, while the image layering Genesis programs contain a single genloop construct with fewer Genesis entities. Thus, the time to generate programs for the former group is an order of

```
(1)    auto task1 = mare::create_task(task_type_0);
(2)    task1->launch(array1);
(3)    auto task3 = mare::create_task(task_type_0);
(4)    task3->launch(array3);
(5)    auto task4 = mare::create_task(task_type_0);
(6)    task4->launch(array4);
(7)
(8)    auto task7 = mare::create_task(task_type_2);
(9)    task4->then(task7);
(10)   task1->then(task7);
(11)   task7->launch(array7,array4,array1);
(12)   auto task2 = mare::create_task(task_type_1);
(13)   task1->then(task2);
(14)   task2->launch(array2,array1);
(15)
(16)   auto task5 = mare::create_task(task_type_3);
(17)   task2->then(task5);
(18)   task3->then(task5);
(19)   task7->then(task5);
(20)   task5->launch(array5,array2,array7,array3);
(21)   task5->wait_for();
```

PROGRAM 13: A simple MARE example. MARE code (created using Genesis).

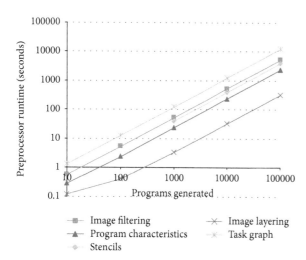

FIGURE 6: Runtimes of the preprocessor.

TABLE 1: Breakdown of program generation time for image filtering.

Programs	File parsing (s)	Instance gen. (s)	File output (s)
10	0.0013	0.52	0.0004
100	0.0013	5.20	0.0043
1000	0.0013	51.37	0.043
10000	0.0013	512.91	0.52
100000	0.0013	5134.51	6.36

amenable to parallelization since the generation of each instance is independent. Such a parallel approach is left to future work.

6.2. Statistical Sampling. We evaluate the statistical quality of the sampled data using Pearson's chi-squared goodness of fit test [20]. The chi-squared (χ^2) test is an indicator of how well a sampled distribution differs from a declared distribution. A χ^2 value is calculated from the samples, where a higher resultant χ^2 value indicates a greater deviation from the declared distributions, and a lower value gives greater confidence that the sampling came from the desired distribution without bias.

A calculated χ^2 value can be converted to a P value, the probability of observing a sample statistic as extreme as that χ^2 value for many degrees of freedom. The degree of freedom is one less than the number of possible outcomes in a distribution [22]. A P value of 0.05 is commonly accepted as a threshold for significant deviance [22]; a sampling with a P value greater than 0.05 is considered reasonable while a sampling with a P value lower than 0.05 is expected to have some bias. Thus, a calculated χ^2 value can be compared to a

magnitude higher than the time for the latter. Nonetheless, even for large numbers of generated instance programs, the time remains in the tens of minutes, leading us to conclude that the time taken to generate programs is reasonable.

The time to generate programs can be broken down into three components: reading and parsing the Genesis program, generating instance programs, and writing instance programs to files. This breakdown is shown in Table 1 for the image filtering case study. Reading the Genesis program is done once for each invocation of the preprocessor, and thus the runtime in this phase remains constant and almost negligible. The other two phases grow linearly as the number of programs generated increases and constitute the bulk of the runtime with the instance program generation component dominating. However, this component is also the most

```
(1)    value depth sample depth_dist
(2)    genloop d:1:${depth}-1
(3)        varlist this_level[0]
(4)        value width sample width_dist
(5)        genloop w:1:${width}
(6)            variable new_task from tasks
(7)            remove new_task from tasks
(8)
(9)            genif ${d} != 1
(10)               value num_fanin sample fanin_dist
(11)               genif num_fanin > ${all_tasks(size)}
(12)                   genmath num_fanin = ${all_tasks(size)}
(13)               end
(14)               ${create_task(${new_task}, ${num_fanin})}
(15)               varlist fanin[0] name(array)
(16)               genloop i:1:${num_fanin}
(17)                   variable input_task from all_tasks
(18)                   add input_task to fanin
(19)                   remove input_task from all_tasks
(20)                   remove input_task from no_fanout_tasks
(21)                   ${express_dependence(${input_task}, ${new_task})}
(22)               end
(23)               value array_count
(24)               genmath array_count = ${num_fanin} + 1
(25)
(26)               /// Write the launch call (omitted for brevity)
(27)               /// And add the fanin back to all_tasks
(28)               ...
(29)           genelse
(30)               /// Create a node with no fanin (omitted for brevity)
(31)               ...
(32)           end
(33)
(34)           add new_task to this_level
(35)       end
(36)
(37)       /// Add this_level to all_tasks and no_fanout_tasks
(38)       genloop w:1:${width}
(39)           variable transfer_task from this_level
(40)           add transfer_task to all_tasks
(41)           add transfer_task to no_fanout_tasks
(42)           remove transfer_task from this_level
(43)       end
(44)   end
```

PROGRAM 14: Varying depth, width, and connectivity.

critical value, defined as the χ^2 value that has a P value of 0.05 for a given degree of freedom. Thus, samplings that have χ^2 higher than the critical value have a P value lower than 0.05.

We report the results for our first case study with 1000 instance programs. Table 2 gives the seven Genesis values in the case study, their distributions, and their degrees of freedom. For a single run to generate the 1000 instance programs, the resulting χ^2 values and their corresponding P value are shown for the generated Genesis values. In all cases, the P value is much larger than 0.05, leading us to conclude that bias due to sampling is unlikely.

Tables 3, 4, 5, 6, and 7 show the same result over 10 runs of the generation of 1000 instance programs for each of the five case studies. The tables show the maximum and minimum χ^2s calculated across the 10 runs and the critical value of each distribution. For example, in the image filtering case study and over the 10 runs, 66 out of 70 χ^2 values, or 94.3%, are below their critical value, implying an unbiased sampling. Similarly, for the other case studies, almost all of runs result in χ^2 below the corresponding critical value. This leads us to conclude that the statistical quality of sampling from distributions is as expected.

```
(1)    variable last_task from tasks
(2)    remove last_task from tasks
(3)    value num_no_fanout = ${no_fanout_tasks(size)}
(4)    ${create_task(${last_task}, ${num_no_fanout})}
(5)    add last_task to all_tasks
(6)    varlist last_fanin[0] name(array)
(7)    genloop t:1:${num_no_fanout}
(8)       variable parent_task from no_fanout_tasks
(9)       add parent_task to last_fanin
(10)      remove parent_task from no_fanout_tasks
(11)      ${express_dependence(${parent_task}, ${last_task})}
(12)   end
(13)   /// Write the launch call (omitted for brevity)
(14)   ...
(15)   ${last_task}->wait_for();
```

PROGRAM 15: Creation of a final task that depends on all tasks with no fan-out.

TABLE 2: Test results for one run of the image filtering Genesis program.

Variable	Distribution	Deg. of freedom	χ^2	P value
numEpochs	Uniform 1–10	9	7.26	0.61
numComps	Uniform 1–20	19	21.88	0.29
numVars	8, 16, 32	2	3.30	0.19
coef1	Uniform 0–7	7	3.57	0.83
coef2	Uniform 0–7	7	5.83	0.56
offs_r	Uniform 0–15	15	19.76	0.18
offs_w	Uniform 0–15	15	10.88	0.76

TABLE 3: Test results for value distributions for image filtering.

Variable	Distribution	Min χ^2	Max χ^2	Critical value	χ^2s over critical
numEpochs	Uniform 1–10	5.02	20.96	16.92	20.96
numComps	Uniform 1–20	8.17	35.05	30.14	35.05
numVars	8, 16, 32	0.18	3.30	5.99	None
coef1	Uniform 0–7	3.19	13.92	14.07	None
coef2	Uniform 0–7	3.07	13.86	14.07	None
offs_r	Uniform 0–15	8.54	20.32	25.00	None
offs_w	Uniform 0–15	8.99	31.20	25.00	29.98, 31.20

TABLE 4: Test results for value distributions for stencils.

Variable	Distribution	Min χ^2	Max χ^2	Critical value	χ^2s over critical
weight_cube	Uniform 1–10	1.94	10.47	16.92	None
weight_star (1)	Uniform 1–10	4.91	12.73	16.92	None
weight_star (2)	Uniform 1–10	3.82	14.91	16.92	None
weight_star (3)	Uniform 1–10	5.27	17.09	16.92	17.09
weight_diamond	Uniform 1–10	4.12	13.53	16.92	None
weight_thumbtack	Uniform 1–10	4.13	14.48	16.92	None
weight_no_corners	Uniform 1–10	6.00	14.85	16.92	None

TABLE 5: Test results for value distributions for static program characteristics.

Variable	Distribution	Min χ^2	Max χ^2	Critical value	χ^2s over critical
offs	Uniform 0–7	2.13	12.13	14.07	None
insntype	"sum", "cp", "ld"	0.00	4.53	5.99	None
numBlocks	Uniform 2–5	0.38	9.96	7.81	9.96
numInsns	Uniform 1–20	8.00	27.19	30.14	None

TABLE 6: Test results for value distributions for image layering.

Variable	Distribution	Min χ^2	Max χ^2	Critical value	χ^2s over critical
background	Uniform 1–3	0.09	5.70	5.99	None
heightValue	Uniform 0–1023	945.63	1087.02	1098.52	None
widthValue	Uniform 0–1023	968.11	1067.90	1098.52	None
sizeValue	Uniform 1–10	2.34	17.11	16.92	17.11
face	Uniform 1–1000	937.60	1031.54	1073.64	None
numberFaces	Uniform 1–10	3.82	19.10	16.92	19.10

TABLE 7: Test results for value distributions for task graphs.

Variable	Distribution	Min χ^2	Max χ^2	Critical value	χ^2s over critical
depth	Uniform 3–5	0.01	4.90	5.99	None
width	Uniform 2–5	1.07	12.12	7.81	12.12
num_fanin	Uniform 1–3	0.22	6.20	5.99	6.20

7. Related Work

Our work related to program generators. CSmith [4] is a tool to generate C programs and is used to find bugs in compilers through stress testing. The generated programs are not fully described by the user and are generally random. CodeSmith Generator [5] creates visual basic code using templates. However, it does not provide sampling like Genesis and, consequently, does not generate multiple similar versions of a program with different characteristics. TestMake [6] generates test harnesses for programs. In contrast, Genesis generates whole programs that vary in their characteristics.

Christen et al. [23] describe a domain-specific language for describing stencil codes and optimizations that can be applied to them. The language is used in Patus, which is an autotuning framework for stencils. Patus uses the program description to generate stencils optimized in different ways for use in their heuristic search for good performing code. Thus, to some extent, our work bears resemblance to theirs. Nonetheless, Genesis is not limited to stencils, although it has been used to describe stencils and their optimizations in a case study. Further, unlike Genesis, the Patus language does not control the random distribution of optimizations parameters.

Voronenko et al. [8] automate the generation of vectorized and multithreaded linear transform libraries, providing users with optimized code for this domain of applications. Similar to Patus, the specific domain of this work is in contrast to Genesis, which can be used in any domain.

Bazzichi and Spadafora [24] create an automatic generator for compiler testing that produces a set of programs covering the grammatical constructions of a context-free grammar language. However, it does not give the user control over the programs generated beyond selecting a random seed.

Kamin et al. [25] created Jumbo, which generates code for Java during the actual running of the program. Poletto et al. [26, 27] have also added language and compiler support to generate code during runtime. In contrast, Genesis generates code but does it during compilation and not runtime. Genesis also generates multiple programs when it is run taken from statistical samples instead of runtime information.

Genesis uses variables whose values are randomly sampled in order to customize generated programs based on given distributions. Hardware description languages, such as Verilog [28] and SystemVerilog [29], also use randomly generated values for variables. For example, the rand keyword in the declaration of a variable in a Verilog program randomly assigns the variable of a value from a specified range with a given distribution. However, unlike Genesis, these variables are used to randomly vary inputs and signals for the purpose of generating test vectors for hardware verification.

Our work also relates to other approaches that describe programs, such as Program Description Language [30], and approaches that customize programs, including lexical [31] and syntactic [32–34] preprocessors. In contrast to all these works, Genesis describes and generates multiple programs whose code is customized using user-specified statistical distributions.

The work presented here extends the authors' initial presentation of Genesis [35] through more detailed description of the constructs and the processing flow of the language, the use of new case studies, and expansion of the experimental evaluation.

8. Conclusion and Future Work

We presented Genesis, a language to express and generate statistically controlled program sets for use in multiple domains and applications. It differs from previous preprocessors by providing the unique ability to sample from distributions. It is not restricted to a specific output language and is also flexible enough to express sets of programs with varying lengths and characteristics. We presented five case studies in different domains to illustrate the utility of Genesis and its ability to easily express programs with different characteristics. We designed and implemented a prototype preprocessor for Genesis, which is released into the public domain as an open source artifact (https://github.com/chiualto/genesis). We evaluated the preprocessor's performance and demonstrated the statistical quality of the samples it generates. We believe that Genesis is a useful tool that eases the expression and creation of large and diverse program sets, which can provide large benefits for its users.

This work can be extended in several directions. More case studies can be used to assess if there is a need to extend the Genesis constructs to increase functionality or usability. The language itself can be extended, for example, by adding return values for features. The efficiency and memory footprint of the preprocessor can be improved, in particular via the parallelization of the program instance generation phase. It may also be beneficial to migrate the preprocessor into a compiler. Finally, language-specific features may be introduced. For example, if the instance programs being generated are known to be written in OpenCL, it might be possible to generate the host program to allow the user to run the programs and get runtime information directly after using Genesis.

Conflicts of Interest

The authors declare that they have no conflicts of interest.

Acknowledgments

This work was funded by research grants from NSERC and Qualcomm.

References

[1] H. Zhu, P. A. V. Hall, and J. H. R. May, "Software unit test coverage and adequacy," *ACM Computing Surveys*, vol. 29, no. 4, pp. 366–427, 1997.

[2] C. Bienia, *Benchmarking modern multiprocessors [Ph.D. dissertation]*, Princeton University, 2011.

[3] S. Woo, M. Ohara, E. Torrie, J. Singh, and A. Gupta, "The SPLASH-2 programs: characterization and methodological considerations," in *Proceedings of the 22nd Annual International Symposium on Computer Architecture (ISCA '95)*, pp. 24–36, S. Margherita Ligure, Italy, June 1995.

[4] X. Yang, Y. Chen, E. Eide, and J. Regehr, "Finding and understanding bugs in C compilers," in *Proceedings of the 32nd ACM SIGPLAN Conference on Programming Language Design and Implementation (PLDI '11)*, pp. 283–294, San Jose, Calif, USA, June 2011.

[5] CodeSmith Tools LLC, CodeSmith Generator, http://www.codesmithtools.com/product/generator.

[6] A. Markus, "Generating test programs with TestMake," in *Proceedings of the Second European Tcl/Tk User Meeting*, pp. 127–138, TU Hamburg-Harburg, June 2001, http://flibs.sourceforge.net/article_testmake.pdf.

[7] J. Schimmel, K. Molitorisz, A. Jannesari, and W. F. Tichy, "Automatic generation of parallel unit tests," in *Proceedings of the 8th International Workshop on Automation of Software Test (AST '13)*, pp. 40–46, IEEE, San Francisco, Calif, USA, May 2013.

[8] Y. Voronenko, F. De Mesmay, and M. Püschel, "Computer generation of general size linear transform libraries," in *Proceedings of the 7th International Symposium on Code Generation and Optimization (CGO '09)*, pp. 102–113, Seattle, Wash, USA, April 2009.

[9] M. Gabbrielli and S. Martini, *Programming Languages: Principles and Paradigms*, Springer, 1st edition, 2010.

[10] G. Fursin, Y. Kashnikov, A. W. Memon et al., "Milepost GCC: machine learning enabled self-tuning compiler," *International Journal of Parallel Programming*, vol. 39, no. 3, pp. 296–327, 2011.

[11] cTuning.org, "Static Features available in MILEPOST GCC V2.1," http://ctuning.org/wiki/index.php/CTools:MilepostGCC:StaticFeatures:MILEPOST_V2.1.

[12] Y. Chen, S. Fang, Y. Huang et al., "Deconstructing iterative optimization," *ACM Transactions on Architecture and Code Optimization*, vol. 9, no. 3, pp. 21:1–21:30, 2012.

[13] OpenCV Dev Team, Face recognition with OpenCV, 2014.

[14] I. Hong, D. Kirovski, G. Qu, M. Potkonjak, and M. B. Srivastava, "Power optimization of variable-voltage core-based systems," *IEEE Transactions on Computer-Aided Design of Integrated Circuits and Systems*, vol. 18, no. 12, pp. 1702–1714, 2006.

[15] P. Chowdhury and C. Chakrabarti, "Static task-scheduling algorithms for battery-powered DVS systems," *IEEE Transactions on Very Large Scale Integration (VLSI) Systems*, vol. 13, no. 2, pp. 226–237, 2005.

[16] A. Andrei, P. Eles, Z. Peng, M. Schmitz, and B. Al-Hashimi, "Voltage selection for timeconstrained multiprocessor systems," in *Designing Embedded Processors—A Low Power Perspective*, Springer, Berlin, Germany, 2007.

[17] M. Ruggiero, D. Bertozzi, L. Benini, M. Milano, and A. Andrei, "Reducing the abstraction and optimality gaps in the allocation and scheduling for variable voltage/frequency MPSoC platforms," *IEEE Transactions on Computer-Aided Design of Integrated Circuits and Systems*, vol. 28, no. 3, pp. 378–391, 2009.

[18] A. Benoit, R. Melhem, P. Renaud-Goud, and Y. Robert, "Assessing the performance of energy-aware mappings," *Parallel Processing Letters*, vol. 23, no. 2, Article ID 1340003, 17 pages, 2013.

[19] Qualcomm Technologies, Inc, Multicore asynchronous rutime environment: Documentation and interface specification, 2013.

[20] R. L. Plackett, "Karl Pearson and the chi-squared test," *International Statistical Review*, vol. 51, no. 1, pp. 59–72, 1983.

[21] A. Chiu, *Genesis: a language for generating synthetic programs [M.S. thesis]*, Department of Electrical and Computer Engineering, University of Toronto, 2015.

[22] G. W. Snedecor and W. G. Cochran, *Statistical Methods*, Iowa State University Press, 8th edition, 1989.

[23] M. Christen, O. Schenk, and H. Burkhart, "A code generation and auto-tuning framework for parallel stencil computations," in *Proceedings of the Cetus Users and Compiler Infrastructure Workshop*, October 2011.

[24] F. Bazzichi and I. Spadafora, "An automatic generator for compiler testing," *IEEE Transactions on Software Engineering*, vol. 8, no. 4, pp. 343–353, 1982.

[25] S. Kamin, L. Clausen, and A. Jarvis, "Jumbo: run-time code generation for Java and its applications," in *Proceedings of the International Symposium on Code Generation and Optimization (CGO '03)*, pp. 48–56, IEEE, San Francisco, Calif, USA, March 2003.

[26] M. Poletto, *Language and compiler support for dynamic code generation [Ph.D. thesis]*, Massachusetts Institute of Technology, 1999.

[27] M. Poletto, W. C. Hsieh, D. R. Engler, and M. F. Kaashoek, "'C and tcc: a language and compiler for dynamic code generation," *ACM Transactions on Programming Languages and Systems*, vol. 21, no. 2, pp. 324–369, 1999.

[28] S. Palnitkar, *Verilog R Hdl: A Guide to Digital Design and Synthesis*, Prentice Hall Press, Upper Saddle River, NJ, USA, 2nd edition, 2003.

[29] C. B. Spear, *Systemverilog for Verification: A Guide to Learning the Testbench Language Features*, Springer, 2nd edition, 2010.

[30] S. Caine and E. Gordon, "PDL: a tool for software design," in *Proceedings of the National Computer Conference and Expo*, pp. 271–276, 1975.

[31] W. Turski, "Software engineering-some principles and problems," in *Programming Methodology by David Gries*, pp. 29–36, Springer, New York, NY, USA, 1978.

[32] X. Leroy, D. Doligez, A. Frisch, J. Garrigue, D. Rmy, and J. Vouillon, The objective Caml system release 3.12, 2010, http://caml.inria.fr.

[33] D. Rémy and J. Vouillon, "Objective ML: an effective object-oriented extension to ML," *Theory and Practice of Object Systems*, vol. 4, no. 1, pp. 27–50, 1998.

[34] G. Steele, *Common Lisp the Language*, Digital Press, 2nd edition, 1990.

[35] A. Chiu, J. Garvey, and T. S. Abdelrahman, "Genesis: a language for generating synthetic training programs for machine learning," in *Proceedings of the 12th ACM International Conference on Computing Frontiers (CF '15)*, Ischia, Italy, May 2015.

Permissions

All chapters in this book were first published in SP, by Hindawi Publishing Corporation; hereby published with permission under the Creative Commons Attribution License or equivalent. Every chapter published in this book has been scrutinized by our experts. Their significance has been extensively debated. The topics covered herein carry significant findings which will fuel the growth of the discipline. They may even be implemented as practical applications or may be referred to as a beginning point for another development.

The contributors of this book come from diverse backgrounds, making this book a truly international effort. This book will bring forth new frontiers with its revolutionizing research information and detailed analysis of the nascent developments around the world.

We would like to thank all the contributing authors for lending their expertise to make the book truly unique. They have played a crucial role in the development of this book. Without their invaluable contributions this book wouldn't have been possible. They have made vital efforts to compile up to date information on the varied aspects of this subject to make this book a valuable addition to the collection of many professionals and students.

This book was conceptualized with the vision of imparting up-to-date information and advanced data in this field. To ensure the same, a matchless editorial board was set up. Every individual on the board went through rigorous rounds of assessment to prove their worth. After which they invested a large part of their time researching and compiling the most relevant data for our readers.

The editorial board has been involved in producing this book since its inception. They have spent rigorous hours researching and exploring the diverse topics which have resulted in the successful publishing of this book. They have passed on their knowledge of decades through this book. To expedite this challenging task, the publisher supported the team at every step. A small team of assistant editors was also appointed to further simplify the editing procedure and attain best results for the readers.

Apart from the editorial board, the designing team has also invested a significant amount of their time in understanding the subject and creating the most relevant covers. They scrutinized every image to scout for the most suitable representation of the subject and create an appropriate cover for the book.

The publishing team has been an ardent support to the editorial, designing and production team. Their endless efforts to recruit the best for this project, has resulted in the accomplishment of this book. They are a veteran in the field of academics and their pool of knowledge is as vast as their experience in printing. Their expertise and guidance has proved useful at every step. Their uncompromising quality standards have made this book an exceptional effort. Their encouragement from time to time has been an inspiration for everyone.

The publisher and the editorial board hope that this book will prove to be a valuable piece of knowledge for researchers, students, practitioners and scholars across the globe.

List of Contributors

Karla Morris
Sandia National Laboratories, 7011 East Avenue, Livermore, CA 94550-9610, USA

Partha Pratim Ray
Department of Computer Applications, Sikkim University, Gangtok, Sikkim 737102, India

Samira Ghayekhloo and Zeki Bayram
Department of Computer Engineering, Eastern Mediterranean University, Famagusta, Northern Cyprus, Mersin 10, Turkey

Joo Hwan Lee, Nimit Nigania, Hyesoon Kim, Kaushik Patel and Hyojong Kim
School of Computer Science, College of Computing, Georgia Institute of Technology, Atlanta, GA 30332, USA

Magne Haveraaen
Department of Informatics, University of Bergen, 5020 Bergen, Norway

Damian Rouson and Clayton Carson
Stanford University, Stanford, CA 94305, USA

Hari Radhakrishnan
EXA High Performance Computing, 1087 Nicosia, Cyprus

Aziz Nanthaamornphong
Department of Information and Communication Technology, Prince of Songkla University, Phuket Campus, Phuket 83120, Thailand

Jeffrey Carver
Department of Computer Science, University of Alabama, Tuscaloosa, AL 35487, USA

Salvatore Filippone
Department of Civil and Computer Engineering, University of Rome 'Tor Vergata', Roma 00173, Italy

Junchang Wang, Shaojin Cheng and Xiong Fu
Department of Computer Science, Nanjing University of Posts and Telecommunications, Nanjing, China

Damian W. I. Rouson
Stanford University, Stanford, CA 94305, USA

Sameer Shende
University of Oregon, Eugene, OR 97403, USA

Stavros C. Kassinos
Computational Sciences Laboratory (UCY-CompSci), University of Cyprus, 1678 Nicosia, Cyprus

Anuj Sharma and Irene Moulitsas
School of Aerospace, Transport and Manufacturing (SATM), Cranfield University, Cranfield, Bedfordshire MK43 0AL, UK

Hiroyuki Takizawa and Shoichi Hirasawa
Tohoku University/JST CREST, Sendai, Miyagi 980-8579, Japan

Makoto Sugawara and Hiroaki Kobayashi
Tohoku University, Sendai, Miyagi 980-8578, Japan

Isaac Gelado
NVIDIA Research, Santa Clara, CA 95050, USA

Wen-mei W. Hwu
The University of Illinois at Urbana-Champaign, Urbana, IL 61801, USA

Kyle L. Spafford and Jeffrey S. Vetter
Oak Ridge National Laboratory, One Bethel Valley Road, Building 5100, MS-6173 Oak Ridge, TN 37831-6173, USA

Renata Vaderna, Željko Vuković, Igor Dejanović and Gordana Milosavljević
Faculty of Technical Sciences, University of Novi Sad, Trg Dositeja Obradovića 6, Novi Sad, Serbia

Bart Janssens and Walter Bosschaerts
Department of Mechanics, Royal Military Academy, Avenue de Renaissance 30, 1000 Brussels, Belgium

Támas Bányai
von Karman Institute for Fluid Dynamics, Chaussée deWaterloo 72, 1640 Rhode-Saint-Genése, Belgium

Karim Limam
LaSIE, La Rochelle University, Avenue Michel Crépeau, 17042 La Rochelle Cedex 1, France

Stergios Papadimitriou
Department of Computer Engineering & Informatics,
Technological Educational Institute of Kavala, 65404
Kavala, Greece

Kirsten Schwark
iDashboards, 900 Tower Drive, Troy, MI 48098, USA

Kostas Theofilatos and Spiridon Likothanasis
Department of Computer Engineering and Informatics,
University of Patras, Greece

Seferina Mavroudi
Department of Computer Engineering and Informatics,
University of Patras, Greece
Technological Educational Institute of Patras, 26332
Patras, Greece

Alton Chiu, Joseph Garvey and Tarek S. Abdelrahman
The Edward S. Rogers Sr. Department of Electrical
and Computer Engineering, University of Toronto,
Toronto, ON, Canada

Index

Printed in the USA
CPSIA information can be obtained
at www.ICGtesting.com
JSHW051432221024
72173JS00006B/1452

9 781639 892662